always up to date

The law changes, but Nolo is always on top of it! We offer several ways to make sure you and your Nolo products are always up to date:

1 **Nolo's Legal Updater**

We'll send you an email whenever a new edition of your book is published! Sign up at **www.nolo.com/legalupdater**.

2 **Updates @ Nolo.com**

Check **www.nolo.com/update** to find recent changes in the law that affect the current edition of your book.

3 **Nolo Customer Service**

To make sure that this edition of the book is the most recent one, call us at **800-728-3555** and ask one of our friendly customer service representatives. Or find out at **www.nolo.com**.

4th edition

Web & Software Development:

A Legal Guide

by Attorney Stephen Fishman

Fourth Edition	JULY 2004
Editor	RICHARD STIM
Illustrations	SASHA STIM-VOGEL
Cover Design	JALEH DOANE
Book Design	TERRI HEARSH
CD-ROM Preparation	ANDRÉ ZIVKOVICH
Index	THÉRÈSE SHERE
Proofreading	ROBERT WELLS
Printing	CONSOLIDATED PRINTERS, INC.

Fishman, Stephen.
    Web & Software development : a legal guide / by Stephen Fishman. -- 4th ed.
        p.   cm.
    Includes index.
    ISBN 1-4133-0087-1
     1. Computer Software--Law and legislation--United States. 2. Web sites--Law and legislation--United States. I. Title: Web and software development. II. Title.

KF390.5.C6F57 2004
346.7304'8--dc22   2004049536

Acknowledgments

My sincere thanks to:

Nolo publisher Jake Warner for his invaluable editorial contributions, patience, and support,

Stan Jacobson for his invaluable research assistance,

Terri Hearsh for her oustanding book design and Jaleh Doane for her terrific cover,

André Zivkovich for preparing the CD-ROM disk.

The following attorneys who provided insightful comments about software contracts (Chapter 17):

- Paul Goodman of Elias, Goodman, and Shanks, P.C. (New York),
- Susan Eiselman of TeleLawyer, Inc.,
- Alan Alberts of Alberts and Associates (Placerville, California), and
- Andrew Weill of Benjamin, Weill, and Mazer (San Francisco).

Donna Demac, fellow, the Freedom Forum Media Studies Center at Columbia University, for her comments on Chapter 13 (Multimedia Projects),

Nick Moffitt of the LNX-BBC Project, Seth Schoen of the Electronic Frontier Foundation, and Eureka Endo for their comments about the Open Source Movement.

Vincent S. Castellucci, Associate Director of Licensing, Harry Fox Agency, for reviewing the material on use of music in multimedia programs (Chapter 13),

William Roberts, President, Media-Pedia Video Clips Inc., for patiently explaining the stock footage business.

Finally, I thank Steve Elias and Richard Stim for their outstanding editing.

About the Author

Stephen Fishman is a San Francisco-based attorney who has been writing about the law for over 20 years. Among his many books are, *The Copyright Handbook, The Public Domain, Working for Yourself*, and *Hiring Independent Contractors*, all published by Nolo.

Table of Contents

4 Copyright Registration

5 Copyright Notice

6 Software and Web Copyright Infringement

7 Trade Secret Basics

8 Establishing a Trade Secret Protection Program

13 Website and Software Permissions

14 Employment Agreements

15 Consulting Agreements

16 Software and Website Licenses

17 Website Development Agreement

18 Custom Software Development Agreement

19 Help Beyond This Book

Appendix: How to Use the CD-ROM

Index

How to Use This Book

Welcome. This book is intended for anyone who develops websites, software, or both. It may also may be used by people who work for software and website developers, whether as employees or independent contractors. Although it is written from the developer's point of view, it should also be useful to companies and people who hire software and Web developers.

A. How This Book Is Organized

Conceptually, this book is divided into four parts:

Chapters 1-10 contain an overview of how to use the book, followed by a detailed discussion of intellectual property protection for software and websites, including copyright, trade secret, patent, and trademark protection. Chapter 12 covers protection for databases.

Chapters 11, 14, and 15 examine the legal relationship between a software or Web developer and its employees and independent contractors; separate chapters cover employment and independent contractor agreements.

Chapters 13, 16, 17, and 18 cover agreements for the development and licensing of software and websites. Included are:

- a detailed custom software development agreement, which governs the development of software for a specific end-user (Chapter 18)
- a detailed website development agreement (Chapter 17)
- software and website license agreements (Chapter 16)
- a discussion of the permissions problems involved in developing websites and software (Chapter 13).

Chapter 19, Help Beyond This Book, tells you how to do further research on your own and, if necessary, find an attorney.

Icons Used in This Book

 A caution to slow down and consider potential problems.

 "Fast track" lets you know that you may be able to skip some material that doesn't apply to your situation.

 Information regarding the CD-ROM included with this book.

 This icon alerts you to a tip that may help you negotiate or draft an agreement.

 This icon refers you to helpful books or other sources.

 The cross reference icon refers you to related topics in this book.

B. Putting Your Agreements Together

Most readers of this book will use it (at least part of the time) to create legal agreements—for example, employment and independent contractor agreements, website development agreements, and software development agreements. You should carefully read and follow the instructions in the chapter covering the particular agreement you want to use.

After you have decided what agreement to use, there are some technical de-tails that have to be dealt with. It's best for you to handle these yourself.

1. The Process of Reaching a Final Agreement

You should create a first draft of the agreement. This and all subsequent drafts should be dated and numbered (e.g., "draft #1, October 6, 2002"). In addition, a legend like the following should be placed at the top of the draft to make clear that it is not the final agreement:

PRELIMINARY DRAFT FOR DISCUSSION PURPOSES ONLY—NOT INTENDED AS A LEGALLY BINDING DOCUMENT.

The draft should be sent to the other party to review. Often, the other party will want to make changes. This can be done in several ways. The other party can discuss the changes with the original drafter in person or by telephone; the original drafter will then make the agreed changes and send a second draft to the other party for review. Alternatively, the other side may suggest its changes in writing; this can be in the form of a letter, interlineations to the original draft, or by completely revising the original draft. The original drafter will then review the changes, perhaps make more changes, and then send another draft back to the other side for review. It is common for contract drafts to go back and forth among the parties many times before a final agreement is reached.

Care must be taken to alert the other side to all changes made in each draft. The normal practice is to underline all additions and to indicate deletions either by leaving them in place with a line drawn through them or using a caret or other sign indicating omissions. This can be easily done with many word processing programs.

2. Print Out and Proofread the Final Agreement

Print out the final agreement on 8.5 x 11-inch paper. Make sure the pages are consecutively numbered (either at the top right corner or the bottom of each page). Read through the entire agreement to make sure it is correct and complete. Minor changes can be made by hand (in ink only) and initialed. However, it's probably just as easy (and neater) to make any changes on your computer and then print out the agreement again. When you're finished proofreading, print out at least two copies of the agreement.

3. Attach All Exhibits

Attach a complete copy of all exhibits (also called "attachments"), if any, to every copy of the agreement. Each exhibit or attachment should be consecutively

numbered or lettered ("A,B,C" or "1,2,3"). Make sure that your references to the exhibits in the main body of the agreement match the actual exhibits.

4. Sign the Agreement

It's best for both parties to sign the agreement and to do it in ink. The two of you need not be together when you sign, and it isn't necessary to sign at the same time. There's no legal requirement that the signatures be located in any specific place in a business contract, but they are customarily placed at the end of the agreement—that helps signify that both parties have read and agreed to the entire document.

It's very important that both parties sign the agreement properly. Failure to do so can have drastic consequences. How to sign depends on the legal form of the business of the person signing.

In this section, we take a look at the possible legal forms and their effects on signature requirements.

a. Sole proprietorships

A person is a sole proprietor if he or she is running a one-person business and hasn't incorporated or formed a limited liability company. The vast majority of ICs and consultants are sole proprietors, as are many clients.

If you or the other party is a sole proprietor, you can each simply sign your own name and nothing more. That's because a sole proprietorship, unlike a corporation or partnership, is not a separate legal entity from the person who owns it. Therefore, if Susie Davis runs custom shopping tours for wealthy tourists, for example, her agreements with her clients, can be signed "Susie Davis."

However, if you use a fictitious business name, it's best for you to sign on behalf of your business.

> **EXAMPLE:** Chris Kraft is an IC sole proprietor who runs a website development business. Instead of using his own name for the business, he calls it AAA Web Development. He should sign his contracts like this:

```
AAA Web Development
By:
Chris Kraft
```

b. Partnerships

If either you or the other party is a partnership, you must sign the agreement on behalf of the partnership, which means that the partnership must be identified in the signature block. Identifying the partnership is very important: If a partner signs only his or her name without mentioning the partnership, the partnership is not bound to the agreement—only the individual partner will be bound. This means that if you contract with a partnership, but the partnership isn't identified in the signature block, you couldn't go after the partnership's money or assets if the signing partner breaches the agreement. Instead, you could obtain only the signing partner's assets, which will likely be less than the partnership's.

Conversely, if you're a partner in a partnership and mistakenly sign an agreement as an individual, you're setting yourself up as the legal target if something goes wrong and the other side decides to sue. Since the other side won't be able to sue the partnership, it will look solely to you for legal recourse.

Which partner should sign? If the partnership is a "general" partnership (every partner invests and participates in managing the business), any partner can sign. But some partnerships are "limited partnerships," which means that there is at least one general partner, but also some partners who invest in but don't participate in the business. Limited partners should never sign agreements. That's because by law they have no authority to bind the partnership. The agreement should always be signed by a general partner.

Only one partner needs to sign. The signature block for the partnership should state the partnership's name and the name and title of the person signing on the partnership's behalf.

EXAMPLE: The Argus Partnership contracts with Sam to create some custom software. Randy Argus is one of the general partners. He signs the contract on the partnership's behalf like this:

The Argus Partnership
A Michigan Partnership

By:
Randy Argus, a General Partner

It's possible for a person who is not a partner to legally sign on behalf of the partnership. In this circumstance, the signature should be accompanied by a partnership resolution stating that the person signing the agreement has the authority to do so. The partnership resolution is a document signed by one or more of the general partners stating that the person named has the authority to sign contracts on the partnership's behalf. Attach the resolution to the end of the agreement.

c.   Corporations

If either you or the other party is a corporation, the agreement must be signed by someone who has authority to sign contracts on the corporation's behalf. The corporation's president or chief executive officer (CEO) is presumed to have this authority.

If someone other than the president or CEO of a corporation signs—for example, the vice-president, treasurer, or other corporate officer—ask to see a board of directors' resolution or corporate bylaws authorizing him or her to sign. If the person signing doesn't have authority, the corporation won't be legally bound by the contract. Attach the resolution to the end of the agreement.

Keep in mind that if you own a corporation and you sign personally instead of on your corporation's behalf, you'll be personally liable for the contract. It's likely that the main reason you've gone to the trouble to form a corporation is to avoid such liability. So signing improperly is self-defeating.

The signature block for a corporation should state the name of the corporation and the name and title of the person signing on the corporation's behalf.

EXAMPLE: Susan Ericson is the president of Acme Web Designers, Inc. Since she is the president, any contracts signed by her need not be accompanied by a corporate resolution showing she has authority to bind the corporation. The signature block for contracts she signs should look like this:

Acme Web Designers
A California Corporation

By:
Susan Ericson, President

---

d. Limited liability companies

The owners of limited liability companies are called members. Members may hire others to run their company for them, who are called managers. An agreement with a limited liability company should be signed by a member or manager.

> **EXAMPLE:** AcmeSoft LLC, a limited liability company, hires Sally to perform freelance programming services. The contract is signed on AcmeSoft's behalf by Edward Smith, the company's manager. The signature block should appear in the contract like this:

```
AcmeSoft LLC
A California Limited Liability Company

By:
Edward Smith, Manager
```

5. Dates

When you sign an agreement, include the date and make sure the other party does, too. You can simply put a date line next to the place where each person signs— for example:

```
Date:
Jamie Alvarez
```

You and the other party don't have to sign on the same day. Indeed, you can sign weeks apart. However, note that unless the agreement provides a specific starting date, it begins on the date it's signed. If the parties sign on different dates, the agreement begins on the date the last person signed. Until the agreement is signed by both parties, they're not bound by it.

6. Faxing and Emailing Agreements

It has become very common for people doing business with each other to communicate by fax machine or email. Especially when you are hashing out the details of contract clauses, it is very convenient to fax or email drafts back and forth. However, there are some potential problems with using faxes and email.

a. Preserving confidentiality

One problem is preserving confidentiality. You never know who might end up receiving or reading a fax or email message. For this reason, it's wise to place a confidentiality legend such as the following on your faxes or emails:

> The messages and documents transmitted with this notice contain confidential information belonging to the sender.
>
> If you are not the intended recipient of this information, you are hereby notified that any disclosure, copying, distribution, or use of the information is strictly prohibited. If you have received this transmission in error, please notify the sender immediately.

This legend can be placed on a fax cover sheet or at the beginning of an email message.

If your negotiations are particularly sensitive, you may wish to encrypt your email messages so others can't read them. Inexpensive encryption programs such as PGP (Pretty Good Privacy) are readily available. To learn how to obtain both free and commercial versions of PGP, log on to the following website: www.pgpi.org.

b.   Signing the finished agreement

When a final agreement is reached, you'll both need to sign the contract. One approach is for one party to sign the contract and fax it to the other, who signs it, makes a photocopy, and faxes it back. This way, you each have a copy of the agreement signed by both sides.

A faxed signature is probably legally sufficient if neither party disputes that it is a fax of an original signature. However, if the other party claims that a faxed signature was forged, it could be difficult or impossible to prove it's genuine, since it is very easy to forge a faxed signature with modern computer technology. Forgery claims are rare, however, so this is usually not a problem. Even so, it's a good practice for you and the other party to follow up the fax with signed originals exchanged by mail or air express.

If both you and the other party are advanced computer users, you can "sign" the contract digitally and send it by email. This involves using encryption technology to create a digital signature. This is a technically complex subject beyond the scope of this book. You can find a good deal of material on digital signatures on the Internet. The American Bar Association has a good discussion of this topic on its website at www.abanet.org/scitech/ec/isc/dsg-tutorial.html. A comprehensive collection of links to digital signature laws in the United States and throughout the world can be found at http://rechten.kub.nl/simone/ds-lawsu.htm.

There is also a comprehensive book on digital signature law called *The Law of Electronic Commerce*, by Benjamin Wright (Aspen Law & Business).

7.   Save the Agreement

Each party should keep one original signed copy of the agreement. Make sure to store it in a safe place. You might want to make additional photocopies to ensure against loss. ■

Introduction to Intellectual Property

This chapter introduces the concept of intellectual property and discusses how a software or Web developer may implement a simple plan to preserve and protect its intellectual property.

A. What Is Intellectual Property?

"Intellectual property" is a generic term used to describe products of the human intellect that have economic value. Software and websites are just two of the many forms of intellectual property. Other examples include text, music, movies, photographs, artwork, inventions, processes, product names, and confidential business information. Intellectual property may be owned and bought and sold the same as other types of property. But in many important respects, ownership of intellectual property is very different from ownership of a house or a car.

Anybody who develops real estate would be a fool not to know something about real estate law. Similarly, everyone who creates software or websites, or hires others to do so, should have a basic understanding of intellectual property laws. These laws define exactly what a software or Web developer owns and doesn't own, what it can sell and what it can and cannot legally take from others.

There are four separate bodies of law that may be used to protect software and websites. These are:
- trade secret law
- copyright law
- patent law, and
- trademark law.

Let's take a brief look at each type of intellectual property law. (All four types of protection are covered in more detail in later chapters.)

B. Trade Secret Law

A trade secret is information that is not generally known in the business community and that provides its owner with a competitive advantage in the marketplace. The information can be an idea, written words, formula, process or procedure, technical design, list, marketing plan, or any other secret that gives the owner an economic advantage.

If a trade secret owner takes reasonable steps to keep the confidential information secret, the courts of most states will protect the owner from disclosures of the secret to others by:
- the owner's employees
- other persons with a duty not to make such disclosures
- industrial spies, and
- competitors who wrongfully acquire the information.

This means that the trade secret owner may be able to sue the infringer and obtain an injunction (a court order preventing someone from doing something, like infringing on another's trade secrets) or damages. However, the trade secret owner must truly take steps to preserve the trade secret; the more widely known a trade secret is, the less willing the courts are to protect it.

> **EXAMPLE:** AcmeSoft, a small software developer, decides to create a program designed to automate and improve the manufacture of widgets. AcmeSoft knows that several of its competitors are working on similar programs, but its star programmer has devised a revolutionary new method to computerize widget making.

AcmeSoft doesn't want its competitors to know about the new method, or that it's developing a new widget manufacturing program, so it keeps this information as a closely guarded trade secret. It requires its employees to sign employment agreements in which they promise not to disclose valuable information to outsiders without AcmeSoft's permission. AcmeSoft also implements other trade secrecy measures (discussed in detail in Chapter 8), such as marking documents with sensitive information "confidential."

All of the trade secret measures implemented by AcmeSoft are designed to:

- prevent outsiders from learning about AcmeSoft's development activities, and
- give AcmeSoft legal grounds to stop the information from being used by a competitor if the competitor learns about them illegally (by hiring away or bribing an AcmeSoft employee).

By relying on trade secrecy principles, AcmeSoft gets a leg up on its competition, all of which are pursuing different, less original and imaginative designs for their own widget manufacturing programs. When AcmeSoft distributes its program, AcmeSoft can continue to maintain the program as a trade secret by providing customers with copies in object code form only (which cannot easily be read) and by requiring them to sign license agreements by which they promise to keep the program confidential.

Trade secrecy is often seen as the most important form of protection for high-technology companies, and in particular for software developers—due to the limitations on copyright protection (discussed briefly below). For website developers, trade secrecy can be used to protect marketing and business plans, cost and pricing information, unpublished computer code, design definitions and specifications, storyboards and concept outlines, technical notes, memoranda and correspondence relating to Web design and development, and Web development tools. (See Chapters 7 and 8 for more information about trade secrets.)

C. Copyright Law

All the elements that make up a website —HTML code, text, graphics, music, and other materials—are protected by federal copyright law, as is virtually all software. A copyright costs nothing, is obtained automatically, and lasts a very long time— over 70 years.

1. Software

The copyright law protects original works of authorship. Computer software is considered to be a work of authorship, as are all types of written works (books, articles, etc.), music, artwork, photos, films, and videos.

But copyright protection for software is relatively weak. Here's why. The owner of a copyright has the exclusive right to copy and distribute the protected work, and to create derivative works based upon it (updated versions, for example). However, this copyright protection extends only to the particular way the ideas, systems, and processes embodied in software are expressed by a given program. Copyright never protects an idea, system, or process itself. In other words, copyright protects against the unauthorized duplication or use of computer code and,

to some extent, a program's structure and user interface, but copyright never protects the underlying functions, methods, ideas, systems, or algorithms used in software.

EXAMPLE: AcmeSoft's widget program· is automatically protected by copyright as soon as it's written. This means no one may make or sell copies of the program without Acme-Soft's permission.

In addition, it is illegal for anyone to create new software similar to AcmeSoft's using a substantial amount of AcmeSoft's program. Nonetheless, AcmeSoft's competitors are free to independently create a new program accomplishing the same purpose.

Because of the complexity of the law and confusion in the courts, the extent of copyright protection for such aspects of AcmeSoft's program as its structure and interface is not entirely clear. However, by treating the program as a trade secret, AcmeSoft can protect these items as well as the program's underlying ideas, inventive functions, methods, systems, and algorithms.

2. Websites

All the elements that make up a website —software, HTML code, text, graphics, and other materials—are protected by federal copyright law. This is so whether they are under development or completed, unpublished or placed on the Internet for all to see and use. Anyone who makes unauthorized copies of such materials beyond the bounds of fair use can be sued by the copyright owner for copyright infringement. Although not mandatory, it is a good idea to register a website with the Copyright Office and to place a copyright notice on it. This provides certain important advantages if a suit is filed. (See Chapter 3 for a detailed discussion of copyright.)

> **EXAMPLE:** Acme Web Development contracts with a rock band, The Burned-Out Hipsters, to create a website to publicize the band's gigs and sell merchandise. All of the content Acme creates for the website is automatically protected by copyright, with Acme the initial owner. Acme signs a written agreement stating that upon full payment of its fee, the Hipsters will own the copyright in the website. If the Hipsters fail to pay, Acme will continue to own this content, not the Hipsters. This means they cannot use it without Acme's permission. If they do, Acme can sue them for copyright infringement.

For more information copyright law, see Chapters 3 through 6.

D. Patent Law

The federal patent law protects inventions. By filing for and obtaining a patent from the U.S. Patent and Trademark Office, an inventor is granted a monopoly on the use and commercial exploitation of an invention, for approximately 17 to 18 years. A patent may protect the functional features of a machine, process, manufactured item, or composition of matter, the ornamental design of a nonfunctional feature, or asexually reproduced plants. A patent also protects improvements of any such items.

To obtain a patent, the invention must be:

- novel—unique over previous technology in one or more of its elements, and
- nonobvious—that is, surprising to a person with ordinary skills in the relevant technology.

1. Software Patents

Most software is not sufficiently novel or nonobvious to qualify for a patent. When a patent is appropriate, obtaining it can be a difficult, expensive, and time-consuming process. It usually takes about two to three years.

A software patent provides broad protection for the ideas, inventive functions, methods, systems, and algorithms that, taken together, constitute the invention, not just the computer code used to express or implement them. In effect, patent protection gives the patent holder an absolute monopoly for 17-18 years over the use of its invention as described in the patent. Where available, patent protection is so strong that it is preferred over both copyright and trade secret protection.

EXAMPLE: Certain features of Acme-Soft's widget manufacturing program are quite revolutionary and have never been used before. If AcmeSoft applies for and obtains a patent on these features, it will have a monopoly on their use in widget manufacturing for approximately 17 to 18 years. In other words, no one else may use the patented features of AcmeSoft's program to manufacture widgets without AcmeSoft's permission. If they do, AcmeSoft could successfully sue for patent infringement.

2. Internet Patents

Website developers use patents to protect
- novel and nonobvious software used on websites, and
- novel and nonobvious new ways of doing business on the Internet; the latter are often called "business methods patents" or "Internet patents." (See Chapter 9 for a discussion of patents.)

EXAMPLE: While developing the website for the band, The Burned-Out Hipsters, Acme Web Development creates a new process for purchasing CDs online. If the new process is both novel and nonobvious, it may qualify for a patent. If Acme obtains a patent from the U.S. Patent and Trademark Office, it will have a monopoly on the process for approximately 17 to 18 years—that is, it will have the right, within the U.S., to stop anyone who uses the process described in its patent without its permission.

For more information on patents, see Chapter 9.

E. Trademark Law

Trade secret, copyright, and patent laws do not protect names, titles, or short phrases. This is where trademark protection comes in. Under both federal and state laws, a business with a product or service can obtain protection for a word, phrase, logo, or other symbol used to distinguish that product or service from others. If a competitor uses a protected trademark, the trademark holder can obtain a court injunction (a court order preventing the infringement) and money damages.

EXAMPLE: AcmeSoft markets its program under the name "WIDGETEER" and registers this trademark with the U.S. Patent and Trademark Office. None of AcmeSoft's competitors can use its name on a widget-manufacturing program without AcmeSoft's consent. If they do, AcmeSoft could get a court to order them to stop and sue for damages.

Web developers can use the state and federal trademark laws to protect their business names, domain names, and other elements of websites used to identify goods or services such as logos and slogans.

See Chapter 10 for more information about trademarks.

F. Implementing an Intellectual Property Plan

Every software and Web developer needs to create and implement an intellectual property plan. This consists primarily of using forms and procedures to identify, establish ownership, and protect the developer's intellectual property.

1. Using the Intellectual Property Forms in This Book

Following are the basic forms any developer should have. Samples of most forms are included in this book.

a. Employment agreement

Every employee engaged in the creation of intellectual property, or who may be exposed to company trade secrets, should sign an employment agreement. Ideally, each employee should sign the agreement no later than the first day of work on the project. The agreement should assign (transfer) to the employer ownership of all software and other work-related intellectual property the employee creates within the scope of employment. The agreement should also include nondisclosure provisions designed to make clear to the employee that she has a duty to protect the company's trade secrets. (See Chapter 14 for a detailed discussion and sample agreements.)

b. Independent contractor agreement

Every independent contractor—that is, each nonemployee who performs work for the company—should sign an independent contractor agreement, ideally no later than the start of work. This agreement includes trade secrecy provisions and provisions designed to make it clear that the worker is an independent contractor, not an employee. (If you're not sure whether a worker is an employee or an independent contractor, see Chapter 15.) Most importantly, the agreement should assign ownership of the contractor's work product to the company. This is absolutely vital. (See Chapter 15 for more information and sample agreements.)

c. Software and website development agreement

It is in the best interests of both a software or Web developer and its clients that a detailed development agreement be negotiated and signed before the project is begun. This agreement should, among other things, describe the project to be developed, contain payment provisions, state who will own the work when it is completed and contain any desired warranties. (See Chapter 17 for a sample software development agreement; see Chapter 18 for a sample website development agreement.)

d. Nondisclosure agreements

No developer should ever reveal its trade secrets to an outsider unless a nondisclosure agreement is signed promising to keep the secrets confidential. "Outsiders" can include potential customers, beta testers and even office visitors. (See Chapter 8 for more information and sample agreements.)

2. Taking Trade Secrecy Measures

In addition to using the form agreements outlined above, certain physical security measures should be taken to prevent outsiders from obtaining access to company trade secrets. For example, documents containing trade secrets should be marked confidential and kept locked in desks, filing cabinets or safes, when not in use. (See Chapter 8 for more information.)

3. Exploring Patenting

If a software program contains a truly innovative approach to a problem that is a significant advance in the field or that has long stymied other programmers, it may qualify for a patent.

In addition, an increasing number of patents have been issued to companies that have devised novel ways of doing business on the Internet—for example, new online ordering processes or a unique Internet advertising scheme. These patents, which usually combine software with business methodology, are commonly referred to as Internet patents or business method patents.

If a company is serious about obtaining patents, its employees should be encouraged to bring any potentially patentable inventions to management's attention. In addition, all employees engaged in research and development should keep an inventor's notebook documenting when and how their inventions were developed.

4. Copyrighting Software and Websites

Relatively little has to be done to preserve copyright protection—it begins automatically the moment a protectible work is created. However, it is highly advisable—but not mandatory—to register the copyright in all software or website materials with the Copyright Office in Washington, DC. For maximum protection, this must be done no later than three months after the work is published. A copyright notice should also be placed on all copies of published work. (See Chapter 3 for more information.)

5. Registering Trademarks

The company should conduct a trademark search before adopting a trademark to see if any similar trademarks are already in use. Trademarks on software should be registered with the U.S. Patent and Trademark Office. Domain names that serve as trademarks should be registered with the U.S. Patent and Trademark Office. (See Chapter 10 for more information.) ■

3

Copyright Basics

This chapter introduces copyright, the law that protects your software and websites. Copyright law establishes who owns program code and Web content and who has the right to develop and market software or a website. Copyright law also usually serves as the first line of defense against pirates—people who steal software or Web content. There are significant limitations on the scope of copyright protection and we discuss these in Chapter 6. Many software developers supplement copyright protection with the protections afforded by trade secrecy law.

A. What Is a Copyright?

Copyright provides the creator of software or a website with the right to control how the work is used. The Copyright Act of 1976 (17 U.S.C. §§ 101 et seq.)—the federal law providing for copyright protection—grants creators (called "authors") a bundle of intangible, exclusive rights including:

- the right to make copies of a protected work
- the right to initially sell, rent, lease, or lend copies to the public (but this right is limited by the "first sale" doctrine, which permits the owner of a particular copy of a work to sell, lend, or otherwise dispose of the copy without the copyright owner's

permission—for example, used bookstores may sell the books they purchase without getting permission)

- the right to prepare new works based on a protected work (called "derivative works")
- the right to show or transmit a copy of a work publicly, and
- the right to perform a protected work in public.

Only the author or someone to whom the author has transferred rights can exercise these rights. If someone infringes the copyrighted material by using it without permission, the owner can sue and obtain compensation for any losses. The owner can also obtain an injunction (court order) requiring the copyright infringer to stop the infringing activity.

B. What Does Copyright Protect?

Copyright protects all kinds of original works including:

- literary works—any work "expressed in words, numbers, or other verbal or numerical symbols or indicia" (17 U.S.C. § 101), including novels, plays, screenplays, nonfiction prose, newspapers and magazines, software, manuals, catalogues, text advertisements, and compilations such as some business directories. The Copyright Act classifies computer programs as "literary works," because the code is commonly expressed in letters and numbers.

- motion pictures, videos, and other audiovisual works—movies, documentaries, training films and videos, television ads, and interactive multimedia works
- photographs, graphic works, and sculpture—maps, posters, paintings, drawings, graphic art, display ads, cartoon strips, statues, and works of fine art
- music—songs, instrumental works, and advertising jingles
- sound recordings—recordings of music, sounds, or words
- pantomimes and choreographic works—ballets, modern dance, and mime works, and
- architectural works—building designs, whether in the form of architectural drawings or blueprints, or the design of actual buildings.

1. Copyright Protection for Computer Software

The Copyright Act officially defines computer programs as "sets of statements or instructions to be used directly or indirectly in a computer to bring about a certain result." (17 U.S.C. § 101.) Copyright protects all forms of software code including source code and object code, as well as program design documents and supporting materials. Program design documents may include schematics, flowcharts, or other specifications that describe a program's structure, sequence, and organization. Supporting materials may include users' manuals, software documentation, and instructions.

EXAMPLE: AcmeSoft, a small software developer, creates a software package called AcmeMap-Website mapping software that allows a webmaster to see a graphical description of all the pages in a website. The package consists of the AcmeMap program and an extensive manual. AcmeSoft is the owner of every copyrightable element of the AcmeMap package. As the owner of the copyright in AcmeMap, AcmeSoft has all of the exclusive rights discussed in Section B and no one else can exercise these without AcmeSoft's permission.

Can Computer Languages Be Copyrighted?

No court has ruled on whether the creator of a high-level computer language such as C++ or Java can acquire copyright in the language—that is, prevent others from using it. The prospect of copyright protection for computer language is extremely unlikely and the Copyright Office apparently believes languages cannot be protected since the office refuses to grant registrations to them.

a. Screen displays protectible as audiovisual works

Copyright defines an audiovisual work as a series of related images intended to be shown through the use of a machine or device. (17 U.S.C. § 112.) Computer screen displays may constitute an audiovisual work that is separate and distinct from the "literary work" comprising the actual computer code. For example, several early software copyright cases held that the computer screen displays contained in video games such as *Pac-Man* were protectible as audiovisual works. In more recent years, copyright owners have attempted—with limited success—to protect the "look and feel" of non-game software—for example, the menu hierarchy of Lotus 1-2-3 and the graphical user interface of the Apple Macintosh.

b. Software distributed online

Software is commonly distributed over the Internet through services such as America Online and C/NET's Download .com. Copyright law protects this software in the same manner as software sold by mail order or in stores. That is, downloading or otherwise using the software without the copyright owner's consent is illegal.

2. Copyright Protection for Websites

Websites, more so even than software, involve combinations of many disparate elements—for example, graphics, music, and text. Copyright can protect these elements separately—for example, a photograph at a website may have its own copyright—and copyright can also protect the way that these diverse elements are arranged to create the total website.

a. Protection for website elements

Each element of a website may be entitled to separate copyright protection. These elements include:

- text
- graphics and other artwork
- music and other sound recordings
- photographs
- videos and movies
- databases
- computer software, and
- the HTML code used to design the website.

Since a website consists of so many elements, it is possible that different people may own diverse elements. For example, a photograph by Annie Leibowitz, an article by Paul Theroux, and a recording by Eric Clapton may each have a separate copyright—yet may all be used at one website if the owners consent. This consent may be a limited license to use the material or a permanent transfer of ownership known as an assignment. For example, a company may create some of the elements at a website and acquire assignments for works that were created by outsiders. In that way, the company acquires ownership of all of the elements.

b. Copyright protection for the overall website selection and arrangement

A company can claim copyright in the particular way that the website elements are selected and arranged even if the company does not own copyright in all the individual elements themselves. A work created by selecting and arranging more than one work of authorship into a single new work is called a "collective work." Examples of collective works are newspapers, magazines, and other periodicals in which separate articles are combined into a collective whole. However, the preexisting material can consist of any work of authorship, including any type of writing, music, photographs or drawings, or other artwork.

Almost all websites qualify as collective works. However, it's important to understand that copyright protection for a collective work is limited. All that is protected is the selection or arrangement of

the preexisting material, not the preexisting material itself.

For example, let's assume that a company called AcmePic creates a website containing the 1,000 most important photographs of the 20th century. The site consists of text, HTML code, and 1,000 photos. Acme employees created the text and code.

What elements of this website does AcmePic own? Obviously, it owns the site's HTML code and text, since its employees created them. It owns none of the photos, since these were licensed from their copyright owners. But AcmePic owns something else—the copyright in the website as a collective work. This copyright protects the particular way AcmePic's employees selected and arranged all the material on the site, including the licensed photos. Anyone who copies all or a substantial part of the site would violate AcmePic's collective work copyright (as well as its copyright in the text). This is so even though AcmePic does not own the copyright in any of the individual photos that were copied.

However, not all websites qualify for even the minimal copyright protection afforded to collective works. A website is protected as a collective work only if the author/compiler had to use creativity and judgment to create it. If not even minimal creativity was employed to select or arrange the materials on a website, it will not be protected as a collective work.

How can you tell if your website contains sufficient creativity to be entitled to copyright protection as a collective work? A website is copyrightable as a collective work if either the selection or arrangement of the material are minimally creative.

As a general rule, a selection of website elements is minimally creative if the website developer uses subjective judgment in selecting the data from a body of relevant material.

For example, AcmePic's editors had to select which 1,000 of all the photos taken during the 20th century should be included on the website. This selection is copyrightable because it required individual judgment. Similarly, a website consisting of a collection of the "greatest" speeches by U.S. presidents would be copyrightable.

Similarly, the way the individual items on a website are ordered or placed is entitled to copyright protection only if done in a way that requires the exercise of the website creator's subjective judgment. An ordering or placement is not entitled to copyright protection if done in a mechanical way. An alphabetical or chronological arrangement is purely mechanical and not entitled to copyright protection. Thus, for example, a collection of the sheet music for Beatles songs placed in alphabetical order by title would not be entitled to copyright protection for the

grouping. But an arrangement on some other basis could be—for example, according to theme or from worst to best in the opinion of the website creator.

C. Three Prerequisites for Copyright Protection

You must satisfy three fundamental prerequisites in order for copyright to protect your work.

1. Fixation

The first requirement for copyright protection is that your work must be fixed in a tangible medium of expression—for example, written on a piece of paper, saved on a computer disk, or recorded or filmed on tape. Copyright protection begins the instant you fix your work. There is no waiting period and it is not necessary to register with the Copyright Office, although important benefits are obtained by doing so (for information on registration, see Chapter 4).

a. When is software fixed?

Software is sufficiently "fixed" to qualify for copyright protection when it is stored on magnetic media such as disks or tapes; imprinted on devices such as ROMs, chips, and circuit boards; or, of course, written down on paper. Several courts have held that fixation also occurs when a program is loaded from a permanent storage device into computer RAM. (*MAI v. Peak*, 991 F.2d. 511 (9th Cir. 1993).) In these cases a program was retained in RAM for several minutes or even longer. It's unclear whether a more ephemeral storage in RAM, say for just a few seconds, also counts as fixation.

b. Website fixation

A website, including its separate elements—for example, text, graphics, sound, data, photos, videos, or other material—is fixed when it is saved on a computer hard disk or other digital storage medium, written down on paper, recorded with a camera, or tape recorded.

2. Originality

A work is protected by copyright only if it is original. This doesn't mean that it must be new to the world. Software or a website is original for copyright purposes if it —or at least a part of it—is original to the author. Many programs and websites consist of some elements that are original and others that are copied. In these cases, copyright will protect only the original elements (although the copied elements might be protected under someone else's copyright).

3. Minimal Creativity

A minimal amount of creativity over and above the originality requirement is often necessary for copyright protection—for example, one court held that a programmer's minute variations on a standard communications protocol for fax machines were not sufficiently creative to be copyrightable. (*Secure Servs. Technology v. Time & Space Processing, Inc.,* 722 F.Supp. 1354 (E.D. Va. 1989).) The amount of creativity required for copyright protection is difficult to quantify.

As a practical matter, the less creativity invested in a software or website, the more difficult it will be to protect in the event of an infringement lawsuit. For example, software consisting primarily of standard programming techniques may receive little or no protection while highly creative programs will receive full protection.

The same holds true for websites. Those portions of a website's design and coding that are standard (that is, commonly used by many website designers) will be hard to protect while it will be easier to assert copyright protection for more inventive code. For example, there is no copyright protection for the format of a Frequently Asked Questions (FAQ) page on a website. The FAQ format, used in thousands of websites, is common property. (*Mist-On Systems, Inc. v. Gilley's European Tan Spa,* 2002 U.S. Dist. LEXIS 9846 (D. Wis. 2002).)

> ### Copyright Does Not Protect "Sweat of the Brow"
>
> The amount of work expended to create a program, website, or other work of authorship has no bearing on copyright protection. In the past, some courts extended copyright protection if the creation of the work required a substantial amount of work even if the work lacked originality or creativity. However, the Supreme Court outlawed this "sweat of the brow" theory when it ruled that the owner of a white pages telephone directory (or similar alphabetical database) could not stop others from copying. (*Feist Publications, Inc. v. Rural Telephone Service Co.*, 111 S.Ct. 1282 (1991).)

D. Limitations on Copyright Protection

Copyright law includes important limitations on the owner's rights. These limitations are intended to protect the public by establishing the ability to use copyrighted materials and by limiting the time periods for copyright ownership.

1. Fair Use

Obviously, the advancement of the arts and sciences cannot be fostered unless there is a free flow of information and ideas. If you are prohibited from making any use of software or websites without the copyright owner's permission, the free flow of ideas is impeded. To avoid this result, the Copyright Act includes a fair use exception that permits limited copying from a copyrighted work for purposes such as research and editorial comment so long as the value of the copyrighted work is not diminished. Fair use is discussed in more detail in Chapter 6.

2. Material in the Public Domain

Any work that is not legally protected is said to be in the public domain. The public domain belongs to everyone, and anyone can use it freely. A work can enter the public domain for a variety of reasons:

- if it was created by the federal government
- if it lacks the prerequisites of copyright—for example, it lacks originality, sufficient creativity, or fixation
- if the term of the copyright expires, or
- if it is a type of work copyright does not protect—for example, laws and court decisions.

If a work is in the public domain, the work can be used freely without violating copyright law.

However, keep in mind there are many different ways to legally protect software such as patent, trademark, and trade secret laws. For example, a novel method or processes that cannot be protected by copyright, may be protected by patent law; website materials such as logos and domain names may be protected by trademark laws. Other materials, such as photos, music, and videos may be protected by licenses. Therefore, don't presume that because all or part of a software product lacks copyright protection it is always free to use; it may be protected by one or more of these other laws.

The Public Domain, by Stephen Fishman (Nolo), provides the final word on whether software, websites, music, artwork, or any other copyrightable work is in the public domain.

3. Copyright Ownership and Transfer of Ownership

The exclusive rights outlined in Section B initially belong to the author. For copyright purposes, the author is not necessarily the person who created it; it can be that person's employer—for example, a corporation. In fact, the majority of software and websites are created by employees or independent contractors who transfer their copyright rights to the hiring companies. As a result, most software and websites are owned by businesses, not by the people who actually create them.

There are four ways a person or business may become an author:

- An individual independently authors the work.
- An employer (whether a person or corporation or partnership) pays an employee to author the work, in which case the employer is the author under the work made for hire rule.
- A person or business entity specially commissions an independent contractor to create the work under a work made for hire contract, in which case the commissioning party becomes the author.
- Two or more individuals or entities collaborate as joint authors.

The copyright owner of a work is free to transfer some or all of his, her, or its copyright rights to other people or businesses—for example, the copyright owner of a video licenses its use to a website.

4. Copyright Duration

The copyright in a work created by an individual after 1977 lasts for the life of the creator plus an additional 70 years. If there is more than one creator, the life-plus-70 term is measured from the year-date the last creator dies.

The copyright in works created by employees for their employers lasts for the earlier of:

- 95 years from the date of publication, or
- 120 years from the date of creation.

This term also applies to works created by individuals under a work made for hire contract, and individuals who choose to remain anonymous or use a pseudonym (pen name) when they publish their work. (For information on the duration of copyright for works created before 1978, see *The Copyright Handbook*, by Stephen Fishman (Nolo).)

As you can see, copyright protection lasts so long that it is highly likely that any software or website you create will have long been obsolete by the time the copyright expires.

E. Copyright Infringement

Copyright infringement occurs when someone exploits one or more of your exclusive rights without permission. The most common types of infringement are unauthorized copying and distribution, or unauthorized derivative works—for example, someone incorporates your software into their work without your permission. Here are some examples of infringement:

EXAMPLE: BigTech creates a plug-in program for a popular Web browser that brings high-quality speech audio to Web pages. In doing so, it obtains a copy of the source code for a program owned by Audiodata and copies hundreds of lines of code from Audiodata's program. BigTech has infringed Audiodata's exclusive right to copy the code.

EXAMPLE: Kerry Kabana creates a website about the Pilates exercise method. Kerry makes a number of drawings showing how to perform Pilates movements and places them on his site. He later discovers that they have been copied without his permission and placed on a website called TheRealPilates.com. The owners of TheRealPilates.com have infringed on Kerry's exclusive right to reproduce his drawings.

The Copyright Act doesn't prevent copyright infringement any more than the laws against auto theft prevent car theft. However, the Copyright Act gives copyright owners a legal remedy to sue the infringer in federal court.

A copyright owner who wins an infringement suit can stop any further infringement, have the infringing work destroyed, obtain damages from the infringer—for example, the amount of any profits obtained from the infringement—and recover other monetary losses. In effect, the law requires the pirate to restore the author to the same economic position she would have been in had the infringement never occurred. In some cases, the copyright owner may even be able to obtain monetary penalties that may far exceed the actual losses.

Software Purchasers' Limited Right to Make Copies and Adaptations

Earlier we said that a software copyright owner has the exclusive right to reproduce his work and create derivatives from it. However, there is an exception to this rule. A person who purchases a computer program has the right to copy or adapt the program if the copy or adaptation is:

- necessary to get the program to work on his computer; or
- for archival purposes (a single back-up copy) and is made and kept only by the person who owns the legally purchased copy. (17 U.S.C. § 117.)

This limited right to make a back-up or archival copy is not very generous. Since the copy is for back-up purposes only, it cannot be used on a second computer. This means, for example, that if you own a desktop computer and a laptop, and want to use your word processor on both, legally you must buy two copies. Some large software publishers are now including provisions in their license agreements permitting their customers to use a program on two different computers. (For more on software licenses, see Chapter 16.)

F. Copyright Formalities

To obtain maximum copyright protection you should comply with two simple technical formalities: copyright notice and registration.

1. Copyright Notice

Before 1989, copyright protected only published works that contained a copyright notice (the © symbol followed by the publication date and copyright owner's name). This is no longer true, and use of copyright notices is now optional. Even so, you should include copyright notice on all software and websites distributed to the public. Besides deterring potential infringers, inclusion of a copyright notice makes it impossible for an infringer to claim he or she didn't know the software was copyrighted, enabling the copyright owner to obtain greater damages in a copyright infringement suit.

It has never been necessary to include a copyright notice on unpublished works. A work is published for copyright purposes when copies are sold, rented, lent, given away, or distributed to the public on an unrestricted basis.

Software that is distributed to the public without a signed license agreement is normally considered published. Software that is under development or licensed to a limited number of users under a signed license agreement is usually considered unpublished. However, since unpublished copies of your work may receive limited distribution—for example, to beta testers—it is a good idea to include a notice on these copies as well.

You should assume that an Internet website (and any material you place on it) has been published for copyright purposes. You should definitely include one or more copyright notices on your websites. (For more on copyright notice, see Chapter 5.)

2. Registration

When people speak of "copyrighting" a work, they usually mean registering it with the Copyright Office. Keep in mind, however, that copyright registration is simply a legal formality, and contrary to what many people think, it is not necessary to register a work to create or establish a copyright. Protection begins the moment your software or website is fixed.

However, registration is required before a copyright owner may file a lawsuit to enforce his or her rights. In addition, registration within three months of publication or before the infringement begins provides some very important advantages in an infringement lawsuit—for example, the court can order the infringer to pay your attorney fees.

G. Masks Used to Manufacture Computer Chips

Until 1985, it was unclear whether the intricate designs imposed on a computer chip in the form of masks were protectible under copyright or patent laws. Congress stepped in and passed the Semiconductor Chip Protection Act, a law that creates a special type of copyright protection for these designs (masks) and the three-dimensional templates (mask works) that are used to create them. To qualify for this ten-year period of protection, the mask or mask work must be original and independently created, and the owner of the mask or mask work must be:

- a U.S. national or resident on the date the work is registered with the U.S. Copyright Office or first commercially exploited anywhere in the world
- a national or resident of a country that is a signatory to a mask work treaty
- the owner of a mask or mask work that is commercially exploited in the U.S., or
- an owner who is made subject to protection through presidential proclamation.

If you want more information on protection of mask works and masks, short of visiting a lawyer, visit the Copyright Office website at www.loc.gov/copyright or call the Copyright Office at 202-707-3000 for more information. ■

Copyright Registration

Ⓞ ne of the great things about copyright protection is that it is free and begins automatically the moment you create a work of authorship. There is no need to go through a lengthy and expensive application process as is required for patent protection, or set up an elaborate regimen to establish and maintain trade secrecy.

However, there are two relatively simple and inexpensive copyright formalities that you should follow: registering your copyright with the Copyright Office and using a copyright notice on your published works. Both procedures are optional (although you must register before filing a copyright infringement lawsuit). But by adopting them you will obtain the maximum copyright protection available—that is, you will be in the strongest legal position you can be if you need to sue a pirate for copyright infringement. If your work is at all valuable, both formalities are well worth the minimal effort they involve. In this chapter we explain how to register your software or website with the Copyright Office. In Chapter 5, we explain how to meet notice requirements.

A. Copyright Registration: The Basics

Copyright registration is a legal formality by which a copyright owner makes a public record in the U.S. Copyright Office in Washington, DC, of some basic information about a copyrighted work.

Where to Get Help. If you have difficulty understanding any aspect of the registration process, you can get help by calling the Copyright Office at 202-707-3000 between 8:30 a.m. and 5:00 p.m. eastern time, Monday through Friday. An Information Specialist will be available to give you advice on selecting the proper form, filling it out, and making the required deposit. Copyright Office Information Specialists are very knowledgeable and helpful; however, they are not allowed to give legal advice. If you have a particularly complex problem that calls for interpretation of the copyright laws, consult a copyright attorney. (See Chapter 19, Help Beyond This Book.)

1. What Is Copyright Registration?

When people speak of "copyrighting" software, a website, or other works, they usually mean registering them with the Copyright Office. To register, you fill out the appropriate preprinted application form, which requires you to provide various information about your work, including:

- the title of the work
- who created the work and when, and
- who owns the copyright.

You then mail the completed application form and a small application fee to the Copyright Office along with (depending on the type of work) one or two copies of all or part of the work. The Copyright Office reviews your application and then issues you a certificate of registration.

Contrary to what many people think, it is not necessary to register a work to create or establish a copyright in it. This is because an author's copyright comes into existence automatically the moment a work is fixed in tangible form. (However, as discussed below, it is a good idea to register any work that may have commercial value.)

2. Why Register?

Although registration is not required, there are several excellent reasons to register any valuable work.

- **Registration Is a Prerequisite to Filing an Infringement Suit.** If you're an American citizen or legal resident and your software or other copyrighted work is first published in the United States (or simultaneously in the U.S. and another country), you may not file a copyright infringement suit in this country unless your work has been registered with the Copyright Office.

- **Registration Protects Your Copyright by Making It a Public Record.** This means you're the presumed owner of the copyright in the material deposited with the registration, and the information contained in your copyright registration form is presumed to be true.

- **Timely Registration Makes It Easier to Win Money in Court.** If you register either before an infringement of your work begins or within three months of publishing the work, you'll become entitled to two additional benefits if you sue an infringer and prevail in the case: attorney fees and court costs, and you may elect to have the court award statutory damages (special damages of up to $150,000 per infringement) without having to establish what damage you actually suffered.

It may seem that all the benefits of prompt registration relate to litigation. You're also probably aware that the overwhelming majority of copyrights are never involved in a lawsuit. Why, then, should you go to the trouble of registering? The answer is that registration is a very inexpensive type of insurance. As with other forms of insurance, you buy protection against fairly unlikely occurrences, but occurrences that are so potentially devastating that you're willing to plan in advance to cushion their impact. Since registration is very easy to accomplish, currently costs only $30 per work registered, and provides significant benefits, it's one of the great insurance deals of all time.

Potential Problems Arising From Copyright Registration of Software

Let's assume you're convinced that registration is wise for your software. Before you register, you should know about a possible downside to making your work a public record by registering it with the U.S. Copyright Office: Your copyright application and at least some part of your work become available for public inspection when you register. Others will have the opportunity to examine your work. They can view everything you send to the Copyright Office, although they cannot normally make copies. If making your material public in this way concerns you, make sure to read Section E.

---

3. When to Register

A work may be registered at any time. However, to receive the benefit of statutory damages and attorney fees in infringement suits, copyright owners must register their works within the time periods prescribed by the Copyright Act. The time periods differ for published and unpublished works.

The copyright owner of a published work is entitled to statutory damages and attorney fees only if the work is registered:

- within three months of the date of the first publication, or
- before the date the copyright infringement began.

If an unpublished program, website material, or other work is infringed upon, its author or other copyright owner is entitled to obtain statutory damages and attorney fees from the infringer only if the work was registered before the infringement occurred.

A work is published for copyright purposes when copies are made available to the public on an unrestricted basis. Obviously, a software product is published when it is made available to the public in stores or by mail order. It's not entirely clear whether software distributed online is considered published. But, to be on the safe side, you should assume that it is.

When a website is published for copyright purposes has yet to be clearly defined by the courts or Copyright Office. You should assume it has been published when it is placed online and can be accessed by Internet users.

4. Who May Register

Not just anyone can register a program or website. The registrant must own all or part of the rights that make up the work's copyright. This means that a program or website may be registered by:

- the person who created it—but only so long as he or she owns all or part of the copyright in the work (which is normally not the case where the work was created for an employer or client)
- a person or company whose employee(s) created it
- a person or company that hired an independent contractor (nonemployee) to create it, provided that it obtained a transfer of all or part of the contractor's copyright rights in the work
- a person or company that obtains a transfer of all or part of the copyright in it from the creator(s)—for example, where an independent software author transfers all or part of his rights in a program to a software publisher.

In some cases, a number of different companies or people may be legally entitled to register a program or website because they all own copyright rights in the work—for example, where a software author transfers the right to distribute a program in the U.S. to one publisher and the right to distribute it outside the U.S. to another.

However, normally only one registration is allowed for each version of a published work (but the work may be registered again if it is revised or updated; see below). It makes absolutely no difference who gets the job done. The single registration protects every copyright owner.

5. Registering All the Elements of a Software Package or Website

Both computer software and Internet websites are multifaceted products that ordinarily consist of several different works of authorship that are combined to create the program or website.

In the case of software, these disparate elements typically include:

- computer code (often including various modules and files that may be able to stand on their own as independent works of authorship)
- documentation, and
- screen displays and other elements of the user interface.

Websites usually contain even more elements, including:

- text
- graphics
- photos
- video
- sounds
- computer programs, and

- HTML code or other similar types of code used to design and format websites.

The question naturally arises: "Do I register each type of authorship separately or everything together at the same time?" Fortunately, you often can register every element of a software program or website together on one application form for one fee, saving you both time and money.

Copyright Office rules provide that you may register any number of separate works of authorship together on one registration application if:

- the copyright claimant is the same for all elements of the work for which copyright registration is sought, and
- all such elements are either unpublished or are published together at the same time as a single unit.

6. The Copyright Claimant

Because the copyright claimant must be the same for all elements of the work being registered, you'll need to know who this is. The copyright claimant is either the author of the work or a person or organization to whom the copyright initially belonging to the author has been transferred.

- **Author:** When a work is first created, it is owned by the author. This is either (1) the person(s) who actually created it; or, (2) if the work is made for hire, the person or company that hired the creators (whether they were employees or independent contractors). If the work is registered at this point, the author is the claimant.

EXAMPLE 1: FrancoSoft publishes a French language instruction software package called *Lingua Franca*. All the elements of the software package—code, documentation, screens—were created by FrancoSoft employees or independent contractors who assigned all their copyright rights in the work to FrancoSoft. FrancoSoft is considered the author of this work made for hire. As such, it initially owns all the copyright rights in every element of *Lingua Franca* and is the copyright claimant for registration purposes. Assuming all the elements are sold together, the entire package can be registered by FrancoSoft on a single application.

EXAMPLE 2: Rich creates a website to promote his band, the Burned-Out Hipsters. He designs the site himself and places on it photos and text and sounds he created. Rich is the author and copyright claimant of his site and may register all the elements together on one application provided they are published at the same time.

- **Author's transferee:** Authors are free to transfer all or part of their exclusive copyright rights to others. These exclusive rights are the right to copy, distribute, display, perform, or create derivative works from an original work. When an author transfers all of his or her exclusive copyright rights in one bundle to a single person or entity (the transferee), the transferee becomes the copyright claimant for registration purposes. Such a transferee must have a written transfer document from the author—for example, a software publishing agreement transferring the original author's "entire right, title, and interest" in the software. (See Chapter 11.)

EXAMPLE 1: AcmeSoft purchases all the copyright rights in a flowcharting program from DataDo. Since the program has not been registered by DataDo, AcmeSoft decides to register it. The entire software package can be registered on one application with AcmeSoft listed as the copyright claimant (owner of all the rights in the work).

EXAMPLE 2: BigWidget, Inc., purchases a small start-up company called Widget.com that sells widgets over the Internet. Among the assets BigWidget purchases are all the copyrights in Widget.com's website

(which was created by Widget.com's employees). The entire website can be registered on one application with BigWidget listed as the copyright claimant (owner of all the rights in the work).

- **Multiple claimants:** Often an author transfers some of his or her copyright rights and retains others, or transfers some rights to one person or entity and others to another person or entity. This may occur where an author transfers fewer than all exclusive rights to a publisher, or where a person or entity that acquired all the author's rights transfers some, but not all, of the rights to a third party. In this event, nobody will own all the copyright rights. If the work hasn't been registered already, any person or entity that owns one or more exclusive rights in the work may register. The original author is listed as the claimant on the application, even if someone else is registering the work. In effect, this means that the authors will always be listed as the copyright claimant unless somebody else ends up owning all the exclusive copyright rights before registration occurs.

EXAMPLE: Assume that AcmeSoft purchases from DataDo in the above example only the exclusive right to distribute the flowcharting program on the Macintosh platform. AcmeSoft may still register the entire software package on one application (or DataDo may do so, it makes no difference who does). DataDo, the initial author of this work made for hire, would be listed as the claimant, since no single person or entity now owns all the rights in the program.

7. How Many Times to Register

Subject to the exceptions noted below, a published software program or website constituting a single integrated unit of publication (that is, all elements of the work are published together) need be and can be registered only once. A work originally registered as unpublished may be registered again after publication, even if the published and unpublished versions are identical.

a. Registering updates and new versions

Most websites and computer software programs are never really finished. They are constantly being updated and otherwise revised and modified. Once you've registered a version of a software program or website, all material contained in that version is covered, regardless of how many new versions are produced. New material contained in new versions, however, is not covered.

A new version of a preexisting program or website is one type of derivative work—a work based upon or recast from preexisting material. To qualify for registration, the new material in a derivative work must be significant enough to constitute copyrightable authorship. If the changes are minor, or merely correct routine errors, registration is probably not necessary—and will not be allowed. This is particularly true where the changes are sprinkled here and there and do not make sense standing alone.

If, on the other hand, your changes are significant, then you'll want to register the updated work as a new version of the original.

Examples of software modifications that can and should be registered include situations where:

- substantial new program code is added to a previously published program to enable it to accomplish new functions
- a previously published program is translated from one computer language to another
- a previously published program is adapted to run on a different model or brand of computer (as long as the changes are not functionally predetermined—that is, the basic software that is being changed was specifically designed to accommodate such changes).

Where modifications such as these are registered, the registration covers only the new material added to the preexisting software. Note carefully that under Copyright Office rules, registering a later version of the same software will not constitute registration of any earlier versions.

Substantial changes to websites such as substantial new text, photos, videos, etc., should likewise be registered. If your website is updated frequently, this means you may have to re-register it frequently, perhaps as often as every few weeks. Unless your website qualifies as an automated database or serial publication (see the following section), each published update must be separately registered.

> **EXAMPLE:** Rich creates a website advertising his band. He registers the original site on Feb. 1, 2005. He publishes significant changes on March 1, April 1, and June 1. He should register each update separately, by filing a new registration application and $30 fee.

b.   Group registration of websites

Two types of websites qualify for group registration: these are automated databases and serial publications. Group registration means that a single blanket registration covers revisions published on multiple dates. This saves both time and money.

- **Automated databases:** Websites that constitute "automated databases" qualify for group registration. This means that all the updates or other revisions made within any three-month period may be registered on one application for one $30 fee. Unfortunately, there is no clear definition of when a website is an automated database. For information on what constitutes an automated database, download Circular 65 from the Copyright Office website. In general, the Copyright Office appears to have no clear guidelines on when a website is an automated database; but, apparently, they "know it when they see it." Obviously, websites like Nexis or Ebay—that contain and organize large collections of facts and data—would qualify as automated databases. If you think your website falls within the definition set forth above, you have nothing to lose by attempting to use the group registration procedure. The worst that can happen is that your application will be rejected and you'll have to refile. For guidance on automated databases, see Chapter 12.
- **Serial publications:** Another class of websites that may use a group registration procedure is online versions of serial publications (magazines, journals, and newsletters published weekly or less often) and daily news-

papers. Examples include *The New York Times* and *Time Magazine* websites. Websites such as these may register three months of issues on one application for one $30 fee.

However, group registration is not available for electronic journals that are published a single article at a time. This is because group registration may be used only for a collective work. Electronic journals published one article at a time are not collective works. For detailed guidance on how to do a group registration of an online serial publication or daily newspaper, see *The Copyright Handbook: How to Protect & Use Written Works*, by Stephen Fishman (Nolo).

8. Registering Computer Screen Displays

Whether and to what extent user interfaces are protected by copyright has been the subject of much litigation and is still an unsettled question. As discussed earlier in this section, it normally is not necessary to separately register computer screens. A single registration of the entire program will extend to the screen displays. The only exception is where the copyright claimant in the underlying program is different than the claimant for the displays—that is, where the code and displays are owned by different parties. In this event, separate registrations by each claimant are required.

Nevertheless, because computer screen displays are so valuable, some software publishers have sought to separately register them. Doubtless the primary motivation for this was to make it clear to the world that the displays were protected by copyright and thereby deter potential copiers and make it easier to win an infringement case. One software publisher, the video game maker Atari, sued the Copyright Office when it refused to register the displays for a video game called *Breakout* as a separate audiovisual work. The court held that the game displays were copyrightable and should be registered by the Copyright Office. (*Atari Games Corp. v. Oman*, 979 F.2d 242 (D.C. Cir. 1992).)

It's rarely worth the trouble to separately register screen displays. If you want to make it clear your displays have been registered, simply mention the displays in the nature of authorship space on your one basic registration application. Also, include photos or other identifying material for them with your deposit. Be aware, however, that this will probably delay approval of your application, because the copyright examiner will have to examine your identifying material to determine whether your computer screens are copyrightable.

9. Registering HTML Code

HTML (Hypertext Markup Language) is the document format used on the World Wide Web. Web pages are built with

HTML tags (codes) embedded in the text. HTML defines the page layout, fonts, and graphic elements as well as the hypertext links to other documents on the Web.

Technically speaking, HTML is not a programming language like Java or JavaScript. Instead, it should be thought of as a "presentation language." Nevertheless, the Copyright Office treats HTML the same as computer code for copyright registration purposes.

This brings up the question: Should you register your HTML code? In most cases the answer would appear to be no. Registration is usually made to protect the substantive content of a website (text, graphics, sounds, videos, etc.), not the HTML code. Registering your HTML code will *not* protect these elements. Conversely, registering such elements will not serve to register the HTML code.

Even if you want to register your HTML code, you may do so only if, and to the extent, it is copyrightable—that is, the code constitutes an original work of authorship. To qualify, your HTML code must be original (not copied from others) and be minimally creative. Most HTML code likely flunks both tests. Much is copied from other websites and much is based on a standard format and likely not minimally creative.

Nevertheless, if you feel your code is copyrightable and want to register it, you may attempt to do so. Follow the same procedures as for regular computer code.

B. Selecting the Proper Application

You can obtain the Copyright Office registration application forms in a number of ways:

- Digital copies of the forms are on the Forms Disk at the end of this book. The forms are in Adobe Acrobat PDF format. You must have the Adobe Acrobat Reader installed on your computer to view and complete the forms. A copy of the Reader is on the Forms Disk. You can complete these forms on your computer and then print them out; but before you do this, read "Printing the Forms on Your Computer," below.
- You can obtain the forms directly from the Copyright Office. Digital copies can be downloaded from the Copyright Office's website at www. copyright.gov. Hard copies can be obtained by calling the Copyright Office's Forms Hotline at 202-707-9100 or by writing to the Copyright Office at the following address:

Library of Congress
Copyright Office
Publications Section, LM-455 101
Independence Avenue, SE
Washington, DC 20559-6000

Printing the Forms on Your Computer

The Copyright Office is very picky about the print quality of the registration application forms you send in. This is because it produces completed registration certificates by electronically scanning the original application you submit. As a result, if you submit an application of poor print quality, you'll get a registration certificate of poor quality as well.

If you complete the digital forms on your computer be sure to follow these instructions when you print them out:

- The forms should be printed head to head (top of page 2 is directly behind the top of page 1) using both sides of a single sheet of paper. This means you'll have to print the first side, take the paper out of the printer, turn it over, put it back in the printer, and then print the second side. Of course, this doesn't apply to those forms that are one-sided.
- Dot matrix printer copies of the forms are not acceptable.
- Inkjet printer copies of the forms require enlarging if you use the Shrink to Fit Page option.
- To achieve the best quality copies of the application forms, it is recommended, but not required, that you use a Laser Printer.

1. Selecting the Application for Software

The Copyright Office has developed several different preprinted registration forms used to register various types of works.

a. Form TX

Software is usually registered on Form TX, the form used to register all types of writings and other literary works. Software is classified as a literary work for registration purposes.

b. Form PA

Where pictorial or graphic authorship predominates, registration may be made on Form PA as an audiovisual work. If your registration consists primarily of display screens or other audiovisual elements, rather than computer code and documentation, you should use Form PA. An arcade game is a good example of a software work that would be registered on Form PA. Form PA is also normally used to register multimedia programs.

2. Selecting the Application for Websites

The registration form to use depends on the type of website material you're registering. If your website material consists of more than one type of authorship, use the form for the type of material that predominates—for example, if your website consists mostly of text, but has a few pictures, use form TX. The Copyright Office will not second-guess you on the type of form you use. So just make your best judgment.

a. Form TX

Use this form if the material being registered consists primarily of text, a computer program, or HTML code or similar works, or is an automated database (see Section A7). For an example of a website consisting primarily of text, see Nolo's website at www.nolo.com.

b. Form VA

Use this form if the material being registered consists primarily of pictorial or graphic works (pictures, drawings, etc.). For an example, see Comstock Images at www.comstock.com.

c. Form PA

Use this form if the material being registered consists primarily of audiovisual materials, such as videos, sounds accompanying images, music or lyrics. For an example, see BMW Films at www.bmwfilms.com.

d. Form SR

Use this form to register sound recordings that do not accompany a series of images on the website. For an example of a website consisting primarily of sound recordings, see Launch.com at www.launch.com.

e. Form SE

Use this form to register a single issue of a serial publication such as a newspaper or magazine. For an example of a website for a serial publication, see *The New York Times* website at www.nytimes.com.

f. Form SE/Group

Use this form to register a group of issues of a serial publication, such as a number of issues of a daily online newspaper.

g. Form SE/CP

Use this form to register a group of contributions to a periodical—for example, a number of online magazine articles.

C. Filling Out the Application

When filling out the form, remember that it could end up being submitted in court to help prove your infringement case. If any part of it is inaccurate, your case could suffer—perhaps greatly. Moreover, a person who intentionally lies on a copyright registration application may be fined up to $2,500.

1. Space 1: Title Information

You must provide information about your work's title in Space 1.

Title of This Work. The Copyright Office uses the title for indexing and identifying your software. If your software has a title, fill in that wording. This should be the same title that appears on your deposit. If your work is untitled, either state "untitled" or make a title up.

a. Software titles

If the title of your software includes a version number (such as, AccountHelper, Version 1.0) list it along with the title.

b. Website titles

If you're registering an entire website, the domain name will ordinarily be the title. If your work is untitled, either state "untitled" or make a title up. Whatever title you use, it should be the same as appears on your deposit. (See Section F, below.)

 Titles and Other Identifying Phrases Cannot Be Copyrighted. This means that registration will not prevent anyone from using the title to your work. You may, however, be able to protect titles under the trademark laws.

Previous or Alternative Titles. Provide additional titles under which someone searching for the registration might be likely to look, if any. You don't need to include additional titles known only to you or a few others, such as working titles.

If you're registering a new version of software or website under a new title that contains substantial new material, you don't need to list the old title here.

2. Space 2: Author Information

Here you must provide information about the work's author or authors. Space 2 is divided into three identical subspaces: "a," "b," and "c." Subspaces b and c are filled out only if there is more than one author.

a. Name of author

Following is a brief review of who the author is for registration purposes. If you need more information, refer to Chapters 3 and 10.

- **Works not made for hire:** Unless the work was made for hire, the person or people who created the work are the authors. Give the full name—full first, middle, and last name—of the first (or only) author.
- **Works made for hire:** If the work to be registered is a work made for hire, the author for registration purposes is the employer or other person or entity for whom the work was prepared. The full legal name of the employer or commissioning party must be provided as the "Name of Author" instead of the name of the person who actually created the work.

EXAMPLE 1: MicroJohnny, Inc., publishes a jury trial simulation game called *Litigator*. The program was created by MicroJohnny employees within the scope of their employment. MicroJohnny, Inc., should be listed in the "Name of Author" space.

EXAMPLE 2: Assume instead that MicroJohnny purchased all the copyright rights in *Litigator* from its creator, a self-employed programmer named Jane Milsap. Jane Milsap should be listed as the program's author, since it was not a work made for hire.

EXAMPLE 3: Assume instead that when Jane Milsap created *Litigator*

she was employed by MicroGames, Inc., and that the game was originally a work made for hire owned by MicroGames. MicroJohnny purchases all the rights in the game from MicroGames. Who should be listed as the author? MicroGames. The employer is the author of a work made for hire for copyright purposes. But a person or company that buys all the copyright rights in such a work for hire from the employer does not become the author (the new owner should just be listed as the copyright claimant in Space 4 below).

EXAMPLE 4: Rich creates a website containing photos and information about his garage band. Rich, the individual creator of the site, should be listed in the "Name of Author" space.

EXAMPLE 5: MicroJohnny, Inc., creates a website advertising its computing products. The website was created by MicroJohnny employees within the scope of their employment. The website is a work made for hire and MicroJohnny, Inc., should be listed in the "Name of Author" space.

While not required, the name of the employee(s) who created a work made for hire may also be included if you want to make this part of the public record—

for example: "MicroJohnny, Incorporated, employer for hire of Ken Grant, Jack Aubrey, Mona Wildman, and Jane Kendall."

b. Anonymous or pseudonymous authors

A work is anonymous if the author or authors are not identified on the published copies of the work. A work is pseudonymous if the author is identified under a fictitious name (pen name).

If the work is published as an anonymous work, you may:

- leave the Name of Author line blank (or state "N/A" for not applicable)
- state "anonymous" on the line, or
- reveal the author's identity.

If the work is pseudonymous, you may:

- leave the line blank
- give the pseudonym and identify it as such—for instance, "Nick Danger, pseudonym," or
- reveal the author's name, making it clear which is the real name and which is the pseudonym—for example, "Harold Lipshitz, whose pseudonym is Nick Danger."

Of course, if the author's identity is revealed on the application, it will be a simple matter for others to discover it, because the application becomes a public document available for inspection at the Copyright Office.

c. Dates of birth and death

If the author is a human being, the year of birth may be provided here, but this is not required (the birth year is used for identification purposes). However, if the author has died, the year of death must be listed unless the author was anonymous or pseudonymous. This date will determine when the copyright expires (70 years after the author's death).

Leave this space blank if the author is a corporation, partnership, or other organization. Corporations, partnerships, and other business entities do not "die" for copyright purposes, even if they dissolve.

d. Was this contribution to the work a "work made for hire"?

Check the "Yes" box if the author is the owner of a work made for hire. Always check this box where the author is a corporation, partnership, or other organization.

e. Author's nationality or domicile

This information must always be provided, even if the author is a business, is anonymous, or used a pseudonym.

If the work is a work made for hire and the author is a corporation, partnership, or other entity, state the country where the business has its principal office or headquarters. If this is anywhere in the U.S., simply state "U.S.A."

If the author is a person, his citizenship (nationality) and domicile could be different. An author's domicile generally is the country where she maintains her principal residence and where she intends to remain indefinitely. An author is a citizen of the country in which she was born or moved to and became a citizen of by complying with its naturalization requirements.

> **EXAMPLE:** Evelyn is a Canadian citizen, but she has permanent resident status and has lived year-round in Boston since 1990 and intends to remain there for the indefinite future. She is domiciled in the United States. She can state "Canada" in the citizenship blank or "U.S.A." in the domicile blank.

f.   Was this author's contribution to the work anonymous or pseudonymous?

Check the "Yes" box if the author is anonymous or used a pseudonym as described above. Check the "No" boxes if the author is identified by her correct name. Don't check either box if the work was made for hire.

g.   Nature of authorship

You must give a brief general description of the nature of the author's contribution to the work. This is the most important box on the registration form. What you put in this box will determine whether your registration sails through without incident or whether you're in for a round of correspondence. The Copyright Office primarily relies on this box to determine whether your work is deserving of registration under the copyright laws.

The Copyright Office maintains a manual for use by its examiners containing specific words and phrases that are, and are not, acceptable to describe the nature of the authorship. The main idea underlying these guidelines is that some descriptions adequately describe a work as something subject to copyright protection while others don't. The advice below is based on these internal Copyright Office guidelines

What you put on the Nature of Authorship line will vary most depending on whether this is:

- your first registration for an original work, or
- a registration for a new version of a previously published work or a derivative work.

h. Software authorship

Most computer programs or code can be described using general descriptive terms such as "entire text of computer program." The Copyright Office takes the view that this simple phrase registers every aspect of the program that is within the scope of copyright protection, including screen displays.

Other terms the Copyright Office will accept include:

"program listing"

"computer program code"

"program text and screen displays"

"program text"

"computer software"

"routine"

"entire program"

"entire program code"

"software"

"entire text"

"subroutine"

"entire work"

"module"

"text of program"

"program instructions"

"wrote program."

If documentation is included with the program registration (which is only appropriate if all items are published as one unit) you should add:

- "with users' manual," or
- "entire text of computer program with accompanying documentation."

Pick a term that accurately describes your work. If your deposit doesn't match the descriptive term you choose, you'll get a letter asking for clarification and your registration will accordingly be delayed.

⚠ Unacceptable Terms. Here is a listing of terms that will cause the Copyright Office to bounce your registration back for another try:

"algorithm"	"analysis"
"chip"	"computer game"
"disk"	"encrypting"
"eprom"	"firmware"
"format"	"formatting"
"functions"	"language"
"logic"	"menu screen"
"mnemonics"	"printout"
"programmer"	"prom"
"rom"	"software methodology"
"structure"	"sequence"
"organization"	"system"
"system design"	"text of algorithm."

Should you mention computer display screens in the nature of authorship statement? If you do, there are two consequences:

- You will have to deposit identifying materials for the screen displays with your application (that is, photos, drawings, or printouts clearly revealing the screens; see Section E5).
- The Copyright Office examiner will look at the identifying material to see

if it is copyrightable (which will probably delay approval of your application).

In general, the elements of many screen displays are not copyrightable. The Copyright Office has expressed the view that menu screens and similar functional interfaces consisting of words or brief phrases in a particular format generally are not registrable.

On the other hand, if you are certain that your computer screens are copyrightable and you really want to protect the screen design, you may wish to indicate that screen displays are part of your authorship and deposit identifying material for the screens with your program code.

In this event, you should state "entire text of computer program and screen displays" in the Nature of Authorship space; or, if you are also registering documentation, state "entire text of computer program and screen displays with user documentation."

Another approach is to include identifying material for your screen displays but not to mention them in your nature of authorship statement. Instead, simply say "entire work," "computer program," or "all." When you do this, the copyright examiner will not examine the displays to see if they are copyrightable. The screens will ride along with the code without comment by the Copyright Office. This has the advantage of avoiding having approval of your application delayed. The disadvantage, however, is that you won't get a de-

termination by the Copyright Office that your screens are copyrightable. But at least they will remain on record with the Copyright Office as part of your deposit.

i. Software authorship for new versions and derivatives

If you're registering a new version of software or other derivative work, you have more to consider in explaining your "Nature of Authorship" under Space 2.

To be eligible for separate registration, a work based on a prior work must involve enough changes in the prior work to be separately copyrightable. If the new material you wish to register consists of changes in or revisions to a prior program, you must use very precise language. Your registration should sail through if you describe the nature of the new material as:

"editorial revisions"

"revised revisions of [name of program]"

"computer program"

"text of program"

"programming text"

"program listing"

"program instructions"

"text of computer game"

"module"

"routine"

"subroutine"

"additional program text and extensively modified text"

"wrote program."

⚠️ **Functionally Predetermined Changes Are Not Registrable.** If you state "error corrections," "debugging," "patching," "features," or "enhancements" in the Nature of Authorship box you'll receive a letter from the Copyright Office requesting that you either submit a new application with a better statement of authorship, or abandon your registration by notifying them that the changes are too minor or "functionally predetermined" to warrant registration as an original work of authorship.

"Functionally predetermined" means the basic software that is being changed has been specifically designed to accommodate such changes. For example, many operating systems, and applications, software are deliberately made to easily accept preplanned changes (patches) that will permit them to compatibly operate with a number of different central processors (i.e., boards or chips). When such patches are made, they're considered functionally predetermined and ordinarily don't either alter the work or stand by themselves sufficiently to warrant a new registration.

Translation Note

Programs that are significantly adapted or translated to another computer language are usually considered to be a derivative work and registrable as such. In this situation, to correctly describe what is going on in the Nature of Authorship box, you need to include the name of the language into which the work has been translated. Thus "translation to C++" is deemed sufficient, while "translation" by itself is not. If, however, it appears to the Copyright Office that your translation really only enables the preexisting program to operate on a different machine without the need for a different language, your registration may or may not be approved as a new version, depending on the magnitude of the changes.

---

j. Website authorship

If you're using Forms TX or PA, you must describe the original authorship you are registering. Do not use common Web-related terms such as "website," "site design," "user interface," "format," "layout," or "design." Instead, use terms that clearly refer to copyrightable authorship such as "text," "artwork," "photographs," "music," "audiovisual material" (including any sounds), "sound recording" (if the sounds do not accompany a series of images), and "computer program." If you're registering HTML code or similar code, use "HTML code," "Java applets," or similar words describing the work.

If you're registering more than one type of authorship, describe each type—for example, "text and photographs."

If you are using form VA to register material consisting primarily of pictorial or graphic works, you need not write a description of your authorship. Instead, simply check the appropriate box or boxes in the Nature of Authorship space—for example, if you're registering photographs, check the Photograph box.

3. Space 3: Relevant Dates

Here, you must provide the date of creation and date of first publication for the work.

a. Year in which creation of this work was completed

Fill in the year in which the software or website you're registering first became fixed in its final form, disregarding minor changes. This year has nothing to do with publication, which may occur long after creation. Deciding what constitutes the year of creation may prove difficult if the work was created over a long period of time. Give the year in which the author(s) completed the particular version of the work for which registration is now being sought, even if other versions exist or further changes or additions are planned.

b. Date and nation of first publication of this particular work

Leave this blank if an unpublished work is being registered. Publication occurs for copyright purposes when a work is made widely available to the public. Give only one date, listing the month, day, year, and country where publication first occurred. If you're not sure of the exact publication date, state your best guess and make clear it is approximate—for example, "November 15, 200x (approx.)." If publication took place simultaneously in the United States and one or more foreign countries, you can just state "U.S.A." Make sure the publication date you list is for the version of the software being registered, not for some previous version.

If the work has been published in both hard copy and digital form—and the two publications occurred at different times—the earlier of the two should be listed in the date and nation of publication spaces.

Internet: What Is the Nation of First Publication?

The nation of publication for a work distributed online is either the nation from which the work is uploaded or the nation containing the server where the work is located. Use the name of a real country such as U.S.A. or Canada. Don't use non-specific terms such as "global," "worldwide," or "Internet" in the nation of publication space.

---

4. Space 4: Information About Copyright Claimants

Here you must properly identify the copyright owners and, if necessary, how ownership was acquired.

a. Copyright claimants

Provide the name and address of each copyright claimant, which must be:

- the author or authors of the work (including the owner of a work made for hire, if applicable), or
- persons or organizations that have, on or before the date the application is filed, obtained in writing ownership of all the exclusive United States copyright rights that initially belonged to the author, or

- persons or organizations that the author or owner of all U.S. copyright rights has authorized by contract to act as the claimant for copyright registration (there is no legal requirement that such contract be in writing, but it's not a bad idea). (37 C.F.R. 202.3(a)(3) (1984).)

(See Section A6 above for a detailed discussion of who qualifies as the copyright claimant.)

A copyright claimant must be listed even for anonymous or pseudonymous works. You can provide the claimant's real name alone, the real name and the pseudonym, the pseudonym alone if the claimant is generally known by it, or, if the claimant wishes to remain anonymous, the name of the claimant's authorized agent.

When the name listed for the claimant is different than the name of the author given in Space 2, but the two names identify one person, explain the relationship between the two names.

> **EXAMPLE:** John Smith is the author of the website he is registering, but all of the copyright rights have been transferred to his corporation, SmithCo, Inc., of which Smith is the sole owner. Smith should not just state SmithCo, Inc. Rather, he needs to explain the relationship between himself and his company claimant— for example, "SmithCo, Inc., solely owned by John Smith."

b. Transfers

If the copyright claimant named just above is not the author or authors named in Space 2, give a brief general description of how ownership of the copyright was obtained. However, do not attach any transfer documents to the application. If there is not enough space to list all the claimants on Form TX, you can list additional claimants on the reverse side of Form/CON.

This statement must indicate that all the author's United States copyright rights have been transferred by a written agreement or by operation of law. Examples of acceptable transfer statements include: "By written contract," "Transfer of all rights by author," "By will," "By inheritance," "Assignment," "By gift agreement."

Note that the transfers space is used only to inform the Copyright Office about transfers that occurred before registration. If a copyright is transferred after registration, there is no need to reregister (indeed, it is not permitted). However, although not required, it is a good idea to record (send) a copy of the postregistration transfer document to the Copyright Office. (See Chapter 11.)

5. Space 5: Previous Registration

If none of the material in the work you're registering has been registered before, check the "No" box and skip ahead to Space 6.

If all or part of the work has been previously registered, check the "Yes" box. Then, you need to check one or more of the next three boxes to explain why a new registration is being sought:

- Check the first box if you are now registering a work you previously registered when it was unpublished.
- Check the second box if someone other than the author was listed as the copyright claimant in Space 4 in the prior registration, and the author is now registering the work in her own name. For example, where an anonymous or pseudonymous author previously listed an authorized agent in Space 4 and now wishes to re-register in her own name.
- Check the third box if the previously registered work has been changed, and you are registering the changed version or new edition to protect the additions or revisions.

Then provide the registration number and year of previous registration in the blanks indicated. The registration number can be found stamped on the certificate of registration. It is usually a multidigit number preceded by the two-letter prefix of the application form used—for example:

TX 012345. The Copyright Office places a small "u" following the prefix if the registered work is unpublished—for example: TXu 567890. If you made more than one prior registration for the work, you only need to give the latest registration number and year.

6. Space 6: Description of Derivative Works or Compilations

If your software or website qualifies as a derivative work or compilation, you'll need to complete Space 6.

a. Software: Space 6

You'll usually need to complete Space 6 if your software is:

- a derivative work—that is, a work based upon or derived from one or more preexisting works—for example, it contains a substantial amount of previously published, previously registered, or public domain material (such as subroutines, modules, or textual images),
- a changed version of another work (this is really just one type of derivative work), or
- a compilation of preexisting works—that is, a work created by selecting, arranging, and coordinating preexisting materials into a new work of authorship.

b. Software: preexisting material (6a)

If your software is a derivative work and the preexisting material was substantial, you must generally describe the preexisting material here. You can simply state "previous version"; you need not provide any more detail. If the derivative work was based on a series of preexisting works, it is not necessary to list every one.

Don't fill out Space 6a if the software is a compilation.

c. Software: material added to this work (6b)

Typical examples of descriptions of new material for derivative works in Space 6b include "revised computer program," "editorial revisions," and "revisions and additional text of computer program." Often, you can simply repeat what you stated in the Nature of Authorship line in Space 2.

> **EXAMPLE:** AcmeSoft created and registered version 1.0 of a database program in 2004. AcmeSoft later thoroughly revises the software, adding many new features and redesigning the user interface. This new version 2.0 is published in 2005. AcmeSoft should state "revised computer program" in Space 6b when it registers version 2.0.

As mentioned earlier, you shouldn't use words such as "enhancements," "error corrections," "patches," "features," or "debugging." This is because the Copyright Office tends to rule that these types of changes aren't significant enough to warrant another registration.

If the work is a compilation, the statement should describe both the compilation itself and the material that has been compiled.

> **EXAMPLE:** *Internet Magazine* compiles a number of previously published and public domain Java applets onto a disk. It should state in Space 6b: "Compilation of Java applets and text."

If your software is both a derivative work and compilation, you may state "Compilation and additional new material."

> **EXAMPLE:** *Internet Magazine* in the example above not only compiles preexisting Java applets, but has its staff create a number of new applets as well. It could state in Space 6b: "Compilation and additional new material (programming and text)."

If the preexisting material in your work is not substantial or was not published, registered, or in the public domain, put "N/A" in Space 6.

> **EXAMPLE 1:** You would not need to complete Space 6 for a computer pro-

gram entitled "X-103 Program, Version 3," incorporating material from two earlier developmental versions that were unpublished and unregistered.

> **EXAMPLE 2:** You would not be required to complete Space 6 for a program containing a total of 5,000 lines of program text, only 50 of which were previously published.

There are two situations where you should provide an explanatory cover letter to the Copyright Office if you don't complete Space 6:

- the title of your work contains a version number other than 1 or 1.0, or
- the deposit for the software has a copyright notice containing multiple year dates.

In either case, the examiner will question (by letter or phone) whether the program is a revised or derivative version if Space 6 has not been completed.

If the software is not a derivative work and the version number or multiple year dates in the copyright notice on the deposit refer to internal revisions or the history of development of the program, put that information in a cover letter to the Copyright Office to help speedup processing.

> **EXAMPLE:** PubSoft developed a desktop publishing program called *Practical Publisher* over a number of years. It produced several versions of

the program that it used for internal testing and development only. The final published version of the program PubSoft registers in 2005 has a copyright notice that says "Copyright (c) 2003, 2004, 2005 by PubSoft, Inc." Although it was not required (see Chapter 5), PubSoft included the multiple year dates in the notice to make clear the copyright covers the earlier versions. PubSoft should include a letter such as the following with its registration application:

Register of Copyrights
Library of Congress
Copyright Office
101 Independence Avenue, SE
Washington, DC 20559-6000

Dear Register:

Enclosed is a copyright registration application for Practical Publisher 1.0 submitted by PubSoft, Inc.

Please note that the deposit material for the program contains a copyright notice with multiple-year dates.

Practical Publisher 1.0 is not a derivative work or revised version for registration purposes. The multiple-year dates in the copyright notice refer to internal revisions that have not been published or registered. I certify that the statements made in this letter are true.

Very truly yours,

Keith Stoke
Software Development Manager

---

d. Websites: Space 6

You'll need to complete Space 6 if the website or other work being registered contains a substantial amount of material (such as text, photos, or graphics) that was:

- previously published
- previously registered with the Copyright Office, or
- in the public domain.

If your site falls into any of these categories, it is likely either a derivative work, a compilation, or both.

A derivative work is a work based upon or derived from one or more preexisting works. Updated or revised versions of preexisting websites are one type of derivative works. Websites based on preexisting works are also derivative works—for example, the *Star Wars* website (www.starwars.com) is a derivative work based upon the movie of the same name.

A compilation is a work created by selecting, arranging, and coordinating preexisting materials into a new work of authorship. Many websites are compilations. For example, the LEXIS/NEXIS website is a compilation of preexisting articles.

e. Websites: preexisting material (6a)

Complete Space 6a if your website is a derivative work. Here, you must generally describe the preexisting material the work you're registering was derived from. In the case of the *Star Wars* website, for example, Space 6a would list the movie *Star Wars* upon which the website was based.

If you're just registering an updated or new version of a website, you can simply state "previous version"; you need not provide any more detail. If the derivative work was based on a series of preexisting works, it is not necessary to list every one.

Don't fill out Space 6a if the website is a compilation, unless it a compilation that is also a derivative—for example, a French translation of website links or an online version of a print encyclopedia.

f. Websites: material added to this work (6b):

If your website is a derivative work or compilation, you must describe in Space 6b the new material you are registering. This is the material you (or somebody you've hired) has added to the preexisting material. Often, you can simply repeat what you stated in the Nature of Authorship line in Space 2.

Typical examples of descriptions of new material for derivative works in Space 6b include "editorial revisions" and "revisions and additional text."

If the work is a compilation, the statement should describe both the compilation itself and the material that has been compiled.

EXAMPLE: The website www.refdesk .com is a collection of weblinks to sites on the Internet containing useful reference materials. Refdesk.com is a compilation. Its authors should state in Space 6b: "Compilation of weblinks and text."

If your website is both a derivative work and compilation, you may state "Compilation and additional new material."

EXAMPLE: The Nolo website (www .nolo.com) consists of a compilation of preexisting Nolo books and articles as well as new material created by the Nolo staff derived from other published Nolo materials. Nolo could state in Space 6b: "Compilation and additional new material (editorial revisions and additional text)."

If the preexisting material in your work is not substantial or was not published, registered, or in the public domain, put "N/A" in Space 6.

7. Space 7: Deposit Account and Correspondence

In Space 7, you provide contact information and indicate whether you elect to use a deposit account.

a. Deposit account

If you plan to have 12 or more trans-actions per year with the Copyright Office, you may establish a money deposit account to which you make advance money deposits and charge your copyright fees against the account instead of sending a separate check each time. You must deposit at least $250 to open an account. For an application, obtain Circular R5 from the Copyright Office by downloading it from the Copyright Office website.

b. Correspondence

Provide the name, address, area code, and telephone number of the person the Copyright Office should contact if it has questions about your application. If the registration is being made by a corporation or other entity, list the name of the person in the organization who should be contacted. If you have a fax number, include that along with your regular phone number (remember to specify which is a fax). The Copyright Office may soon start corresponding by fax.

8. Space 8: Certification

Check the appropriate box indicating your capacity as the person registering the work:

- Check the Author box if you are the person (or one of several people) named in Space 2. If there are several authors, only one need sign.
- Check the Other Copyright Claimant box if you are not named in Space 2 as the author, but have acquired all the author's rights.
- Check the Owner of Exclusive Right(s) box if you only own one or more—but not all—of the exclusive rights making up the entire copyright.
- Check the Authorized Agent box if you are not signing for yourself as an individual, but as the authorized representative of the author, the copyright claimant who owns all the copyright rights, or the owner of some exclusive rights. State the name of the person or organization on whose behalf you're signing on the dotted line following the box.

Check the Authorized Agent box if you, as an individual, are signing on behalf of a corporation, partnership or other organization that is the author, copyright claimant, or holder of exclusive rights.

Type or print your name and date in the appropriate blanks, then sign your name on the line following "Handwritten signature."

⚠ **Watch Your Dates.** If you are registering a published work, the Copyright Office will not accept your application if the date listed in the certification space is earlier than the date of publication shown in Space 3.

9. Space 9: Return Mailing Address

Fill in your name and the return mailing address for your copyright registration certificate in the last box on the form. Make sure the address is legible, since the certificate will be returned to you in a window envelope.

Now that you've completed the form, you'll need to prepare your deposit, covered in Section E, below.

D. Complying With Copyright Deposit Requirements

To register your work with the U.S. Copyright Office, you're required to submit (deposit) one or two copies of the work itself. Deposit requirements serve three primary functions:

- Deposits show the Copyright Office that your work is eligible for copyright protection (that it is an original work of authorship).

- Deposits show the Copyright Office that your work is adequately described on your application form.
- Deposits serve as an identifier for your work in the event a dispute arises involving your copyright.

Deposit requirements differ for computer programs and websites, so they are discussed separately. (Note, however, that the deposit requirements for HTML code and similar code are the same as for computer programs.)

Whether or not your registration application is accepted, your deposit becomes the property of the U.S. government and will never be returned to you.

E. Software Deposits

Except where the software is embodied on a CD-ROM disk, you may not deposit floppy disks or other magnetic media (or computer chips in the case of firmware). Rather, the Copyright Office wants a hard-copy printout of all or part of your code (when it comes to the registration of long programs, Copyright Office rules usually allow you to send a portion of the work instead of the whole thing). There are four alternative types of deposits for you to choose from:

- a printout of all or part of your software source code (Section E1, below)
- a copy of part of the source code with any trade secrets blacked out so

no one can read them (Section E2, below)

- a combination of source code and object code (Section E2, below), or
- object code only (Section E3, below).

These requirements are the same however software is distributed—whether in stores, by mail order, or online over the Internet or commercial online services. However, there are special requirements when software is contained on a CD-ROM.

Please read this entire section through at least once before making a decision as to what you wish to deposit. This material is potentially confusing, and you may well find yourself changing your mind several times.

> ## Special Relief From Deposit Requirements
>
> In some cases, you may be unwilling or unable to make a deposit in any of the forms described in this section. For example, if you need to register immediately for litigation purposes, it's possible that the required computer code may not be available. In this event, you may be able to deposit something else—for example, pictures of the screen displays.
>
> To get permission to file a special kind of deposit, you must request that the Copyright Office grant you special relief from their deposit requirements. Send a signed letter to the Chief of the Examining Division, Copyright Office, Library of Congress, Washington, DC 20559. Explain why you need special relief—for example, to preserve the confidentiality of your computer code, to avoid a severe financial burden, or because the normally required material is unavailable. Also explain exactly what you wish to deposit instead.

1. Depositing Straight Source Code

Your first alternative is to deposit all or part of your program source code—that is, the computer program instructional code that the programmer writes using a particular programming language such as C++ or Java.

This is what most people do and what the Copyright Office prefers. The advantage to depositing source code is that it better identifies the nature of your original work of authorship than does object code. Depositing your source code serves to register your object code as well even though the object code is not deposited. (*CGA Corp. v. Chance*, 217 U.S.P.Q. 718 (N.D. Cal. 1982).)

Under Copyright Office regulations (37 C.F.R. 202.70), you generally don't have to deposit your entire program source code. To satisfy the deposit requirement for program source code, you must deposit either:

- the entire program source code if the source code is no more than 50 pages, or
- if the source code is longer than 50 printed-out pages, the first and last 25 pages.

A page isn't precisely defined, but in practice, standard 8½-inch by 11-inch paper is most often used.

There are no requirements as to the format or spacing of the code—that is, it may be single- or double-spaced.

As an alternative to a printout, you may deposit a microfiche of the identifying material. If you do this, deposit the entire program code or, if it's longer than 50 pages, microfiche the first and last 25 pages.

If the code contains a copyright notice, you must include the page or equivalent unit containing the notice. A photograph or drawing showing the form and location of the notice is acceptable. Whatever you do, it's always a good idea to sprinkle many copyright notices throughout the code.

If the deposit material does not give a printed title and/or version indicator, add the title and any indicia that can be used to identify the particular program.

Deposits and Trade Secrets

If you deposit the first and last 25 pages of your source code, you may wish to arrange the source code modules so that the most innovative and/or secret portions of the code do not appear in the first or last 25 pages. Copyright Office rules do not prevent this. You may also take out any comment statements that might help an infringer. The downside to this is that your deposit may not provide the best possible evidence of your work to prove copyright infringement. So there is a trade-off involved.

Determining the First and Last 25 Pages of Your Software

Being able to deposit only the first and last 25 pages of a program is very convenient, but there is one problem—most software systems are broken into multiple files residing in multiple folders. How do you determine which are the first and last 25 pages? The Copyright Office doesn't seem concerned with this issue and has left it up to you to decide which 25 pages should be "first" and which 25 should be "last." You could do it by ordering your files in alphabetical order (according to the file names) and send the first 25 pages from the alphabetically first file and the last 25 pages from the alphabetically last file. Or, you could do it some other way that you think makes sense. The Copyright Office will not question your decision.

---

a. Revised programs

If the program you're registering is a revision of a previously registered program, and the revisions are uniformly (more or less) spread throughout the program, deposit the first and last 25 pages as indicated above and the page containing the copyright notice, if any.

If, on the other hand, the revisions are concentrated in a part of the program that isn't fairly represented by the first and last 25 pages requirement, you may deposit

any 50 pages that are representative of the revised material in the new program together with the page containing the copyright notice.

b. Programs created in scripted language

For programs created in scripted language such as HTML and JavaScript, the script is considered the equivalent of source code. Thus, the same number of pages of script are required as are required for source code.

2. Depositing Source Code With Trade Secrets Blacked Out or Depositing Source Code and Object Code

As discussed in Chapter 7, trade secret protection can be used in conjunction with copyright protection to protect the ideas, concepts, and algorithms embodied in software. Source code is usually a software developer's or publisher's most closely guarded trade secret. Software is normally distributed in object code form only. The source code is usually kept locked away and shown only to employees and others who have agreed to keep it secret.

If you plan to keep your source code a trade secret, there's a danger that you'll compromise this status by using the source code as a registration deposit. Your deposit becomes a public record on file at the Copyright Office in Washington, DC, and if you deposit source code, it could conceivably be studied by a competitor or pirate, and reproduced in an infringing program. This is not supposed to happen, but it has.

In one well-known case, an attorney employed by Atari Games Corporation gained access to, and made a copy of, source code that Nintendo of America had deposited. The attorney accomplished this feat by falsely claiming the code was involved in litigation. Using this information, Atari was able to create a key to open the ROM-based lock that controlled access to the Nintendo game system. Nintendo brought a copyright infringement suit against Atari for making the unauthorized copy of the code and won. (*Atari Games Corp. v. Nintendo of America, Inc.*, 980 F.2d 857 (Fed.Cir. 1992).) No one can say how many other times this has occurred.

To avoid revealing trade secrets in your deposit, Copyright Office rules permit you to deposit source code with any trade secrets blacked out, or a combination of source code and object code. Under these rules, you have the option of depositing:

- the first and last 25 pages of source code with up to 49% of the source code blacked out (in other words,

you deposit 50 pages with only 26 being readable; this obviously helps you to protect source code against infringement), or

- the first and last ten pages of source code with no blacked out portions (this smaller deposit may, depending on the length of the program, or program package, pretty well frustrate pirates), or

- the first and last 25 pages of object code, plus any ten or more consecutive pages of source code with no blacked out portions (because object code is unreadable by humans, this should frustrate potential infringers), or

- for programs consisting of less than 50 pages, the entire source code with up to 49% of the code blacked out.

In all cases, the visible portion of the code must represent an "appreciable amount" of computer code.

If the code contains a copyright notice, you must include the page or equivalent unit containing the notice. A photograph or drawing showing the form and location of the notice is acceptable.

If the deposit material does not give a printed title or version indicator, add the title and any indicia that can be used to identify the particular program.

If you're depositing a revised program with the revisions contained in the first and last 25 pages, you may select any of the four options described just above.

If the revisions are not contained in the first and last 25 pages of code, your deposit must consist of either:

- 20 pages of source code containing the revisions with no blacked out portions, or
- any 50 pages of source code containing the revisions with up to 49% of the code blacked out.

3. Depositing Object Code Only

If you do not want to deposit any source code (even with portions blacked out), you may deposit object code only—that is, the machine language version of the program which the computer executes. Because object code is unreadable by most mortals, a deposit in this form won't likely be examined for ideas and code by a competitor. Also, if you're treating your work as a trade secret, an object code deposit doesn't reveal it.

However, depositing object code only has a down side. Because Copyright Office personnel can't read object code to determine whether it constitutes an original work of authorship, the Copyright Office registration will be made under the Office's "rule of doubt," and you'll receive a warning letter to that effect. The rule of doubt means the Copyright Office is unable to independently verify that your deposit is a work of original authorship.

Having your registration issued under the rule of doubt results in loss of one of the benefits of registration: the presumption that your copyright is valid. (*Freedman v. Select Information Sys.*, 221 U.S.P.Q. 848 (1984) (N.D. Cal. 1983).) This means that if you end up suing someone for copyright infringement, you will have to prove to the court that your software is an original work of authorship and otherwise qualifies for copyright protection. Usually this is not too difficult, but it will complicate matters. Loss of this presumption may be particularly damaging if you wish to obtain a quick pretrial injunction forcing an alleged infringer to stop distributing a pirated work.

Programs Not Compiled Into Object Code

When you compile a program written in C++ or most other languages, the compiler translates the source code into machine code or processor instructions—this is what the Copyright Office terms object code. However, not all programs are compiled into object code. For example, programs written in the Java programming language are compiled into bytecode instead of machine code. The bytecode is then executed by a program called a bytecode interpreter. For programs such as Java, you may deposit the bytecode or similar intermediate code instead of your source code.

---

a. What to deposit

Deposit the same amount of object code as is required when depositing straight source code as described in Section E1, above. In other words, you must deposit either:

- The entire program in object code, or
- If the object code is longer than 50 printed-out pages, the first and last 25 pages.

Make sure you deposit 50 pages of object code, and not the equivalent of 50 pages of source code translated into object code form.

If the code contains a copyright notice, you must include the page or equivalent unit containing the notice. A photograph or drawing showing the form and location of the notice is acceptable. Where the copyright notice is encoded within the object code so that its presence and content are not easily readable, the notice should be underlined or highlighted and its contents decoded.

If the deposit material does not give a printed title or version indicator, add the title and any indicia that can be used to identify the particular program.

b. Letter to Copyright Office

All deposits consisting solely of object code must be accompanied by an assurance to the Copyright Office that the work contains copyrightable authorship.

If you fail to include this assurance with your deposit, the Copyright Office will write you and state that since they can neither read your deposit nor verify that its subject material is copyrightable, you must either send human-readable source code or a letter assuring the Copyright Office that your deposit contains copyrightable material. Obviously, it makes sense to anticipate this request.

A letter such as the following will provide the needed assurance if you deposit object code.

Sample Letter Declaring Your Work Is Copyrightable

Register of Copyrights
Library of Congress
Copyright Office
101 Independence Avenue, SE
Washington, DC 20559-6000

Dear Register:

Enclosed is a copyright registration application for Website Maker submitted by Julia Youngster. Julia Youngster is submitting the deposit in object code form in order to protect trade secrets that are contained in the computer code.

Website Maker as deposited in object code form contains copyrightable authorship.

I certify that the statements made in this letter are true.

Very truly yours,

Julia Youngster

4. Special Deposit Requirements for Software Embodied on CD-ROMs

The Library of Congress wants to establish a collection of CD-ROMs, so a regulation was enacted in 1991 requiring applicants of works embodied on CD-ROMs to deposit the CD-ROM disk along with a printout of the program code.

CD-ROMs are often used for multimedia works—that is, works containing text, audiovisual elements like photos and video, and music or other sounds, in addition to software (usually operating software or software that produces screen displays).

A single copyright registration and deposit can cover all these elements—that is, the software plus the "content."

However, a separate registration and deposit for the software used for a multimedia work embodied on a CD-ROM is required when the software:

- was previously published or was previously registered as an unpublished work, or
- was, or will be, sold or otherwise distributed separately.

When you make a separate registration for only the software on a CD-ROM, you need to make clear in your application that this is all you're registering—that is, that you're not registering the content or

other elements on the CD-ROM. Otherwise, the copyright examiner will ask you whether you want to register these other elements. To avoid this, include a letter with your application stating that you wish to register the software only.

You must deposit one copy of the entire CD-ROM package. Everything that is marketed or distributed together must be deposited, whether or not you're the copyright claimant for each element. This includes:

- the CD-ROM disk(s)
- instructional manual(s), and
- any printed version of the work that is sold with the CD-ROM package—for example, where a book accompanies a CD-ROM.

In addition, you must deposit a printout of all or part of the source code or object code for the software you're registering as described in Sections E1, E2, and E3 above.

5. Deposit Requirements for Computer Output Screens

You don't have to deposit identifying material for your screens unless you make specific reference to them in Space 2 (Nature of Authorship) of your registration form. (See Section B.) If you specifically mention the screens, you must deposit them.

To deposit application software screens, use a printout, photograph, or drawing of the screens. These reproductions should be no smaller than 3" by 3" and no larger than 9" by 12". The Copyright Office will also accept a manual accompanying the program as a deposit for the computer output screens if it contains clear reproductions of the screens.

Where the authorship on the screens is predominantly audiovisual (for example, an arcade game), a 1.5" VHS format videotape that clearly shows the copyrightable expression should be deposited. In the case of arcade games, you should deposit your "attract" and "play" modes together as part of a single registration in videotape form. For game screens, you should include any sound component, either as part of the videotape recording or separately on a cassette. Don't neglect this. The uniqueness of the sound that accompanies game programs has been helpful in establishing ownership of these types of works in several court decisions.

Don't deposit a videotape if the computer screens simply show the functioning of the program. Instead, deposit printouts, photos, or drawings as described above.

As part of this type of registration, you should also explain your deposit in a letter.

Sample Letter Explaining Deposit

June 11, 200X

Dear Chief Examiner:

Please find enclosed my deposit consisting of identifying material related to my computer program Celestial Tease. The material consists of videotape and photographs. These represent the output screens and accompanying sound from the above-mentioned program. I request you accept this material as a deposit accompanying my copyright registration.

Sincerely,

Crystal Star

Senior Programmer

6. Deposit Requirements for Documentation

Documentation includes user manuals, training manuals, instruction sheets, textual flowcharts, film, slide shows, and all other works that are used to support a program in some way. Written documentation can be anything from two pages stapled together to a bound, full-color, 500-page book.

If you register your documentation separately, you must deposit two copies of your entire work if it's in written, sound recording, or graphic form.

If your documentation isn't registered separately and you include a reference to it on your registration form, you must deposit one copy of the documentation. If you don't refer specifically to the documentation, the deposit is optional.

F. Website Deposits

The Copyright Office gives you two deposit options when you register a website:

- *Option 1:* Under the first deposit option, you must provide a computer disk containing the entire work clearly labeled with title and author information *and* a representative hard-copy sample of the work being registered.

If the work consists of less than five pages of text or graphics, or three minutes of music, sounds, or audiovisual material, you must deposit a copy of the entire work along with a confirmation that it is complete.

If the work is longer, you must deposit five representative pages or three representative minutes. This identifying material must include the work's title and author, and a copyright notice, if any.

- *Option 2:* Alternatively, you may deposit a hard-copy version of the entire work. No computer disk is required in this case.

Your deposit should be in a format appropriate for the type of work being registered. For example, a hard-copy printout of text or graphics or an audio-cassette of music or sounds.

If a work is published both online and by distributing physical copies, you must deposit the physical copies, not the online materials. For example, if a work is published as a hardbound book and also transmitted online, two copies of the hardbound book must be deposited.

G. Sending Your Application to the Copyright Office

By now, you have completed your application form and have your deposit ready to go. Make a photocopy of your application form and retain it in your records along with an exact copy of your deposit.

1. Application Fee

You must submit a check or money order for the nonrefundable application fee payable to the Register of Copyrights. Clip—don't staple—your check or money order to the application.

At this writing, the registration fee is $30. Be sure to check to see if the registration fee has been raised. You can do this by checking the Copyright Office website at www.copyright.gov, checking the update section of the nolo.com website, or by calling the Copyright Office at 202-707-3000.

2. Send Single Package to Copyright Office

Put your application, deposit, and check or money order for the appropriate application fee in a single package. If you send them separately, all the packages will be returned by the Copyright Office. But, if you send a deposit of a published work separately, the Copyright Office will turn it over to the Library of Congress rather than return it to you, so you'll get the application and fee back, but not the deposit.

Send your single package to:

Library of Congress
Copyright Office
101 Independence Avenue, SE
Washington, DC 20559-6000

Watch Your Dates. If you're registering a published work, your application must be received by the Copyright Office after the publication date listed in Space 3 of your application. Reason: A published work cannot be registered prior to the date of publication.

Screening of Mail to the U.S. Copyright Office

All mail (whether by U.S. Postal Service or private carrier) is carefully screened for biological and other harmful substances before being delivered to the Copyright Office. This process can add three to five days to the delivery time for all mail sent to the Copyright Office. The effective date of registration of a work is still the day the work is received, but relief from this may be available under special Copyright Office regulations (see www.copyright.gov/fedreg/2001/66fr62942.html).

3. Registration Effective When the Application Is Received

Your registration is effective on the date the Copyright Office receives all three elements: application, deposit, and application fee in acceptable form. This means you don't need to worry about how long it takes the Copyright Office to process the application and send you a certificate of registration. You'll be eligible to obtain statutory damages or attorney fees from anyone who copies your work while your application is being processed.

H. Expedited Registration

In a few special circumstances, you may request that your application be given special handling by the Copyright Office. Special handling applications are processed in five to ten days, rather than the normal six to eight months or more. Special handling is available only if needed:

- for copyright litigation: under current law, a work must be registered before a copyright infringement suit may be filed; you'll need to have a certified copy of your registration certificate to show the court
- to meet a contractual or publishing deadline, or
- for some other urgent need.

The requirements for special handling are explained in Circular 10, *Special Handling,* which can be downloaded from the Copyright Office website. You must pay an additional $530 fee for special handling (the $30 application fee plus a $500 special handling fee).

I. Dealing With the Copyright Office

The Copyright Office has an enormous workload: they handle over 600,000 applications per year. It can take anywhere from six to eight months or even longer for your application to be processed.

Be patient and remember that the registration is effective on the date it is received by the Copyright Office (assuming the forms were filled out properly), not the date you actually receive your registration certificate.

The Copyright Office will eventually respond to your application in one of three ways:

- If your application is acceptable, the Copyright Office will send you a registration certificate, which is merely a copy of your application with the official Copyright Office seal, registration date, and number stamped on it. Be sure to retain it for your records.
- If your application contained errors or omissions the Copyright Office believes are correctable, a copyright examiner may phone you for further information. Or he may return the application or deposit with a letter explaining what corrections to make.
- If the Copyright Office determines that your work cannot be registered, it will send you a letter explaining why. Neither your deposit nor fee will be returned.

If you don't hear anything from the Copyright Office within six to eight months after your application should have been received, you may wish to write them to find out the status of your application. They may have lost the application, it may have never been received or—

most likely—they may be very far behind in their work. In your letter, identify yourself, the author, and the copyright owner; give the date of your application and the form you used; and describe the work briefly. If the Copyright Office cashed your check, you'll know that they did receive the application. Include a copy of the canceled check with your letter. It will contain a number that will help the Copyright Office trace your application.

You'll have to pay the Copyright Office a fee if you want to find out about the status of an application fewer than 16 weeks after the Copyright Office received it. Call the Copyright Office at 202-707-3000 to ask about this.

1. Review of Copyright Office's Refusal to Register Application

If you think the Copyright Examiner has wrongfully refused to register your work, you may submit a written objection and request that the Copyright Office reconsider its action. The appeal letter should be addressed to Chief, Receiving and Processing Division, Copyright Office, P.O. Box 71380, Washington, DC 20024-1380. The first request for reconsideration must be received in the Copyright Office within 120 days of the date of the Office's first refusal to register, and the envelope containing the request should be clearly marked: FIRST APPEAL/.

If the claim is refused after reconsideration, the head of the appropriate Examining Division section will send you written notice of the reasons for the refusal. After this, you may again request reconsideration in writing. This second appeal must be received in the Copyright Office within 120 days of the date of the Office's refusal of the first appeal, and be directed to the Board of Appeals at the following address: Copyright GC/I&R, P.O. Box 70400, Southwest Station, Washington, DC 20024.

The second appeal is handled by the Copyright Office Board of Appeals, which consists of the Register of Copyrights, the General Counsel, and the Chief of the Examining Division. The Chair of the Board of Appeals will send you a letter setting out the reasons for acceptance or denial of your claim. The Appeals Board's decision constitutes the Copyright Office's final action. You may then bring a legal action to have a court review the Copyright Office's decision. In addition, you can bring a copyright infringement action notwithstanding the Copyright Office's refusal to register your work. You'll need to see a lawyer about this. (See Chapter 19.)

2. Examining Deposits From Copyright Office Files

The Copyright Office is located in Washington, DC, so anyone who wants to look at any records must go there. Direct copying from Copyright Office files by nonagency employees is prohibited by law. Because the Copyright Office stores great masses of information, it normally takes from one to five days even to get access to a particular deposit.

To look at any specific deposit, a person normally needs:

- the registration number or the exact name of the work and author, and
- a signed, written statement as to why access is needed.

This written statement is placed in a file associated with the copyright deposit and is available to the copyright owner for examination.

When a deposit is retrieved, a Copyright Office employee is assigned to stay with the deposit at all times and to prevent the requester from taking notes or copying the deposit in any way. As a practical matter, this means that it's unlikely that your code will be directly copied from Copyright Office files. However, it won't stop an intelligent pirate from getting a pretty good overview of your approach.

If you suspect that your deposit has been copied, you may well want to have the Copyright Office conduct a search of your file for evidence of an examination of your deposit. The Copyright Office charges $75 an hour to conduct searches. Call the Copyright Office at 202-287-8700, explain that you want a search of your file to see whether it has been examined by anyone else, and ask what the charge will be. Then, mail this amount and a written request to have your file examined to:

Library of Congress

Copyright Office

Reference and Bibliography Section, LM-451

101 Independence Avenue, SE

Washington, DC 20559-6000

J. Corrections and Changes After Registration Is Completed (Supplemental Registration)

The same published work normally can only be registered once with the Copyright Office. However, a second supplemental registration may be necessary to augment your original basic registration if you later discover that you forgot something important, supplied the Copyright Office with the wrong information, or if important facts have changed. A special form, Form CA, is used for this purpose.

Remember that your registration is a public record. By keeping your registration accurate and up-to-date you will make it easier for those searching the Copyright Office records to discover your work and locate you or your company. This may result in new marketing opportunities and help to prevent an infringement. For information on completing the Form CA, download the form from the Copyright Office website and follow the instructions that accompany the form.

Supplemental Registration Not Needed to Correct Obvious Errors

It is not necessary to file a formal supplemental registration to correct obvious errors the Copyright Office should have caught when it reviewed your application. This includes, for example, the omission of necessary information, such as the names of the author or claimant, and obvious mistakes (like a publication date of 1098). If, when you receive your registration certificate, you discover that such errors have been overlooked by the copyright examiner, simply notify the Copyright Office and the mistake will be corrected with no need for a supplemental registration additional fee. ∎

Copyright Notice

This chapter is about copyright notice—the "c" in a circle—©—followed by a publication date and name, usually seen on published works. The purpose of such a notice is to inform the public that a work is copyrighted, when it was published, and who owns the copyright. A copyright notice is not required as a condition of obtaining or keeping a copyright. Nevertheless, it's a very good idea to include a notice anyway on all your published software, websites, and other copyrightable works.

A. Why Use a Copyright Notice?

Contrary to what many people believe, a copyright notice is not required to establish or maintain a copyright in the United States or most foreign countries. Nor is a notice necessary to register a work with the Copyright Office. However, notice was required for software and other copyrightable works published in the U.S. before March 1, 1989.

So if a notice is not mandatory, why bother to include one on your published software and other copyrightable works? There are several excellent reasons.

1. Notice Helps Makes Infringement Suits Economically Feasible

Copyright infringement lawsuits are often only economically feasible if the author can obtain substantial financial damages from the infringer and use some of this money to pay the attorney. The easiest way to get substantial damages is to prove that the infringement was willful—that is, that the infringer knew that he or she was breaking the law but did so anyway. Proving "willfulness" can be difficult if a published work lacks a valid copyright notice. The reason for this is what's known as the innocent infringement defense. If a person infringes upon a published work that does not contain a copyright notice, the infringer can claim in court that the infringement was innocent—that is, he or she didn't know the work was protected by copyright. On the other hand, if there is a valid copyright notice on the work, the infringer cannot claim innocence and will be treated as a willful infringer.

2. Copyright Notice May Deter Potential Infringers

Another important reason to place a copyright notice on all copies of your published software is that it may help deter copyright infringement. The notice lets users know that the work is protected by copyright and may not be copied without the owner's permission. Moreover, since copyright notices appear on the vast majority of published works, including software and websites, a user of software or a website not containing a notice might mistakenly assume that it is not protected by copyright, and feel free to copy it or otherwise infringe upon your copyright.

3. Notice Informs the World Who the Copyright Owner Is

A copyright notice contains the name of the copyright owner(s) of the work. This information will help third parties—who might want to obtain permission to use or purchase the work—to identify and locate the owner.

B. When to Place a Copyright Notice on Software and Websites

Many people are confused about exactly when to place a copyright notice on their software or other copyrighted works. Should you use a copyright notice from the day you write the first line of code, when you test the first module, or only when you first market your software to the public? Should you place a notice on your website when you're developing it or only when you place it online?

The best practice is to put a modified informal copyright notice on your work (described in Section C4 below) even before it is published, and put a formal copyright notice on your work when it is published.

1. Copyright Notices for Published Software

A full-blown formal copyright notice of the type described in Section C below should be used for all published software and other published works. A work is published for copyright purposes when copies are sold, licensed, rented, lent, given away, or otherwise distributed to the public. Selling copies to the public through retail outlets or by mail order, publishing code in a magazine, selling a program at a widely attended computer show, and allowing a number of educational institutions to use your program without restriction are all examples of publication.

However, publication occurs only when software is made available to the general public on an unrestricted basis. Distributing copies of software to a restricted group of users does not constitute publication. For example, sending copies to a few friends or beta testers would not constitute a publication.

2. Software Distributed Online

It is common to distribute software by uploading it to sites on the Internet and commercial online services such as America Online or C/Net. It's not entirely clear whether making a program available online constitutes publication. However, you should assume it does. Accordingly, all such programs should carry a proper copyright notice to achieve maximum copyright protection.

3. Copyright Notices for Unpublished Software

Placing a copyright notice on unpublished software provides all the benefits discussed in Section A, above, except that technically it will not prevent an infringer from raising the innocent infringement defense discussed above. For these reasons, it is sensible to place a copyright notice on unpublished software before sending it to beta testers, potential publishers, product reviewers, and other third parties. See Section C4 for a form of notice to use with unpublished materials.

4. Copyright Notices for Websites

Courts, Congress, and the Copyright Office have yet to decide exactly when a website is published for copyright purposes. You should assume that any website that can be accessed by Internet users has been published, and include a copyright notice on it. Online materials that can be accessed only on a very limited basis—for example, over a private network—might not be considered published. But even in these cases it is wise to include a copyright notice. It costs nothing to do so and may help to deter infringements.

Web materials you have not yet placed online or otherwise made available to the general public would be considered unpublished. But, as with unpublished software, it's a good idea to place a notice on such materials before you make them available to others in the offline world. Such a notice should not include a publication date. See Section C4 for a form of notice to use with unpublished materials.

C. Form of Notice

There are strict technical requirements as to what a copyright notice must contain if it is to serve its purpose of preventing an innocent infringer defense. A valid copyright notice contains three elements:

- the copyright symbol—©—or the words "Copyright" or "Copr."
- if the software, website, or other work is published, the year of publication, and
- the name of the copyright owner.

It is not required that these elements appear in any particular order in the notice, but most notices are written in the order set forth above—for example, © 2001 Nolo.

Errors in Copyright Notice

If you discover an error in the copyright notice for your published work, it's wise to have it corrected when subsequent copies are produced. However, it is not necessary to recall any copies already distributed.

---

1. Copyright Symbol or the Words "Copyright" or "Copr."

In the United States either the © symbol or the words "Copyright" or "Copr." may be used. Or you can use the © symbol and the words Copyright or Copr. (This will help make it clear to even the dullest minds that your work is copyrighted.)

However, in those foreign countries that require that a copyright notice appear on a published work for it to be protected by copyright at all, you must use the © symbol (you can also use the words Copyright or Copr. if you wish). So, in the case of websites (which can be accessed all over the world) and software that might be distributed outside the U.S., be sure to always use the © symbol.

Virtually all word processing programs come with alternate character sets that include the c in a circle. However, if, for some reason, your computer is unable to make a © symbol, the word Copyright or abbreviation Copr. should be used along with a c in parentheses—like this: (c). This will be a valid notice in the U.S., but there might be problems in some foreign countries. So if your work has particular international application, use a © symbol.

A different copyright symbol is used for sound recordings copyrights. A capital P in a circle—℗—is used instead of the © symbol.

2. Year of Publication

The copyright notice must also state the year the work was published. For initial versions of software, this is easy. Also, as discussed in the preceding section, a publication date should not be provided in a notice for unpublished software or website materials.

a. Updates

Of course, most websites and software programs are continually revised and updated. The copyright notice doesn't have to be changed if an update consists only of minor revisions.

However, if an update contains a substantial amount of new material, it is considered to be a separate work of authorship in its own right. The notice for such a derivative work should contain the date the new work was published. The notice need not contain the date or dates of the prior version or versions. However, it is common practice to include such dates in the copyright notice. One reason is to let the user know when the earlier versions were created. Another reason to do this is that it is not always possible to tell if a work qualifies as a derivative work under copyright office rules.

> **EXAMPLE 1:** AcmeSoft, Inc., published version 1.0 of a VRML authoring tool in 2001. The copyright notice read "Copyright © 2001 by AcmeSoft, Inc." The software was revised and republished as a new 2.0 version in 2002. If the 2.0 version qualifies as a derivative work, the notice need only state "Copyright © 2002 by AcmeSoft, Inc." However, AcmeSoft is not sure whether the changes it made were substantial enough to make the 2.0 version a new derivative work. AcmeSoft decides to err on the side of caution and writes the notice like this: "Copyright © 2001, 2002 by AcmeSoft, Inc."

If AcmeSoft revises the program again in 2003, it may write the copyright notice like this: "Copyright © 2001-2003 by AcmeSoft, Inc."

> **EXAMPLE 2:** AcmeSoft has its employees create a website to advertise and sell its software products. The site went live in 2001. The copyright notice read "Copyright © 2001 by AcmeSoft, Inc." AcmeSoft thoroughly revises the site in 2002, adding substantial new text, graphics, and sounds. AcmeSoft changes its copyright notice to: "Copyright © 2002 by AcmeSoft, Inc." Because it's not required, AcmeSoft decides to drop the 2001 date from its notice. This way, the site looks newer.

b. Form of date

The date is usually written in Arabic numerals—for instance, "2002." But you can also use:

- abbreviations of Arabic numerals—for instance, "'02";
- Roman numerals—for instance, "MMII"; or
- spelled-out words instead of numerals —for instance, "Two Thousand Two."

3. Copyright Owner's Name

The name of the copyright owner must also be included in the notice. Briefly, the owner is one of the following:

- the person or persons who created the work
- the legal owner of a work made for hire, or
- the person or entity (partnership or corporation) to which all the author's exclusive copyright rights have been transferred.

a. Person or persons who created the work

Unless a work is made for hire (see below), the original creators initially own all the copyright rights. Where all these rights are retained, the creator's name should appear in the copyright notice.

> **EXAMPLE:** Eli Yale creates a database used by charities and places it on his website. Eli is the sole copyright owner of the database and website. The copyright notice on the website should state: "Copyright © 2001 by Eli Yale."

If there are multiple creators, they should all be listed in the copyright notice. The names can appear in any order.

b. Works made for hire

A work made for hire is a work made by an employee as part of his or her job, or a work specially ordered or commissioned under a written work for hire contract. (See Chapter 11.) The creator's employer or other person for whom the work was prepared is considered the author of such a work for copyright purposes and that person's (or entity's) name should appear in the copyright notice as owner unless the copyright has been assigned to someone else. The creator-employee's name should not be included in the notice.

c. Transferees

If all of the copyright rights owned by an author or authors (whether the author is the actual creator or the owner of a work made for hire) are transferred to another person or entity, that name should appear in the copyright notice on all copies produced and distributed after the transfer. However, any copies produced before the transfer occurred may be distributed without updating the notice.

d. Name on notice where rights are transferred to different people or entities

A copyright is completely divisible—that is, the owner may transfer all or part of her exclusive copyright rights to whomever and however she wishes. For example, a copyright owner can transfer less than all of his or her rights and retain the others, or transfer some rights to one person or entity and all the others to other transferees. (See Chapter 11.)

Because copyrights are divisible, it can be confusing to determine just who the owner of copyright is for purposes of the copyright notice. The general rule is that unless the author, whether it is the actual creator or the owner of a work made for hire, transfers all of his or her copyright rights to a single person or entity, the author's name should appear in the notice.

EXAMPLE: Dick and Jane create an educational computer game for young children. They sell to Moppet Publishing Co. the right to publish the game in North America. Dick and Jane sell the right to publish the game outside North America to Foreign Press, Inc. They sell TV, video, and film rights based on the game to Repulsive Pictures. Dick and Jane's names alone should appear in the copyright notice in all published versions of the game. In contrast, had Dick and Jane sold all their rights to Moppet, its name should appear alone in the notice.

The one exception to this general rule is where a collective or derivative work is created from preexisting material (see Section D, below).

e. Form of name

Usually, the owner's full legal name is used. However, it is permissible to use an abbreviation of the owner's name, a last name alone, a trade name, nickname, fictitious name, pseudonym, initials, or some other designation as long as the copyright owner is generally known by the name or other words or letters used in the notice. For example, International Business Machines Corporation may use the abbreviation IBM. Remember, however, that the point of a notice is to notify, so avoid being cryptic or cute.

If You Want to Remain Anonymous

The word "anonymous" should not be used in a copyright notice because an author is obviously not generally known by that name. Likewise, it is not advisable to use a pseudonym by which you are not generally known. You can avoid revealing your name in a copyright notice, and still ensure the notice's validity, by transferring all of your copyright rights to a publisher. This way, the publisher's name may appear in the notice. Another approach would be to form a corporation, transfer your entire copyright to it, and then use the corporation's name in the notice.

If the copyright owner is a corporation, it is not necessary to include the abbreviation "Inc." in the name, even if this is part of the corporation's full legal name. Nor is it necessary for the word "by" to precede the copyright owner's name, although it is commonly used—for example, a notice can be written as "Copyright © 2002 by WidgetCo, Inc." or "Copyright © 2002 WidgetCo."

---

4. Form of Notice for Unpublished Works

All the rules discussed above should be followed for notices on unpublished software or unpublished website materials

except that you don't include a publication date in the copyright notice. Instead,
the notice should indicate the work's unpublished status. A copyright notice for
an unpublished work should be in one of
the following forms:

Copyright © AcmeSoft, Inc.
(This work is unpublished.)

Copyright © AcmeSoft, Inc.
(Work in progress.)

D. Notice on Compilations and Derivative Works

Compilations and adaptations are created
partially or completely from preexisting
material. However, it is usually not necessary that the copyright notice for this type
of work refer to the preexisting material.

1. Compilations

A compilation may be a collective work—
that is, a work that consists of separate
and independent works assembled into a
collective whole. A good example is an
online encyclopedia such as that found at
www.britannica.com. Online versions of
serial publications, such as periodicals,
magazines, and newspapers, are also collective work compilations.

A compilation may also be a work in
which preexisting materials—for example
data of various types—are selected, coor-
dinated, and arranged so that a new work
is created. A catalogue is one example. If
you create a compilation you must either
own the preexisting material used in the
work or obtain the permission of those
who do own it (unless of course, the material is in the public domain).

If you do not own the preexisting material, all you own is the copyright in the
compilation as a whole—that is, the
copyright in the creative work involved in
selecting, combining, and assembling the
material into a whole work. Nevertheless,
a compilation need only contain one
copyright notice in the name of that
copyright owner. That notice will extend,
for the purposes of defeating the innocent infringer rule, to the individual components of the compilation.

EXAMPLE: Hardsell, Inc., compiles a
group of the 100 best new Java applets
and sells them through its website.
The copyright owners of each program
gave Hardsell permission to publish
them on the website, but still retain all
their copyright rights. The website
need contain only one copyright notice in Hardsell's name: "Copyright ©
2002 by Hardsell, Inc." Separate copyright notices need not be provided for
the 100 Java programs.

Although an individual contribution to a compilation does not have to have its own copyright notice, a notice is permissible where the copyright in the contribution is owned by someone other than the owner of the compilation as a whole. This may help deter a potential infringer and make clear that the owner of the copyright in the compilation does not own that particular contribution. It will also make it clear to end-users whom to contact for permission to use the particular contribution.

> **EXAMPLE:** The owner of a Java applet program included on Hardsell's website above could include a copyright notice on the user's computer screen upon start-up of the program.

⚠️ **Advertisements Appearing in Collective Works.** Copyright notice for a collective work does not extend to advertisements. For example, the copyright notice in an online newspaper will protect the editorial content such as the stories and news photos, but it will not extend to any portion of an advertisement. Therefore, the owner of copyright of an advertisement should *always* include a separate notice.

a. Publication date for compilations

The copyright notice for a compilation need only list the year the compilation itself is published, not the date or dates the preexisting material was published.

> **EXAMPLE:** The publication date for the notice on Hardsell's website would be 2002, the year the website was published (went live).

2. Derivative Works

A derivative work is a work that is created by recasting, transforming, or adapting a previously existing work into a new work of authorship. Software examples include revised versions of preexisting programs. "Porting" a program from one type of hardware to another—for example, from a Mac to a PC—is another type of derivative work.

Websites are often derivative works as well. They will qualify as such whenever they are based upon or derived from preexisting materials. For example, the online version of the King James Bible that can be found at http://etext.lib.virginia.edu/kjv.browse.HTML is a derivative based on the original version of that religious work.

Unless the preexisting material used by a derivative work is in the public domain or owned by the creator of the derivative work, the creator must obtain the copyright owner's permission to use it.

As with compilations, the copyright notice for a derivative work need only contain the name of the owner of the copyright of the derivative work itself, not the owner of the preexisting material upon which the derivative work was based.

EXAMPLE: Inumeracy Software published a mathematical equation-writing program for the Macintosh in 2001. Oxymoron Software, Inc., obtains permission to create an updated and revised PC version of the program. The PC program is a derivative work based upon the preexisting Macintosh program. However, only Oxymoron's name need appear on the copyright notice for its program, since Oxymoron is the owner of the copyright in the derivative work.

As with collective works, the publication date in the notice for a derivative work should be the year the derivative work was published, not the year or years the preexisting material was published.

3. Work Containing Previously Copyrighted Material

If your software or website is not a derivative work but nevertheless includes material that was previously published by another copyright owner, you needn't include a separate copyright notice for the work unless this is required by the other copyright owner. Your single copyright notice protects the entire work as a whole. However, if the copyright owner of the earlier work you use wishes his or her copyright to be specifically noted, you would do it like this:

- © Copyright 2001 Sid Simm
- © Copyright 2002 Mary Michaels

When your work, whether a website or software program, contains other people's copyrighted material, it is not necessary for you to state in your notice what elements of the work you are claiming copyright in. You can simply use a standard notice as described above. However, you have the option of explaining in your notice just what parts of the work you claim to hold a copyright in.

EXAMPLE: The website Arts and Letters Daily (www.aldaily.com) consists of short descriptions of and links to interesting articles appearing all over the Internet. The copyright owner of the site owns a copyright in the coding, format, and content on the site, but not in any of the articles the site links to. To help make this clear, the site's copyright notice provides: "Coding, format, and on-site content copyright © 2001 Arts and Letters Daily."

4. Works Containing United States Government Materials

The rule that a single general notice is sufficient for a compilation or derivative work does not always apply to publications incorporating United States government works. United States government publications are in the public domain. They are not copyrighted and anyone can use them without asking the federal government's permission. However, if a work consists preponderantly of one or more works by the U.S. government, the copyright notice must affirmatively or negatively identify those portions of the work in which copyright is claimed—that is, that part of the work not consisting of U.S. government materials. This enables readers of such works to know which portions of the work are government materials in the public domain.

It's up to you to decide if your work consists preponderantly of U.S. government materials. Certainly, if more than half of your product consists of federal government materials, your notice should enable readers to determine which portions of the work are copyrighted and which are in the public domain.

> **EXAMPLE:** Databest Inc. creates a website containing analyses of U.S. census data and including several files containing U.S. Census Bureau mate-

rial. The website is a collective work in which independently created contributions have been combined to form a collective whole. The U.S. census materials amount to over half the material on the website. The copyright notice for the work could state: "Copyright © 2001 by Databest Inc. No protection is claimed in works of the United States Census Bureau."

Alternatively, the notice could affirmatively identify those portions not containing government materials. In this event, the notice might look like this: "Copyright © 2001 by Databest Inc. Copyright claimed in Sections 1 through 10."

Failure to follow this rule will result in the copyright notice being found invalid. This means that an infringer of the material in which you claim a copyright would be allowed to raise the innocent infringement defense at trial. (See Section A1 above.)

E. Where to Place Copyright Notice

Although it's not strictly required by law, you should place your copyright notice in lots of different places to ensure that it serves its intended purposes—to be seen and give notice of your copyright to the world.

1. Software

Every component of a published software package should contain a copyright notice. This includes:

- the package or box the software comes in, if any
- the manual and other written documentation
- the computer disks or other media containing the software, and
- the appropriate computer screens.

a. Packaging

Most published software that is not distributed online is sold in some sort of box or other package. A copyright notice should appear somewhere on the box. It is often placed on the back of the box, but you can also place it on the front or sides. The notice will apply to your cover art and graphics as well as to the software and other materials inside the box or package.

b. Computer diskettes, CD-ROMs

A copyright notice should also be printed on a label permanently affixed to the computer diskettes, CD-ROM disks, or other magnetic media containing the software.

c. Computer code

If you license or otherwise distribute your source code, at a minimum include a copyright notice on the first and last page. Even better, include a notice on every page.

Also, place a copyright notice on the first page and liberally sprinkle notices throughout the remainder of the code. This way, anyone who prints out the code will see that you claim copyright in it.

In addition, use a confidentiality legend in conjunction with your copyright notice. (See Section F.)

d. Computer screens

According to Copyright Office regulations, providing a copyright notice on the box or disk containing published software is sufficient. But it shouldn't be sufficient for you. Remember, you want to make sure that users do really see your notice. It should appear somewhere on the computer screen when the software is used. This can be done in one or more of the following ways:

- by printing the notice in or near the title of the program or at the end of the program
- displaying the notice when the program is first activated (on the opening screen or in an about or credit box), or
- displaying the notice continuously while the program is being used (for example, in a status bar).

A good rule is to display it on the screen at the beginning and end of a program, as well as every time the program title is displayed. Also include a notice in any "read me" files.

Certain programs have more than one mode or version when they are running or performing their task. For example, many complicated programs have a training mode, separate from the program itself. Each mode should have a correct copyright notice.

e. Software documentation and other materials in book or pamphlet form

Documentation includes everything that accompanies, explains, illustrates, or otherwise complements your program. Many manuals, such as user manuals, programmer reference manuals, and training manuals, look more or less like books. Short manuals and program documentation often take the form of a pamphlet. The rules for placing your copyright notice are the same for both, as long as the pamphlet consists of at least two pages.

The copyright notice for a manual or other similar written work may be placed in any of the following locations:

- the title page
- the page immediately following the title page (this is the most commonly used location for books)
- either side of the front cover

- if there is no front cover, either side of the back leaf of the copies—that is, the hinged piece of paper at the end of a book or pamphlet consisting of at least two pages
- the first or last page of the main body of the work.

2. Websites

It is legally sufficient to place one copyright notice for a website on the home page (usually at the bottom). This single notice is all that's required, no matter how big the website. However, you are perfectly free to use more than one notice. If you wish, you can include a notice on the bottom of every page.

Sometimes, website designers turn the copyright notice into a hyperlink. When users click on the link, they are sent to a page setting forth copyright and other restrictions on use of the site in more detail. One example can be found at http://web.lexis.com/xchange/Misc/copyright.asp. This is not required, but may help deter infringements.

F. Other Information Near Notice

Certain other information in addition to the copyright notice itself is commonly included on the same page as the notice.

1. All Rights Reserved

Until recent years, some Central and Latin American countries required that the words "All rights reserved" be used along with a copyright notice. This is no longer true. These words are unnecessary, but do no harm if they are used.

2. Warning Statements

Since many people do not really understand what a copyright notice means, many copyright owners include various types of warning or explanatory statements near the copyright notice. The purpose is to make clear to users that the work is copyrighted and may not be reproduced without the copyright owner's permission. It does not cost anything to place this type of statement near the copyright notice, and it may help deter copyright infringement. But remember, such statements do not take the place of a valid copyright notice as described earlier in this chapter.

a. Statements used on websites

Here are some examples of warning statements you can use near a copyright notice on a website:

No part of this work may be reproduced in whole or in part in any manner without the permission of the copyright owner.

No part of the materials available through the [DOMAIN NAME] site may be copied, photocopied, reproduced, translated, or reduced to any electronic medium or machine-readable form, in whole or in part, without prior written consent of [COPYRIGHT OWNER'S NAME]. Any other reproduction in any form without the permission of [COPYRIGHT OWNER'S NAME] is prohibited.

All materials contained on this site are protected by United States copyright law and may not be reproduced, distributed, transmitted, displayed, published, or broadcast without the prior written permission of [COPYRIGHT OWNER'S NAME].

On the other hand, some website owners are happy to permit certain types of unauthorized copying, while prohibiting others. To make it clear to Web users what types of copying are permissible, you can include a statement like the following along with the copyright notice:

The materials on this website may be copied online, but may not be reproduced in print or on a CD-ROM without written permission.

The materials on this website may be copied for noncommercial personal use only.

The materials on this website may be freely copied and distributed so long as our copyright notice and website address are included.

This manual, and the software described in this manual, are copyrighted. No part of this manual or the described software may be copied, reproduced, translated, or reduced to any electronic medium or machine-readable form without the prior written consent of [Name of Copyright Owner], except that you may make one copy of the program disks solely for back-up purposes.

b. Statements used in software

Here's a simple warning statement that could be used near a copyright notice on diskette labels and on the computer screen when the program is activated (for example, it could be placed inside an about or credit box or near the program's title):

A growing number of software publishers are departing from negative-sounding statements like those above. Rather, they employ friendly language that is positive and inviting. The reasoning behind this approach is that appealing to an end-user's sense of fair play will get better results than attempting to scare him. Here's an example of such language:

This software is copyrighted. The software may not be copied, reproduced, translated, or reduced to any electronic medium or machine-readable form without the prior written consent of [Name of Copyright Owner], except that you may make one copy of the program disks solely for back-up purposes.

We have worked very hard to create a quality product and wish to realize the fair fruits of our labor. We therefore insist that you honor our copyright. However, we want to encourage the use of our product in all possible circumstances and will work very hard to meet your needs if you will call and ask us for permission.

Here is an example of the type of warning statements that are commonly used in software manuals:

3. Trade Secret Notices on Software

Most software qualifies for trade secret protection as well as copyright protection. For this reason, it's a good idea to include a trade secret notice along with a copyright notice. (For more information on trade secrets, see Chapter 8.)

a. Unpublished programs

A confidentiality notice such as the following can be used for unpublished programs and other unpublished materials:

THIS IS AN UNPUBLISHED WORK CONTAINING [your or your company name]'s, CONFIDENTIAL AND PROPRIETARY INFORMATION. DISCLOSURE, USE, OR REPRODUCTION WITHOUT AUTHORIZATION OF [your or your company name] IS PROHIBITED.

b. Published programs

When you publish a program—for example, market it in computer stores or over the Internet—include a combined confidentiality notice such as the following in the program itself and on any diskettes, manuals, and other documentation:

THIS [choose one: program, document, material] IS CONFIDENTIAL AND PROPRIETARY TO [your company name] AND MAY NOT BE REPRODUCED, PUBLISHED, OR DISCLOSED TO OTHERS WITHOUT COMPANY AUTHORIZATION. ■

Software and Web Copyright Infringement

Previous chapters have provided an overview of copyright law and have discussed the steps a software copyright owner must take to give his or her work maximum protection under the copyright laws. This chapter explores how these protections are enforced. This subject is referred to as copyright infringement.

Copyright infringement is where the rubber hits the road in the copyright law. It concerns how authors and other copyright owners enforce their legal rights. However, the right to bring copyright infringement suits is a two-edged sword: you may have the right to sue others, but others may also have the right to sue you. Consequently, this chapter is divided into two parts. Part I discusses how to avoid being sued for copyright infringement. Part II provides an overview of infringement lawsuits from the plaintiff's point of view.

PART I. Avoiding Copyright Infringement

Some activities always constitute copyright infringement and should always be avoided. Others may be permissible because the copyright laws do not give copyright owners an absolute monopoly over the use of their works. For this reason, Part I is divided into three sections.

Section A covers the type of things you should never do. Section B explains certain types of copying and other activities that may be legally allowed. Section C shows you ways to avoid being accused of copyright infringement.

A. Things You Should Never Do

The clearest cases of copyright infringement involve direct copying of a copyrighted work, particularly where you copy all or most of the work. If you're caught doing these types of copying you likely won't have a legal leg to stand on should the copyright owner elect to sue you for infringement. Indeed, your best course would probably be to seek to settle the case as cheaply as possible without going to court.

Creating derivative works without permission and going beyond the restrictions contained in license agreements also usually present clear cases of copyright infringement.

It goes without saying that you should never become involved in these types of copyright infringement. The risks will usually be greater than the rewards. See Section H for a detailed discussion of the many unpleasant legal consequences of copyright infringement.

1. Wholesale Unauthorized Copying of Copyrighted Works

Copying all or most of a copyrighted work—wholesale copying—for the purpose of distributing it to others is referred to as piracy and is prohibited under copyright law.

a. Works found on the Internet

The Internet is filled with millions of copyrighted works, including text files, graphics, photographs, videos, and sounds. Contrary to what some people seem to think, the majority of the content on the Internet is copyrighted. Unless your intended use of such material falls within the fair use rule, you must obtain permission to use such works.

That said, it's likely that making a single copy of a text file posted on the Internet solely for *personal* use—for example, printing out an article posted on a website—will be excused as a fair use.

Can You Copy HTML Code?

It is a common practice for Web developers to copy HTML code from other websites. This activity may be copyright infringement, although it is not likely to be. As is the case with computer code, HTML code is theoretically entitled to copyright protection to the extent it is original and minimally creative. However, it's likely that much HTML code flunks both tests. Much is not original. Even if it is, the copyright protection it receives is likely subject to the same limitations as for computer code. Because of these limitations, it's likely that the vast majority of HTML code receives little or no copyright protection.

---

b. Computer code

Subject to important limitations discussed below, copyright protects source code (code written in high-level computer languages consisting of English-like words and symbols readable by humans, such as C++ and Java), object code (the series of binary ones and zeros read by the computer itself to execute a program, but not readable by ordinary humans), microcode (instructions that tell a microprocessor chip how to work), and other forms of computer code such as Java bytecode.

Copyright protects both applications programs (programs that perform a specific task for the user, such as word processing, will and trust writing, accessing the World

Wide Web, bookkeeping, or playing a video game) and operating systems and utility programs (programs that manage a computer's internal functions and facilitate use of applications programs).

Wholesale copying or software piracy takes a variety of forms, including:

- Creating "new" software from old. Creating a "new" program by copying a substantial amount of the protected expression in a preexisting program, is a classic example of software piracy.

- End-user piracy by companies and individuals.

  EXAMPLE: AcmeSoft, Inc., a large software developer, makes 100 unauthorized copies of a well-known HTML editor program and distributes them to its employees.

- Counterfeiting published software.

  EXAMPLE: Fly By Night Software, Inc., a software distributor, makes 50,000 unauthorized copies of the popular computer arcade game, *Kill or Die*, and distributes them throughout the world.

- Online piracy. This includes uploading and downloading computer programs to and from the Internet without the copyright owners' permission.

What About Copying Only a Small Amount of Code?

Copying only a small portion of a program's code could constitute copyright infringement, particularly if it is a highly creative or important example of the programmer's art. For example, copyright infringement has been found to exist where only 14 lines of source code out of a total of 186,000 lines were copied verbatim. (*SAS Inst., Inc. v. S&H Computer Sys., Inc.*, 605 F. Supp. 816 (M.D. Tenn. 1985).)

However, there are instances when copying a small amount of code—for example, a particular routine or subroutine—may not constitute infringement if the portion of code is not protected under copyright law (see Section B1). In this event, copying would be permitted.

---

2. Creating Unauthorized Derivative Works

If a new work contains a substantial amount of copyrighted material from an existing work, it may constitute a derivative work. You need permission to create a derivative work from someone else's copyrighted material.

Open Source Software Is Different

Today, much software is distributed under open source licenses—for example, the Linux operating system. You don't need permission from the copyright owner to modify or otherwise create a derivative work from open source software. Indeed, the source code is provided to users to help them create derivative works. However, many open source licenses require all derivative works that are publicly distributed to also be open source. See Chapter 16, Section F, for a discussion of open source.

---

a. What is a derivative work?

A derivative work is "a work based upon one or more preexisting works." It includes any "form in which a work may be recast, transformed, or adapted." (17 U.S.C. § 101.) To be derivative, a work must incorporate in some form a portion of the protected expression of a preexisting copyrighted work.

A derivative work stands on its own for copyright purposes and is entitled to its own copyright protection independent of the original work it was derived from.

Of course, all works are derivative to some extent. Authorship, whether of a novel or a computer program, is more often than not a process of translation and recombination of previously existing elements—ideas, facts, discoveries, proce-dures, concepts, principles, systems, and so forth. Rarely, if ever, does an author create a work that is entirely new. For example, writers of fiction often draw bits and pieces of their characters and plots from other fictional works they have read. The same is true of software authors. For example, it's likely that any spreadsheet program could be said be derived to some extent from VisiCalc, the first computer spreadsheet.

A substantial amount of expression must be copied to make a work derivative. How much is substantial? Enough so that the average intended user of the work would conclude that it had been adapted from or based upon the previously existing work. Enough so that, absent consent to use the material from the preexisting work, the second work would constitute an infringement on the copyright in the first work. This is, of course, a judgment call, and in close cases opinions may differ as to whether one work is derivative of another.

Common examples of derivative works include:

- **Updates and new versions.** An updated or new version of an existing program, website, book, or other work is a most common example of a derivative work. Only the person who owns the derivative work's rights in a work may create an updated or new version of it or permit others to do so.

- **Translations.** A translation of a work from one language to another—whether a human or computer language—is a very common type of derivative work. It is usually necessary, for example, to obtain permission from the copyright owner to translate a program into a new source code language.
- **Transferring a work from one medium to another.** Changing the medium in which an original work is fixed normally creates a derivative work consisting of the expression as fixed in the new medium. And, regardless of what new medium is used, a copyright infringement occurs if you don't first obtain permission from the owner. For example, a person who uses a scanner to create a digital version of a copyrighted photograph is creating a derivative work.
- **New works based on other underlying works.** Any work based upon a preexisting work is a derivative work. Computer games are good examples. A computer game based on a movie, television show, board game, or other underlying work is a derivative work. Naturally, you need permission from the owner of the derivative work's rights in the underlying work to create a new work based upon it.

b. Why you need permission to create derivative works

With the exception of open source software, permission must be obtained from the owner of the exclusive right to prepare derivative works based upon the underlying work. Usually the owner is the author or publisher, but not always. If you intend to create a derivative work from someone else's copyrighted work, be sure to get permission before you go to the time and trouble of adapting it into a new work.

3. Going Beyond License Restrictions

Yet another form of copyright infringement is going beyond the restrictions of a license agreement. Today, most software is licensed rather than sold outright. But software is not the only type of copyrighted work that is licensed. Any work of authorship can be licensed, including text, photos, graphics, videos, and sounds. Content appearing on websites is often licensed from other sources. For example, a photo on a website may be licensed from a stock photo house.

License agreements typically contain many restrictions on what a licensee may do with his or her copy. For example, software licensees are typically barred from using the software on a local area network (LAN). You must obtain a special license for this sort of use. Using a program on a LAN in violation of a license agreement constitutes copyright infringement. Similarly, a webmaster who licenses a photo for use on one website may be barred from using it on another without obtaining an additional license and perhaps paying an additional fee.

4. Impermissible Linking, Framing and Inlining

Linking allows you to click on a highlighted word, phrase, picture, or icon, and be immediately taken to another website. You can also, of course, use the same click process to reach other pages *within* the site you're already viewing. Framing is a form of linking in which visitors to one site view content from a second site inside a frame supplied by the first site. Inlining is the process of displaying a graphic file on one website that originates at another. For example, inlining occurs if a user at site A can, without leaving site A, view a "cartoon of the day" featured on site B. In some cases, linking, framing, and inlining can get you into copyright or other legal trouble and should not be done without obtaining permission.

It is not a violation of copyright to create a hyperlink, but courts have held that it is a violation of the law to create a link that contributes to unauthorized copying of a copyrighted work if the linking party *knew or had reason to know* of the unauthorized copying and encouraged it.

EXAMPLE: A website posted infringing copies of a church's copyrighted handbook at its site. The website was ordered to remove the handbook, but subsequently provided links to other sites that contained infringing copies of the handbook. These links were different from traditional hyperlinks because the website knew and encouraged the use of the links to obtain unauthorized copies. The linking activity constituted contributory copyright infringement. (*Intellectual Reserve, Inc. v. Utah Ministry, Inc.*, 75 F. Supp. 2d 1290 (D. Utah 1999).)

EXAMPLE: A group of computer hackers posted on their website a computer program called DeCSS that could crack the Content Scramble System (CSS)—an encryption system the provides anticopying protection for movies distributed on DVD. The court issued an injunction barring the hackers from posting DeCSS on the Internet and preventing them from electronically "linking" their site to others. (*Universal City Studios, Inc. v. Reimerdes*, 82 F. Supp. 2d 211 (S.D. N.Y. 2000).)

Limiting Liability With Disclaimers

If a website owner is concerned about liability for links but is unable or unwilling to seek permission from the linkee, a prominently placed disclaimer may reduce the likelihood of legal problems. A disclaimer is a statement denying an endorsement or waiving liability for a potentially unauthorized activity. A disclaimer is rarely a cure-all for legal claims, but if a disclaimer is prominently displayed and clearly written, a court may take it into consideration as a factor limiting damages. In some cases, such as trademark disputes, it may help prevent any liability. For example, in a case involving a dispute between two websites for restaurants named Blue Note, one factor that helped the lesser-known restaurant avoid liability was a prominently displayed disclaimer stating that it was not affiliated with the more famous restaurant. (*Benusan Restaurant v. King*, 937 F. Supp. 295 (S.D. N.Y. 1996).) To minimize liability for any activities that occur when a visitor is taken to a linked website, a webmaster may want to include a linking disclaimer on its home page or on any pages with otherwise troublesome links.

Here is a sample linking disclaimer:

By providing links to other sites, [name of your website] does not guarantee, approve, or endorse the information or products available at these sites, nor does a link indicate any association with or endorsement by the linked site to [name of your website].

A link that bypasses a website's home page and instead goes to another page within the site is often called a "deep link." Some website owners object to the use of deep links. They want the people who use their website to go first to the home page, either because advertising is posted there, because that page provides the site's terms and conditions, or because the site's popularity—for purposes of determining advertising revenue—is based upon home page visits.

Many copyright experts believe that deep linking is not copyright infringement. After all, the author of a novel can't prevent readers from reading the end first if they so desire, so why should a website owner have the right to determine in what order a user can access a website? Nevertheless, it's prudent to be careful before deep linking to advertising-rich commercial sites. Many such sites have linking policies posted. Some well-known websites such as Amazon.com welcome deep links. If a commercial website has no posted linking policy or says that deep links are not allowed, it's wise to ask for permission before deep linking.

Framing may trigger a dispute under copyright and trademark law theories because a framed site arguably alters the appearance of the content and creates the impression that its owner endorses or voluntarily chooses to associate with the framer. One court fight involving two dental websites also failed to fully resolve the issue. Applied Anagramic, Inc., a dental services website, framed the content of a competing site. The frames included information about Applied Anagramic as well as its trademark and links to all of its Web pages. A district court ruled that a website containing a link that reproduced Web pages within a "frame" may constitute an infringing derivative work. The court reasoned that the addition of the frame modified the appearance of the linked site and such modifications could, without authorization, amount to infringement. (*Futuredontics Inc. v. Applied Anagramic Inc.*, 46 U.S.P.Q. 2d 2005 (C.D. Cal. 1997).)

IMG links, a special type of programming HTML link, can be used to display graphic files on one site that are stored on another. In one case, Dan Wallach, a fan of the "*Dilbert*" comic strip, did not like the design of the official "*Dilbert*" site owned by United Media and designed his own, The Dilbert Hack Page. He used IMG links to display the cartoon images from the United Media site so that a visitor to the Dilbert Hack Page viewed "*Dilbert*" cartoons (inlined from the United Media Page) within Wallach's "improved" page design. United Media demanded that Wallach stop, because the display violated copyright law and the process could destroy the integrity of the comic strip (if for example, the strip were displayed at an adult or racist site). The parties avoided a lawsuit when Wallach agreed to drop the IMG links, and used traditional hypertext links to the United Media home page. Subsequently, a federal court of appeals ruled that an image search engine violated copyright law when it used inline links to reproduce full-size photographic images. Smaller inlined reproductions ("thumbnails") were permitted under fair use principles. (*Kelly v. Arriba Software,* (9th Cir. 2002) CV-99-0560-GLT.)

5. Removing Copyright Management Information

In 1998, Congress created a new basis for suing copyright infringers. The Digital Millennium Copyright Act makes it illegal to remove "copyright management information" (CMI) from copyrighted works and gives copyright owners the right to sue for damages people who do so. This is in addition to any rights they may already have to sue such people for copyright infringement for copying their works.

The main intent behind the new law was to prevent infringers from removing copyright notices and other ownership information from material placed in the online world. However, the law applies both to online and other digital works and to old fashioned paper and ink works such as published computer manuals or programs.

As a result of this law, U.S. authors and other copyright owners have an ironclad right of attribution—that is, the right to be identified as the owners of their works.

a.   What is CMI?

Copyright management information includes:

- the title and other information identifying the work
- a work's copyright notice
- the author's name and any other identifying information about the author
- the copyright owner's name and any other identifying information about the owner
- any terms and conditions for use of the work, and
- identifying numbers or symbols on the work referring to any of the above information or Internet links to such information.

b.   What can't you do with copyright management information?

It is now illegal to do any of the following if you know or have reasonable grounds to know that it will induce, facilitate, or conceal a copyright infringement:

- intentionally remove or alter any copyright information

- distribute, import for distribution, or publicly perform a work whose copyright management information has been removed or altered without permission from the copyright owner or legal authority
- provide false copyright management information, or
- distribute or import for distribution a work containing false copyright management information.

For example, it is illegal to remove the copyright notice from a program and then copy and place it online without the copyright owner's permission.

c.   Penalties for CMI violations

Any person injured by a violation of the law may sue the violator for damages and seek to obtain a court injunction ordering the violator to stop distributing the work from which the copyright management information was removed, altered, or falsified. Such a suit may be brought in addition to any suit for copyright infringement the person may have against the violator.

d.   Exceptions for fair use and public domain works

There are some situations where it is permissible to remove copyright management information without the copyright owner's permission.

First, the new law provides that such an action is permissible if permitted by law. One case where the law may permit removing copyright management information is when material is copied on the grounds of fair use—for example, when creating a parody of a copyrighted work. In this event, its removal would likely not be considered a legal violation.

Law enforcement, intelligence, and other government agencies are permitted to alter or remove copyright management information in order to carry out lawful investigative, protective, information security, or intelligence activities.

6. Cracking Copyright Protection Measures

Copyright owners are fearful that infringers may devise means of circumventing their anti-infringement technological measures—for example, devise means of "cracking" encryption codes. The Digital Millennium Copyright Act (DMCA) enacted by Congress in late 1998 includes a complex provision designed to prevent this. Following is an overview of the types of activities the DMCA prohibits.

a. Importing or selling circumvention devices

First, subject to the exceptions noted below, the DMCA makes it illegal for anyone to make, import, or sell software, devices, or services whose primary purpose is to circumvent technological measures used to prevent unauthorized access to or copying of a work, and (1) the technology or services have no commercially significant purpose other than such circumvention, or (2) the person marketing the technology or services knows they are being used for such circumvention. Circumventing such "technological measures" includes descrambling a scrambled work, decrypting a decrypted work, "or otherwise to avoid, bypass, remove, deactivate, or impair a technological measure without the authority of the copyright owner." (17 U.S.C. § 1201(a)(3)(A).)

b. Obtaining access to a work through circumvention of technological measures

Also, subject to several exceptions noted below, the DMCA also makes it illegal for anyone to circumvent any technological measure (such as encryption) that effectively controls access to the work. Note that the law doesn't make it illegal to break anticopying technology *per se*. It makes it illegal to crack code in order to gain access. This subtle distinction supposedly preserves fair use rights. However, many copyright experts believe it is a meaningless difference, since one must first gain access to a work before it can be copied.

c. Exemptions from anticircumvention prohibitions

None of the DMCA's anticircumvention prohibitions discussed above apply to:

- nonprofit libraries, archives, and educational institutions that wish to gain unauthorized access to works solely to make a good faith determination of whether to acquire a copy
- a person who has lawfully obtained the right to use a copy of a computer program and circumvents such technological measures to gain access to the code to identify and analyze "those elements of the program that are necessary to achieve interoperability of an independently created computer program with other programs"
- people engaged in research to identify flaws and vulnerabilities in encryption technologies, and
- people engaged in testing the security of an individual computer, computer system, or network (with the owner's or operator's authorization).

Exemptions are also given to law enforcement, intelligence, and other government activities.

Each of these exceptions has its own set of conditions that must be satisfied for it to apply to you. Before relying on one of the exceptions outlined above, read the DMCA carefully and seek legal advice. A copy of the DMCA is contained in Sections 1201-1205 of the Copyright Act, which can be accessed at the U.S. Copyright Office website.

d. Penalties for violations

Penalties for violations of these provisions are the same as for removal of copyright management information. It's important to understand that these penalties may be imposed whether or not you have committed copyright infringement.

B. Things You May Be Able to Do

You may be surprised to learn that in many ways copyright protection is limited in scope. You may be free to copy or otherwise use those elements of a copyrighted work that are unprotected by copyright. Additionally, copying of protected material may be permissible under the fair use doctrine. Finally, the copyright laws do not prevent you from independently creating a new work, even if it's similar to a work already in existence.

Software May Be Protected by Means Other Than Copyright

Just because all or part of a program is not protected by copyright doesn't necessarily mean it isn't legally protected at all. Software developers usually supplement their copyright protection with other forms of protection. These include:

- Patents—the federal law that protects inventions (see Chapter 9)
- Trade secrets—state and federal laws protecting valuable information that is not generally known (see Chapter 7), and
- Trademarks—federal and state laws protecting product names, logos, and designs (see Chapter 10).
- Software developers and publishers also use licenses—contracts restricting how you may use software, including when you can copy it. (See Chapter 16.)

1. Using Software Elements Unprotected by Copyright

All works of authorship—particularly functional works such as computer programs—contain some elements that are protected by copyright and other elements that are not. Anyone is free to use the unprotected elements without obtaining permission from the copyright owner. Unfortunately, there is no system available to an interested party to precisely identify which aspects of a given work are protected by copyright.

The Copyright Office makes no such determination when software is registered. The only time we ever obtain a definitive answer as to how much any particular program (or other work of authorship) is protected is when it becomes the subject of a copyright infringement lawsuit. In this event, a judge or jury determines the question. Of course, such litigation is usually very expensive and time-consuming.

Courts in different parts of the country sometimes disagree with each other on the extent of copyright protection for software. However, a growing consensus has been developing in recent years that many of the most important elements of software should receive little or no copyright protection.

The following software elements are never protected by copyright and may be freely copied by anyone unless they are protected by another form of intellectual property such as trade secrecy, patent law, or trademark law.

a. Ideas embodied in software

Copyright only protects a creative person's particular expression of an idea, system, or process, not the idea, system, or process itself. Ideas, procedures, processes, systems, mathematical principles, formulas or algorithms, methods of operation, concepts, facts, and discoveries are not protected by copyright. (17 U.S.C.

§ 102(b).) Copyright is designed to aid the advancement of knowledge. If the copyright law gave a person a legal monopoly over his or her ideas, the progress of knowledge would be impeded rather than helped. Consider the following real-life example:

> **EXAMPLE:** While a student at the Harvard business school in the late 1970s, Daniel Bricklin conceived the idea of an electronic spreadsheet—a "magic blackboard" that recalculated numbers automatically as changes were made in other parts of the spreadsheet. Eventually, aided by others, he transformed his idea into VisiCalc, the first commercial electronic spreadsheet. The program, designed for use on the Apple II, sold like hotcakes and helped spark the personal computer revolution.

Of course VisiCalc was protected by copyright. Nevertheless, others were free to write their own original programs accomplishing the same purpose as VisiCalc. The copyright law did not give Bricklin et al. any ownership rights over the idea of an electronic spreadsheet, even though it was a revolutionary advance in computer programming. The copyright in VisiCalc extended only to the particular way VisiCalc expressed this idea.

Very soon, many competing programs were introduced. The most successful of these was Lotus 1-2-3, originally created by Mitchell Kapor and Jonathan Sachs. Building on Bricklin's revolutionary idea, Kapor and Sachs expressed that idea in a different, more powerful way. Designed for the IBM PC, Lotus 1-2-3 took advantage of that computer's more expansive memory and more versatile screen display capabilities and keyboard. In short, Lotus 1-2-3 did all that VisiCalc did, only better. VisiCalc sales plunged and the program was eventually discontinued.

Of course, it's easy to say that copyright does not protect ideas, only expression. But what does this mean in the real world? Almost all computer programs embody systems or processes. When does the unprotectible system end and the protectible expression begin? In point of fact it can be very difficult to tell the difference between an unprotected idea, system, or process and its protected expression.

Legal Protection for Ideas, Processes, and Systems

What if Bricklin in the above example had wanted to protect his idea or system of an electronic spreadsheet itself, not just Visicalc? He would have had to look to laws other than copyright. If the electronic spreadsheet had qualified as a patentable invention, it could have been protected under the federal patent law. In this event, Bricklin would have had a 17-year monopoly on its use. Anyone else seeking to write a program implementing the spreadsheet idea would have had to obtain Bricklin's permission or been liable for patent infringement. Bricklin did not apply for a patent, and it is far from clear whether, at the time, he could have obtained one had he done so.

b. When an idea and its expression merge

Part of the essence of original authorship is the making of choices. Any work of authorship is the end result of a whole series of choices made by its creator. However, the choices available to the creators of many works of authorship are severely limited. In these cases, the idea or ideas underlying the work and the way they are expressed by the author are deemed to "merge." The result is that the author's expression is either treated as if it were in the public domain (given no protection at all) or protected only against virtually verbatim or "slavish" copying. If this were not so, the copyright law would end up discouraging authorship of new works and thereby retard the progress of knowledge.

The range of choices available to creators of functional works such as computer programs are often especially constrained, resulting in especially limited copyright protection.

EXAMPLE: Data East USA created a video game called *Karate Champ* for the Commodore computer. Data East sued the creator of a competing karate video game called *World Karate Champ* for copyright infringement. Data East claimed that *World Karate Champ* had impermissibly copied the audiovisual elements of *Karate Champ*. Data East lost because of the merger doctrine.

The court found that the similarities between the two games—similar game procedures, common karate moves, a time element, a referee, computer graphics, and bonus points—necessarily followed from the idea of creating a martial arts karate combat game: they were "inseparable from, or indispensable to … the idea of the karate sport."

As a result, the idea of a karate video game for the Commodore computer and its expression by Data East were deemed to merge, and Data East's game received very limited copyright protection. If this were not so, no one other than Data East could ever create a karate video game. (*Data East USA, Inc. v. Epyx, Inc.*, 862 F.2d 204 (9th Cir. 1988).)

The result of the merger doctrine is that the fewer choices a programmer has when setting out to create a given element of a piece of software, the less copyright protection that element will receive. Or, to put it another way: The scope of copyright protection is proportional to the range of expression available to articulate the underlying ideas communicated by the program.

In recent years, courts have been finding that more and more elements of computer programs are not protectible because of the merger doctrine. The seminal court decision of *Computer Associates Int'l v. Altai, Inc.*, 982 F.2d 693, (2d Cir. 1992), identified the following constraints on the range of software expression (this list is not exclusive):

- elements dictated by efficiency
- elements dictated by external factors, and
- standard programming techniques and program features.

Combinations of Public Domain Elements May Be Copyrightable

Although, as discussed in this section, many individual elements of computer programs are not protected by copyright, copyright protection may nevertheless exist for a programmer who combines these elements. In other words, there may be a copyright in the selection and arrangement of these elements. In one case, for example, a court held that the individual design elements in a point-and-draw computer graphics program were not copyrightable because they were dictated by efficiency concerns and external factors. However, the way these elements—including an external file structure, English language commands, functional modules, and a hierarchical series of menus with a touchscreen—were combined could have been copyrightable. (*Softel Inc. v. Dragon Medical and Scientific Communications, Inc.*, 118 F.3d 955 (2d Cir. 1997).)

But, to be copyrightable, this selection and arrangement must be original, minimally creative, and not itself driven by the constraints of computer programming, including functional considerations or external factors. It seems likely that many such combinations will fail to meet these requirements.

c.   Elements dictated by efficiency

Programmers usually strive to create programs that meet the user's needs as efficiently as possible. The desire for maximum efficiency may operate to restrict the range of choices available to a programmer. For example, there may only be one or two efficient ways to express the idea embodied in a given program, module, routine, or subroutine. If a programmer's choices regarding a particular program's structure, interface, or even source code are necessary to efficiently implement the program's function, then those choices will not be protected by copyright. In other words, no programmer may have a monopoly on the most efficient way to write any program. Paradoxically, this means that the better job a programmer does—the more closely the program approximates the ideal of efficiency—the less copyright protection the program will receive.

> **EXAMPLE 1:** A court held that Lotus 1-2-3's basic spreadsheet screen display resembling a rotated "L" was not protected by copyright because there are only a few ways to make a computer screen resemble a spreadsheet; nor was the use of "+," "-," "*," and "/" for their corresponding mathematical functions; or use of the Enter key to place keystroke entries into cells. The use of such keys was the most efficient means to implement these mathematical functions. (*Lotus Dev. Corp. v. Borland Int'l, Inc.*, 799 F. Supp. 203 (D. Mass. 1992).)

> **EXAMPLE 2:** Another court held that a cost-estimating program's method of allowing users to navigate within screen displays (by using the Space bar to move the cursor down a list, the Backspace key to move up, the Return key to choose a function, and a number selection to edit an entry) was not protectible. The court noted that there were only a limited number of ways to enable a user to navigate through a screen display on the hardware in question while facilitating user comfort. The court also found that the program's use of alphabetical and numerical columns in its screen displays was not protectible. The constraints of uniformity of format and limited page space (requiring either a horizontal or vertical orientation) permitted only a very narrow range of choices. (*Manufacturers Technologies, Inc. v. Cams*, 706 F. Supp. 984 (D. Conn. 1989).)

d.   Elements dictated by external factors

A programmer's freedom of design choice is often limited by external factors such as:

- the mechanical specifications of the computer on which the program is intended to run
- compatibility requirements of other programs which the program is designed to operate in conjunction with
- computer manufacturers' design standards, and
- the demands of the industry being serviced.

EXAMPLE 1: Intel Corp. charged that NEC Corp. had unlawfully copied the microcode to Intel Corp.'s 8086/88 microprocessor chip to create compatible microprocessor chips of its own. (Microcode is a series of instructions that tells a microprocessor chip how to work.) NEC sued Intel to obtain a judicial declaration that it did not infringe on Intel's microcode. The court held that NEC had not committed infringement. Although some of the simpler microroutines in NEC's microcode were substantially similar to Intel's, the court held that machine constraints were largely responsible for the similarities; that is, NEC's programmers had very limited choices in designing their microcode to operate a chip compatible with Intel's 8086/88. Given these constraints, Intel's microcode was protected only against "virtually identical copying." (*NEC Corp. v. Intel Corp.*, 10 U.S.P.Q. 2d 1177 (N.D. Cal. 1989).)

EXAMPLE 2: A cotton cooperative developed a program for mainframe computers called Telcot that provided users with cotton prices and information, accounting services, and the ability to consummate cotton sales transactions. Former employee-programmers of the cooperative created a PC version of the cotton exchange program. The two programs were similar in their sequence and organization. The cooperative sued for infringement and lost. The court held that many of the similarities between the two programs were dictated by the externalities of the cotton market. The programs were designed to present the same information as contained in a cotton recap sheet, and there were not many different ways to accomplish this. (*Plains Cotton Cooperative Assoc. v. Goodpasture Computer Service, Inc.*, 807 F.2d 1256 (5th Cir. 1987).)

e. Standard programming techniques and software features

Certain programming techniques and software features are so widely used as to be standard in the software industry. To create a competitive program, a software developer may have no choice other than to employ such techniques and features because users expect them. Courts treat such material as being in the public domain—it is free for the taking and cannot be owned by any single software author even though it is included in an otherwise copyrightable work.

EXAMPLE 1: A court held that the following basic elements of the Macintosh user interface were unprotectible because they were common to all graphical user interfaces and were standard in the industry:

- overlapping windows to display multiple images on a computer screen
- iconic representations of familiar objects from the office environment, such as file folders, documents, and a trash can
- opening and closing of objects in order to retrieve, transfer, or store information
- menus used to store information or control computer functions, and
- manipulation of icons to convey instructions and to control operation of the computer. (See *Apple Computer v. Microsoft Corp.*, 779 F. Supp. 133 (N.D. Cal. 1992).)

EXAMPLE 2: The owner of an outlining program called PC-Outline sued the owner of a competing program called Grandview for copyright infringement. Grandview had nine pull-down menus functionally similar to those of PC-Outline. Nevertheless, the court held that Grandview did not infringe on PC-Outline. The court reasoned that use of a pull-down menu was commonplace in the software industry. The court declared that a copyright owner cannot claim "copyright protection of an ... expression that is, if not standard, then commonplace in the computer software industry." (*Brown Bag Software v. Symantec Corp.*, 960 F.2d 1465 (9th Cir. 1990).)

f. Copying user interfaces

The user interface of a computer program is the way a program presents itself to and interacts with the user. It consists principally of the sequence, flow, and content of the display screens that appear on a computer's monitor (permitting the user to select various options or input data in a prescribed format) and the use of specific keys on the computer keyboard to perform particular functions. The look and feel of a program's interface can be very important to the user (a well-designed interface makes a program much easier to use) and therefore very valuable to the program's owner. It's possible to copy the way a user interface looks and works without copying any computer code.

After years of litigation involving some of the most famous software interfaces in the world it seems clear that copyright provides very little protection for most of the elements of a user interface. Anything less than slavish copying of an entire interface is likely not an infringement. As a result, developers need not go to the trouble of devising different words to convey simple menu commands and may use commands that are familiar to users of competing works.

The two most important cases involve the Macintosh interface and the Lotus 1-2-3 computer spreadsheet program.

Apple sued Microsoft, claiming that the user interface of Microsoft's Windows system violated Apple's copyright in the Macintosh user interface. Ultimately, all of Apple's claims were dismissed and the case was upheld on appeal. The trial court held that the "desktop metaphor" underlying the Macintosh user interface—suggesting an office with familiar office objects such as file folders, documents, and a trash can—was an unprotectible idea. The court also ruled that most of the individual elements of the user interface at issue in the case were not protectible, either because Apple had licensed them to Microsoft, because they were not original, or because they lacked copyrightable expression. However, the court also held the Macintosh interface might be protected as a whole, at least from virtually identical copying, even though its individual elements were not protected. In other words, although many of the individual elements of the interface were not protectible standing alone, they still formed part of a larger arrangement, selection, or layout that was protected expression. (*Apple Computer, Inc. v. Microsoft Corp.*, 35 F.3d. 1435 (9th Cir. 1994).)

Lotus Development Corp. sued Borland International, Inc., claiming that its Lotus 1-2-3 spreadsheet program had been infringed by Borland's Quattro and Quattro Pro spreadsheet programs. In order to enable users familiar with Lotus 1-2-3 to switch to Quattro without having to learn new commands or rewrite their Lotus macros, Borland included in its programs an alternate command menu structure that was a virtually identical copy of the Lotus 1-2-3 menu command hierarchy. Borland did not copy any of Lotus's code. It copied only the words and structure of Lotus's menu commands. After losing at trial, Borland finally won on appeal. The Court of Appeal held that 1-2-3's command hierarchy was a method of operation that was not protected by copyright. The court stated that a software developer should be able to create a program that users can operate in exactly the same way as a competing program. (*Lotus Development Corp. v. Borland International, Inc.*, 49 F.3d 807 (1st Cir. 1995).)

2. Copying Web Elements Unprotected by Copyright

Although no court has ruled on the issue, it's likely that the limitations on copyright protection for software discussed in the preceding section also apply to the Web. Copyright law will not protect common elements of HTML and similar codes—for example, the method of making text blink in HTML (<BLINK>*YOUR TEXT*</BLINK>). Copyright will not protect the basic format and layout elements of websites.

In general, the ideas embodied in websites are not protected. For example, the idea of creating a website about how to invest wisely in the stock market is not copyrightable. Anyone else is free to take the same idea and create their own website without infringing. However, the concrete way that someone expresses that idea can be protected—for example, the words, graphics, and other works created to express that idea can be protected by copyright.

Similarly, elements of a website that are not original or that are dictated by efficiency or standard Web design techniques are not protectible. Some examples might include the simple navigation bar found at the bottom of a Web page or the use of a house icon to represent a website's home page.

3. Copying Elements in the Public Domain

There are some categories of works that copyright can never protect. These works are in the public domain and freely available to anyone unless they are protected by some body of law other than copyright—for example, patent or trademark law.

Following is a brief description of some of the works that are in the public domain. For a comprehensive discussion of the public domain, see *The Public Domain: How to Find & Use Copyright-Free Writings, Music, Art & More*, by Stephen Fishman (Nolo).

a. Purely functional items

Copyright only protects works of authorship. Things that have a purely functional or utilitarian purpose are not considered to be works of authorship and are not copyrightable. For example, there is no copyright protection for the purely functional aspects of machinery, refrigerators, lamps, or automobiles. However, if the design of a useful article incorporates artistic features that are independent of the article's functional aspects, such features are protectible.

b. Words, names, titles, slogans, and other short phrases

No matter how highly creative, novel, or distinctive they may be, individual words and short phrases are not protected by copyright, and will not be registered by the Copyright Office (37 C.F.R. § 202.1(a)). For this reason, the use of words and short phrases in the menus and icons of the Macintosh user interface—"Get Info" and "Trash," for example—were found not to be protectible.

c. Blank forms designed solely to record information

Blank forms designed solely to record information are not protected by copyright. The Copyright Office will not register such items. (37 C.F.R. § 202.1(c).) According to the Copyright Office, this includes such items as time cards, graph paper, account books, bank checks, scorecards, address books, diaries, report forms, and order forms.

This rule may also apply to computer screen templates designed to fit with electronic spreadsheets or database programs. If such templates are designed solely to record information, and do not convey information, they should not be protected.

However, it can be difficult in many cases to determine if a form is designed solely to record information. Even true blank forms—that is, forms consisting mainly of blank space to be filled in—may convey valuable information. For example, the columns or headings on a blank form may be interlaced with highly informative verbiage. Moreover, the configuration of columns, headings, and lines itself may convey information.

d. Typeface designs

The Copyright Office and courts have concluded that typeface designs—whether digital or analog—are industrial designs and are therefore not protected by copyright. The reasoning for this is that typeface styles or fonts are purely utilitarian. The Copyright Office, therefore, will not register a work consisting solely of a typeface design. However, copyright can protect typeface software (computer programs designed to produce fonts). In addition, some typefaces have been protected by design patents, including ITC Stone, Adobe Garamond, and Adobe Minion.

e. Works for which copyright has expired

As discussed in Chapter 3, copyright protection does not last forever. When it expires the work enters the public domain. In effect, public domain works belong to everybody. Anyone is free to use them but no one can ever own them. All works published in the U.S. before 1923 are in the public domain because their copyrights have expired. Many works first published during 1923-1963 are also in the public domain because their copyrights were never renewed.

f. Works dedicated to the public domain

The author of a copyrightable work is free to decide that he or she doesn't want it protected by copyright and may dedicate it instead to the public domain. By doing so, the author gives up all ownership rights in the work and permits anyone to copy or otherwise use the work without permission. There are no official forms to file to do this. The author merely needs to state clearly somewhere on the work that no copyright is claimed in the work. The Copyright Office will not register a work for which copyright has been expressly disclaimed. Without such registration, a copyright infringement suit cannot be filed.

Probably more software has been dedicated to the public domain than any other type of work. Much of this public domain software can be found on the Internet. However, it's important to understand that software distributed for free is not necessarily in the public domain. Following is a list of terms commonly used to describe software that is distrib-

uted for free but is *not* in the public domain. The software is copyrighted and users are often required to agree to license agreements (whose terms are usually quite generous). If the software you're interested in is described with one of these terms, it isn't in the public domain.

There is nothing wrong with using such software, but you should be aware that it comes with legal restrictions on how it is used. Make sure you understand these restrictions. They will usually be spelled out in a Read Me file, license agreement, manual, or other documentation included within the software or inside its packaging.

- *Free software*: Free software—also called freeware—is software that is made available to the public for free. Although it's free, it is not in the public domain because the author retains his or her copyright rights and places restrictions on how the program is used. Ordinarily, it can't be modified or incorporated into other software without the owner's permission.

- *Shareware*: Shareware refers to a method of marketing software by making trial copies available to users for free. If the user wishes to keep the software, he or she is supposed to pay the shareware owner a fee. Shareware is fully protected by copyright and may be used only in the manner and to the extent permitted by the owner.

- *Open source software*: Open source software is copyrighted and it can either be sold or given away. However, it must be distributed under an open source license that guarantees users' rights to read, use, modify, and redistribute the software freely. The source code must be made available so users can improve or modify the program. Many parts of the UNIX operating system, (including the Linux program) were developed this way. (See Chapter 16, Section F, for a discussion of open source.)

- *Copyleft software*: "Copyleft" is a term devised by famed programmer Richard Stallman and the Free Software Foundation. It's very similar to open source software. For more information, see www.fsf.org.

- *Semi-free software*: This is software that is not free, but comes with permission for individuals to use, copy, distribute, and modify it so long as they do so solely for nonprofit purposes. PGP (Pretty Good Privacy), a popular program used to encrypt email, is one example.

g. U.S. government software

Any work created by U.S. government employees as part of their job duties is in the public domain, including software and websites. Creative works made for the U.S. government by outside contractors are also in the public domain unless the government allows the contractor to retain ownership in the product.

Thousands of software programs have been created by U.S. government employees and contractors and are in the public domain. These include, for example, weather forecasting programs created by the National Weather Service, mapmaking programs created by the U.S. Geological Survey, and aeronautical programs created by NASA.

Likewise, there are thousands of U.S. government websites, most of whose material is in the public domain. This includes, for example, the IRS and NASA websites (www.irs.gov), (www.nasa.gov). You can find a directory of U.S. government websites at http://firstgov.gov.

4. Creating Similar Works Independently

So long as a work is independently created, it is entitled to copyright protection even if other similar works already exist. This means that if an author can prove he or she independently created the work in question, he or she cannot be guilty of infringing on a preexisting work, even if it is very similar to that work. This rule has been particularly important for the software industry where software developers create programs that perform the same functions as preexisting competing programs.

Of course, proving that a program was independently created can be difficult. The creators of the program must be able to show they did not have access to the preexisting program; or, even if they could have had access to it, they never saw it. One approach taken by some software developers who wish to create programs similar to or compatible with preexisting software is the use of clean room procedures to establish independent creation. Clean room procedures are used to isolate the persons who actually develop the software. In some cases such persons are denied access to any information about the preexisting software. In other cases they may be given only information about the preexisting program's purpose or functions.

The federal appeals court in *Computer Associates v. Altai*, 982 F.2d 693 (2d Cir. 1992) indicated that clean room procedures can really work and serve as a good defense to copyright infringement claims. Here's what happened in that case: Altai hired a programmer formerly employed by CAI to create a job scheduling program. Unbeknownst to Altai, the programmer used substantial chunks of CAI code to create Altai's software. When Altai learned what happened, it decided to create a clean version of its scheduling program. Altai hired eight new programmers to create the new version. They

were denied access to the infringing version of the software and forbidden to talk to the programmer who created that version. The new programmers were only provided with a specification developed from an earlier noninfringing version of the software. It took about six months to create the new program. It accomplished everything the prior version did, but used none of CAI's code. Altai was sued for copyright infringement by CAI, but the court held that this version of the program did not infringe on CAI's copyright.

For clean room procedures to be effective, great care must be taken not to give the clean room personnel information protected by copyright. For example, an overly specific description for a user interface might contain protected expression which, if used, could taint the clean room. Before implementing a clean room procedure of your own, you should consult with a knowledgeable software attorney.

5. Copying Within the Bounds of Fair Use

The Copyright Act contains several exceptions to the general rule that copyright rights are exclusive to their owners. These exceptions are generally referred to as fair use.

If a particular use of a copyrighted item comes within the legal definition of fair use, the copyright owner's permission isn't necessary, nor is the user required to pay the owner compensation for the use. Often, whether a particular act is or isn't fair use is a major issue in a copyright infringement case, with the defendant claiming, "I didn't infringe your copyright, I only made fair use of it."

The Copyright Act contains several broad categories of what constitutes fair use. A more specific description is found in the congressional committee report that accompanied the act as it was being considered by Congress. According to this report, examples of when unauthorized copying of a copyrighted work is considered fair use include:

- quotations or excerpts in a review or criticism for purposes of illustration or comment
- quotation of a short passage in a scholarly or technical work for illustration or clarification of the author's observation
- use in a parody of some of the content of the work parodied
- summary of an address or article, with brief quotations, in a news report
- reproduction by a library of a portion of a work to replace part of a damaged copy
- reproduction by a teacher or student of a small part of a work to illustrate a lesson
- reproduction of a work in legislative or judicial proceedings or reports, and

- incidental and fortuitous reproduction, in a newsreel or broadcast, of a work located at the scene of an event being reported.

As you may glean from these examples, fair use has historically been used to allow the media broad latitude in reporting on items of public interest, even if they're otherwise subject to copyright protection. Fair use has also been important to educational, scientific, and political pursuits. Note also that, with the exception of uses by the for-profit press and mass media, most of these examples involve nonprofit uses of copyrighted material. Authors of works created primarily for financial gain usually have had a difficult time successfully invoking the fair use privilege.

a. Four factors considered in fair use analysis

Four primary factors are considered to determine whether an unauthorized use is a fair use, rather than copyright infringement:

- *The character and purpose of the use*: The test here is to see whether the subsequent work merely serves as a substitute for the original or "instead adds something new, with a further purpose or different character, altering the first with new expression, meaning, or message." (*Campbell v. Acuff-Rose Music, Inc.*, 114 S.Ct. 1164

(1994).) The Supreme Court calls such a new work "transformative". This is the most significant fair use factor. The more transformative a work, the less important are the other fair use factors, such as commercialism, that may weigh against a finding of fair use. Why should this be? It is because the goal of copyright to promote human knowledge is furthered by the creation of transformative works. "Such works thus lie at the heart of the fair use doctrine's guarantee of a breathing space within the confines of copyright." (*Campbell v. Acuff-Rose Music, Inc.*)

- *The nature of the copyrighted work*: Legal, scientific, historical, and other factual works are more often subject to the fair use defense than fanciful works like novels or movies.
- *The amount and substantiality of the portion of the copyrighted work used in relation to the entire work*: Using a small part of a large work is more likely to be considered fair use than if most of the work is used. Similarly, a part of a work that is somewhat tangential to the whole will qualify as fair use more easily than a portion of core importance.
- *The effect of the use on the potential market for the copyrighted work, or the work's value*: The fact that the use actually competes with the copyrighted work (for example, creating a competing program) weighs against fair use. However, the more transformative the subsequent work, the less important this factor is. In other words, if an author borrows some copyrighted material to create a new and better work, the fact that it may harm the market for the previous work will not necessarily bar a finding of fair use.

b. Making archival copies is a fair use

Congress has specifically authorized two fair uses that relate to computer programs. A person who purchases a computer program has the right to copy or adapt the program if the copy or adaptation is either:

- "An essential step in the utilization of the computer program in conjunction with a machine and that it is used in no other manner"—in other words, the purchaser has to copy the program from a floppy disk to his hard disk or adapt the program to get it to work on his computer; or
- The copy or adaptation is for archival purposes only (a single back-up copy) and is made and kept only by the person who owns the legally purchased copy. (17 U.S.C. § 117.)

This limited right to make a back-up or archival copy is not really very generous. Since the copy is for back-up purposes only, it cannot be used on a second computer. This means, for example, that if you own a desktop computer and a laptop, and want to use your word processor on both, legally you must buy two copies. In an effort to make their customers happy, some large software publishers are now including provisions in their license agreements permitting their customers to use a program on two different computers.

c.   Reverse engineering as a fair use

Reverse engineering is the process of taking a product or device apart and reducing it to its constituent parts or concepts to see how it works. Reverse engineering has long been used by manufacturers of all types of products to help them create new products. Reverse engineering is perfectly legal so long as it doesn't violate another's patent or copyright rights.

Computer hardware may be reverse engineered by unscrewing the box and looking inside. The best way to reverse engineer a computer program is usually to read the source code. To prevent competitors from reading their valuable source code, software owners normally distribute their programs in object code form only, while the source code is kept locked away. However, it is possible, though often difficult, to reverse engineer object code by translating it into human-readable

assembly language which programmers then read to understand the object code. This process is called decompilation or disassembly.

The information gained by reverse engineering can be put to a variety of uses, each with a different economic effect on the owner of the original program. For example, the information can be used to develop a competitive product. In other cases, decompilation can be used to create a program that is functionally compatible—a clone program. Decompilation can also be used to help develop a program that is not competitive, but complementary to the original program—for example, creating a video game cartridge to run on a video game system like Nintendo or *Genesis*.

Decompilation and disassembly involve the making of at least a partial reproduction or derivative work of the object code. Typically, a copy of the original program is made, decompiler software is then used to load the program into computer memory, and the copy is then transformed into human-readable form, which is then fixed on disk or paper.

The most important of these cases involved Sega Enterprises, manufacturer of the *Genesis* video game system. (*Sega Enterprises, Ltd. v. Accolade, Inc.*, 977 F.2d 1510 (9th Cir. 1992).) Accolade, Inc., wanted to manufacture a video game cartridge to be used with the *Genesis* system. Rather than pay Sega for a license to do so, Accolade reverse engineered the *Genesis* system. It disassembled the object code stored in commercially available read-only memory (ROM) chips in Sega's games to learn the requirements for creation of a *Genesis*-compatible game cartridge. This process required that Accolade make unauthorized copies of Sega's code for study and analysis (called intermediate copies). Sega sued Accolade for copyright infringement, claiming that Accolade's copying violated its copyright. Sega lost.

The federal appeals court held that disassembly of object code is a fair use if:

- it is the only means available to obtain access to the unprotected elements of a computer program—ideas, functional principles, and so forth (see Section B1), and
- the copier has a legitimate reason for seeking such access.

In *Sony Computer Entertainment, Inc. v. Connectix Corp.*, 203 F.3d 596 (9th Cir. 2000), a California federal appeals court extended the fair use rule further. Connectix Corporation developed an "emulator"—a software program that could be used to play Sony *PlayStation* games on a computer without using the Sony *PlayStation* game console. To develop the emulator, Connectix disassembled the *PlayStation* BIOS (the basic input-output software) from an internal *PlayStation* ROM chip. Connectix used this BIOS code to develop its own BIOS code. The final version of the Connectix emulator contained all new code created by Connectix.

Nevertheless, Sony claimed that the copies Connectix had made of its BIOS during the development process constituted copyright infringement. The court disagreed, holding that the intermediate copies were a fair use of the Sony BIOS and were necessary to permit Connectix to make its noninfringing emulator function with *PlayStation* games. Unlike in *Sega*, the Connectix emulator directly competes with the Sony *PlayStation* and could harm Sony's console sales. But the *Sony* court held that because the emulator program was "modestly transformative"—that is, a new product rather than a mere copy of the original *PlayStation*—it was a legitimate competitor in the market for platforms capable of playing *PlayStation* games.

Reverse Engineering May Be Barred by License Agreements

Reverse engineering may be legal under the copyright law, but it might still be barred by software license agreements. This lesson was learned by a company called Baystate Technologies that created and marketed a template to improve computer-aided design software. To create its product, the company obtained a copy of a preexisting template created by Bowers and reverse engineered it. Bowers's software template contained a shrink-wrap license agreement that barred such reverse engineering. Bowers sued Baystate for violating the license and won. The court held that the license was valid and not preempted (superseded) by the fair use provisions of the copyright law. (*Bowers v. Baystate*, 320 F.3d 1317 (Fed. Cir., 2003).) The moral is that if you want to reverse engineer a program, be sure that the shrink-wrap license doesn't bar the activity.

Reverse Engineering and the DMCA

As a general rule, the Digital Millennium Copyright Act (DMCA), passed by Congress in 1998, prohibits programmers from circumventing copy protection schemes and other technological measures designed to prevent access to program code. (See Section A6.) However, the DMCA makes an exception for some reverse engineering. It provides that a person who has lawfully obtained the right to use a copy of a computer program may circumvent such technological measures to gain access to the code if it is done to identify and analyze "those elements of the program that are necessary to achieve interoperability of an independently created computer program with other programs." Moreover, programmers can develop tools to permit such reverse engineering and share the information they learn with others provided these activities don't constitute copyright infringement. (17 U.S.C. § 1201(f).)

---

d. Limitations on decompilation as a fair use

The *Sega* and *Sony* cases do not create a blanket rule permitting all decompilation. Decompilation can be a fair use only when it is the only available means to study the unprotected elements of a program. Often, there are means available other than decompilation to study such elements—simply studying the screen display will reveal the ideas and concepts of many programs. The *Sega* court stated that the need for disassembly "arises, if at all, only in connection with operations systems, system interface procedures, and other programs that are not visible to the user when operating."

The fair use factors discussed above are subject to varying interpretations and it is often difficult to predict the outcome of any particular case. This fact is illustrated by another court decision on fair use, involving decompilation of security system source code for the Nintendo video game system by Atari Games. (*Atari Games Corp. v. Nintendo of America, Inc.*, 980 F.2d 857 (Fed. Cir. 1992).) The court reached the same legal conclusion as the *Sega* and *Sony* decisions—decompilation can be a fair use in the proper circumstances. But the court held that Atari's decompilation was *not* a fair use because it obtained the Nintendo source code from the Copyright Offices under false pretenses. It is also likely that Atari's bad faith and lack of fair dealing precluded a finding of fair use.

The question of whether a use qualifies as a fair use must always be decided on a case-by-case basis. For these reasons, anyone wishing to reverse engineer any program to create a new product should first consult with a qualified software attorney.

e. Fair use on the Internet

The fair use rule applies to the Internet, just as it does to the physical world. However, the rule does not give you a blanket license to copy other people's work—a fact Napster learned the hard way (see below). The four fair use factors listed above must be carefully analyzed.

Also, always remember that the fair use rule is a *defense* to copyright infringement. It does not prevent you from getting sued. Moreover, the fair use factors are inherently ambiguous and given to differing interpretations. Thus, what you view as a fair use can easily be seen as copyright infringement by a court. Here are some real examples:

> **EXAMPLE:** Arriba Soft Corporation operated an Internet search engine that displayed thumbnail image pictures copied from other websites. Kelly, a photographer, discovered his photographs were part of Arriba's database and filed suit for copyright infringement. The Court of Appeal held that using thumbnail reproductions of copyrighted photographs on a website was a fair use because the use was "transformative" and did not interfere with the photographer's economic expectations. (*Kelly v. Arriba Soft Corporation*, 336 F3d. 811 (9th Cir. 2003).)

EXAMPLE: Napster, operator of an extremely popular Internet-based "peer-to-peer" digital music file-sharing service, was sued by various record companies for contributory copyright infringement. The court rejected Napster's fair use defense. The court found that Napster flunked all four fair use factors listed above because: (1) the use was not transformative—Napster merely helped users transfer the music recordings into a new medium; (2) the sound recordings were creative works; (3) entire works were copied, not just portions of them; and (4) the copying harmed the record companies' market for CD sales to college students. (*A&M Records, Inc. v. Napster, Inc.*, 239 F.3d 1004 (9th Cir. 2001).)

EXAMPLE: Critics of the Church of Scientology posted copies of entire publications of the church without permission. When the church sued them for copyright infringement, the critics unsuccessfully claimed fair use. The court held that fair use is intended to permit the copying of portions of a work, not complete works. (*Religious Technology Center v. Lerma*, 40 U.S.P.Q. 2d 1569 (E.D. Va. 1996).)

EXAMPLE: The *Washington Post* newspaper used three brief quotations from Church of Scientology texts posted on the Internet in the case discussed in the example above. This time when the church sued for copyright infringement, the claim of fair use was upheld. Important factors in the favorable ruling were that only a small portions of the church publications were excerpted and the purpose was for news commentary. (*Religious Technology Center v. Pagliarina*, 908 F. Supp. 1353 (E.D. Va. 1995).)

EXAMPLE: The *Washington Post* and *Los Angeles Times* sued a website called FreeRepublic.com that encouraged users to post verbatim copies of news articles on the site so that users could comment on them. The court held that this was not a fair use because such extensive copying was not necessary for users to comment on the news of the day. Such comment only required a summary of the underlying facts in the news stories, not the verbatim copy of them in their entirety. (*Los Angeles Times v. Free Republic*, 2000 U.S. Dist. Lexis 5669 (C.D. Cal. 2000).)

C. Protecting Against Infringement Claims

To protect yourself against infringement claims, you must not only avoid committing copyright infringement yourself, but also guard against infringement by your employees, independent contractors, and other people you deal with.

1. When You Can Be Held Liable for Infringement

Unfortunately, you don't have to commit copyright infringement yourself to be held liable. You can be held legally responsible for infringements carried out by your employees, consultants, and others you deal with.

a. Employers liable for infringement by employees

A copyright infringer's employer (whether a corporation, partnership, or individual) will be held liable for any infringing acts by employees within the scope of employment. This is based on the general legal principle that an employer has the right to supervise and control employees' activities and is therefore responsible for their wrongful acts.

b. Hirers of independent contractors

You don't have to be an employer of someone to be held liable for their infringement. The hirer of an independent contractor may be liable for the contractor's infringement if the hirer actively participated in, materially contributed to, or furthered the hired party's infringing acts.

Liability may also be imposed if a contractor had a direct financial interest in the infringing activities and the right to supervise the contractor or at least police his or her conduct.

c. Corporate officers and partners

The president and other officers of a corporation may be held personally liable for infringement by the corporation if the officer caused the infringement, participated in it, or benefited financially from it.

Partners in a partnership may also be held personally liable for infringement by their fellow partners if they participated in it, benefited from it, or arranged it.

d. Employee liability

An employee who commits infringement on his or her own initiative will be held liable. However, liability usually will not be imposed where an employee is ordered to commit an infringement by the employer. But the employer would of course be liable.

e. Anyone who induces an infringement

In addition, any person who induces, causes, or helps another to commit copyright infringement may be held liable as a contributory infringer and subjected to the same penalties as the person who actually committed the infringement.

f. Internet Service Providers (ISPs)

Companies that provide access to the Internet (often called Internet Service Providers or ISPs) are liable for infringement where they or their employees actively engage in the infringement—that is, copy, distribute, or display a copyright owner's work without permission.

ISPs may also be liable even when they don't actively participate in the infringement and instead one of their subscribers or users commits the infringement. Courts have held that an ISP is liable for copyright infringement committed by its subscribers if:

- the ISP knew about, or should have known about, the infringing activity and induced, caused, or contributed to the infringing actions, *or*
- the ISP had the right and ability to control the infringer's acts and received a direct financial benefit from the infringement.

EXAMPLE: Dennis Erlich, a former member of the Church of Scientology uploaded copyrighted church material onto the Internet using the ISP Netcom to obtain Internet access. The church sued both Erlich and Netcom for copyright infringement. The court held that Netcom was not liable for direct copyright infringement because it did not directly participate in copying and posting the church materials on the Internet. Netcom simply operated an ISP and did not receive a direct financial benefit from the alleged infringement—it only charged Erlich a flat fee for Internet access. Netcom would have been liable for Erlich's acts only if it knew about them and induced, caused, or materially contributed to Erlich's allegedly infringing conduct. (*Religious Technology Center v. Netcom On-Line Communication Serv. Inc.*, 907 F. Supp. 1362 (N.D. Cal. 1995).)

2. Preventing Illegal Copying in the Development Process

There are a number of things you can do to prevent illegal copying while software or a website is being developed. These steps will also put you in the best possible legal position if you are later sued for copyright infringement.

a. Keep good records

It is important for software and Web developers to keep detailed records of the entire development process, from the initial idea stage to coding, debugging, and testing. This includes copies of storyboards and prototypes, interim versions, flowcharts, and internal memoranda documenting the many decisions that must be made in the course of development.

b. Registering works under development

If you're especially concerned about being sued for copyright infringement, you may wish to register your work with the Copyright Office while it's still under development. The advantage of this is that you deposit a copy of the software with the Copyright Office as part of the registration process. The existence of this registered copy can serve as proof that you didn't copy from someone else. If your work was deposited before the work you are alleged to have copied was created, then you couldn't have copied it.

c. Don't indemnify clients for infringement claims

Another thing a developer can do to help reduce his or her exposure is to refuse to indemnify customers for infringement claims. Indemnification means the developer promises to defend the customer in court if it is sued for infringement and to pay any damages awarded. Indemnification provisions have been commonly included in development agreements in the past; but, in light of the risks involved, more and more developers are refusing to agree to them or insist on limiting their exposure.

Insurance Coverage for Infringement Claims

Your business may be insured for intellectual property infringement claims and not even know it. The Comprehensive General Liability (CGL) insurance policies typically obtained by businesses may provide such coverage. Several courts have held that the advertising injury provision included in many CGL policies covers infringement claims. However, not all CGL policies provide such coverage. You should ask your insurance broker whether your policy provides this coverage. If the broker doesn't know, you may need to consult with an insurance attorney who represents policyholders. If your CGL policy doesn't cover infringement claims, you may be able to obtain such coverage by purchasing a rider to your policy that covers such claims.

D. What to Do If You're Accused of Copyright Infringement

What should you do if you're accused of copyright infringement? First, see how serious the claim is. If it's minor—for example, a photographer claims you used one of her pictures on a website without permission—the matter can usually be settled very quickly for a small amount of money. This kind of thing happens all the time. There is no need to see a lawyer (who'll probably charge you at least $200 per hour) to deal with this type of minor annoyance. Have the copyright owner sign a letter releasing you from liability in return for your payment. (See Section F4 for an example of a settlement letter.)

On the other hand, if you receive a letter from a copyright owner or owner's attorney alleging a substantial claim—for example, that your popular spreadsheet program is an unauthorized derivative work and its sale should be halted immediately—it's probably time to find a copyright lawyer. If, even worse, you are served with a court complaint (a document initiating a lawsuit), you must act quickly because you may have as little as 20 days to file an answer (response) in court. If you don't respond in time, a judgment can be entered against you. Finding a lawyer is discussed in Chapter 19.

Even if the case is serious, don't despair. The fact is, many infringement suits

are won by the defendant, either because the plaintiff did not have a valid claim to begin with or because the defendant had a good defense. This chapter is not a substitute for a consultation with an experienced attorney; rather, it is designed to give you an idea of some of the things you need to discuss when you see an attorney.

If a substantial claim is involved, the decision whether to settle the case or fight it out in court should only be made after consulting with an attorney who is familiar with the facts of your particular case. However, in making this decision you need to carefully weigh the following factors:

- how likely is it that the plaintiff will prevail
- how much is the plaintiff likely to collect if the plaintiff does win
- what are the costs of contesting the case, not only in terms of money, but also in terms of the time it will take, and the embarrassment and adverse publicity it will generate, and
- how much may the plaintiff be willing to settle for.

In cases where a settlement can't be reached, you may be able to have his suit dismissed very quickly by filing what's called a summary judgment motion. Under this procedure the judge examines the plaintiff's claims and decides whether there is any possibility he could prevail if a trial were held. If not, the judge will dismiss the case. Of course, you must pay a lawyer to file a summary judgment motion, but, if successful, it will cost far less than taking the case to trial. Summary judgment motions are frequently used—and are frequently successful—against plaintiffs who bring patently frivolous infringement suits. Moreover, if the plaintiff's claim was clearly frivolous or brought in bad faith, the judge might order the plaintiff to pay all or part of your attorney fees.

On the other hand, if the plaintiff does have a valid claim, paying an attorney to fight a losing battle will only compound your problems. Valid claims should be settled whenever possible. If the plaintiff was able to obtain a preliminary injunction from a federal judge, he or she probably has a valid claim.

1. Defenses to Copyright Infringement

Even if there are substantial similarities between the plaintiff's work and your work, you will not necessarily be found liable for infringement. The similarities may simply be the result of coincidence; in this event there is no liability. But, even direct copying from the plaintiff's work may be excused if it constitutes a fair use or there is another valid defense.

Possible defenses to an infringement action include many general legal defenses that often involve where, when, and how the lawsuit was brought, who was sued, and so on. We obviously can't cover all of this here. This section is lim-

ited to outlining the major defenses that are specific to copyright infringement actions. Again, if you find yourself defending a serious copyright infringement action, retain a qualified attorney.

a. Material copied was not protected by copyright

Many elements of copyrighted works are not protected by copyright at all or are given very limited protection. (See Section B.) Most courts require that these elements be eliminated from consideration when the plaintiff's work is compared with the allegedly infringing software to determine whether they are substantially similar. This means that if you've only copied or paraphrased these unprotected elements, you won't be found to have committed copyright infringement.

b. The use was authorized

In some cases, you may not be an infringer at all, but a legal transferee. For example:

- You might legitimately claim to have received a license to use the plaintiff's work, and that the work the plaintiff claims to infringe on his copyright falls within that license. For instance, Programmer A orally tells Programmer B he can copy his work, then later claims never to have granted the permission.

- Conflicting or confusing licenses or sublicenses are granted and you claim to be the rightful owner of the right(s) in question.
- You received a transfer from the plaintiff and weren't restricted in making further transfers, and transferred the copyright to individuals unknown to the original owner.
- Several examples of lawful transfers are presented in Chapter 11. If any of these transferees were sued they would have a good defense—that is, that their use was lawful.

c. Statute of limitations

A plaintiff can't wait forever to file an infringement suit. As discussed in Section G4, the statute of limitations is three years from the time the infringement should reasonably have been discovered (but applying this rule can be extremely tricky). If the plaintiff waited too long, you may be able to have the case dismissed.

d. Other defenses

Some of the other possible defenses to copyright infringement include such things as:

- the notion that if the plaintiff is guilty of some serious wrongdoing himself or herself—for example, falsifying

evidence—he or she cannot complain about your alleged wrongs
- the notion that the plaintiff waited so long to file suit that it would be unfair to find the defendant guilty of infringement—"it is inequitable for the owner of a copyright, with full notice of an intended infringement, to stand inactive while the proposed infringer spends large sums of money on its exploitation, and to intervene only when his speculation has proved a success. Delay under such circumstances allows the owner to speculate without risk with the other's money; he cannot possibly lose, and he may win." (*Hass v. Leo Feist, Inc.*, 234 Fed. 105 (S.D. N.Y. 1916).)
- The idea that the copyright owner knew of your acts and expressly or impliedly consented to them.

2. Collecting Your Attorney Fees If You Prevail

If the plaintiff (the person who sues you for infringement) loses his or her suit, the court has discretion to award you all or part of your attorney fees. In the past, many courts would award such fees to a defendant only if they found that the plaintiff's suit was frivolous or brought in bad faith. But these courts would not use this criterion when making fees awards to plaintiffs. In 1994 the Supreme Court held that this approach was incorrect and that attorney fees must be awarded to plaintiffs and defendants in an evenhanded manner. In other words, the same criteria must be applied to both plaintiffs and defendants. (*Fogerty v. Fantasy, Inc.*, 114 S.Ct. 1023 (1994).)

What this means is that if you defeat your accuser in court, you have a good chance of getting an award against him or her for some or all of your attorney fees. The actual amount you'll be awarded, if any, is up to the judge. However, such an award will be useless unless the plaintiff has the money or insurance to pay it.

Part II. Suing Others for Copyright Infringement

The other side of the copyright infringement equation involves suing others for infringing on your protected work. When a copyright dispute arises, there are often several self-help steps a copyright owner can take. These generally amount to telling the infringer to stop the infringing activity and pay for the infringement. If the infringement has occurred online, you may also be able to get the ISP to remove the infringing material. When push comes to shove, however, there is only one remedy with teeth in it: to ask a federal court to order the infringing activity halted and to award a judgment for damages. Because this type of litigation is procedurally complex, an attorney skilled in copyright litigation is required. (See Chapter 19.)

This discussion is not intended as a substitute for a good copyright attorney. Rather, its aim is to:

- help you recognize when copyright infringement has occurred
- suggest some steps you—as a software or website author or other copyright owner—might take on your own to deal effectively with infringement without resorting to lawyers and the courts
- tell you what to expect in the event of a court action, and
- help you estimate what damages and other types of court relief are potentially available to you in an infringement suit.

E. How to Know Whether You Have a Valid Infringement Claim

When a civil copyright infringement action is filed, the person bringing the action (called the plaintiff) must prove certain facts in order to prevail. This is called the burden of proof. While a detailed discussion of court procedure is beyond the scope of this book, here are the major things you must establish to prove infringement:

- you are the lawful owner of all or part of a work protected by a valid copyright
- one or more of the copyright rights you own has been infringed, and
- the person, partnership, or corporation being sued has actually done the infringing act or contributed to it (called a contributory infringer).

Once you've proven infringement, the next step is to establish what remedies you're entitled to. If you can show that the infringer profited from the infringement, or negatively affected your profits, you may be able to recover these profits (what the infringer gained or what you lost) from the infringer, subject, of course, to any defenses the infringer may have (discussed in Section D1). Or you may be eligible to elect to receive statutory damages instead of your actual damages caused by the infringement. In addition, the judge has discretion to award you attorney's fees. Finally, you can have the court order the infringer to stop future infringement and destroy all existing copies.

Let's look at these proof requirements one at a time:

1. Ownership of a Work Protected by Copyright

The question of infringement does not even arise unless the work allegedly infringed is protected by copyright. This means that the work must meet the three prerequisites for copyright protection discussed in detail in Chapter 3; that is, the work must be:

- *Fixed in a tangible medium of expression*: A work is sufficiently fixed if it exists on paper, on disk, or even just in computer RAM.
- *Independently created*: You cannot sue someone for copying software, a website, or other materials that you copied from others.
- *Minimally creative*: The work you believe has been infringed upon must have been the product of a minimal amount of creativity.

2. Infringement of Your Copyright Rights

To prevail in an infringement lawsuit, the plaintiff must prove that an infringement actually occurred. If someone is caught with an exact copy of a copyrighted work, or is seen copying it, the plaintiff has what is aptly called a smoking gun. The infringing villain has been caught red-handed.

Unfortunately, this type of evidence usually isn't available. Most infringers are smart enough to attempt to disguise their copying. Where source code is involved, for example, it is easy for an infringer to use a text editor to disguise its origin by rearranging lines or blocks of code, changing variable names, or altering certain sequences of operations. Moreover, there are rarely any witnesses to copyright infringement. Infringement usually happens behind closed doors and the participants rarely admit their involvement.

This means that in most cases you must prove two things to establish infringement:

- that the claimed infringer had access to your work, and
- that the infringing work is substantially similar to your work.

If these are proven, copying is inferred because there is no other reasonable explanation for the similarities. However the defendant can rebut (defeat) the inference by proving independent creation—that is, that his or her work was created without copying your work. Let's take a closer look at these two infringement criteria.

a. Access

To prove access, you must show that the alleged infringer had the opportunity to view and copy your work. This requirement is easy to show if the work is published or available to the public on the Internet. It may be more difficult if the work has only been accessible to a very few people or has been protected as a trade secret. Problems can develop, for example, when software that is very narrowly distributed under a license agreement is pirated. In one legal decision, access was established when a marketing firm changed clients and showed a copy of the former

client's product to the new clients, resulting in copyright infringement. (*Synercom Technology, Inc. v. University Computing Company*, 462 F. Supp. 1003 (1978).)

b. Substantial similarity

Proving substantial similarity is usually the crux of any copyright infringement case. Assuming the alleged infringer had access to your work, the similarities between your work and his must be compared to see if copying may reasonably be inferred. The similarities must be such that they can only be explained by copying, not by factors such as coincidence, independent creation, or the existence of a prior common source for both programs.

The first step most courts take is to filter out the unprotectible elements of the plaintiff's work before comparing it with the allegedly infringing work. Under this filtration test, those elements of the plaintiff's work that are not protected by copyright are identified and eliminated from consideration. This includes, for example, ideas, elements dictated by efficiency, or external factors or taken from the public domain. (See Section B1.) After this filtration process is completed, there may or may not be any protected elements left. If there are, this core of protected expression is compared with the allegedly infringing program of the defendant to see if there has been impermissible copying. (*Computer Associates Inter-*

national, Inc. v. Altai, Inc. 982 F.2d 692 (2d Cir. 1992); *Gates Rubber Co. v. Bando Ltd.*, 9 F.3d 823 (10th Cir. 1993).)

The clearest cases of copyright infringement involve wholesale copying of your computer code as described in Section A1 above. You'll likely have far more difficulty proving infringement when you allege that nonliteral elements of your program have been copied—that is, things other than computer code such as the user interface. (See Section B.)

The bottom line is that it is virtually impossible for even the most experienced software attorney to predict with confidence whether a nonliteral infringement claim will succeed. In effect, plaintiffs who bring these cases enter a crap shoot: You pay your money and take your chance.

F. Self-Help Remedies for Copyright Infringement

If you suspect your copyright has been infringed, you should discuss your problem with a copyright attorney, even if you plan to try to settle or compromise with the infringer without court action. A preliminary conference shouldn't be expensive. However, whether you see an attorney at this stage or not, there are some preliminary things you can safely do on your own.

1. Determine Scope of the Problem

Your first step is to make a commonsense assessment of how large the problem is. Who is the infringer? What are the infringer's motives? How much infringement is occurring?

If you believe your copyright has been infringed by an ex-employee who created a work substantially similar to your own without authorization, the possible ways of dealing with the infringement are different than if you're dealing either with an unauthorized posting on the Internet or with an international pirate based in Taiwan. In one situation (the Internet), a cease and desist letter might be sufficient, whereas in another (the international pirate), nothing short of a large-scale lawsuit will probably work. And something in between may be the correct approach for the infringement by the ex-employee.

2. Collect Information About Your Copyright Registration

It is a good idea to make sure your copyright records are complete in the event a visit to a lawyer is necessary to stop the infringer. Hopefully, you've registered your copyright and have retained copies of all filed documents and correspondence with the Copyright Office. You should also have retained copies of all copyright transfers you've made.

Because you're human, however, one or more of these documents may have slipped through your fingers. If so, you'll need to obtain a copy of the missing documents from the Copyright Office. Fortunately, Copyright Office records are public records. This means that any member of the public can obtain copies of the information, application, deposit, or other documents relating to registration or ownership. However, you must provide the Copyright Office with specific information, including:

- The type of record you're interested in (for instance, the correspondence between the Copyright Office and the copyright owner, a copy of the deposit, a certificate of registration).
- Whether you require certified or uncertified copies (you would want certified copies in case you need to introduce them in a lawsuit).
- Complete identification of the record, such as the type of work (program, novel, manual, etc.), the complete registration number, the year or approximate year of registration, the complete title of the work as it appears on the application, the author, including any pseudonym by which the author may be known, the claimants, and the volume and page number where the document is recorded; if you're seeking a copy of an assignment, any exclusive license or other recorded contract.

- Any additional information that may be required for the specific record you want. For instance, obtaining copies of deposits requires that you comply with some additional conditions.
- $25 for each certification requested and $25 for additional copies of the application. The fees for all other requests will be added up by the Copyright Office on a case-by-case basis.
- Your telephone number and address, so the Copyright Office can contact you for additional information.

If you don't provide the year or the title of the work, a search of the records may be required for verification of your request. The fee for this search is $65 per hour.

Mail your request to:

Certification and Documents Section LM-402
Copyright Office
Library of Congress
Washington DC 20559

---

3. Cease and Desist Letter

Once you've mailed your request for any missing copyright records, you may want to send the alleged infringer a cease and desist letter. This sort of letter serves several functions:

- First, it lets the infringer know that you believe he or she is infringing your copyright.

- Second, it dates your discovery of the infringing activity, should more serious action be warranted later. This is important for purposes of the statute of limitations on copyright infringement lawsuits discussed below.
- Third, it tells the infringer that you have every intention of stopping him or her.
- Fourth, and perhaps most important, it gives the infringer a chance to explain her conduct and perhaps offer a satisfactory compromise, before you've spent a lot of money initiating a lawsuit. Even if you're sure you're right, it doesn't hurt to listen to the other person's story. In addition, by giving the infringer a chance to respond, you may find out a lot about how he or she plans to defend a court action.

Here is what is normally covered in a cease and desist letter:

- who you are, including your business address and telephone number, or, if you want to protect your privacy, some way to contact you—such as a P.O. box
- the name of your work, date of first publication, and the copyright registration certificate number, if your work is registered
- the nature of the activity you believe to be an infringement of your copyright
- a demand that the infringer cease and desist from the activity, and

- a request for a response within a stated period of time.

Your letter can threaten legal action, but you're probably wiser not to at this stage. The specter of courts and lawyers usually does little but make the other person paranoid, defensive, and unwilling to cooperate.

If you act as if your lawsuit is only hours away, the answer to your letter is likely to come from the infringer's lawyer. Once two lawyers are involved, the chances of any compromise settlement is greatly reduced, as lawyers, by the very nature of their profession, usually get paid more to fight than to compromise.

When you draft your letter, remember that you may end up wanting to use it in court. Accordingly, avoid being cute, nasty, tentative, or overly dramatic. The following example contains about the right tone and level of information.

Sample Cease and Desist Letter

January 10, 200X

Ms. Oleo Oboe, President

Oboe, Inc.

567 Symphony Drive

Anywhere, USA 11111

Dear Ms. Oboe:

I recently became aware of your manufacture and sale of a CD-ROM called 100 Best Java Applets. I am the owner of the copyright in a Java Applet entitled Java 1-2-3, copyright registration No. 22222222. I believe that your CD-ROM contains a copy (or a substantial copy) of Java 1-2-3. Since I have not authorized you or your company to make or sell copies of Java 1-2-3, it follows that you're infringing my copyright by doing so.

This letter is to demand that you and Oboe, Inc., immediately cease and desist from the manufacture and sale of Java 1-2-3, on the CD-ROM 100 Best Java Applets or by any other means. In addition, I request reasonable compensation for the copies you have already sold and your remaining inventory.

Please respond to this letter by January 15, 199X.

Sincerely,

Carl Jones

123 Action Street

Hollywood, CA

Cease and desist letters should be sent by certified mail, return receipt requested. If the infringer refuses to accept your letter, arrange to have it delivered personally, by someone who isn't involved in the dispute and who'll be available to testify that the letter was delivered to the party, if that should become necessary.

What you do next depends on the response you receive, as well as the nature of the infringer and the infringing conduct. Reasonable and routine solutions to many infringements include:

- payment for profits previously made on the infringing work
- making the infringement legal through a license under which you're paid an agreed-upon fee for all future copies, or
- getting the infringer to agree to stop future infringements.

4. Settlement Letter

Any compromise settlement should be in writing, and signed by all parties. At this point, you should definitely get the help of a lawyer with experience in the area.

Here is a sample of the way the Java 1-2-3 dispute might be settled:

Sample Settlement Letter

Ms. Oleo Oboe, President
Oboe, Inc.
567 Symphony Drive
Anywhere, USA 11111

Dear Ms. Oboe:

This letter embodies the terms and conditions to settle all outstanding disputes between Oboe, Inc., and Carl Jones and to authorize Oboe, Inc., to market the computer program, Java 1-2-3.

Carl Jones and Oboe, Inc., hereby agree:

1. Oboe, Inc., will pay Carl Jones the sum of $10,000 for copies of Java 1-2-3 sold up to the date of our agreement, January 20, 200X.

2. Oboe, Inc., will place the following copyright notice on all copies of Java 1-2-3 sold from January 20, 200X, until termination of our Standard Resellers Agreement: © copyright Carl Jones 200X.

3. Oboe, Inc., will execute and be bound by the terms of our Standard Resellers Agreement attached hereto.

4. Carl Jones agrees that this agreement completely settles the matter in dispute between Carl Jones and Oboe, Inc., and releases Oboe, Inc., from any further liability for the sale of Java 1-2-3 prior to January 20, 200X.

Carl Jones
123 Action Street
Hollywood, CA

---

5. Special Self-Help Procedure for Online Infringements

In 1998, Congress adopted the Digital Millennium Copyright Act (DMCA). Among other things, this complex legislation provides copyright owners a very powerful self-help tool to fight online copyright infringement.

Among the DMCA's many provisions are "safe harbors" exempting Internet Service Providers (ISPs) from liability for monetary damages for copyright infringements by their users. However, to obtain safe harbor protection for storage of or linking to infringing material, ISPs must comply with a notice and take-down procedure. If a copyright owner believes that its copyrighted material has been unlawfully stored in an ISP's system or the ISP's system contains links or other locators to a site containing infringing material, the owner can send a notice to the ISP's designated agent notifying it of the claimed infringement. Any ISP receiving such a notice will have a very strong incentive to remove or disable access to the material, since doing so will relieve it of damages liability for the alleged infringement (provided that it meets all the requirements for safe harbor protection).

Using this notice and take-down procedure is not mandatory. You can always forego it and go straight to court and file a copyright infringement lawsuit against the infringer and ISP. However, anyone who believes that his or her work has been infringed on the Internet should first try to use this procedure.

Filing a Notice of Claimed Infringement is not difficult and can easily be accomplished by any copyright owner without paying a lawyer. If the Notice is successful and the ISP removes the infringing material or disables access to it there will often be no need to file an expensive action. If the infringing material is removed by the ISP, you will still have the right to sue the infringer for damages; but, in this event the ISP will not be liable for damages.

This procedure involves three separate steps:

- First, the copyright owner drafts and sends to the ISP a notice claiming that infringing material is present on its system or that there are links to infringing material.
- Second, the ISP must respond to the notice in one of two ways: (1) either remove the infringing material or disable access to it, or (2) do nothing.
- Third, if the ISP has removed or disabled access to the allegedly infringing material, the user or subscriber involved can send the ISP a Counter Notice stating that the material is not infringing or has been misidentified. In this event, the ISP must put the material back or restore access to it unless the copyright owner goes to court to obtain an injunction against the alleged infringer.

Who Is an ISP?

"ISP" is defined very broadly by the DMCA as "a provider of online services or network access, or the operator of facilities" for such services or access. This includes virtually any provider of Internet access or online network services, such as:

- conventional ISPs—for example, companies like MCI, AT&T, Netcom, and Mindspring that provide access to the Internet to paying members of the general public
- commercial online services like AOL and CompuServe
- companies that operate in-house "intranets" or have bulletin boards where customers can post comments about their products
- educational institutions such as universities and colleges that have their own computer networks enabling students and faculty to send email or access the Internet, and
- libraries that provide their patrons with Internet access.

a. Notice of Claimed Infringement

If you're convinced infringement has occurred, you must determine what ISP is involved. Remember, ISPs are companies and institutions that provide people with Internet access and host websites and other materials on the Internet. The ISP is the conduit by which the infringer uses the Internet to disseminate unauthorized works. In some cases it will be apparent who the ISP is—for example, if the infringing material is found anywhere on the AOL system, AOL is the ISP. However, in some cases it may not be clear which ISP the alleged infringer uses. One way to determine this is to check the domain name registration records for the website where the infringing material is found. You can do this at the following website: www.whois.net.

Type in the domain name in the search field and you can access the registration records for the domain name. Click on the link in the "technical information" portion of these records and you will usually (but not always) find the name of the ISP for the website using that domain name.

Next, you must determine if the ISP has designated an agent to receive notifications of claimed infringement. The ISP is supposed to post this information at its website. ISPs are also required to file with the Copyright Office an "Interim Designation of Agent" form. This form gives the agent's name and address. Digital copies of these forms are posted on the Copyright Office's website at: www.loc.gov/copyright /onlinesp/list/index.html.

Not all ISPs have designated agents. This may be because they're unaware of the safe harbor rules or have elected not to take advantage of them. This is perfectly legal. ISPs' compliance with the safe harbor requirements is voluntary.

If the ISP does not have an "Interim Designation of Agent" form on file with the Copyright Office, it cannot take advantage of the safe harbor liability limitations and the procedures discussed in this section will not apply. However, you are still entitled to complain about the alleged infringement and ask the ISP to remove the infringing material. You can also sue the ISP. The normal copyright infringement liability rules will be used to determine the ISP's liability for the infringement.

If the ISP has designated an agent, you must draft and sign a Notice of Claimed Infringement and send it to the agent. The notice must:

- identify the copyrighted work you claim was infringed (if the infringement involves many different works at a single online site, you can include a representative list rather than listing each one)
- identify the online site where the alleged infringement has occurred and identify specifically what material on the site you claim is infringing (include copies, if possible); if a link is involved, it must be identified
- give the name and contact information for the person signing the notice
- state that the information in the notice is accurate and that the complaining party "has a good faith belief that use of the material in the manner complained of is not authorized by the copyright owner, its agent or the law"

- state, under penalty of perjury, that the signer of the notice is authorized to act on behalf of the copyright owner of the material claimed to have been infringed, and
- be signed with either a physical or electronic signature.

The notice can either be emailed or sent by postal mail to the ISP.

 A form Notice of Claimed Infringement is contained on the forms disk under the file name Notice.

b. ISP's response to Notice of Claimed Infringement

An ISP that receives a Notice of Claimed Infringement must examine it to see whether it complies with the requirements set forth in the preceding section. The Notice is deemed legally void if it fails to identify the infringed and infringing works or fails to give adequate contact information for the sender. In this event, the ISP need take no action and the notice will not be construed as putting the ISP on notice of any infringement.

However, if the Notice is defective in any other way, the ISP has a legal duty to contact the person who sent the notice or take other reasonable steps to find out the missing information.

If the Notice is in compliance with the rules, the ISP must decide whether to remove or disable access to the allegedly infringing material. The ISP does not have to remove or disable access to such material, but if it does so, the safe harbor relieving the ISP from damages liability for infringements by its subscribers or users will apply. Moreover, the ISP is immune from all legal liability for removing or disabling access to the material—meaning that neither the subscriber or user or anyone else can sue it for doing so. This is so even if it turns out that the material complained of was not infringing. All this would seem to mean that an ISP would always remove or disable access to material that a copyright owner claims is infringing in a Notice of Claimed Infringement.

The law imposes no specific time limit on how quickly the ISP must act. It simply says the ISP must act "expeditiously" (quickly). If the ISP does remove or disable access to the allegedly infringing material, it must "promptly" notify the subscriber or user of the action. The ball then enters the subscriber's court.

c. User's Counter Notice

An ISP's subscriber or user doesn't have to take the removal of the material lying down. If the user believes that the material is not infringing or has been mistakenly identified, it can take action to have the material put back by the ISP. To do this, the user must send the ISP a Counter Notice. The Counter Notice must:

- identify the allegedly infringing material and give its Internet address
- state, under penalty of perjury, that the material was removed or disabled by the ISP as a result of mistake or misidentification of the material
- state that the user consents to the legal jurisdiction of the federal district court in the judicial district where the user's address is located; or, if the user lives outside the U.S., consent to jurisdiction in any federal district court where the ISP may be sued
- state that the user agrees to accept service of legal process from the copyright owner or other person who signed the Notice of Claimed Infringement
- give the user's name and contact information for the person signing the notice, and
- be signed with either a physical or electronic signature.

The Counter Notice can either be e-mailed or sent by postal mail to the ISP's designated agent.

A form Counter Notice is contained on the forms disk under the file name Counter Notice.

Upon receipt of a Counter Notice satisfying the above requirements, the ISP must "promptly" send the copyright owner or other person who sent the Notice of Claimed Infringement a copy of the Counter Notice and inform such person that the ISP will replace the removed material or stop disabling access to it in ten business days (business days do not include weekends or holidays).

The ISP must replace the removed material or stop disabling access to it not less than ten or more than 14 business days after it received the user's Counter Notice *unless* the copyright owner brings a court action as described below.

By sending a Counter Notice, the user in effect forces the copyright owner to put up or shut up. The copyright owner will have to go to court and convince a judge that it's likely that a copyright infringement has occurred. If the copyright owner doesn't want to go to court, the ISP will have to replace the removed material or stop disabling access to it.

d. Copyright owner's response to Counter Notice

If the subscriber sends the ISP a Counter Notice, you will have to file a copyright infringement lawsuit against the subscriber in federal court and ask the court to grant you an injunction ordering the subscriber to stop the infringing activity on the ISP's system. To obtain such an injunction, you'll have to convince the court that it is likely that the subscriber has committed copyright infringement.

If you don't want the ISP to put the material back or stop disabling access to it, you'll have to act quickly. Access to the material will have to be restored by the ISP no more than 14 business days after the subscriber sent it the Counter Notice. It is sometimes possible, however, to obtain an injunction very quickly. (See Section H1 for a detailed discussion of injunctions in copyright infringement cases.)

To file your lawsuit, you'll have to know the subscriber or user's identity. The DMCA contains a procedure allowing you to subpoena the ISP and require it to give you this information.

If you miss the 14-day deadline, but later obtain an injunction, the ISP will have to remove or disable access to the material again.

G. Nuts and Bolts of Infringement Lawsuits

If you can't satisfactorily resolve the matter yourself (perhaps through mediation or with a short consultation with a copyright lawyer), you have two alternatives: forget about it, or hire a lawyer and bring an infringement suit in federal court.

1. Who Can Sue

A person or entity who files an infringement suit is called the plaintiff. The plaintiff must be someone who owns the copyright rights at issue, or holds an exclusive license to them. This will typically be the creator of the work or a person or entity to whom the creator has transferred ownership—for example, a publisher.

A civil lawsuit based on a claim of copyright infringement of a U.S. copyright cannot be brought unless and until the copyright has been registered with the U.S. Copyright Office. Registration can occur after an infringing act and you can still sue for that infringement.

Copyright registration can take anywhere from six to nine months or even longer. If you need to register immediately so that you can sue, there is an expedited "special handling" procedure by which registration can be accomplished in a much shorter period. (See Chapter 4.)

2. Criminal Prosecutions for Copyright Infringement

Willful (purposeful) copyright infringement is a federal crime. This is so whether or not it is done for financial gain. (17 U.S.C. § 506.) Accordingly, the United States Attorney General has the power to prosecute infringers. Both fines and prison time can be imposed for convictions. The penalties are greater if infringement is done for financial gain and can range up to a $250,000 fine and ten years in prison in the case of multiple offenses. If you wish to have someone criminally

prosecuted for copyright infringement, contact the local U.S. Attorney's office.

3. Who Is Liable for Infringement

Although a primary goal may be simply to stop an infringer from distributing any more copies of an infringing software, you are also entitled to collect damages from those liable for the infringement. You may also be able to receive special statutory damages, which is an important right when your actual damages are very small or difficult to prove, and attorney fees as well. Everybody who participates in or contributes to copyright infringement may be liable for such damages and fees.

4. How Much Time You Have to Sue: Statute of Limitations

There are strict time limits on when copyright infringement suits may be filed. If you fail to file in time, the infringer may be able to have your suit dismissed, even though you have a strong case.

The general rule is that an infringement suit must be filed within three years after the date the copyright owner should reasonably have discovered the infringing act occurred. This is usually plenty of time. However, in some cases, it can reasonably take the copyright owner a long time to discover that the infringement took place, especially where the infringer attempted to conceal the act of infringement. For this reason, if more than three years have passed since the infringing work was first published, don't jump to the conclusion that your suit is barred by the statute of limitations. Again, see a copyright attorney.

H. What You Can Get If You Win: Remedies for Copyright Infringement

Once you've proven the elements of infringement discussed in Section E above, the next step is to establish what remedies you're entitled to. The potential remedies include:

- **Injunctive relief.** This typically consists of a court order requiring the infringer (the defendant) to stop the infringing activity and destroy all remaining copies of the infringing work.
- **Actual damages and infringer's profits.** The plaintiff is entitled to be compensated for the value of lost sales (often difficult to prove) and for other monetary losses resulting directly from the infringement. The plaintiff is also entitled to collect the amount of the defendant's profits from the infringement.
- **Statutory damages.** If the plaintiff's work was timely registered and he or she so chooses, she is entitled to receive special statutory damages provided in the copyright law (statute)

instead of actual damages and other economic damages.
- **Attorney fees.** A copyright owner may also be awarded attorney fees by the judge.

We'll examine each remedy in turn. Again, this isn't a complete description of the legal procedures involved, but is designed to give you an overview of the available remedies.

1. Injunctive Relief

An injunction is a court order telling someone to stop doing something. In a copyright infringement action, the order usually is simply for the defendant to stop the infringing activity. This is commonly a quick, effective remedy because, in many cases, it is possible to get positive action from the court long before the actual trial is held to decide who wins.

Indeed, it is possible to get a temporary restraining order (TRO) almost immediately with very short notice to the defendant. A TRO may last ten days at most. A hearing must then be held on whether the judge should issue a preliminary injunction. A preliminary injunction operates between the time it is issued and the final judgment in the case. This interim court order is available when it appears likely to a federal judge, on the basis of written documentation and a relatively brief hearing at which the lawyers for each side present their view of the dispute, that (1) the plaintiff will most likely win the suit when the trial is held, and (2) the plaintiff will suffer irreparable injury if the preliminary injunction isn't granted. Ordinarily, irreparable injury is presumed to exist where someone infringes upon a copyright owner's exclusive rights. (*Apple Computer, Inc. v. Franklin Computer Corp.*, 714 F.2d 1240 (3d Cir. 1983).)

2. Damages

If you win a copyright infringement suit, you usually have the right to collect money (called damages) from the infringer.

a. Actual damages and infringer's profits

Actual damages are the lost profits or other losses sustained as a result of the copyright infringement. In other words, actual damages are the amount of money that the plaintiff would have made but for the infringement. This may include compensation for injury to plaintiff's reputation due to the infringement and for lost business opportunities (often difficult to prove). To obtain actual damages, the plaintiff must prove in court that the alleged losses actually occurred.

As stated above, the plaintiff is also entitled to recover the amount of the defendant's profits from the infringement to the extent they exceed the plaintiff's recovery for her lost profits.

EXAMPLE: Plaintiff is awarded $10,000 for lost sales due to defendant's infringement. The defendant earned $15,000 in profits from the infringement. Plaintiff is entitled to $5,000 of defendant's profits.

To establish the defendant's profits, the plaintiff is required only to prove the defendant's gross revenue from the infringing work. The defendant's business records (obtained by the plaintiff through formal "discovery" procedures) would usually be presented for this purpose. The defendant must then prove what its actual net profit from the infringement was—that is, the defendant must produce records or witnesses to show the amount of expenses deductible from the infringing work's gross revenues.

b. Statutory damages

Statutory damages are set by the copyright law and require no proof of how much the loss was in monetary terms. However, statutory damages are only available if the work was timely registered—that is, before the infringement began or within three months of publication. Statutory damages are awarded at the judge's discretion and don't depend on having to prove a loss in any specific amount due to the infringement. You have to decide whether you want statutory damages or your actual damages and the defendant's profits. You can't collect both.

3. Seizing the Infringing Work

Another civil remedy for copyright infringement consists of an impound and destroy order from the court. This tells the federal marshal to go to the infringer's place of business (or wherever the infringing material is located) and impound any infringing works. If the plaintiff wins, the court may order the sheriff to destroy the infringing material. To obtain such an order, however, the plaintiff must post a bond at a value at least twice the reasonable value of the infringing software.

Seizure can happen at any time after the suit has been filed. It's usually done as soon as a complaint is filed, but before the defendant is served with a copy of the suit. This way, the defendant learns he or she has been sued only when the marshal comes to the defendant's premises to impound the infringing works.

4. Attorney Fees and Costs

If your suit is successful and you timely registered your copyright, the court may also order the defendant to pay your attorney fees and other costs of going to court, such as filing fees. However, this is not required. It's up to the judge to decide whether to make such an award and how much it should be (the amount must be reasonable). The criteria some courts use to decide whether to award attorney fees include whether the defendant acted in bad faith, unreasonably, or was otherwise blameworthy. Many courts will be especially likely to award fees to a plaintiff whose actions helped to advance the copyright law or defend or establish important legal principles.

If the plaintiff loses his or her suit, the court has discretion to award the defendant all or part of his attorney fees. In 1994 the Supreme Court held that attorney fees must be awarded to plaintiffs and defendants in an evenhanded manner. In other words, the same criteria must be applied to both plaintiffs and defendants. (*Fogerty v. Fantasy, Inc.*, 114 S.Ct. 1023 (1994).)

 Plaintiffs Should Only File Legitimate Infringement Cases. You should never file a copyright infringement case in order to get even with somebody even though you know you don't have a good case. Likewise, don't file clearly frivolous claims in the hope the defendant will pay you something merely to get you off his or her back and avoid having to pay for expensive litigation. In either instance, you will not only lose your case, but the judge will likely order you to pay all or part of the defendant's attorney fees. ■

Trade Secret Basics

Trade secrecy is a do-it-yourself form of intellectual property protection. It is based on this simple idea: By keeping valuable information secret, one can prevent competitors from learning about and using it and thereby enjoy a competitive advantage in the marketplace. Trade secrecy is by far the oldest form of intellectual property, dating back at least to ancient Rome. It is as useful now as it was then.

Trade secrecy should be an integral part of any software or Web developer's intellectual property protection program. The fundamentals of trade secret protection are introduced in this chapter. How to establish your own trade secret protection program is covered in Chapter 8.

A. What Is a Trade Secret?

A trade secret is born in secrecy and spends its life in concealment, disclosed only to those bound to maintain confidentiality. Trade secrets typically include such items as:

- unpublished computer code
- product design definitions and specifications
- product development agreements and other related agreements
- business plans
- financial projections
- marketing plans
- sales data
- unpublished promotional material
- cost and pricing information
- customer lists, and
- pending patent applications.

For business information to qualify as a trade secret, the information must:

(1) not be generally known or ascertainable through legal methods;

(2) provide a competitive advantage or have economic value; and

(3) be the subject of reasonable efforts to maintain secrecy.

Let's look at each of these requirements in detail.

Trade Secrets Governed by State Law

Unlike copyrights and patents, whose existence is provided and governed by federal law that applies in all 50 states, trade secrecy is not codified in any federal statute (although theft of trade secrets can be a federal crime). Instead, it is made up of individual state laws.

Nevertheless, the protection afforded to trade secrets is similar in every state. This is largely because some 42 states have based their trade secrecy laws on the Uniform Trade Secrets Act (UTSA), a model trade secrecy law designed by legal scholars.

1. Information Not Generally Known or Legally Ascertainable

If your competitors already knew the material you want to protect, it isn't much of a secret. Once it's generally known or can be learned by the people within the software or Internet industries, the information loses its special status as a trade secret.

There is no clear line that shows when information is "generally known" in a particular industry. In most cases, information is generally known if it has been published or publicly displayed or is commonly used within an industry. For example, information you place on a website accessible by the general public cannot be a trade secret.

Information is "readily ascertainable" if it can be obtained legally within an industry—for example, if you can find it through an online database, at a library, or through other publicly available sources. A trade secret is not readily ascertainable if bribery, fraud, or other deceptive procedures are required to get it.

2. The Information Provides Economic Value or a Competitive Advantage

To qualify as a trade secret, information must have some economic value or provide an advantage over competitors. For most trade secrets, this requirement is easy to fulfill and can be demonstrated by benefits derived from the use of the trade secret, the costs of developing the secret, or by business or licensing offers for use of the secret.

3. The Company Has Taken Reasonable Steps to Protect the Information

You cannot have a trade secret unless you have taken reasonable precautions to keep the information confidential. These precautions usually involve reasonable security procedures as well as the use of nondisclosure agreements. If you don't maintain reasonable security, the information will lose its trade secret status.

In general, a business is considered to have taken reasonable steps if it uses a sensible system for protecting information—for example, locking its facilities, monitoring visitors, and labeling confidential information. (We provide some suggestions for a trade secret maintenance system in Chapter 8.)

A crucial part of your company's trade secret maintenance should be to require contractors, employees, investors, and others exposed to confidential information to enter into a nondisclosure agreement. If the secret is disclosed you can sue the loose-lipped person for money damages and ask for a court order preventing further disclosure.

4. Examples of Trade Secrets

Some examples of protectible trade secrets include computer software, designs and specifications, business strategies and methods, formulas and customer lists, collections of data, know-how, pricing information, new product names, information regarding new business opportunities, personnel performance, sales information. Two of these items, customer lists and databases, require additional analysis.

a. Customer lists

Companies are often very eager to protect their customer lists as trade secrets, particularly when a former employee might use a customer list to contact clients. If a dispute over a customer list ends up in court, a judge generally considers the following elements to decide whether or not a customer list qualifies as a trade secret:

- Is the information in the list ascertainable by other means? A list that is readily ascertainable cannot be protected.
- Does the list include more than names and addresses? For example, a customer list that includes pricing and special needs is more likely to be protected, because this information adds value.
- Did it take a lot of effort to assemble the list? A customer list that requires more effort is more likely to be a trade secret.

- Did the departing employee contribute to the list? If the departing employee helped create it or had personal contact with the customers, it is less likely to be protected as a trade secret.
- Is the customer list personal, long-standing, or exclusive? If a business can prove that a customer list is special to its business and has been used for a long time, the list is more likely to be protected.

b. Collections of data

A database—information of any type organized in a manner to facilitate its retrieval—is often protected as a trade secret. For example, a court ruled that a database for inventorying and cost economies on wholesale sandwich production for fast food retailers was a protectible trade secret. (*One Stop Deli, Inc. v. Franco's, Inc.*, 1994-1 CCH Trade Cas. p. 70,507 (W.D. Va. 1993).) A collection of data that is readily ascertainable, however, is not a trade secret.

5. Ownership of Trade Secrets

Only the person or entity that owns a trade secret has the right to seek relief in court if someone else improperly acquires or discloses the trade secret. Also, only the trade secret owner may grant others a license to use the secret.

As a general rule, any trade secrets developed by an employee in the course of employment belong to the employer. However, trade secrets developed by an employee on her own time and with her own equipment can sometimes belong to the employee. To avoid possible disputes, it is very good idea for employers to have all employees who may develop new technology sign an employment agreement. The agreement should assign in advance all trade secrets developed by the employee during her employment. Courts generally will enforce such agreements.

6. Duration of Trade Secrets

Trade secrets have no definite term. A trade secret continues to exist as long as the requirements for trade secret protection remain in effect. In other words, as long as secrecy is maintained, the secret does not become generally known in the industry, and the secret continues to provide a competitive advantage, it will be protected. Some trade secrets have lasted for a very long time indeed. For example, the formula for Coca-Cola has been maintained as a trade secret by the Coca-Cola Company for over 100 years.

B. Trade Secret Owner's Rights

A trade secret owner has the legal right to prevent the following four groups of people from copying, using, and benefiting from its trade secrets or disclosing them to others without the owner's permission:

- people who are bound by a duty of confidentiality not to disclose or use the information
- people who acquire the trade secret through improper means such as theft, industrial espionage, or bribery
- people who knowingly obtain trade secrets from others—that is, third parties—who acquired them through improper means or who were bound by a duty of confidentiality not to disclose them, and
- people who learn about a trade secret by accident or mistake but had reason to know that the information was a protected trade secret.

For example, if a software or Web developer's employee signs an agreement establishing a duty of confidentiality (see below) but later discloses the developer's trade secrets to a competitor without the developer's permission, the developer will be able to sue both the employee and competitor for damages and may be entitled to obtain a court order preventing the competitor from using the information. The employee would have breached his or her duty of confidentiality to the developer. At the same time the competitor would have acquired the trade secret from a person who had a duty not to disclose it.

1. Duty of Confidentiality

Persons who learn about a trade secret through a confidential relationship with its owner may not use or disclose the trade secret without permission. A duty of confidentiality may be deemed by the courts to arise automatically (is "implied in law") from many types of relationships, including those between employers and employees who routinely receive trade secrets as part of their jobs. (See "Employees Have a Duty of Confidentiality Imposed by Law," below.) But by far the best way for a trade secret owner to establish a duty of confidentiality is to have each person to whom trade secrets are disclosed agree in writing to preserve their confidentiality. This type of agreement is called a confidentiality agreement or nondisclosure agreement.

a. Employees

The cornerstone of any trade secret protection program is to have all employees who are exposed to trade secrets read and sign nondisclosure agreements. Such an agreement should require the employee to treat as confidential any trade secrets he or she learns in the course of employment. If the employer later tries to prevent the employee from using infor-

mation considered to be a trade secret, the existence of a signed nondisclosure agreement will establish that the employee knew that he owed a duty of confidentiality toward his or her employer. Many courts consider the use of employee nondisclosure agreements the single most important reasonable precaution an employer can take to establish and maintain the secrecy of confidential information.

However, there are limitations on the effectiveness of nondisclosure agreements with employees. In particular, the general knowledge, skills, and experience an employee acquires during her term of employment are not trade secrets and therefore are not covered by a nondisclosure agreement.

Employees Have a Duty of Confidentiality Imposed by Law

All is not lost if an employer fails to have an employee sign a nondisclosure agreement. Even if an employee has never signed such an agreement, he or she will usually be deemed by the courts to have a confidential relationship with the employer if the employee routinely comes into contact with the employer's trade secrets as part of the employee's job. Such an employee is duty bound not to disclose or use, without the employer's permission, information that:

- the employer tells the employee is confidential (preferably in writing), or
- the employee knew or should have known was confidential because of the context in which it was disclosed, the measures the employer took to keep the information secret, and/or the fact that the information was of a type customarily considered confidential in the industry.

However, an employer's failure to use nondisclosure agreements will tend to show that the employer was not protecting any trade secrets and will surely not impress a judge if the company goes to court to enforce its claimed trade secret rights. Employers have won trade secret cases against employees in the absence of nondisclosure agreements, but it is much easier to do so with them.

b. Independent contractors and consultants

People who perform services for a trade secret owner but who are not employees—freelance programmers, Web designers, graphic artists, photographers, technical writers, or beta testers, for example—may have a duty of confidentiality implied by law just as employees may (see "Employees Have a Duty of Confidentiality Imposed by Law," above). However, as is the case with employees, independent contractors should always sign nondisclosure agreements.

c. End-users and other third parties

A trade secret owner can protect his or her trade secrets from unauthorized disclosure or use by end-users and other third parties by having them agree not to disclose or use the information without permission. Such nondisclosure agreements are legally enforceable contracts. This is accomplished in the typical software transaction by licensing the software to the user, rather than selling it outright. The license gives the user permission to use the software under the terms of the license, which includes a nondisclosure provision. Nondisclosure agreements work best for programs that are distributed to a specialized market where licenses can be negotiated and signed with each individual end-user.

> **EXAMPLE:** AcmeSoft develops and markets a highly specialized program used to automate the manufacture of widgets. AcmeSoft negotiates and signs license agreements with all the purchasers of the program (about 50 in all). Each license includes a non-disclosure provision stating that the existence and attributes of the program are not to be disclosed to persons other than those employees of the manufacturer that use the program. The widget manufacturers do not have a confidential relationship with AcmeSoft, but are contractually bound by the license agreements.

Shrink-wrap licenses: Let's assume that there are only about 200 widget manufacturers in the whole country, so it was easy for AcmeSoft to have all the manufacturers who purchased its widget manufacturing program sign license agreements. But what about mass-marketed software? A software publisher cannot negotiate and sign a nondisclosure agreement with every end-user of a widely distributed program. In an attempt to get around this problem, mass-marketed programs often contain "shrink-wrap licenses." These are license agreements that are usually printed on or inside the mass-marketed software package.

Such licenses attempt to convert what would appear to the average person to be a simple purchase of a piece of software into a licensing transaction. The shrink-wrap license typically provides that, by opening the package and using the program, the purchaser agrees to possess the software under the terms of the license. Agreement to the license's terms is also often elicited from the user on-screen when the program is first used. Among other things, a shrink-wrap license usually prohibits the purchaser from disclosing any trade secrets learned from the program and contains various limitations on the seller's liability.

Although a recent court decision upheld the validity of shrink-wrap licenses. there are still questions as to whether they are enforceable in court. (See Chapter 16.) Distributors of mass-marketed software should not rely exclusively on such licenses. They should also distribute the software in a form that makes reverse engineering difficult (compiled code), use copyright protection, and, where available, obtain software patents. Of course, up to the time a program is made available to the public, it can and should be protected by an effective internal trade secrecy program.

Click-wrap licenses: "Click-wrap" licenses serve the exact same function as shrink-wrap licenses except they are used for software that is distributed to end-users over the Internet and commercial online services. The user downloads the software directly into his or her computer, so there is no package or physical written license agreement the user can read. Instead, the user is asked to read the terms of the license on the computer screen and then click an "ACCEPT" button to initiate the software download.

Website confidentiality agreements: More and more people and companies are placing trade secrets on the Web—for example, confidential pricing and product information or investor information. If such information is made freely available to anyone who logs on to the site, its trade secret status will be lost. To preserve secrecy, some websites require users to register and obtain a password to access the site. During the registration process, users are required to agree to a confidentiality agreement.

No court has ruled on the question, but requiring users to have a password and agree to a confidentiality agreement should be at least somewhat effective in preserving the trade secret status of such confidential information. However, problems could occur if too many people gain access to the information—it might be claimed that the information has become "generally known" and no longer qualifies as a trade secret. The moral is that it is not wise to place your most valuable trade secrets on a website, even if access

is limited to those who agree to nondisclosure agreements.

2. Obtaining Trade Secrets by "Improper Means"

Even in the absence of a confidential relationship (whether implied by law or created by contract), a trade secret owner is protected from persons who discover a trade secret by "improper means." This includes anyone who:

- obtains trade secrets through theft, bribery, fraud or misrepresentations, or industrial espionage
- knowingly obtains or uses trade secrets that have been improperly disclosed by a breach of a nondisclosure agreement or breach of a confidential relationship, or
- obtains trade secrets by inducing someone (an employee, for example) to breach an express or implied agreement not to disclose them.

C. Limitations on Trade Secret Protection

There are two important limits on trade secret protection: It does not prevent others from discovering a trade secret through "reverse engineering"; nor does it apply to persons who independently create or discover the same information.

1. Reverse Engineering

One of the most significant limitations on trade secret protection is that it does not protect against "reverse engineering." This is the process of taking a product or device apart and reducing it to its constituent parts or concepts to see how it works and to learn any trade secrets it contains. Any information learned through reverse engineering is considered to be in the public domain and no longer protectible as a trade secret. Reverse engineering is an accepted business practice and is perfectly legal so long as it does not violate anybody's copyright or patent rights. (See Chapter 6 for a discussion of whether reverse engineering constitutes copyright infringement.)

To prevent end-users from reverse engineering object code, software licenses often contain a provision prohibiting the practice. For example, the standard IBM license agreement states that the "customer shall not reverse assemble or reverse compile the licensed programs in whole or in part." Some view such restrictions as invalid because they attempt to preempt (replace) the federal copyright and patent laws. For example, one court has held invalid on ground of federal preemption a Louisiana state law providing that restrictions on reverse engineering contained in "shrink-wrap licenses" were enforceable. (*Vault Corp. v. Quaid Software Ltd.*, 847 F.2d 255 (5th Cir. 1988).)

However, another court has held that shrink-wrap licenses can be legally enforced. (*ProCD, Inc. v. Zeidenberg*, 86 F.3d 1447 (7th Cir. 1996).)

Even if enforceable, it is unclear how effective such provisions are. They may not be binding on anyone who has not signed the license agreement—for example, a freelance programmer invited to work on the licensee's premises who obtains access to the object code program.

2. Independent Creation

The other significant limitation on trade secrecy is that it does not protect against independent creation. A trade secret owner has no rights against a person who independently discovers or develops his or her trade secret. Moreover, if such person makes the information generally available to the public, it will lose its trade secret status.

> **EXAMPLE:** New Ideas, Inc., develops a new method of translating existing forms into HTML code. New Ideas, Inc., markets its NewConversion program to the public, but keeps the conversion method as a trade secret. Dave, a freelance programmer, independently develops the conversion technique and writes an article describing it in a computer programming journal. New Ideas, Inc., has no claim against Dave. In addition, its

conversion method is no longer a trade secret because it is now generally known in the software industry.

One legal expert has described trade secret protection as a leaky sieve because over time many of the most valuable trade secrets are lost when others independently discover them. Few people have or develop information that is incapable of being independently discovered by others.

D. Enforcement of Trade Secrets

Consider this scenario. You arrive at work and learn that the company email account has been hacked and secret files have been copied. You suspect a recently fired employee. What do you do? If you suspect theft of trade secrets, we suggest taking the following steps.

1. Contact an Attorney

Battling over trade secrets is a high-risk activity. An experienced attorney can minimize your risks, preserve your trade secret rights, and provide a realistic perspective of your chances in the dispute. (Chapter 19 discusses hiring an attorney and keeping your legal costs down.)

2. Acquire Evidence

Whenever trade secrets are lost you will need to investigate, or hire an investigator, to learn as much as possible about the trade secrecy loss. These investigations commonly require surveillance of employees. Consult your attorney before hiring an investigator or using undercover surveillance, because these actions may make you liable for claims such as invasion of privacy. Most investigations are performed surreptitiously because your employees may have ties to a former employee accused of trade secret theft and the presence of investigators may tip your hand.

Criminal Prosecution

Several states and the federal government have passed laws that make the unauthorized disclosure, theft, or use of a trade secret a crime. Under these laws the government, not private businesses, arrests the perpetrators and brings criminal charges. The penalties—including imprisonment—can be much more severe than in a civil suit. A person convicted of violating the federal Electronic Espionage Act of 1996 can be imprisoned up to ten years.

The filing of a criminal case does not prevent you from suing. For example, in a case involving the Avery-Dennison company, a Taiwanese competitor was ordered to pay $5 million in fines to the government as a result of criminal charges and $60 million to Avery-Dennison as a result of a civil lawsuit involving claims of trade secret misappropriation, RICO (Rackateer-Influenced and Corrupt Organizations Act) violations, and conversion.

Criminal prosecutions of trade secret theft are rare because many businesses prefer not to bring law enforcement officials into the fray. Also, in some cases, law enforcement officials don't wish to prosecute because there may not be sufficient evidence to obtain conviction. Keep in mind that the standards of proof for criminal cases are higher than for civil battles.

3. Determine What You Lost and What You Want

How has the trade secrecy loss affected your business? You need to know in order to figure out what you want from the perpetrators. For example, if you intended to patent an invention, disclosure of confidential information may ruin your chances.

As with medical injuries, your course of action in a trade secret dispute is dictated by the available cures (or "remedies"). You need to figure out your remedies before your attorney sends a letter to the other party. These potential remedies can be used as leverage to end the dispute before a lawsuit is filed. Potential remedies include:

a. Injunctions

An injunction is a court order directed at those who have stolen your secrets. Asking for an injunction is common, since the primary goal of trade secrecy is to keep information secret.

Courts are authorized to issue emergency injunctions, called temporary restraining orders (TROs), in a matter of days, when you show that a trade secret is at risk of being lost as a result of the misappropriation. The court must then schedule a hearing at which all sides may be heard. If, after this hearing, the court still believes that a trade secret is at stake and that you will probably win at trial, it can issue a "preliminary" injunction. This order will continue to prevent further use or disclosure of the trade secret pending a final decision in the case.

Sometimes injunctions are permanent —that is, they are final court orders in the case. More commonly, courts give the rightful owner of the trade secret a "head start" by prohibiting the information's use by the competitor for such period of time as the court decides it would have taken the competitor to independently develop the information.

If a court determines that an injunction would not be appropriate—for example, the competitor has already engaged in widespread use of your secret and has ruined your competitive advantage—the court can instead order your competitor to pay you a reasonable royalty for further use of the trade secret.

b. Compensatory and punitive damages

If you suffer a financial loss as a result of a breach of trade secrecy, you may be able to get a court to award money damages to you. Your damages are measured by either:

- the profits a competitor earned by using the trade secret, or
- the profits you lost due to the improper trade secret leak.

If the person or company you're suing acted with spite or ill will or a disregard for the probable injury (defined as "willful and malicious"), courts in many states can impose punitive damages. These are damages awarded to you for the purpose of punishing the wrongdoer and providing an example to other would-be trade secret thieves.

c. Attorney fees

If the trade secret infringer signed a nondisclosure agreement including an attorney fee provision (see Chapter 1), you can ask the court to direct the other party to pay your lawyer's bills if you prevail. If you settle the case, neither side has to pay the other (unless the attorney fee payment was negotiated as part of the settlement). Even if there is no nondisclosure agreement or if it lacks an attorney fee provision, a court may require the other side to pay your attorney fees if it is engaged in "willful and malicious" misappropriation. This decision is up to the judge.

E. Avoiding Trade Secret Misappropriation Claims

There are several relatively simple steps you can take to avoid trade secret misappropriation claims.

1. Hiring New Employees

Software and Internet companies have frequently been sued for trade secrecy violations when they hire competitors' employees. For example, Borland filed such a suit against Microsoft when it hired several Borland employees, and Wal-Mart sued Amazon.com alleging that it had misappropriated confidential information relating to online retailing in part by hiring some of Wal-Mart's key IT personnel.

This is particularly likely to occur where a company hires a large number of employees from a single competitor to obtain a competitive advantage (a practice known as "raiding"). Of course it is improper to hire anyone for the purpose of gaining access to anther's trade secrets.

To prevent or defeat trade secrecy claims, it's important to hire employees in a way that shows that you did not hire any particular person for the purpose of obtaining access to trade secrets. In other words, you want to be able to show that all your employees were hired because of their qualifications and expertise, not because they knew competitors' trade secrets.

Here are some simple steps a company should take when hiring its employees:

- Spread your hiring around—avoid targeting a specific company.
- Place advertisements for new employees that list the required qualifications and expertise; consider using a professional recruiter for particularly sensitive positions.

- Make all job applicants complete an employment application and present a resume.
- Interview all job applicants, even if you already know them.
- Maintain thorough records of your hiring program.
- If you hire someone who has been exposed to a competitor's especially sensitive information, consider placing him or her in a position where that information will not be used for a period of time—this helps show that you did not hire the person to steal trade secrets.
- Require all employees to sign employment agreements containing a promise that they will not use or disclose their prior employer's confidential information (the employment agreements in this book contain such a clause).
- Make sure new employees don't bring any confidential records or other materials from their old job.
- Require the employee to document all work done in the new employment.

2. Educate Employees About Trade Secrets

You should also make clear to your employees that they should not engage in trade secret misappropriation. Make clear both orally and in writing that they should not use or disclose any trade secrets of former employers or colleagues in other companies or engage in industrial espionage or trade secret theft.

3. Be Careful About Signing Confidentiality Agreements

Software and Web developers not only hire employees, they also work for clients who are concerned about protecting their own trade secrets. Many software developers' or computer consultants' clients routinely include confidentiality provisions in their development agreements. It's not unreasonable for a client to want you to keep its secrets away from the eyes and ears of competitors.

If, like many developers or consultants, you make your living by performing similar services for many firms in the same industry, insist on a confidentiality provision that is reasonable in scope and defines precisely what information you must keep confidential. Such a provision should last for only a limited time—five years at the most.

a. Unreasonable provision

A general provision barring you from making any unauthorized disclosure or using any technical, financial, or business information you obtain directly or indirectly from the client is unreasonable. Such broad restrictions can make it very

difficult for you to do similar work for other clients without fear of violating the duty of confidentiality clause. Here's an example:

> Developer may be given access to Client's proprietary or confidential information while working for Client. Developer agrees not to use or disclose such information except as directed by Client.

Such a provision doesn't make clear what information is and is not the client's confidential trade secrets, so you never know for sure what information you must keep confidential and what you can disclose when working for others.

Also, since this provision bars you from later using any of the client's confidential information to which you have access, it could prevent you from using information you already knew before working with the client. Always attempt to delete or rewrite such a provision.

b. Reasonable provision

A reasonable nondisclosure provision makes clear that, while you may not reuse confidential information the client provides, you have the right to freely use any information you obtain from other sources or that the public learns later.

Specifically, do not sign a contract requiring you to keep confidential any information:

- you knew about before working with the client
- you learn from a third person who has no duty to keep it confidential
- you develop independently even though the client later provides you with similar or identical information, or
- that becomes publicly known though no fault of your own—for example, you wouldn't have to keep a client's manufacturing technique confidential after it is disclosed to the public in an article in a trade journal written by someone other than you.

4. Document Development Efforts

As discussed above, trade secrecy does not protect against independent creation or reverse engineering. Carefully document your attempts at independent development or reverse engineering by keeping meticulous records of the entire development process, from the initial idea stage to coding, debugging, and testing.

F. Using Trade Secrets With Other IP Protections

Trade secrecy is a vitally important legal protection for software and websites, but,

because of the limitations discussed in Section A, above, it should be used in conjunction with copyright and, in some cases, patent protection.

1. Trade Secrets and Copyrights

Trade secrecy and copyright are not incompatible. To the contrary, they are typically used in tandem to provide the maximum legal protection available for most programs and websites.

a. Development phase

Typically, trade secrecy is most important during a program's or website's development phase. As discussed in Chapter 3, the copyright laws grant a copyright owner the exclusive right to copy, distribute, adapt, or display protected expression, but not ideas. The moment a program, website, or other work of authorship is fixed in a tangible medium of expression (saved on disk or other media, written down, etc.) it is protected by the federal copyright laws to the extent it is original (independently created). Provided that secrecy is maintained, trade secret protection can still continue.

Because an item is automatically protected by copyright upon its fixation, rather than when it is first published, there usually is a substantial time period during which both trade secret and copyright protection apply. This is because a program or website is usually tested and modified for some time after it is first "fixed," but before it is distributed or placed online. As long as it is maintained as a trade secret during this period, the program and website enjoys both trade secret and copyright protection.

b.   Distribution phase

Once a program or website is made available to the general public, it will lose trade secret status unless steps are taken to preserve secrecy. In the case of software, such steps may include distributing the program only in object code form and having each person who receives the work sign a license restricting disclosure of the secrets it contains. (See Chapter 16.) Website owners may require users to obtain passwords and agree to nondisclosure agreements.

2.   Trade Secrets and Patents

The federal patent laws provide the owner of a patentable invention with far greater protection than that available under trade secrecy or copyright laws—in effect, a total 17- to 18-year monopoly (20 years from the filing date) on the use of the invention as described in the patent. Patent protection is available for some computer programs and methods of doing business on the Internet.

Many companies use trade secrecy to protect these and other patentable inventions or processes as trade secrets in the initial stages of development and then seek patent protection. A patent application is published verbatim when the patent issues or earlier, as discussed below, and at that point all of the trade secrets and know-how become public. This public disclosure doesn't usually hurt the inventor, because the patent can be used to prevent anyone else from commercially exploiting the underlying information.

Every pending patent application filed on or after November 29, 2000 is published for the public to view 18 months after its filing date (or earlier if requested by the applicant). The only exception is if the applicant, at the time of filing, informs the PTO that the application will not be filed abroad. If the patent application is published and later rejected you will be in the unfortunate position of having lost both trade secret and patent rights.

If you file a patent application and want to keep it as a trade secret even if the patent isn't granted, you will have to withdraw the application before publication to prevent loss of trade secret status. ■

8

Establishing a Trade Secret Protection Program

Trade secret protection is based on the commonsense notion that keeping information close to the chest can provide a competitive advantage in the marketplace. But simply saying that a computer program or other information is a trade secret will not make it so. You must affirmatively behave in a way that manifests your desire to keep the information secret. This chapter shows you how to establish and maintain an adequate trade secret protection program.

This chapter is divided into two parts. Part I shows you how to identify your trade secrets and establish basic and advanced programs to protect them from unauthorized disclosure. Part II shows you how to draft nondisclosure agreements, the cornerstone of any trade secret protection program.

PART I: Identifying and Protecting Your Trade Secrets

Some companies go to extreme lengths to keep their trade secrets secret. For example, the formula for Coca-Cola (perhaps the world's most famous trade secret) is kept locked in a bank vault in Atlanta, which can be opened only by a resolution of the Coca-Cola Company's board of directors. Only two Coca-Cola employees ever know the formula at the same time; their identities are never disclosed to the public and they are not allowed to fly on the same airplane.

Fortunately, such extraordinary secrecy measures are seldom necessary. You don't have to turn your office into an armed camp to protect your trade secrets, but you must take reasonable precautions to prevent people who are not subject to confidentiality restrictions from learning them.

How much secrecy is "reasonable"? This depends largely on two factors:
- the physical and financial size of your company, and
- the value of your trade secrets.

A small start-up company need not implement the same type of trade secrecy program as a Microsoft or Amazon.com. A trade secret's value also affects how much secrecy the courts will deem reasonable. For example, more care should be taken to protect extremely valuable source code than relatively unimportant personnel information.

Someone needs to be in charge of a company's secrecy program. In some companies, management devises a security plan and then designates someone to serve as the company's security officer to manage and enforce it. Another approach taken by some hi-tech firms is to have the employees involved with each new project devise and enforce their own security plan. Either approach can work. The key to any trade secret protection program is to devise a secrecy plan you and your employees can live with—and then stick to it.

A. Identifying Your Trade Secrets

The first step in any trade secret protection program is to identify exactly what information and material is a company trade secret. As discussed in Chapter 7, a trade secret can be any information used by the company that gives it an advantage over competitors who do not know or use the information.

For software and Web development companies, trade secrets typically include such items as:

- unpublished computer code
- design definitions and specifications
- flow diagrams and flowcharts
- storyboards and concept outlines
- technical notes, memoranda, and correspondence relating to the design and development of computer code
- software development tools
- formulas and algorithms embodied in software
- system and user documentation
- data structures and data compilations
- product development agreements and other related agreements
- business plans
- marketing plans
- sales data

- unpublished promotional material
- cost and pricing information
- customer lists, and
- pending patent applications.

It makes no difference in what form a trade secret is embodied. Trade secrets may be stored on computer hard disks or CD-ROMs, written down on paper, or kept only in employees' memories.

Some companies conduct periodic trade secret "audits" or inventories in which they attempt to identify all the company information that should be protected as a trade secret. If you do this, it's best not to attempt to make such audits too detailed. If you overlook an important trade secret and it doesn't show up on a supposedly exhaustive list, someone might be able to claim it really wasn't a trade secret. To avoid this, don't attempt to create a detailed inventory of every piece of paper or computer file containing trade secrets. Rather, create a simpler inventory describing your trade secrets in more general terms—for example "all documents relating to XYZ Project." Be sure to periodically update this list.

⚠ Not Everything Is a Trade Secret. Some companies make the mistake of assuming that virtually all information about the company and its products is a trade secret that must be protected from disclosure to outsiders. They then find that attempting to protect such a morass of information is very expensive and burdensome, and they may end up abandoning their protection program. Use your common sense in deciding whether disclosure of a particular item of information to a competitor would really harm the company.

B. Basic Trade Secret Protection Program

Trade secrecy measures take time, cost money, can result in aggravation, and in some cases lower employee morale and productivity if workers perceive that the company is spying on them or maintaining a fortress mentality. Don't adopt an overly ambitious security program that you'll be unable or unwilling to follow. It is much better to have a modest security program that you and your employees will stick to rather than an extravagant program that will be ignored or resented.

Presented below are the absolute minimum safeguards a software or Web development company should take to protect its trade secrets. Such a basic secrecy program is adequate for small companies, particularly start-ups. In other words, if you file suit in court to prevent unauthorized disclosure or misappropriation of your trade secrets, a judge would likely conclude that you took the minimum reasonable precautions to prevent

the public or competitors from learning about your secrets absent improper acquisition or theft. (See Chapter 7.)

As your company grows, you'll want to implement some or all of the advanced secrecy measures discussed in Section C, below.

1. Use Nondisclosure Agreements

A nondisclosure agreement (often called an "NDA" for short) is a document in which a person who is given access to trade secrets promises not to disclose them to others without permission from the trade secret owner. Before you give any person access to your trade secrets, make sure that he or she has signed a nondisclosure agreement. This includes people both inside and outside your company.

Don't neglect the important step of preparing nondisclosure agreements. Using nondisclosure agreements consistently is the single most important element of any trade secret protection program.

Using a nondisclosure agreement accomplishes these basic purposes:

- It conclusively establishes that the parties have a confidential relationship. As discussed in detail in Chapter 7, only persons who are in a confidential relationship with a trade secret owner have a legal duty not to disclose the owner's trade secrets without permission.

- Signing such an agreement makes clear to a person who receives a trade secret that it is to be kept in confidence. It impresses on him or her that the company is serious about maintaining its trade secrets.
- If it's ever necessary to file a lawsuit, a signed nondisclosure agreement precludes a court from concluding that the company didn't bother to use nondisclosure agreements because it really didn't have any trade secrets.

Part II below provides detailed guidance on how to draft NDAs and includes sample forms.

a. Employees

All employees who may have access to trade secrets should be required to sign nondisclosure agreements before they begin work, or on their very first day of work. If you have employees who have not signed nondisclosure agreements, you should ask them to do so if they are given access to any trade secrets. A nondisclosure provision may be part of an employment agreement, which covers all aspects of employment, including confidentiality issues. Chapter 14 contains sample employment agreements including nondisclosure provisions.

Top management should sign nondisclosure agreements as well. Although such individuals owe a duty of loyalty to their company, which includes a duty not to disclose information that would harm the business, it's prudent to put it in writing. Potential customers or investors may wish to have the extra safeguard of a signed nondisclosure agreement before buying your product or investing in your company. If your business is a partnership, all partners should sign a partnership agreement containing a nondisclosure provision.

b. Independent contractors (consultants)

The consultant you hire today may end up working for a competitor tomorrow. Never expose a nonemployee consultant to trade secrets without having a signed nondisclosure agreement on file. The nondisclosure agreement may be contained in an independent contractor agreement, which covers all aspects of the work relationship. This is discussed in detail in Chapter 15; sample forms are included.

The sample agreements in Chapter 15 limit the consultant's confidentiality obligation to information in writing that is marked confidential, or information orally disclosed that is later reduced to writing and appropriately marked. This is a reasonable limitation because it enables the consultant to know exactly what is and is not a trade secret. However, it means that whenever trade secrets are orally disclosed to a consultant, a follow-up letter must be sent stating that the information is confidential. If you're an employer, make sure that your employees understand this policy and confirm all oral disclosures to outside consultants in writing.

c.   Licensees and purchasers

Nondisclosure provisions are routinely included in software and Web license and sale agreements. (See Chapter 16.)

d.   Other outsiders

Have any other outsider who may be exposed to your trade secrets sign a nondisclosure agreement as well. This may include people interviewing for jobs with your company, suppliers, outside beta testers, product reviewers, potential investors, bankers, accountants and outside auditors, as well as people who visit your company.

2.   Maintain Physical Security

Although employees or ex-employees, not industrial spies, most often misappropriate trade secrets, courts usually require that a company take at least some steps

to ensure the physical security of its trade secrets. At a minimum, a software company should implement a "clean desk" and "locked file cabinets and desk drawers" policy. Documents containing trade secrets—such as hard-copy printouts of source code—should not be left hanging about on desks when not in use; rather, they should be locked in desk drawers or filing cabinets. Your office should also be securely locked at the end of the day. Also, consider making periodic copies of valuable source code and place them in an office safe or bank safety deposit box for security and back-up purposes.

3.   Computer Security

Your computer system likely not only contains the software or Web materials you develop, but other sensitive information as well, such as financial records. It's vital to take reasonable measures to prevent unauthorized people from gaining access to your computer system. Here's a list of some of the security measures that can be employed; you can probably think of others. Some of these measures may be too much of a hassle, particularly for small companies. By no means are all required. But the more you employ, the safer your trade secrets will be.

- Use secret passwords, access procedures, and firewalls to prevent trade secret theft from your company's file server. The passwords should be periodically changed, especially when an employee who knows the current passwords quits or is fired.

- If practical, place computers, terminals, and other peripherals in a physically secure location to which access is restricted—for example, in a locked office or room to which only those people who need to use them have the key.

- Put "fuses" into software to detect unauthorized access and to stop or erase the program if unauthorized access occurs.

- Program your computers not to duplicate or reproduce software unless special programming instructions are input.

- Keep trade secrets in coded or encrypted form so outsiders can't read them. Inexpensive encryption programs such as PGP (Pretty Good Privacy) are readily available.

- Include secret codes in software identifying the employees who created it.

- Consider using separate computer systems, without Internet or other network access, for your most sensitive information.

Take Care With Email

Make certain that both you and your employees take care not to inadvertently disclose trade secrets in email. Always keep in mind that an email recipient can easily forward copies of a message to any number of others. Given the enormous volume of email and the fact that it is transmitted over the Internet in small packets rather than all at once, it's unlikely that anyone will intercept a specific email message in transit. Email is most likely to be read by unauthorized people when it is stored on a computer after it's composed and sent. It's wise to encrypt any email that contains any particularly sensitive information. This will make it difficult or impossible for your email to be read without your permission.

---

4. Label Information Confidential

Documents (both hard-copy and electronic), software, and other materials containing trade secrets should always be marked "confidential." This is the best way to alert employees and others that a document contains trade secrets. Moreover, nondisclosure agreements—including those in this book—require that trade secret documents be marked this way.

Here is some language you can use on any type of trade secret material:

> THIS [choose one: program, document, database] IS CONFIDENTIAL AND PROPRIETARY TO [your company name] AND MAY NOT BE REPRODUCED, PUBLISHED, OR DISCLOSED TO OTHERS WITHOUT COMPANY AUTHORIZATION.

You should also obtain a rubber stamp reading CONFIDENTIAL and use it to mark documents when it's inconvenient to use the longer notice above.

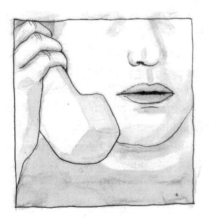 **Don't Mark Everything Confidential.** Don't go overboard and mark everything in sight confidential. If virtually everything, including public information, is marked "confidential," a court may conclude that nothing was really confidential. It is better not to mark anything than to mark everything.

a. Computer code

It's wise to combine a confidentiality notice with a copyright notice, like this:

> THIS PROGRAM IS CONFIDENTIAL AND PROPRIETARY TO [your company name] AND MAY NOT BE REPRODUCED, PUBLISHED, OR DISCLOSED TO OTHERS WITHOUT COMPANY AUTHORIZATION.
>
> COPYRIGHT © [year] BY [your company name]

Or, if the work is unpublished, use a notice like this:

> THIS PROGRAM IS CONFIDENTIAL AND PROPRIETARY TO [your company name] AND MAY NOT BE REPRODUCED, PUBLISHED, OR DISCLOSED TO OTHERS WITHOUT COMPANY AUTHORIZATION.
>
> COPYRIGHT © [your company name]. THIS WORK IS UNPUBLISHED.

Mark all copies of source code with such a notice. Also, when you create source code, flowcharts, or data compilations on your computer, include a notice at the beginning and end of the work and a few places in between.

b. Faxes and email

Try to keep faxing and emailing of trade secrets to a minimum. When it's unavoidable, be sure to include a confidentiality notice such as this one:

THE MESSAGES AND DOCUMENTS TRANSMITTED WITH THIS NOTICE CONTAIN CONFIDENTIAL INFORMATION BELONGING TO THE SENDER.

IF YOU ARE NOT THE INTENDED RECIPIENT OF THIS INFORMATION, YOU ARE HEREBY NOTIFIED THAT ANY DISCLOSURE, COPYING, DISTRIBUTION, OR USE OF THE INFORMATION IS STRICTLY PROHIBITED. IF YOU HAVE RECEIVED THIS TRANSMISSION IN ERROR, PLEASE NOTIFY THE SENDER IMMEDIATELY.

This notice will make it clear to people receiving the fax or email that it contains trade secrets and should be treated with care. It can be placed on a fax cover sheet or at the beginning of an email message.

5. Don't Write Down Trade Secrets

Perhaps the best way to maintain a trade secret is not to write it down at all. Particularly in small companies, a good deal of sensitive information—marketing plans, for example—can be transmitted orally to those who need to know.

C. Advanced Trade Secret Protection Program

Presented below are some additional security precautions that will help ensure the safety of your trade secrets. As your company grows and you develop increasingly valuable trade secrets, you'll want to consider making some or all of these precautions a part of your security plan.

1. Limit Employee Access to Trade Secrets

Obviously, the fewer people who know a trade secret, the less likely it will leak out. In very small companies, particularly start-ups, it may not be possible or desirable to limit access to trade secrets, since everyone is involved in every facet of the company's operation. However, as a company grows, it's a good idea to restrict access to trade secrets to only those employees who really need to know them.

One way to control employees' access to trade secrets is to use project logs. Start by making a list of which employees need to have access to confidential materials for each of your company's ongoing projects. Create a log for each project and have every employee sign in and out each time they use confidential materials.

The log should contain room for the date, the employee's name, the time in, the time out, and perhaps additional information, depending on the project. The log can be maintained manually or via computer.

Using such logs won't necessarily prevent your trade secrets from being stolen by someone bent on committing trade secret theft, but they will help you keep track of what who has what trade secret materials and when they have them.

> **EXAMPLE:** An ex-employee stole a stack of paper on which software code was printed. The company did not file a lawsuit until more than two years after the theft when it finally discovered the loss of the papers. The lawsuit was dismissed because the court ruled that the company should have detected the theft by using document control logs—a common practice among high-technology companies dependent upon trade secrets. (*Computer Assocs. Int'l v. Altai, Inc.,* 918 S.W.2d 453 (1996).)

Trade Secret Project Log

Date

Document Title/Subject

Employee's Name

Time Out

Time In

---

2. Beef Up Physical Security

In larger companies, you can take additional physical security precautions. Company trade secrets can be kept in a specified protected location or even in geographically separate facilities. Access to these areas can then be restricted. Large companies also employ security guards, surveillance cameras, and perimeter fencing.

3. Restrict Photocopying

If trade secrets are written down, one of the principal means by which they can be lost is through unauthorized photocopying. Try to restrict access to photocopiers, particularly at night. One excellent method is to require key cards and passwords to use company photocopiers. Such systems allow you to keep a record of who uses the photocopier, how much, and when.

In the absence of such a system, keep a logbook next to the copier and require anyone who copies a document marked "confidential" to record the following information: the date, name of person making the copy, name of the person for whom the copy is made, number of copies, and the subject matter and name of the document. In addition, a record should be kept of anyone who receives confidential copies—for example, the names could be written on a cover transmittal sheet. As always, those people should sign nondisclosure agreements.

Photocopy Log

Date

Person making copy

Person for whom copy made

Number of Copies

Title/Subject of Document

A photocopy log such as this is not nearly as effective as key cards and passwords, but it's still better than nothing. It won't prevent someone from making unauthorized copies, but will at least show you who has been making authorized copies of confidential material. It also helps make it clear to your employees that photocopying trade secret materials is a big deal and should be done with care.

4. Shred Documents

Don't leave documents containing valuable trade secrets lying around in your wastepaper bins. Companies have been known to hire investigators to engage in Dumpster diving at their competitors' premises. Obtain a shredding machine to effectively dispose of any documents containing trade secrets.

5. Consider Using Noncompetition Agreements

We've already mentioned above that all employees and consultants should be required to sign nondisclosure agreements before being exposed to trade secrets (see Section D below for detailed guidance on how to draft NDAs). However, nondisclosure agreements are not a panacea. It can be very difficult for an employer to know whether an ex-employee has disclosed trade secrets to a competitor. Moreover, even if the employer is sure trade secrets have been disclosed, it can be difficult to obtain court relief for violations of a nondisclosure agreement. The ex-employer must prove that the employee actually disclosed confidential information. This can be an onerous task, especially where the ex-employee claims that the information allegedly disclosed didn't qualify as a trade secret.

One way to avoid these problems is to have employees and consultants sign noncompetition agreements. These are agreements by which an employee or independent contractor promises not to compete with the employer's business for a stated time period (usually no more than two years).

It's usually easy to discover whether an ex-employee has gone to work for a competitor. To enforce a noncompetition agreement in court, the ex-employer need only show that the ex-employee went to work for a competitor in violation of the agreement's terms. But, the best part about a noncompetition agreement from an employer's point of view is that it will deter both the employee from seeking employment with a competitor and the competitor from hiring him or her. This significantly reduces an employee's incentive and opportunity to divulge trade secrets.

From the company's point of view, this all sounds great, but there is a down side. Noncompetition agreements are very unpopular with many employees and consultants, and some will refuse to sign them. You could lose an outstanding prospective employee or consultant by insisting on it. Moreover, they are unenforceable in a number of states, including California. Even in those states where such agreements are enforceable, they must be carefully drafted to withstand judicial scrutiny. (For a detailed discussion and sample forms, see Chapters 14 and 15.)

6. Screen Employee Publications and Presentations

A trade secret is lost if it is disclosed to the public on an unrestricted basis. Employers may inadvertently disclose trade secrets in speeches and presentations at trade shows and professional conferences. Trade secrets can even be lost through advertising—for example, a company that lists its clients in an advertising brochure cannot claim later that its customer list is a trade secret.

Companies with advanced trade secret programs screen all papers, articles, and advance texts of speeches and presentations. The screening can be done by a formal committee consisting of members who, taken together, are familiar with all the company's products and trade secrets, or by individuals who specialize in a particular area.

Special care must be taken to avoid disclosing patentable inventions in articles or other publications. Patent protection in some foreign countries can be lost through such inadvertent disclosures, and in all countries disclosure starts the one-year period running during which a patent application must be filed or the right to do so is lost forever.

7. Control Visitors

Visitors to your company should not be allowed to wander unsupervised in areas where confidential materials are kept. Visitors who might be exposed to trade secrets should be asked to sign a nondisclosure agreement before leaving the reception area.

Many companies require visitors to sign a logbook—but that's a mistake. Visitors who sign in may be able to see who else has been visiting your company, which is often very sensitive information in itself.

8. Deal With Departing Employees

The primary source of trade secret leaks is former employees. It is very important to take special precautions when an employee who has signed an NDA decides to leave or is fired.

a. Exit interviews and acknowledgment of obligations form

Before an employee leaves, your company's security officer or other person in charge of the trade secrecy program should conduct an exit interview. Use this opportunity to remind the employee of the obligation not to disclose company trade secrets to others, particularly the new employer. Wherever possible, prepare a list generally describing the specific trade secrets the employee has knowledge of and review it together. Give the employee a copy of the list. Also, remind the employee to return all company documents and materials before leaving. If the employee wants to keep a work sample, make sure it contains no confidential information. Finally, try to find out as much as possible about the worker's new employer and job responsibilities. This will help you determine whether the employee might be tempted to reveal trade secrets to a new employer. If you think this is possible, you may want to send the new employer the letter in Subsection b below.

Give the employee a copy of any nondisclosure and/or noncompetition agreement you and the employee have signed. Go over the agreement and make sure the employee understands the provisions and appreciates that the company is serious about protecting its trade secrets. Finally, ask the employee to sign an acknowledgment of obligations (a sample form is shown below). If the employee refuses to sign, be sure to note that in your personnel files. The refusal may be helpful if you later attempt to obtain a court order to prevent the employee from disclosing company trade secrets.

 The full text of the Acknowledgment of Obligations agreement is on the CD-ROM. See the Appendix for instructions on using the CD-ROM.

Acknowledgment of Obligations

1. I acknowledge that during my employment with Mystery Web Development, Inc. (the Company), I have received or been exposed to trade secrets of the Company including, but not limited to, the following: [CHECK APPLICABLE BOXES]

❑ Financial data

❑ Price or costing data

❑ Customer and vendor lists

❑ Marketing plans and data

❑ Personnel data

❑ Technical information concerning Company research and development projects, including _____ [DESCRIBE]

❑ Product design and specification data, including _____ [DESCRIBE]

❑ Patent applications and disclosures, including _____ [DESCRIBE]

❑ Product information, including _____ [DESCRIBE]

❑ Other _____[DESCRIBE]

2. I have read, signed, and been furnished with a copy of my [Employment OR Nondisclosure] Agreement with the Company. I have complied with and will continue to comply with all of the provisions of the Agreement, including my obligation to preserve as confidential all of the Company's trade secrets.

3. I do not have in my possession original documents, copies of them, or any other thing containing Company trade secrets. I have not disclosed Company trade secrets to anyone not authorized by the Company to receive them.

4. I have returned to my supervisor all identification badges, keys, and other access devices issued to me by the Company.

/s/

Jennifer Jones

Date: 2/15/0X

b. Informing new employers about nondisclosure agreement

If, as a result of your exit interview or for some other reason, you're concerned that a departing employee may reveal company trade secrets to a new employer, consider sending the new employer a polite warning letter. You can let the company know that your ex-employee has signed a nondisclosure agreement and that you are serious about enforcing it. Your letter serves two purposes:

1. It may help deter both the employee and new employer from breaching the nondisclosure agreement.

2. If a breach does occur, it will establish that the new employer knew that the employee possessed your trade secrets and had a duty not to disclose them without your permission. This will make the new employer, along with your ex-employee, liable for any unauthorized disclosure. And if the ex-employee makes an unauthorized disclosure, it will enable you to obtain a court order barring the new employer from using any of your trade secrets.

Be careful how you write this letter. Don't accuse anyone of trying to steal trade secrets; just stick to the facts. A letter making wild accusations could get your ex-employee fired because the other company fears you might sue. If this occurs, your ex-employee might sue your company for defamation or slander. Also, don't describe the trade secrets involved in detail; a general description of the subject matter is sufficient.

The full text of this sample letter is on the CD-ROM. See the Appendix for instructions on using the CD-ROM.

Send this letter by certified mail, return receipt requested. A copy should also be sent to the former employee.

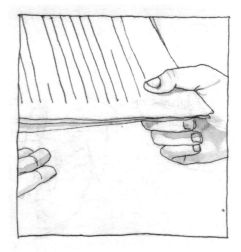

Letter to New Employer

July 12, 20XX

To Whom It May Concern:

We understand that Olivia Williams has decided to join your company. We would like to inform you of the following facts:

During her employment by the PineTree Robotics Company, Olivia Williams had access to our trade secrets including, but not limited to, advanced information about robotic visual scanning algorithms.

In connection with her employment, Ms. Williams signed an Employment Agreement in which she promised not to disclose or utilize any of our trade secrets without our permission. The Agreement remains in full force and effect.

At the time Ms. Williams left our company, she was informed of her continuing obligations under the Employment Agreement. She signed an acknowledgment of these obligations, a copy of which is enclosed.

We are confident that Ms. Williams intends to comply with her obligations and respect our trade secrets. We also trust that your company will not assign her to a position that might risk disclosure of our trade secrets.

If you have any questions regarding these matters, we will be happy to clarify them for you. In addition, if at any time you wish to know whether information provided you by Ms. Williams is a trade secret owned by us, we will be happy to work out a procedure for providing you with this information.

Very truly yours,

Jane Matthews

cc: Olivia Williams

Trade Secrets and the Government

Information that is held by the U.S. government may be disclosed upon request of citizens under the Freedom of Information Act (5 U.S.C. § 552). If you disclose trade secret information to the government—for example, your company creates software for government use—how can you prevent further disclosure of those software secrets under the Freedom of Information Act? There is a way the information will not be disclosed if the trade secret documents are clearly marked with the following notice:

This material is subject to exemption under the provisions of the Freedom of Information Act, specifically, 5 U.S.C. § 552(b)(4).

In addition, if you contract with the federal government, any proprietary materials you license or transfer should be marked with a legend that restricts rights.

This is particularly important in the case of software. We suggest the following legend, for example, in the case of software licensed to the federal government:

The software is furnished with RESTRICTED RIGHTS. Use, duplication, or disclosure is subject to restrictions as set forth in paragraph (b)(3)(B) of the Rights in Technical Data and Computer Software Clause in DAR 7-104.9(a) and in subparagraph (c)(1)(ii) of 252.227-7013; 52.227-19(a) through (d) and applicable ADP Schedule Contract. Unpublished rights are reserved under the copyright laws of the United States. The U.S. government agrees that any such products licensed, which have appropriate RESTRICTED RIGHTS legends applied on them, shall be provided only with RESTRICTED RIGHTS.

PART II. Drafting Nondisclosure Agreements

Part I explained why and when you should use nondisclosure agreements (NDAs). Part II provides detailed guidance on how to draft them yourself. Following are instructions and samples of five nondisclosure agreements:

- General Nondisclosure Agreement
- Nondisclosure Agreement With Prospective Licensees
- Beta Tester's Nondisclosure Agreement
- Visitor's Nondisclosure Agreement, and
- Prospective Employee's Nondisclosure Agreement.

For nondisclosure agreements to be used with employees, use the employment agreements in Chapter 14. For independent contractors, use the consulting agreements in Chapter 15.

One NDA or Many?

When you are disclosing information to a company and you are concerned about dissemination within the company you have two choices. You can have everyone who will have access to your trade secrets sign your nondisclosure agreement or you can have an executive or officer of the company sign it and include a requirement that all of the company's employees and contractors who are exposed to the trade secrets be bound by similar agreements.

If each person exposed to the information signs your agreement, you can sue each person individually in the event of a breach. This option is better suited for small entities such as sole proprietorships or a partnership—business forms in which each signatory can be individually liable. The second option is better for larger businesses that operate as corporations or LLCs and are usually only liable as corporate entities. You can sue only the company for breaking its promise not to disclose; you cannot sue the individual who disclosed the information. It is the one used in the sample agreement with this language:

"Receiving Party shall carefully restrict access to Confidential Information to employees, contractors and third parties as is reasonably required and shall require those persons to sign nondisclosure restrictions at least as protective as those in this Agreement."

D. General Nondisclosure Agreement

The General Nondisclosure Agreement can be used with any outside individual or company to whom you disclose your trade secrets, including contractors, potential customers or investors.

 The full text of the General Nondisclosure Agreement is on the CD-ROM. Call up the agreement on your computer and read it along with the following discussion, which explains the wording of the form and describes what information you'll need to insert.

A sample NDA is shown below. In subsequent sections we provide alternative versions of many of the provisions in this agreement.

Sample Nondisclosure Agreement

This Nondisclosure Agreement (the "Agreement") is entered into by and between Acme Web Development, Inc., a California corporation with its principal offices at 1282 47th Avenue, San Francisco, California ("Disclosing Party"), and Sasha Lorenz, a sole proprietor, located at 412 Mission Street, San Francisco, California ("Receiving Party"), for the purpose of preventing the unauthorized disclosure of Confidential Information as defined below. The parties agree to enter into a confidential relationship with respect to the disclosure of certain proprietary and confidential information ("Confidential Information").

1. Definition of Confidential Information. For purposes of this Agreement, "Confidential Information" shall include all information or material that has or could have commercial value or other utility in the business in which Disclosing Party is engaged. If Confidential Information is in written form, the Disclosing Party shall label or stamp the materials with the word "Confidential" or some similar warning. If Confidential Information is transmitted orally, the Disclosing Party shall promptly provide a writing indicating that such oral communication constituted Confidential Information.

2. Exclusions From Confidential Information. Receiving Party's obligations under this Agreement do not extend to information that is: (a) publicly known at the time of disclosure or subsequently becomes publicly known through no fault of the Receiving Party; (b) discovered or created by the Receiving Party before disclosure by Disclosing Party; (c) learned by the Receiving Party through legitimate means other than from the Disclosing Party or Disclosing Party's representatives; or (d) is disclosed by Receiving Party with Disclosing Party's prior written approval.

3. Obligations of Receiving Party. Receiving Party shall hold and maintain the Confidential Information in strictest confidence for the sole and exclusive benefit of the Disclosing Party. Receiving Party shall carefully restrict access to Confidential Information to employees, contractors, and third parties as is reasonably required and shall require those persons to sign nondisclosure restrictions at least as protective as those in this Agreement. Receiving Party shall not, without prior written approval of Disclosing Party, use for Receiving Party's own benefit, publish, copy, or otherwise disclose to others, or permit the use by others for their benefit or to the detriment of Disclosing Party, any Confidential Information. Receiving Party shall return to Disclosing Party any and all records, notes and other written, printed, or tangible materials in its possession pertaining to Confidential Information immediately if Disclosing Party requests it in writing.

4. Time Periods. The nondisclosure provisions of this Agreement shall survive the termination of this Agreement and Receiving Party's duty to hold Confidential Information in

Sample Nondisclosure Agreement (continued)

confidence shall remain in effect until the Confidential Information no longer qualifies as a trade secret or until Disclosing Party sends Receiving Party written notice releasing Receiving Party from this Agreement, whichever occurs first.

5. Relationships. Nothing contained in this Agreement shall be deemed to constitute either party a partner, joint venturer, or employee of the other party for any purpose.

6. Severability. If a court finds any provision of this Agreement invalid or unenforceable, the remainder of this Agreement shall be interpreted so as best to effect the intent of the parties.

7. Integration. This Agreement expresses the complete understanding of the parties with respect to the subject matter and supersedes all prior proposals, agreements, representations, and understandings. This Agreement may not be amended except in a writing signed by both parties.

8. Waiver. The failure to exercise any right provided in this Agreement shall not be a waiver of prior or subsequent rights.

This Agreement and each party's obligations shall be binding on the representatives, assigns, and successors of such party. Each party has signed this Agreement through its authorized representative.

Acme Web Development, Inc.

_____ Date:

by: Chandler Bartlett III

Vice President

_____ Date:

Sasha Lorenz

1. Who Is Disclosing? Who Is Receiving?

In the sample agreement, the "Disclosing Party" is the person disclosing secrets, and "Receiving Party" is the person or company who receives the confidential information and is obligated to keep it secret. The terms are capitalized to indicate they are defined within the agreement. The sample agreement is a "one-way" (or in legalese, "unilateral") agreement—that is, only one party is disclosing secrets.

If both sides are disclosing secrets to each other you should modify the agreement to make it a mutual (or "bilateral") nondisclosure agreement. To do that, substitute the following paragraph for the first paragraph in the agreement.

This Nondisclosure Agreement (the "Agreement") is entered into by and between _____ [insert your name, business form, and address] and _____ [insert name, business form, and address of other person or company with whom you are exchanging information] collectively referred to as the "parties," for the purpose of preventing the unauthorized disclosure of Confidential Information as defined below. The parties agree to enter into a confidential relationship with respect to the disclosure by one or each (the "Disclosing Party") to the other (the "Receiving Party") of certain proprietary and confidential information (the "Confidential Information").

---

2. Defining the Trade Secrets

Every nondisclosure agreement defines its trade secrets, often referred to as "confidential information." This definition establishes the subject matter of the disclosure. There are three common approaches to defining confidential information: (1) using a system to mark all confidential information; (2) listing trade secret categories; or (3) specifically identifying the confidential information.

What's best for your company? That depends on your secrets and how you disclose them. If your company is built around one or two secrets—for example a famous recipe or formula—you can specifically identify the materials. You can also use that approach if you are disclosing one or two secrets to a contractor. If your company focuses on several categories of secret information, for example, computer code, sales information, and marketing plans, a list approach will work with employees and contractors. If your company has a wide variety of secrets and is constantly developing new ones, you should specifically identify secrets.

Here's an example of the list approach.

"Confidential Information" means information or material that is commercially valuable to the Disclosing Party and not generally known or readily ascertainable in the industry. This includes, but is not limited to:

(a) technical information concerning the Disclosing Party's products and services, including product know-how, formulae, designs, devices, diagrams, software code, test results, processes, inventions, research projects and product development, technical memoranda, and correspondence;

(b) information concerning the Disclosing Party's business, including cost information, profits, sales information, accounting and unpublished financial information, business plans, markets and marketing methods, customer lists and customer information, purchasing techniques, supplier lists and supplier information, and advertising strategies;

(c) information concerning the Disclosing Party's employees, including salaries, strengths, weaknesses, and skills;

(d) information submitted by the Disclosing Party's customers, suppliers, employees, consultants, or co-venture partners with the Disclosing Party for study, evaluation, or use; and

(e) any other information not generally known to the public that, if misused or disclosed, could reasonably be expected to adversely affect the Disclosing Party's business.

Using a list approach is fine, provided that you can find something on the list that fits your disclosure. For example, if you are disclosing a confidential software program, your nondisclosure agreement should include a category such as "programming code" or "software code" that accurately reflects your secret material.

Although the final paragraph in the example above includes "any other information," you will be better off not relying solely on this statement. Courts that interpret NDAs often prefer specificity.

If confidential information is fairly specific—for example, a unique method of preparing income tax statements—define it specifically.

EXAMPLE: Definition of Confidential Information

The following constitutes Confidential Information: *business method for preparing income tax statements and related algorithms and software code.*

Another approach to identifying trade secrets is to state that the disclosing party will certify what is and what is not confidential. For example, physical disclosures such as written materials or software will be clearly marked "Confidential." In the case of oral disclosures, the disclosing party provides written confirmation that a trade secret was disclosed. Here is an appropriate provision taken from the sample NDA in the previous section:

EXAMPLE: Definition of Confidential Information

(Written or Oral.) For purposes of this Agreement, "Confidential Information" includes all information or material that has or could have commercial value or other utility in the business in which Disclosing Party is engaged. If Confidential Information is in written form, the Disclosing Party shall label or stamp the materials with the word "Confidential" or some similar warning. If Confidential Information is transmitted orally, the Disclosing Party shall promptly provide a writing indicating that such oral communication constituted Confidential Information.

When confirming an oral disclosure, avoid disclosing the content of the trade secret. An email or letter is acceptable, but the parties should keep copies of all such correspondence. A sample letter is shown below.

Letter Confirming Oral Disclosure

Date:

Dear Sam, .

Today at lunch, I disclosed information to you about my kaleidoscopic projection system—specifically, the manner in which I have configured and wired the bulbs in the device. That information is confidential (as described in our nondisclosure agreement) and this letter is intended to confirm the disclosure.

William

3. Excluding Information That Is Not Confidential

You cannot prohibit the receiving party from disclosing information that is publicly known, legitimately acquired from another source, or developed by the receiving party before meeting you. Similarly, it is not unlawful if the receiving party discloses your secret with your permission. These legal exceptions exist with or without an agreement, but they are commonly included in a contract to make it clear to everyone that such information is not considered a trade secret.

EXAMPLE: Exclusions From Confidential Information

Receiving Party's obligations under this Agreement do not extend to information that is: (a) publicly known at the time of disclosure under this Agreement or subsequently becomes publicly known through no fault of the Receiving Party; (b) discovered or created by the Receiving Party prior to disclosure by Disclosing Party; (c) otherwise learned by the Receiving Party through legitimate means other than from the Disclosing Party or Disclosing Party's representatives; or (d) is disclosed by Receiving Party with Disclosing Party's prior written approval.

In some cases, a business presented with your nondisclosure agreement may request the right to exclude information that is independently developed *after* the disclosure. In other words, the business might want to change subsection (b) to read, "(b) discovered or independently created by Receiving Party prior to *or after* disclosure by Disclosing Party."

By making this change, the other company can create new products after exposure to your secret, provided that your secret is not used to develop them. You may wonder how it is possible for a company once exposed to your secret to de-velop a new product without using that trade secret. One possibility is that one division of a large company could invent something without any contact with the division that has been exposed to your secret. Some companies even establish clean room methods.

Although it is possible for a company to independently develop products or information without using your disclosed secret, we recommend avoiding this modification if possible.

4. Duty to Keep Information Secret

The heart of a nondisclosure agreement is a statement establishing a confidential relationship between the parties. The statement sets out the duty of the Receiving Party to maintain the information in confidence and to limit its use. Often, this duty is established by one sentence: "The Receiving Party shall hold and maintain the Confidential Information of the other party in strictest confidence for the sole and exclusive benefit of the Disclosing Party." In other cases, the provision may be more detailed and may include obligations to return information. A detailed provision is provided below.

The simpler provision is usually suitable when entering into an NDA with an individual such as an independent contractor. Use the more detailed one if more than one individual within a business may use your secrets. The detailed provision provides that the receiving party has to restrict access to persons within the company who are also bound by this agreement.

EXAMPLE: Provision Establishing a Duty of Nondisclosure

Receiving Party shall hold and maintain the Confidential Information of the Disclosing Party in strictest confidence for the sole and exclusive benefit of the Disclosing Party. Receiving Party shall carefully restrict access to Confidential Information to employees, contractors, and third parties as is reasonably required and only to persons subject to nondisclosure restrictions at least as protective as those set forth in this Agreement. Receiving Party shall not, without prior written approval of Disclosing Party, use for Receiving Party's own benefit, publish, copy, or otherwise disclose to others or permit the use by others for their benefit or to the detriment of Disclosing Party, any Confidential Information.

In some cases, you may want to impose additional requirements. For example, the Prospective Software Licensee Nondisclosure Agreement contains a prohibition against reverse engineering, decompiling, or disassembling the software. This prohibits the receiving party (the user of licensed software) from learning more about the trade secrets.

You may also insist on the return of all trade secret materials that you furnished under the agreement. In that case, add the following language to the receiving party's obligations:

EXAMPLE: Return of Materials

Receiving Party shall return to Disclosing Party any and all records, notes, and other written, printed, or tangible materials in its possession pertaining to Confidential Information immediately if Disclosing Party requests it in writing.

5. Duration of the Agreement

How long does the duty of confidentiality last? The sample agreement offers three alternative approaches: an indefinite period that terminates when the information is no longer a trade secret; a fixed period of time; or a combination of the two.

EXAMPLE: Unlimited Time Period

This Agreement and Receiving Party's duty to hold Disclosing Party's Confidential Information in confidence shall remain in effect until the Confidential Information no longer qualifies as a trade secret or until Disclosing Party sends Receiving Party written notice releasing Receiving Party from this Agreement, whichever occurs first.

EXAMPLE: Fixed Time Period

This Agreement and Receiving Party's duty to hold Disclosing Party's Confidential Information in confidence shall remain in effect until _____.

EXAMPLE: Fixed Time Period With Exceptions

This Agreement and Receiving Party's duty to hold Disclosing Party's Confidential Information in confidence shall remain in effect until _____ or until one of the following occurs:

(a) the Disclosing Party sends the Receiving Party written notice releasing it from this Agreement, or

(b) the information disclosed under this Agreement ceases to be a trade secret.

The time period is often an issue of negotiation. You, as the disclosing party, will usually want an open period with no limits; receiving parties want a short period. For employee and contractor agreements, the term is often unlimited or ends only when the trade secret becomes public knowledge. Five years is a common length in nondisclosure agreements that involve business negotiations and product

submissions, although many companies insist on two or three years.

We recommend that you seek as long a time as possible, preferably unlimited. But realize that some businesses want a fixed period of time and some courts, when interpreting NDAs, require that the time period be reasonable. Determining "reasonableness" is subjective and depends on the confidential material and the nature of the industry. For example, some trade secrets within the software or Internet industries may be short-lived. Other trade secrets—for example, the Coca-Cola formula—have been preserved as a secret for over a century. If it is likely, for example, that others will stumble upon the same secret or innovation or that it will be reverse engineered within a few years, then you are unlikely to be damaged by a two- or three-year period. Keep in mind that once the time period is over, the disclosing party is free to reveal your secrets.

6. Miscellaneous Provisions

The sample NDA includes four miscellaneous provisions. These standard provisions (sometimes known as "boilerplate") are included at the end of most contracts. They actually have little in common with one another except for the fact that they don't fit anywhere else in the agreement. They're contract orphans. Still, these provisions are very important and can affect how disputes are resolved and how a court enforces the contract.

Relationships. Your relationship with the receiving party is usually defined by the agreement that you are signing—for example an employment, licensing, or investment agreement. To an outsider, it may appear that you have a different relationship, such as a partnership or joint venture. It's possible that an unscrupulous business will try to capitalize on this appearance and make a third-party deal. That is, the receiving party may claim to be your partner to obtain a benefit from a distributor or sublicensee. To avoid liability for such a situation, most agreements include a provision like this one, disclaiming any relationship other than that defined in the agreement. We recommend that you include such a provision and take care to tailor it to the agreement. For example, if you are using it in an employment agreement, you would delete the reference to employees. If you are using it in a partnership agreement, take out the reference to partners, and so forth.

EXAMPLE: Relationships

Nothing contained in this Agreement shall be deemed to constitute either party a partner, joint venturer, or employee of the other party for any purpose.

Severability. The severability clause provides that if you wind up in a lawsuit over the agreement and a court rules that one part of the agreement is invalid, that part can be cut out and the rest of the agreement will remain valid. If you don't include a severability clause and some portion of your agreement is deemed invalid, then the whole agreement may be canceled.

EXAMPLE: Severability

If a court finds any provision of this Agreement invalid or unenforceable, the remainder of this Agreement shall be interpreted so as best to effect the intent of the parties.

Integration. In the process of negotiation and contract drafting, you and the other party may make many oral or written statements. Some of these statements make it into the final agreement. Others don't. The integration provision verifies that the version you are signing is the final version, and that neither of you can rely on statements made in the past. *This is it!* Without an integration provision, it's possible that either party could claim rights based upon promises made before the deal was signed.

A second function of the integration provision is to establish that if any party makes promises after the agreement is signed, those promises will be binding only if they are made in a signed amendment (addendum) to the agreement.

EXAMPLE: Integration

> This Agreement expresses the complete understanding of the parties with respect to the subject matter and supersedes all prior proposals, agreements, representations, and understandings. This Agreement may not be amended except in a writing signed by both parties.

 Watch Out for "We'll Fix It Later" Promises. The integration clause closes the door on any oral or written promises. Don't sign an agreement if something is missing and don't accept an assurance that the other party will correct it later.

Waiver. This provision states that even if you don't promptly complain about a violation of the NDA, you still have the right to complain about it later. Without this kind of clause, if you know the other party has breached the agreement but you let it pass, you give up (waive) your right to sue over it. For example, imagine that the receiving party is supposed to use the secret information in two products but not in a third. You're aware that the receiving party is violating the agreement, but you are willing to permit it because you are being paid more money and don't have a

competing product. After several years, however, you no longer want to permit the use of the secret in the third product. A waiver provision makes it possible for you to sue. The receiving party cannot defend itself by claiming it relied on your past practice of accepting its breaches. Of course, the provision swings both ways. If you breach the agreement, you cannot rely on the other party's past acceptance of *your* behavior.

EXAMPLE: Waiver

> The failure to exercise any right provided in this Agreement shall not be a waiver of prior or subsequent rights.

 Signatures. The parties don't have to be in the same room when they sign the agreement. It's even fine if the dates are a few days apart. Each party should sign two copies, and keep one. This way, both parties have an original signed agreement. See Chapter 1 for a detailed discussion on how to sign legal agreements.

7. Additional Contract Provisions

Here are some other provisions that you can add to your agreement. These provisions are not essential, but we recommend including at least some of them if you have sufficient bargaining power. They can give you additional rights and create additional obligations on the other party.

a. Injunctive relief

An injunction is a court order directing a person to do (or stop doing) something. If someone violated your NDA, you would want a court order directing that person to stop using your secrets. To get an injunction, you must demonstrate to the court that you have suffered or will suffer irreparable harm as a result of the unauthorized use of your secrets. Irreparable harm is harm that can't be compensated for later by money.

Proving that in court is expensive and time-consuming. In order to cut through some of that legal work, some nondisclosure agreements include a provision similar to the one below. In it, the receiving party agrees that the harm caused by a breach is irreparable, so you will have less to prove if and when you seek a court order. This provision only makes it easier to obtain an injunction; by itself, it will not compel a judge to order an injunction. In other words, don't expect that a judge will automatically stop the disclosure simply because this provision is in your agreement. To get an injunction, you will always need to demonstrate that you are likely to prevail in your dispute. That said, this clause provides some tactical advantages and it's a good idea to include it.

EXAMPLE: Injunctive Relief

> Receiving Party acknowledges that any misappropriation of any of the Confidential Information in violation of this Agreement may cause Disclosing Party irreparable harm, the amount of which may be difficult to ascertain, and therefore agrees that the Disclosing Party shall have the right to apply to a court of competent jurisdiction for an order enjoining any such further misappropriation and for such other relief as the Disclosing Party deems appropriate. This right of Disclosing Party is to be in addition to the remedies otherwise available to Disclosing Party.

b. Indemnity

Some NDAs require the receiving party to pay for all damages (lost profits, attorney fees, or other expenses) incurred by the other party as a result of the receiving party's breach of the nondisclosure agreement. This obligation is known as indemnification. Leaving out the indemnity provision does not prevent you from suing and collecting damages for a breach (contract law holds the receiving party responsible for a breach), but the clause makes it easier to claim damages. To include indemnity in your nondisclosure agreement, add the following language at the end of the obligations section:

EXAMPLE: Indemnity

Receiving Party agrees to indemnify the Disclosing Party against any and all losses, damages, claims, or expenses incurred or suffered by the Disclosing Party as a result of the Receiving Party's breach of this Agreement.

c. Attorney fees

What if the other party breaches the NDA, and you are forced to sue? The rate for business lawyers is $200 to $400 an hour. The filing and initial stages of a lawsuit cost $5,000 to $50,000 and can quickly escalate to more than $100,000, depending on the length of the suit and the subject matter. The amount you pay lawyers could quickly overshadow any amount you might win.

In the United States (unlike many other countries), the loser of a lawsuit is not required to pay the winner's attorney fees. In other words, each party has to pay its own lawyer, regardless of the outcome of the suit. There are two exceptions to this rule:

1) a court may award fees if a specific law permits it; and

2) a court must award attorney fees if a contract provides for it.

If you don't include an attorney fees clause in your agreement, a judge may

(in most states) order the award of attorney fees in cases where the theft of the trade secret was willful and malicious. It's up to the judge, which makes things unpredictable. You are far better off using an attorney fees provision like the one below. Because lawyers are so expensive, having an attorney fee provision—that is, having each side afraid it will get stuck paying someone's attorney fees—can prove crucial to ending a dispute.

However, don't be surprised if the other party is opposed to the idea. Why? Because it is the receiving party that is usually sued, not vice versa, and the receiving party may believe that the provision will encourage you to sue.

EXAMPLE: Attorney Fees and Expenses

In a dispute arising out of or related to this Agreement, the prevailing party shall have the right to collect from the other party its reasonable attorney fees and costs and necessary expenditures.

This attorney fees provision is mutual—that is, whoever wins the lawsuit is awarded attorney fees. This is fair, and encourages the quick resolution of lawsuits. We discourage a provision that allows only one party to receive attorney fees. No matter which side they favor, such provisions create an uneven playing field for resolving disputes. One state (California) recognizes this unfairness and automatically converts a one-way attorney fees contract provision into a mutual one.

d.   Arbitration and mediation

Arbitration and mediation are referred to as alternative dispute resolution (ADR) procedures because they offer ways to end squabbles without litigation. These ADR procedures have become popular over the last decade because they avoid the court system and can save time and money. However, taking a dispute out of the court system may not always be the right decision, because you may be bound by a decision from which there is no means of appeal. Below we discuss both options and offer examples of appropriate contract provisions.

Arbitration. Arbitration is like going to court with less formality and expense. Instead of filing a lawsuit, the parties hire one or more arbitrators to evaluate the dispute and make a determination. The arbitration process can be relatively simple; usually arbitration involves some document preparation and a hearing. A lawyer is not required to arbitrate, but many parties use attorneys for help in presenting the strongest legal arguments.

The arbitrator's determination may be advisory (in which case either party can disregard it and file a lawsuit) or it may be binding. A binding decision can be enforced by a court and cannot be overturned unless something especially unfair

happened—for example, the arbitrator ruled against you and you later learn that the arbitrator owned stock in your opponent's company.

In order to arbitrate a dispute, both parties must consent. Unfortunately, when you are in the midst of a dispute, it's hard to get the parties to agree to anything. So, the best method of guaranteeing arbitration is to include an arbitration provision in your nondisclosure agreement.

Arbitration is not, however, always preferable to litigation. Even though ADR is quicker than going through a trial, it may take several weeks to initiate ADR proceedings. By going to court, however, a business may obtain a temporary court order restraining disclosure (TRO) in less time than it takes to initiate arbitration. This initial period of the dispute can be crucial when you're concerned about the loss of secrecy. For this reason, you need to weigh the potential cost of litigation versus the speed of obtaining relief. For a small company with limited resources, arbitration is usually the preferable route.

Many businesses are opposed to arbitration for other reasons as well. They may have recently lost an arbitration proceeding and refuse to participate in another one. They may be fearful that the dispute will be placed in the hands of an inappropriate arbitrator, or they may prefer the litigation process in order to intimidate the other party. In addition, some arbitrations can be expensive and end up being appealed in the court system.

EXAMPLE: Arbitration

> If a dispute arises under or relating to this Agreement, the parties agree to submit the dispute to binding arbitration in the state of ___ [insert state in which parties agree to arbitrate] or another location mutually agreeable to the parties. The arbitration shall be conducted on a confidential basis pursuant to the Commercial Arbitration Rules of the American Arbitration Association. Any decision or award as a result of any such arbitration proceeding shall be in writing and shall provide an explanation for all conclusions of law and fact and shall include the assessment of costs, expenses, and reasonable attorney fees. Any such arbitration shall be conducted by an arbitrator experienced in ___[insert industry experience required for arbitrator] and ____ [insert area of law that is the subject of your dispute, for example licensing law] law and shall include a written record of the arbitration hearing. The parties reserve the right to object to any individual who is employed by or affiliated with a competing organization or entity. An award of arbitration may be confirmed in a court of competent jurisdiction.

Mediation. In mediation, a neutral evaluator (the mediator) attempts to help the parties reach a resolution of their dispute. Both sides sit down with the mediator and tell their stories. The mediator advises ways to resolve the dispute, and the two parties try to agree. If they do, they sign an enforceable settlement agreement. Because it is not binding and because it is less expensive than litigation or arbitration, some businesses prefer mediation, at least as a first step. You can locate a mediator through the American Arbitration Association (www.adr.org) or local bar associations.

Mediation is the most inexpensive and peaceable method of solving problems. You can arrive at a settlement rather than being told how to resolve the dispute by an arbitrator or judge. It's less likely to exacerbate bad feelings between the parties, as lawsuits inevitably do.

By itself, however, mediation is often not enough, because it doesn't force the parties to end the dispute. If you cannot resolve the dispute with mediation, you must find some binding method of ending the battle, either arbitration or litigation. Sometimes one party chooses mediation simply to buy more time. Keep in mind, as we mentioned in the preceding section, that time is generally of the essence in disputes over the disclosure of information.

If you want to use a mediation clause, we suggest a provision like the one below, which progresses from informal meeting to mediation and then to arbitration.

EXAMPLE: Mediation & Arbitration

The parties agree that any dispute or difference between them arising under this Agreement shall be settled first by a meeting of the parties attempting to confer and resolve the dispute in a good faith manner.

If the parties cannot resolve their dispute after conferring, any party may require the other to submit the matter to nonbinding mediation, utilizing the services of an impartial professional mediator approved by both parties.

If the parties cannot come to an agreement following mediation, they will submit the matter to binding arbitration at a location mutually agreeable to the parties. The arbitration shall be conducted on a confidential basis under the Commercial Arbitration Rules of the American Arbitration Association. Any decision or award as a result of any such arbitration proceeding shall include the assessment of costs, expenses, and reasonable attorney fees and shall include a written record of the proceedings and a written determination of the arbitrators. Absent an agreement to the contrary, an arbitrator experienced in intellectual property law shall conduct any such arbitration. The parties may object to any individual who is employed by or affiliated with a competing organization or entity. In the event of any such dispute or difference, either party may give to the other notice requiring that the matter be settled by arbitration. An award of arbitration shall be final and binding on the parties and may be confirmed in a court of competent jurisdiction.

e. Which state's law will govern disputes

Every state has laws regarding contract interpretation and trade secrecy. You can choose any state's laws to govern the agreement, regardless of where you live or where the agreement is signed. Most businesses favor the state where their headquarters are located.

Does it matter which state you choose? Some states have a reputation of being favorable for certain kinds of disputes. For example, California's state and federal courts have resolved many high-tech disputes; as a body of law has developed, judges' decisions have become more predictable. Generally, however, the differences in state law are not great enough to make this a major negotiating issue.

EXAMPLE: Governing Law

This Agreement shall be governed in accordance with the laws of the State of _____.

⚠ **Don't Confuse Jurisdiction and Governing Law.** Selecting where a dispute will be settled, described below, is more important than selecting which state's laws will apply. Sometimes these two provisions are grouped in one paragraph, so read them carefully.

f. Choosing jurisdiction

Jurisdiction (sometimes referred to as personal jurisdiction) is the power of a court to bind you by its decision. If a court doesn't have this authority over you, any judgment it issues isn't worth anything. A court can get jurisdiction over you in three ways: 1) you are a resident of the state in which the court is located; 2) you have sufficient contacts in the state, such as selling considerable merchandise there; or 3) you consent to jurisdiction.

The purpose of adding a jurisdiction provision to an NDA is to get each party to consent in advance to jurisdiction in one county or state and to give up the right to sue or be sued anywhere else. Consider the couple who opened a Burger King franchise in Florida. In their agreement with Burger King, they consented to jurisdiction in Michigan. Later, when problems arose, the couple argued that it wasn't fair to have to travel to Michigan and that they had not understood this provision. The courts upheld the jurisdiction clause and the couple was forced to fight Burger King in a Michigan court.

This may seem like a trivial issue at the time you are negotiating an agreement, but it will be a major issue if there is ever a dispute. In fact, the prospect of hiring lawyers and traveling to another state is often enough to dissuade companies from pursuing a lawsuit. We recommend the following strategies:

- If you have sufficient bargaining power, obtain jurisdiction in your home county.
- If you cannot obtain jurisdiction in your home county, don't say anything about jurisdiction. If there is no reference to jurisdiction, the location of the case is usually determined by whoever files the lawsuit.
- If you *do* include a jurisdiction clause it may be helpful to choose the same state you chose for governing law, as discussed above. It's simpler and more efficient for a court to apply the familiar laws of its own state.

EXAMPLE: Jurisdiction

The parties consent to the exclusive jurisdiction and venue of the federal and state courts located in ___[insert county and state in which parties agree to litigate] in any action arising out of or relating to this Agreement. The parties waive any other jurisdiction to which either party might be entitled by domicile or otherwise.

⚠️ **In Some States, Jurisdiction Clauses Are Invalid.** Idaho, Montana, and Alabama refuse to honor jurisdiction provisions in contracts. In those states, if you use a jurisdiction provision, it will be invalid. The states' reasoning? They think law, not by people shopping around for the most convenient or advantageous forum, should determine jurisdiction.

g. Successors and assigns

It's possible that someone else may succeed either party. For example, a sole proprietor's heirs may inherit the business. In that case you would make want to sure that the heirs were bound by the same nondisclosure requirements.

In other cases, a party may assign its rights to another company. For example, another company—maybe even a competitor of yours—may acquire the business you sign an NDA with. So, if you have the bargaining power, prohibit any assignment of your contract unless you give written consent. But understand that in today's world of acquisitions and mergers, many companies want the freedom to assign agreements and oppose a complete prohibition on assignments.

EXAMPLE: Successors & Assigns

> This Agreement shall bind each party's heirs, successors, and assigns. Disclosing Party may assign this Agreement to any party at any time. Receiving Party shall not assign any of its rights or obligations under this Agreement without Company's prior written consent. Any assignment or transfer in violation of this section shall be void.

If the other party is concerned that this language gives you too much control, you can soften the effect by agreeing to withhold consent only if you have a valid business reason. What's a valid reason? Perhaps the potential assignee has a poor reputation for maintaining trade secrets, or maybe it is in poor financial shape. You cannot, however, withhold consent for an arbitrary reason, such as that someone from the company once treated you rudely.

EXAMPLE: Assignability—Consent Not Unreasonably Withheld

> This Agreement shall bind each party's heirs, successors, and assigns. Receiving Party may not assign or transfer its rights or obligations pursuant to this Agreement without the prior written consent of Disclosing Party. Such consent shall not be unreasonably withheld. Any assignment or transfer in violation of this section shall be void.

If you don't have much bargaining power and the other party wants freedom to transfer to affiliates or new owners, you can use a provision such as the one below:

EXAMPLE: Assignability—Consent Not Needed for Affiliates or New Owners

This Agreement shall bind each party's heirs, successors, and assigns. Receiving Party may not assign or transfer its rights or obligations pursuant to this Agreement without the prior written consent of Disclosing Party. However, no consent is required for an assignment or transfer that occurs: (a) to an entity in which Receiving Party owns more than fifty percent of the assets; or (b) as part of a transfer of all or substantially all of the assets of Receiving Party to any party. Any assignment or transfer in violation of this Section shall be void.

E. Prospective Licensee Nondisclosure Agreement for Software Company

If your company produces software, you'll need a nondisclosure agreement when you provide a copy of a finished software product to a prospective licensee or other customer for evaluation.

 This agreement may be found on the CD-ROM at the back of the book. Call up the agreement on your computer and read it along with the following discussion, which explains the wording of the form and describes what information you'll need to insert.

1. Introductory Paragraph

Fill in the date you want the agreement to take effect. Next, fill in your company name. Fill in the name of the outside individual or company being granted access to your trade secrets (called the "Customer"). Finally, describe the software or other information disclosed or fill in the name of the product.

2. Nonexclusive License

Fill in the number of days you are allowing the customer to use the software for evaluation purposes.

3. Software a Trade Secret

This clause makes it clear that the software is a trade secret. There is nothing to fill in here.

4. Nondisclosure

This provision is the heart of the agreement. The customer promises to treat your trade secrets with a reasonable degree of care and not to disclose them to third parties without your written consent. The customer also promises not to make commercial use of the information without your permission.

Finally, the customer may not disclose the information to its employees or consultants unless they have signed confidentiality agreements protecting your trade secrets. If the customer breaks these promises, you can sue to obtain monetary damages and possibly a court order to prevent the customer from using the information.

5. Return of Software and Materials

This clause outlines when the product must be returned to your company.

6. Limitation of Liability

This clause makes it clear to the customer that the software is being provided only for evaluation purposes and that you are not liable for any damages caused by the customer's use of the software.

7. General Provisions

If you would like explanations of any of the following provisions, review Sections D6 and D7:

- Relationships
- Severability
- Integration
- Waiver
- Injunctive Relief
- Indemnity
- Attorney Fees
- Governing Law
- Jurisdiction
- Assignments
- Successors
- Signatures.

F. Software Beta Tester Nondisclosure Agreement

If you develop software (including Web applications) and give beta versions to outside testers, here is a nondisclosure agreement for you to use.

 This agreement may be found on the CD-ROM at the back of the book.

1. Introductory Paragraph

Fill in the date. Next, fill in your name. Fill in the name of the outside individual or company that is beta testing your software (the "Tester").

2. Software

Here, fill in the name of the software being tested.

3. Company's Obligations

Typically, a beta tester is given a free copy of the finished version of software as payment. That is what this agreement provides, although you can make some other arrangements for payment—for example, an hourly rate or a fixed fee.

4. Tester's Obligations

This clause describes the software tester's duties, which are to gather and report test data. There is nothing to add here.

5. Software a Trade Secret

This clause makes clear to the tester that the software is a trade secret. The tester is not allowed to copy the software except as necessary to perform or test it and may not reverse engineer or disassemble it to see how it works.

6. Security Precautions

This clause requires the tester to take reasonable precautions to make sure the software isn't seen by unauthorized people. There is nothing to add here.

7. Term of Agreement

Fill in the time frame during which the testing will occur.

8. Return of Software and Materials

This clause requires the tester to return the software when the testing is done and delete it from any computer on which it's been installed.

9. Disclaimer of Warranty

This clause states that the software is being provided to the tester "as is." You do not guarantee the software for any purpose and the tester waives any potential legal claims against your company arising from the use of the software—for example, if it does not perform the claimed functions.

10. Limitation of Liability

This clause makes it clear to the beta tester that the software is being provided only for evaluation purposes, and that you are not liable for any damages caused by the beta tester's use of the software—for example if it damages the tester's hard drive.

11. No Rights Granted

This clause makes it absolutely clear that the software belongs to you and that the tester is acquiring no ownership rights in it whatsoever and cannot sell or transfer the software to others.

12. No Assignments

This clause provides that the tester must perform the testing services personally. The tester may not get anyone else to do the testing.

13. General Provisions

If you would like explanations of any of the following provisions, review Sections D6 and D7:

- Relationships
- Severability
- Integration
- Waiver
- Attorney Fees
- Governing Law
- Jurisdiction
- Signature.

G. Visitor Nondisclosure Agreement

If visitors to your company might have access to company trade secrets, ask them to sign a nondisclosure agreement. We've removed many of the provisions from other NDAs in order to make this a short, easy-to-understand agreement; one

that visitors shouldn't object to signing. Give visitors a signed copy.

 This Agreement may be found on the CD-ROM. Call up the agreement on your computer and read it along with the following discussion, which explains the wording of the form and describes what information you'll need to insert.

1. Introductory Material

Visitor's Name:
[Fill in the name of the person who is visiting your company.]

Affiliation:
[Fill in the name of the company or organization the individual represents.]

Place Visited:
[Fill in your company's name and the address of the location visited.]

Date Visited:
[Fill in the date or dates of the visit.]

2. Access to Confidential Information

Fill in your company's name.

3. Definition of Confidential Information

This clause defines what information the visitor must keep confidential. You have the option of listing any specific items in section 2(d).

4. Obligation to Keep Trade Secrets Confidential

This clause spells out the visitor's confidentiality obligations. There's nothing to fill in here.

5. Successors

This clause makes the confidentiality obligations binding on the visitor even if the company is sold or goes out of business.

6. Entire Agreement

This clause makes clear that the agreement can't be changed except by a writing signed by the parties. There's nothing to fill in here.

7. Signature

Each visitor should sign and date the agreement, preferably before gaining access to trade secrets.

H. Interview Nondisclosure Agreement

You may end up divulging trade secrets when interviewing prospective employees, especially for sensitive jobs. Any person you hire should be required to sign an employee NDA (or an employment agreement containing a nondisclosure provision). But, of course, the interviewees you don't hire won't be signing an employment NDA or employment agreement. For this reason, have applicants for sensitive positions sign a simple nondisclosure agreement at the beginning of a job interview.

 This agreement may be found on the CD-ROM. Call up the agreement on your computer and read it along with the following discussion, which explains the wording of the form and describes what information you'll need to insert.

1. Company Name

Fill in your company's name and the name of the job applicant.

2. Job

Describe the position or projects the applicant is being interviewed for.

3. Possible Disclosure of Confidential Information

This just states that the applicant might learn trade secrets during the interviewing process. There is nothing to fill in.

4. Definition of Confidential Information

This describes the kinds of material the applicant might see that you consider trade secrets. Fill in Section (d) if the information to be disclosed is not listed elsewhere in this section.

5. Obligation to Keep Trade Secrets Confidential

This informs the applicant that he or she cannot disclose the information.

6. Other Companies' Trade Secrets

Here, the applicant promises not to reveal confidential information from any other company during the interview or at another time.

7. Signatures

See Chapter 1 for details on signatures. ■

Software and Internet Patents

This chapter provides the briefest possible overview of the subject of software and Internet patents. This is an extremely complex area of the law. If you're serious about obtaining a patent, it's highly advisable to seek the assistance of a patent lawyer. But reading this chapter first will help you decide whether to apply for a patent and, if you do, communicate intelligently with your lawyer.

A. Patent Basics

Following is a brief overview of patent law. For more information about patents, refer to either *Nolo's Patents for Beginners,* by David Pressman and Richard Stim (Nolo), or *Patent It Yourself*, by David Pressman (Nolo).

1. What Is a Patent?

A patent is a document issued by the U.S. Patent and Trademark Office (PTO) that grants a monopoly for a limited period of time on the use and development of an invention which the PTO finds to qualify for patent protection. For most patents, this right lasts approximately 17 to 18 years. The monopoly right conferred by a patent extends throughout the United States and its territories and possessions. It's also possible to obtain patents in most foreign countries.

The U.S. Patent and Trademark Office (PTO) issues three different kinds of patents: utility patents, design patents, and plant patents.

- Utility patents are inventions that have some type of usefulness—this includes virtually all software and Internet patents.
- Design patents protect a device's ornamental characteristics—some design patents have been obtained to protect computer screen icons.
- Plant patents protect certain types of plants and obviously have no bearing on software or Internet patents.

2. Types of Inventions That Can Be Patented

Most inventions must pass several basic tests to qualify for a patent:

- The invention must fall within one or more of five statutory classes of inventions (that is, it must be "statutory subject matter").
- The invention must have some utility, no matter how trivial.
- The invention must be novel (this means that it must have one or more new main elements).
- The invention must be nonobvious (a significant development) to somebody positioned to understand the technical field of the invention.

a. Statutory subject matter

To qualify for a utility patent an invention must be:

- a process or method of getting something useful done (such as a genetic engineering procedure, a manufacturing technique, or computer software)
- a machine (usually something with moving parts or circuitry, such as a cigarette lighter, sewage treatment system, laser, or photocopier)
- an article of manufacture (such as an eraser, tire, transistor, or hand tool)
- a composition of matter (such as a chemical composition, drug, soap, or genetically altered life form), or
- an improvement of an invention that fits within one of the first four categories.

Often, an invention will fall into more than one category. For example, computer software can usually be described both as a process (the steps that it takes to make the computer do something) and as a machine (a device that takes information from an input device and moves it to an output device). Regardless of the number of categories a particular invention falls under, only one utility patent may be issued on it.

b. Utility

Patents may issue on inventions that have some type of usefulness (utility), even if the use is humorous, such as a musical condom or a motorized spaghetti fork. However, the invention must work—at least in theory. For this reason, no patent has ever issued on a perpetual motion machine (a device that does more work than the energy supplied to it).

c. Novelty

In the context of a patent application, an invention is considered to be novel when it is different from all previous inventions (called "prior art") in one or more of its basic elements. When deciding whether an invention is novel for purposes of issuing a patent, the PTO will consider all prior art that existed as of the date the inventor files a patent application on the invention, or if necessary, as of the date the inventor can prove he or she first built and tested the invention, or conceived the invention and then followed up with diligence by building and testing it or filing a patent application. An invention will flunk the novelty test if it was described in a published document or put to public use more than one year prior to the date the patent application was filed (this is known as the one-year rule).

d. Nonobviousness

In addition to being novel, an invention must be nonobvious to qualify for a patent. An invention is considered nonobvious if someone who is skilled in the particular field of the invention would view it as an unexpected or surprising development. In deciding whether an invention is nonobvious, the PTO may consider all previous developments in the field (called "prior art") that existed when the invention was conceived. As a general rule, an invention is considered nonobvious when it does one of the following:

- solves a problem that people in the field have been trying to solve for some time
- does something significantly faster than was previously possible, or
- performs a function that could not be performed before.

3. How to Obtain a Patent

To obtain patent protection, an inventor must file an application (with the appropriate filing fees) and be issued a patent. To apply for a U.S. patent, the inventor must file an application with a branch of the U.S. Department of Commerce, known as the U.S. Patent and Trademark Office (PTO). A U.S. patent application typically consists of:

- an explanation of why the invention is different from all previous and similar developments (the "prior art")
- a detailed description of the structure and operation of the invention (called a patent specification) that teaches how to build and use the invention
- a precise description of the aspects of the invention to be covered by the patent (called the patent claims)
- all drawings that are necessary to fully explain the specification and claims

- a statement under oath that the information in the application is true, and
- the filing fee.

In addition, small inventors often include a declaration asking for a reduction in the filing fee.

Provisional Patent Applications

Often inventors want to have a patent application on file when they go out to show their invention to prospective manufacturers, because it will discourage rip-offs. Also, inventors like to get their invention on record as early as possible in case someone else comes up with the same invention. To accomplish both these goals an inventor may file what is known as a Provisional Patent Application (PPA). The PPA need only contain a complete description of the structure and operation of an invention and any drawings that are necessary to understand it—it need not contain claims, formal drawings, a Patent Application Declaration (a statement under penalty of perjury that everything in the application is true), or an Information Disclosure Statement (a statement of all prior art known to the applicant).

---

a. Patent examinations

When the PTO receives an application, a patent examiner is assigned to it. Because a patent grants the inventor a monopoly on the invention for a relatively long period of time (14 years for design patents and 17-18 years for utility patents), patent applications are rigorously examined. Typically the application process takes between one and three years.

The examiner is responsible for deciding whether the application meets all technical requirements, whether the invention qualifies for a patent, and, assuming it does, what the scope of the patent should be. Typically, a patent application travels back and forth between the applicant and the patent examiner until an agreement is reached. Then, the applicant pays a patent issue fee and receives an official copy of the patent, and the PTO issues a patent deed.

To keep a patent in effect, three additional fees must be paid over the life of the patent. At present, the total patent fee for a small inventor, from application to issue to expiration, is well over $3,000. For large corporations, it is twice this amount.

b. Multiple applications for the same invention

If the patent examiner discovers that another pending application involves the same invention, and that both inventions appear to qualify for a patent, the patent examiner will declare that a conflict (called an interference) exists between the two applications. In that event, a hearing is held to determine who is entitled to the patent.

Who gets the patent depends on such variables as who first conceived of the invention and worked on it diligently, who first built and tested the invention, and who filed the first provisional or regular patent application. Because of the possibility of a patent interference, it is wise to document all invention-related activities in a signed and witnessed inventor's notebook, so that you can later prove the date the invention was conceived and the efforts taken to build and test the invention or quickly file a patent application.

4. Enforcing a Patent

Should you receive a software or Internet-based patent, your program and its unique, novel approach cannot be used by others without your permission. In other words, independent creation, which is sufficient to beat a claim that a copyright or trade secret has been infringed, isn't good enough to defend against a charge of patent infringement. As long as you patent it first, it's yours and yours alone for approximately 17-18 years.

However, patents are not self-enforcing; and the U.S. government will not help you enforce yours. Patents are a little like hunting licenses. If someone uses your invention as described in your patent without your permission you have the right to sue them in federal court. Patent suits are among the most expensive of all forms of litigation. However, the potential rewards can be enormous if a patent suit is successful (treble damages may be recovered in the case of willful infringement).

It is very common for a company or person accused of patent infringement to agree to license (pay for the use of) the invention rather than face the uncertainties and expenses of litigation. However, some accused infringers elect to fight and seek to have the patent overturned in court. Many patent experts believe that the Patent Office has issued a number of software and Internet-related patents that should have been rejected on grounds of failure to satisfy the nonobviousness test. Such patents are particularly likely to be subject to court challenge.

5. Patent Duration and Expiration

Patent protection usually ends when the patent expires. For utility patents, the statutory period is 20 years after the date of filing of the regular patent application. Thus, for example, if it takes two to three years to obtain a patent after the application is filed, you would have 17-18 years of effective patent protection. For design patents, the statutory period is 14 years from date of issuance.

A patent may expire if its owner fails to pay required maintenance fees. Usually this occurs because attempts to commercially exploit the underlying invention have failed and the patent owner chooses not to throw good money after bad.

Finally, patent protection will end if a patent is found to be invalid. This may happen if someone shows that the patent application was insufficient, that the applicant committed fraud on the PTO (usually by lying about or failing to disclose the applicant's knowledge about prior art that would legally preclude issuance of the patent), or that the inventor engaged in illegal conduct when using the patent —such as conspiring with a patent licensee to exclude other companies from competing with them.

Once a patent has expired for any reason, the invention described by the patent falls into the public domain: it can be used by anyone without permission from the owner of the expired patent. The basic technologies underlying television and personal computers are good examples of valuable inventions that are no longer covered by in-force patents.

B. Patents for Software

Ten or 15 years ago there was no apparent reason for a software developer to worry about software patents. Only a tiny number of highly specialized patents had ever been issued on software innovations. The general legal view was that software innovations weren't patentable, because software technology itself did not appear to fit comfortably within any of the patentable subject matter groups discussed in Section A2 above. All this has changed. Thousands of software and software-related patents have now been issued and thousands more are in the application stage.

1. Brief History of Software Patents

When first faced with applications for patents on software-based inventions in the 1950s, the United States Patent and Trademark Office (PTO) routinely rejected the applications on the grounds that software consists of mathematical algorithms (that is, a series of mathematical relationships, like differential equations). Mathematical algorithms were considered a law of nature, or "pure thought." Patents cannot be granted for a law of nature or mental process. For example, no one can legally have a patent on the use of "1 + 1 = 2" because it would create too huge (and fundamental) a monopoly. Thus, software by itself was considered to be nonpatentable.

However, in 1981 the Supreme Court held that an algorithm may be patentable if it works in connection with a specific apparatus—that is, a physical structure of some type—and is described that way in the patent claims (the precise statements in the patent application that describe the parameters of the invention). (*Diamond v. Diehr*, 450 U.S. 171 (1981).)

The *Diamond v. Diehr* decision cleared the way for patentability of software-based inventions. Nevertheless, there continued to be great controversy and uncertainty about when software could be patented. The PTO in particular, was opposed to software patents and adopted a restrictive view of what software was patentable.

All this changed in July 1998, when a federal court upheld a patent for a computer program used to calculate the net asset value of mutual funds. (*State Street Bank & Trust Co. v. Signal Financial Group, Inc.,* 149 F.3d 1368 (Fed. Cir. 1998) *cert. denied* 119 S.Ct. 851 (1999).) The court ruled that patent laws were intended to protect any method, whether or not it required the aid of a computer, so long as it produced a "useful, concrete and tangible result." The court found that software—even if it merely manipulates numbers—produces something tangible. Thus with one stroke, the court legitimized both software patents and methods of doing business (see Section C below). In the six months following the ruling, patent filings for software/Internet business methods increased by 40%.

2. When Software Is Patentable

Software itself—that is, computer code by itself—is not considered statutory subject matter. In other words, it's not patentable. For this reason, patents don't issue on software itself; rather, they issue on inventions that use software to produce a useful result—that is, "software-based" inventions. The term "software patent" is somewhat confusingly used to describe these software-based inventions.

This useful result can occur outside the computer. These inventions often involve software connected to and running hardware components. The essence of these inventions is found in the functional combination of their software and hardware.

> **EXAMPLE:** A software program calculates the time needed to cure a certain type of rubber in a certain type of mold, and then directs the mold to open when the curing is completed.

Patents are also obtainable for software-based inventions that involve feeding information into a computer and acting on that information so as to transform it into instructions that produce a specific action by the computer—or by a machine linked to the computer—that in turn produces a useful result.

> **EXAMPLE:** Raw information from a heart monitoring device is fed into a

computer. The software program analyzes the information according to a set of principles and causes the results of this analysis to be displayed in a format that shows whether the person is at risk for a heart attack.

Following are several examples of software-based inventions (and their patent numbers) that have received patents. These software inventions perform the following functions:

- translates between natural languages (U.S. Pat. No. 4,502,128)
- determines boundaries of graphic regions on a computer screen (U.S. Pat. No. 4,788,438)
- governs removable menu windows on a computer screen (U.S. Pat. No. 4,931,783)
- generates and overlays graphic windows for multiple active program storage areas in the computer (U.S. Pat. No. 4,555,775)
- qualifies and sorts file record data in a computer (U.S. Pat. No. 4,510,567)
- operates a system that valuates stocks, bonds, and other securities (U.S. Pat. No. 4,334,270).

Design Patents

In some instances, software inventors can apply for what is known as a design patent. A design patent provides a 14-year monopoly to industrial designs that have no functional use. That is, contrary to the usefulness rule discussed just above, designs covered by design patents must be purely ornamental.

C. Internet Business Method Patents

Since 1998, an increasing number of patents have been issued to software and Internet companies that have devised novel ways of doing business—for example, new online ordering processes or a unique Internet advertising scheme. These patents, which usually combine software with business methodology, are commonly referred to as Internet patents or business method patents. These patents are important for software and Web developers because any company that develops or acquires such a patent can stop others from using the patented business method for approximately 17-18 years. And, of course, the owner of the patent can exploit it by licensing the method—that is, charging a fee for others to use it.

EXAMPLE: Amazon.com devised a method for expediting online orders known as the "1-Click" system. The method allows a repeat customer to bypass address and credit card data entry forms, because Amazon can access that information directly from the customer's computer. Amazon was granted a patent on this business method in September 1999 (U.S. Pat. No. 5,960,411).

1. Business Methods Patents Are Valid

Traditionally, the PTO rarely granted business method patents, claiming that a process could not be patented if it was simply an abstract idea, something the PTO believed described most business methods. Similarly, software patents were usually held to be unpatentable by the PTO and the courts, based on the view that they were unprotectible algorithms. However, all this changed when a federal court ruled in the *State Street* case (see Section B1, above) that a business method was patentable if it produces a useful, concrete, and tangible result.

The *State Street* case opened the way for Internet business method patents, and the PTO created a new classification for applications: "Data processing: financial, business practice, management or cost/price determination."

Since the *State Street* case, patents have been issued for:

- an online shopping rewards program, referred to as the "ClickReward" (U.S. Pat. No. 5,774,870)
- a system that provides financial incentives for citizens to view political messages on the Internet (U.S. Pat. No. 5,855,008)
- an online auction system by which consumers name the price they are willing to pay and the first willing seller gets the sale (also known as "name your price" or as a "reverse auction" (U.S. Pat. No. 5,794,207), and
- a process that supposedly blocks the auction practices described in the previous patent (U.S. Pat. No. 5,845,265).

2. Legal Requirements for Getting a Business Method Patent

In order to qualify for patent protection, a business method must novel and nonobvious.

a. Novelty

A business method is considered novel when it is different from all previous methods—known in patentspeak as the "prior art"—in one or more of its essential elements. Prior art consists of:

- any published writing (including any patent) that was made publicly available either (1) before the date of invention, or (2) more than one year before the patent application is filed
- any U.S. patent that has a filing date earlier than the earliest date of invention
- any relevant method or process (whether described in writing or not) existing publicly before the method was conceived, or
- any public or commercial use, sale, or knowledge of the business method more than one year before the patent application is filed.

The PTO will consider all prior art, whether Internet-related or not. As noted, an Internet method will flunk the novelty test if it was described in a published document or put to public use more than one year before the patent application was filed. For this reason, a business that is seeking to acquire a patent must research the prior art and promptly file its patent application or it risks losing valuable patent rights.

b. Nonobviousness

Meeting the nonobviousness requirement turns on whether or not the differences between the business method subject to the patent application and the prior art would be obvious to someone with ordi-

nary skill in the field of the business. Or put another way, whether or not the method provides a new or unexpected result.

> **EXAMPLE:** An economist devised a method of avoiding taxes by using a credit card to borrow money from a 401(k) fund. The method did not exist previously and differed substantially from previous methods of avoiding taxes. Since the method was new and was not obvious to accountants or tax experts, the economist acquired a patent (U.S. Pat. No. 5,206,803).

c. Determining who gets a business method patent

What happens if a competing business claims that it was already using the particular method that is the subject of a patent application? If Business A files for a business method patent, but Business B can show that it was using the method publicly more than a year prior to the filing, Business B can thwart the patent application or, if necessary, invalidate the patent later. The key is that Business B's use of the method must have been public. If Business B used the method confidentially, the patent will be issued to Business A. However, under a 1999 amendment to the patent law, Business B retains the right to continue using the method without liability for infringement.

EXAMPLE: Company A has been using a business accounting method for years but has never publicly disclosed it. Company B independently develops the method and obtains a patent on it. Company B sues Company A. Under the amendment to the patent law, Company A has not infringed the patent.

If Company A had been using the method publicly for more than year before the patent application was filed, Company B's patent would be invalidated.

3. Using Internet Patents as a Sword or Shield

Internet patents can be used offensively against a major competitor or they can be used defensively as a bargaining chip against an aggressive competitor who threatens to sue based on one of its patents. Experience has shown that rivals are less likely to go to court when they know that their opponent can also wield a patent. Such competitors often prefer to reach a truce under which each company cross-licenses the other's patents.

EXAMPLE: Company A and Company B both sell concert tickets online, including services for exchanging un-

wanted tickets and earning rewards for frequent purchases. Company A holds a patent on a method of exchanging concert tickets. Company B has a patent on a method of offering rewards to concert promoters for group ticket purchases. Although each company believes the other is infringing its patent, neither seeks to enforce its rights in court, fearing that the other is almost sure to file a lawsuit in response. Instead, after a few months of legal posturing, Company A and B agree to share or "cross-license" their technology.

4. Challenging a Business Method Patent

There are two ways to challenge business method patents after they are granted. A disgruntled competitor can sue in federal court or can institute a procedure in the PTO known as a reexamination.

Filing a lawsuit can be expensive (often costing hundreds of thousand dollars and sometimes running into the millions) but some companies choose to fight it out in the hopes that they can invalidate the adversary's business method patent. The challenging party normally seeks to prove the patented process was not novel or was obvious, and therefore that the PTO shouldn't have issued the patent. This is usually done by demonstrating that the patent examiner overlooked important prior art.

Initiating a reexamination procedure with the PTO can also invalidate a patent. The PTO will reconsider the patent in light of recently uncovered prior art. A reexamination is not as costly as litigation. But if reexamination fails and the patent survives, it will be "strengthened" to the extent that others will be less likely to challenge it and the patent owner will feel more confident enforcing it.

The result of many current PTO and court challenges may be that at least some recent business method patents will be invalidated. One of the most vocal critics of business method patents, Gregory Aharonian of the Internet Patent News Service (www.bustpatents.com), provides an archive of questionable business method and software patents.

D. Should You Apply for a Software or Internet Patent?

The fact that your software or Internet business method may qualify for a patent doesn't necessarily mean that you should apply for one. There are several reasons to hesitate.

1. By the Time You Get a Patent Your Invention May Be Worthless

It generally takes two to three years to obtain a software or business-method patent. Due to the incredible pace of change in the software and Internet industries, your invention may be obsolete and worthless by the time you receive your patent. For a patent to add real value to your business, you need to feel confident that the invention you are patenting will not soon be outdated by newer technology.

2. Software and Internet Patents Are Suspect

Because the United States Patent and Trademark Office (PTO) has had problems deciding what kinds of software and Internet business methods really are patentable, patents on these inventions are suspect. The fact that the PTO issues a patent doesn't mean the patent is valid. It only means that a particular examiner has decided that a patent should issue on your invention. If you should later go to court to enforce the patent, the infringer may be able to successfully prove that the patent never should have issued in the first place. In other words, a judge can (and often does) second-guess the patent examiner and—assuming your adversary appeals—an appellate judge can second-guess the first judge.

This second-guessing routine, which is potentially a problem for all patents, is especially troublesome for software and Internet business methods patents. This is primarily because the PTO lacks both sufficient personnel who are qualified to examine software-related applications and comprehensive information about previous software developments (the prior art in this particular field).

Simply, it's well known that many software and Internet business method patents have been and continue to be improperly issued. The fact that you get such a patent may be little more than an invitation to spend piles of money on lawyers and courts in an unsuccessful effort to enforce it against attacks on its validity.

3. Only the Powerful (or Very Determined) Can Play the Patent Game

Seeking and then enforcing a patent can cost a bundle. The cost depends on several factors, including the subject matter of the patent, the complexity of the examination process, and lawyer's fees. Unless you do it yourself—in which case the costs are much reduced—you can expect to pay between $3,000 and $15,000 to acquire a software or Internet business method patent. After a patent is issued, the owner must pay maintenance fees to the PTO after 3.5, 7.5, and 11.5 years. Of course, if the patent is challenged—and many are—the costs can skyrocket.

Therefore you will want to make a cost-benefit analysis, weighing the costs of obtaining and maintaining the patent over its up to 17-18-year life against the probability that you really will be able to commercially profit from it.

As a general rule, seeking a software or Internet business method patent is unwise unless you are reasonably sure that your invention deserves a patent and at least one of the following is true:

- You are economically strong enough to fund patent litigation should the need for it arise (patent litigation is hellishly expensive because you must hire lawyers—commonly in excess of $100,000).

- You are stubborn and savvy enough to take time to understand how the patent system works and willing to do some or all of your own legal work (a good-sized hill to climb, but others have done it, with huge rewards).

- The innovation is sufficiently important to another company to cause it to come to terms with you if you have the patent (by purchasing your patent rights or paying you for a license to use the innovation).

- You own a lot of patents and are a big enough player in the industry to wheel and deal with other patent holders by trading them the right to use your patents in exchange for your being able to use theirs.

- You know your idea will change the course of a particular field, and without a patent on it you risk forfeiting the credit and profit from the idea to others, who may then obtain their own patent and freeze you out.
- You think the patent will impress prospective financial backers that your business really is special (venture capitalists have been known to tell start-ups to come back and see them after they have obtained a patent).
- You are looking ahead to possibly selling your business and want to increase its value.

4. What to Do If You Want to Apply for a Software or Internet Patent

As the above discussion illustrates, the subject of software and Internet business method patents is an exceedingly complex one, beyond the competence of most lawyers, let alone laypeople. There are two things you should do if you're really serious about obtaining a software-based patent:

- Obtain a copy of *Nolo's Patents for Beginners,* by David Pressman and Richard Stim (Nolo), or *Patent It Yourself,* by David Pressman (Nolo). This will give you an excellent grounding in the entire patent pro-

cess and help you deal with your patent attorney.

- Seek out a patent attorney who has not only applied for software or Internet business method patents, but has actually obtained them. Most patent attorneys have no experience with such patents—make sure you find one who does. Your attorney will prepare the patent application and deal with the PTO examiner.

Beware of the One-Year Rule.
Under what is called the one-year rule, an invention must be filed within one year of the time it is first offered for sale or commercially or publicly used or described. Otherwise, the invention will be considered no longer novel at the time the application is filed and therefore unpatentable. File your patent application as soon as possible but in any event no later than one year after the invention has become known to the public in some way. As a general rule, the limited testing of software by the public in a structured beta test program should not start the one-year period running. But the year period might start running if the beta test release were widespread enough, or if one of the testers posted it on a widely accessed bulletin board or website and as a result it became well known. In any event, you are always better off to assume the worst and get your patent application in as soon as possible.

E. Avoiding Patent Violations (Infringement)

Determining whether someone has infringed a patent depends on a close examination of the patent "claims," a brief statement in the body of the patent application that defines the scope of the business method. You can read claims for any U.S. patent by visiting the PTO website (www.uspto.gov) and searching the patent database by name, subject matter, or other criteria.

Think of the claims as the boundaries of the patent owner's rights. Or put another way, if the elements or steps in your business method match all of the elements or steps elaborated in someone else's patent claims, then you have infringed their patent. Even if the other owner's claims don't literally match your business method, a court may still find infringement if the methods are very similar. In doing this, courts will apply what's known as the "doctrine of equivalents." This means if the steps in the patent and the allegedly infringing software or business method are sufficiently alike, a court will find that infringement has occurred. ■

Trademarks and Domain Names

This chapter provides a brief overview of what you need to know about trademarks and Internet domain names—which often double as trademarks. But for step-by-step guidance on all important aspects of selecting and protecting a trademark, turn to *Trademark: Legal Care for Your Business & Product Name*, by Stephen Elias (Nolo). For detailed guidance on obtaining a domain name, see *Domain Names: How to Choose & Protect a Great Name for Your Website*, by Stephen Elias and Patricia Gima (Nolo).

A. What Are Trademarks and Service Marks?

A trademark is a distinctive word, phrase, logo, graphic symbol, or other device that is used to identify the source of a product and to distinguish a manufacturer's or merchant's products from anyone else's. Some examples are IBM computers and Microsoft software.

A service mark fulfills the same function as a trademark, but for a company's services rather than a particular product. For example, America Online provides a service and AOL is therefore a service mark, as is Amazon.com. The same law applies to both service marks and trademarks, and in this chapter we use the term trademark to refer to both types of marks.

In the trademark context, "distinctive" means unique enough to reasonably serve as an identifier of an underlying product or service in the marketplace. The more distinctive a trademark is, the more legal protection it will receive from the courts and the better job it will do of identifying the goods or services it's being used for.

A trademark can be more than just a brand name or logo. It can include other nonfunctional but distinctive aspects of a product or service that tend to promote and distinguish it in the marketplace, such as shapes, letters, numbers, sounds, smells, or colors.

Each state has it own set of laws establishing when and how trademarks can be protected. There is also a federal trademark law called the Lanham Act (15 U.S.C. §§ 1050 et seq.), which applies in all 50 states. Generally, state trademark laws are relied upon for marks used only within one particular state, while the Lanham Act is used to protect marks for products that are sold in more than one state or across territorial or national borders.

1. Trade Names

A trade name is the formal name of a business or other organization. For example, Apple Computer Inc. and eBay, Inc., are trade names. A trade name is used to identify a business for such purposes as opening bank accounts, paying taxes, ordering supplies, filing lawsuits, and so on. However, a trade name may become a trademark when it is used to identify individual products (or services) sold in the marketplace. Businesses often use shortened versions of their trade names as all or part of a trademark; a good example is the trademark Lotus 1-2-3.

2. Trademarks Compared With Copyrights and Patents

Trademarks coexist with copyrights and patents and may protect different aspects of the same work.

a. Copyright law

Copyright law and trademark law most commonly intersect in advertising copy. The trademark laws protect the product or service name or logo, any distinctive slogans used in the advertising, and the distinctive features associated with the name or logo, such as its color or lettering style. The copyright laws protect any additional literal expression that the ad contains, such as the artwork and overall composition of the ad. Copyright law does not protect names, titles, or short phrases; these are covered by trademark law.

Copyright law and trademark law also meet on occasion in regard to graphic designs used as logos. Trademark law protects the aspect of the logo that is used as a trademark, while copyright law protects the creativity in the design. This means that a similar design can't be used as a trademark by anyone else when customer confusion would result (trademark law), and even absent customer confusion the identical design can't be used without the design owner's permission (copyright law).

b. Patent law

Trademarks or service marks consisting of words, logos, or slogans are not patentable no matter how creative they are. However, it is sometimes possible to get a design patent on the ornamental aspects of a functional device as long as the ornamental aspects are merged with—that is, inseparable from—the device itself. In some situations the feature that is covered by the design patent may also be protected as trade dress (see Section H). See Chapter 9 for a detailed discussion of patents.

B. Trademark Ownership

For most purposes, the "owner" of a trademark doesn't have a total monopoly on the use of the mark. Rather, the owner has the legal right to prevent others from using the mark in such a way as to cause confusion about the products or services the owner provides, or about their origins. However, if the trademark is famous enough, the owner can prevent other uses even if no customer confusion would result. (See Section G1.)

As a general rule, the first user of a trademark owns it. There are two ways to qualify as a first user:

- by being the first to actually use the trademark on products or to market a service
- by applying to register the trademark on the federal principal trademark register (see Section D4) on the grounds that you intend to use it in the future (if you do actually use it later, your date of first use will be considered to be the date of your application).

The fact that a mark is not registered or that a registration is canceled or not renewed does not affect the basic ownership of the mark, which is primarily based on use. However, additional remedies provided by federal registration will not be available to the owner if an infringement occurs.

There is no outside time limit on how long trademark ownership can last. However, ownership rights end if a mark is abandoned. Abandonment commonly occurs when:

- a mark is not used over an extended period of time
- a mark's owner fails to protest the unauthorized use of the mark by others, or

- a mark's owner authorizes others' use of the mark without adequate supervision of how it is used.

In each of these instances, the connection between the mark and the product or service it was originally intended to identify may become so weak that the mark no longer is entitled to protection.

Ownership of a mark also ceases if the mark becomes generic—that is, the mark becomes so widely used as a synonym for the underlying product or service that it no longer is able to distinguish one product or service from another. (See Section C1.)

C. Selecting a Trademark

Not all trademarks are treated equally by the law. The best trademarks are "distinctive"—that is, they stand out in a customer's mind because they are inherently memorable. The more distinctive a trademark is, the "stronger" it will be and the more legal protection it will receive. Less distinctive marks are "weak" and may be entitled to little or no legal protection. For example, marks that describe the attributes of the product or service or its geographic locations are weak. However, a weak mark can become strong with sufficient sales and advertising. When selecting a trademark, it's advisable to choose a strong mark.

1. Inherently Distinctive Marks

Arbitrary and fanciful marks are deemed to be very strong marks. Arbitrary marks consist of common words used in an unexpected or arbitrary way so that their normal meaning has nothing to do with the nature of the product or service they identify. For example, the trademark *Lotus 1-2-3* in no way describes any aspect of a computer spreadsheet program. Similarly, the trademark *Yahoo* does not describe any aspect of a Web portal. Other examples of arbitrary marks include *Peachtree* software and *Apple* computer.

Fanciful or coined words are words made up solely to serve as trademarks. Examples include the marks *eBay*, *Intel*, and *Flooz*.

Suggestive marks are also inherently distinctive. A suggestive mark indirectly describes the product it identifies but stays away from literal descriptiveness. That is, the consumer must engage in a mental process, to associate the mark with the product it identifies. For example, the trademark *WordPerfect* indirectly suggests word processing. *PageMaker* indirectly suggests desktop publishing. *CrossTalk* suggests communication between different computers.

2. Descriptive Marks

Descriptive marks are initially considered to be weak and not distinctive. They are not deserving of much, if any, judicial protection unless they acquire a "secondary meaning"—that is, become associated with a product in the public's mind through long and continuous use.

There are three basic types of descriptive marks:

- Marks that directly describe the nature or characteristics of the product they identify—for example, the mark *Quick Mail* used for an electronic mail program, *Website Maker* for an html editor, *ChessMaster* for a computer chess game.
- Marks that describe the geographic location from which the product emanates—for example, *Oregon* Web Development.
- Marks consisting primarily of a person's last name—for example, *Norton* Utilities.

A mark that is in continuous and exclusive use by its owner for a five-year period is presumed to have acquired secondary meaning and qualifies for federal registration as a distinctive mark. It is also possible to demonstrate secondary meaning by proving sufficient sales and advertising in a period shorter than five years.

EXAMPLE 1: Pinnacle Software, Inc., develops and markets a desktop publishing program called "Self-Publisher." This name is clearly descriptive of the nature of the product. However, over time, and with the help of an advertising campaign, the name loses its sole meaning as a description and instead becomes associated with the Pinnacle program.

EXAMPLE 2: Norton Utilities (named after Peter Norton), which started out as a descriptive mark, has acquired a secondary meaning and is distinctive.

3. Generic Marks

A generic term is a word or symbol that is commonly used to describe an entire category or class of products or services, rather than to distinguish one product or service from another. Generic terms are in the public domain and cannot be registered or enforced under the trademark laws. Words and phrases that are inherently generic in the software field undoubtedly include: "software," "computer," "CD-ROM," "mouse," "crt," "cpu," "floppy disk," "hard disk," "modem," "ROM," "RAM," "menu," "pull-down menu," "footprint," "laptop," and "icon." Generic words in the Internet field likely include "Web," "website," "HTML," "online," or "cyberspace."

D. Federal Trademark Registration

A trademark is federally registered by filing an application with the United States Patent and Trademark Office (PTO) in Washington, DC. The PTO keeps two lists of registered trademarks along with their owners, dates of registration, and other information. These lists are called the *Principal Register* and the *Supplemental Register*.

Registration is not mandatory; under both federal and state law, a company may obtain trademark rights in the parts of the country in which the mark is actually used. However, placement of a mark on the federal register (especially the *Principal Register*) provides important protections that make registration worthwhile. It is placement on this register that is usually meant by the phrase "federally registered."

1. Advantages of Registration

Placement of a mark on the *Principal Register* provides many important benefits. These include:

- The mark's owner is presumed to have the exclusive right to use the mark nationwide.
- Everyone in the country is presumed to know that the mark is already taken (even if they haven't actually heard of it).
- The trademark owner obtains the right to use the Registered symbol– ®—after the mark (see Section E).
- Anyone who begins using a confusingly similar mark after the mark has been registered will be deemed a willful infringer. This means that the

trademark owner can collect more damages in a lawsuit than if the mark were not registered.

- The trademark owner obtains the right to make the mark "incontestable" by keeping it in continuous use for five years. This substantially reduces others' ability to legally challenge the mark on grounds it's insufficiently distinctive to warrant protection.

2. Marks Qualifying for Registration on the *Principal Register*

To qualify for registration on the *Principal Register*, a mark must actually be used in commerce (but not solely within one state's borders) and be sufficiently distinctive to reasonably operate as a product identifier.

However, a mark will not qualify for registration on the *Principal Register* if it is:

- confusingly similar to an existing federally registered trademark
- consists primarily of a surname or geographical name, unless the mark has become well known over time or unless the geographical name is used in an arbitrary or evocative way
- the name of a living person without his or her consent, the U.S. flag, or other government insignias.

3. How to Register

The registration process involves filling out a simple application, paying an application fee ($335, current in 2004), and being willing to work with an official of the PTO to correct any errors that he or she finds in the application. Registration can be accomplished online through the PTO's website at www.uspto.gov.

4. Intent-to-Use Registration

If you seriously intend to use a trademark on a product in the near future, you can reserve the right to use the mark by filing an intent-to-use registration. If the mark is approved, you have six months to actually use the mark on a product sold to the public and file papers with the PTO describing the use (with an accompanying $100 fee). If necessary, this period may be increased by five additional six-month periods if you have a good explanation for each extension

You should promptly file an intent-to-use registration as soon as you have definitely selected a trademark for a forthcoming product. Your competitors are also trying to come up with good trademarks, and they may be considering using a mark similar to the one you want.

For step-by-step guidance on how to register a trademark, refer to *Trademark: Legal Care for Your Business & Product Name*, by Stephen Elias (Nolo).

E. Trademark Notice

The most commonly used notice for trademarks registered with the PTO is an "R" in a circle—®—but "Reg. U.S. Pat. & T.M. Off." may also be used. The "TM" superscript—(tm)—may be used to denote marks that have been registered on a state basis only or marks that are in use but which have not yet officially been registered by the PTO. Only marks that are federally registered can use the "®" symbol. Any business that uses a mark can place the "TM" symbol after it to publicly claim ownership of the mark. The "TM" mark has no legal significance.

F. Trademark Searches

A mark you think will be good for your product or service could already be in use by someone else. If your mark is confusingly similar to one already in use, its owner may be able to sue you for trademark infringement and get you to change it and even pay damages. (See Section G.) Obviously, you do not want to spend time and money marketing and advertising a new mark, only to discover that it infringes on another preexisting mark and must be changed. To avoid this you should do a trademark search or hire someone to do a search for you.

For more on trademark searches, refer to *Trademark: Legal Care for Your Business & Product Name*, by Stephen Elias (Nolo).

A trademark search is a systematic hunt for the existence of any registered or unregistered trademark or service mark that:

- is the same or similar to a mark proposed for use by the business initiating the search
- is being used anywhere in the country (or world if the proposed mark is to be used internationally), and
- is being used in a context that would likely result in customer confusion if the proposed mark is also put into use.

1. Hiring a Trademark Search Firm

Next to hiring a trademark attorney, paying a trademark search firm is the most expensive means of clearing your mark. To initiate a commercial search, call the search company and tell them the name you want searched. Typically, you won't see a written agreement. And the search service won't guarantee the results—in fact, it will specifically disclaim any guarantee. The following three companies are commonly used for professional trademark searches:

- *Thomson & Thomson*, (www.thomson
  -thomson.com), 500 Victory Road,
  North Quincy, MA 02171-1545; 800-
  692-8833
- *CCH Coresearch Corporation*, (www
  .cch-coresearch.com), 800-732-7241
- *Sunnyvale Center on Innovation,
  Invention and Ideas* (Sc[i]³)—pro-
  nounced Sigh-Cubed), (www.sci3
  .com), 665 W. Olive Avenue, Sunnyvale, CA 94086; 408-730-7300.

The last company mentioned—Sc[i]³—
is especially attractive because it's affiliated with the USPTO and provides lower
prices than most other searching companies. As of 2004, Sc[i]³ charged $199 for a
complete online analytical search (including state and federal trademark registers
and common law sources). As with most
trademark search firms, Sc[i]³ doesn't interpret its results; it leaves that to you.

2. Using the Internet to Do Your Own Trademark Search

The PTO maintains a trademark database
called TESS that you can use for free
through the PTO's website (www.uspto
.gov). You can use TESS to compare your
proposed mark with registered trademarks and trademarks that are pending
registration. You'll get a list of the trademarks that meet your search parameters,
and information on how to contact the
owners of those trademarks. You'll also
learn how the trademark is being used
(on what products or for what services)
and what "international class" (category
of goods or services) the mark has been
assigned to by the trademark owner or
applicant. This will help you determine if
you can use the name without creating
the likelihood of customer confusion.

If you want to go beyond the information available at the USPTO site and perform your own high-end search on the
Internet, consider using Saegis at
www.thomson-thomson.com. Saegis is
the most comprehensive trademark
searching service. It provides access to
all state, federal, and international trademark databases, domain name databases, common law sources on the
Internet, and access to newly filed United
States federal trademark applications.
There's a fee for using the service.

You won't find a list, anywhere, of unregistered trademarks, but you can use
the Web to locate almost all the product
and service names that may qualify as unregistered trademarks. Use any of the numerous business directories on the Web—
for example, BigYellow.com, BigBook.com,
SuperPages.Com, Switchboard.com, or
YellowPages.com—and enter your preferred domain name. A Web search engine
may also yield helpful information.

3. Evaluating Your Search Results

A trademark search, whether you perform it yourself or hire a service to do it for you, is rarely conclusive. If you turn up trademarks that might conflict with yours, you need to decide if there'd be a likelihood of customer confusion. (See Section G1.) For additional peace of mind, you may want to review the results of your trademark search with a lawyer who specializes in intellectual property law, a branch of law that includes not only trademarks but also copyrights and patents.

G. Enforcing Trademark Rights

Depending on the strength of the mark and whether and where it has been registered, a trademark owner may be able to bring a court action to prevent others from using the same or similar marks on competing or related products. In some cases—known as dilution—a trademark owner may be able to bring a court action for using the mark on goods that are not competing or related.

1. Trademark Infringement

Trademark infringement occurs when an alleged infringer uses a mark that is likely to cause consumers to confuse the infringer's products with the trademark owner's products. A mark need not be identical to one already in use to infringe upon the owner's rights. If the proposed mark is similar enough to the earlier mark to risk confusing the average consumer, its use will constitute infringement.

Determining whether an average consumer might be confused is the key to deciding whether infringement exists. The determination depends primarily on whether the products or services involved are related (that is, sold through the same marketing channels), and, if so, whether the marks are sufficiently similar to create a likelihood of consumer confusion.

If a trademark owner is able to convince a court that infringement has occurred, he or she may be able to get the court to order the infringer to stop using the infringing mark and to pay monetary damages. Depending on whether the mark was registered, such damages may consist of the amount of the trademark owner's losses caused by the infringement or the infringer's profits. In cases of willful infringement (infringement occurring where the infringer is aware of the existence of the infringed mark—which is presumed if the infringed mark was on the federal principal trademark register), the courts may double or triple the damages award.

> **EXAMPLE:** AcmeSoft develops a computer program designed to automate the manufacture of widgets. AcmeSoft markets the program under the name

"Widgeteer." AcmeSoft registers this descriptive mark with the U.S. Patent & Trademark Office—having demonstrated sufficient sales to prove secondary meaning. One year later, Badd Software, Inc., markets a widget manufacturing program under the name "Widgeter." AcmeSoft sues Badd for using a mark confusingly similar to its own on a similar product. AcmeSoft is able to convince a judge that a substantial number of consumers are being confused by Badd's use of the "Widgeter" mark. The judge orders Badd to stop using the mark on its widget manufacturing programs and awards AcmeSoft damages for willful infringement.

A trademark owner must be assertive in enforcing its exclusive rights. Each time a mark is infringed upon it loses strength and distinctiveness and may eventually become so common as to lose its protection. (See Section C1, above.)

2. Trademark Dilution

Dilution means the lessening of the capacity of a famous mark to identify and distinguish goods or services, regardless of the presence or absence of:

- competition between the owner of the famous mark and other parties, or
- likelihood of confusion, mistake, or deception.

Dilution is therefore different than trademark infringement because trademark infringement always involves a probability of customer confusion, whereas dilution can occur even if customers wouldn't be misled. For example, if Fred starts selling a line of sex aids named "Microsoft," no consumer is likely to associate Fred's products with the original Microsoft. However, because Microsoft has become such a strong and famous mark, the use of the word on sex aids would definitely trivialize the original Microsoft mark (dilute its strength by tarnishing its reputation for quality or blurring its distinctiveness).

In January 1996, however, the Federal Trademark Dilution Act of 1995 was signed into law. (15 U.S.C. § 1125(c).) As with the state statutes, this new federal law applies only to famous marks, and provides primarily for injunctive relief (a court order requiring the infringing party to stop using the mark). However, if the famous mark's owner can prove the infringer "willfully intended to trade on the owner's reputation or to cause dilution of the famous mark," the court has discretion to award the owner attorney's fees and defendant's profits as well as actual damages.

H. Trade Dress Protection

The overall appearance and image of a product or its packaging is known as its "trade dress." Trade dress may include product shapes, designs, colors, advertising, and graphics, and, under the law, may be treated in the same manner as a more traditional trademark.

As with other types of trademarks, trade dress can be registered with the PTO, and receive protection from the federal courts. To receive protection:

- the trade dress must be inherently distinctive, unless it has acquired secondary meaning (becomes associated with a product in the public's mind through long and continuous use), and
- the subsequent use of the trade dress by another person or entity (called the junior user) must cause a likelihood of consumer confusion.

For trade dress to be considered inherently distinctive, one court has required that it "must be unusual and memorable, conceptually separable from the product and likely to serve primarily as a designator of origin of the product." (*Duraco Products Inc. v. Joy Plastic Enterprises Ltd.*, 40 F.3d 1431 (3d Cir. 1994).)

Functional aspects of trade dress cannot be protected under trademark law. Only designs, shapes, or other aspects of the product that were created strictly to promote the product or service are protectible trade dress.

Trade dress protection can be important to software and Web developers in three ways:

- It can be used to protect the distinctive design of the packaging used to sell software.
- Some trademark experts believe that trade dress protection may be available for graphical user interfaces (GUIs). As discussed in Chapter 6, little or no copyright protection is available for GUIs, so trade dress may be the only way to protect them. However, no court has yet ruled that such protection is available.
- Trade dress protection may also be available to protect the nonfunctional and distinctive design of Web pages.

This is a very complex area of trademark law. If you wish to seek trade dress protection for a GUI, you should obtain guidance from an experienced trademark lawyer.

I. Internet Domain Names

Domain names are like trade names in that they identify business entities. And like trade names, they can also function as trademarks or service marks by identifying the source of goods or products. Like trade names, domain names are registered. And, like trade names, a domain name registration does not guarantee trademark status. If you choose a domain name that is the same or similar to a business name that is already in use as a trademark anywhere in the country (in physical or virtual space), you are courting a trademark infringement dispute and possible lawsuit.

1. What Is a Domain Name?

Every website has what's called a domain name—a unique "address" that computers understand. You're already aware that a domain name looks like this: *www .webdevelopment.com*. The letters *www*, of course, stand for World Wide Web; those letters are automatically a part of every domain name. The middle part— *webdevelopment* in our example—is the unique name that you select and register for your business. In technical parlance, it's a second-level domain name or SLD.

The last part of a domain name— *.com*, in our example—is the top-level domain name or TLD. For up-to-date information about the status of the new TLDs, go to www.icann.org/tlds.

2. Registering a Domain Name

Before you can use a domain name, you need to register it with a domain name registry. Obtaining a domain name is easy and fairly automatic provided someone else hasn't already acquired it. You just provide some minimal information to the registry and pay a modest fee (approximately $35 per .com name). All of this can be done online, using a credit card.

There Are Two Kinds of Registration. We discuss two types of registration in this section: domain name registration and trademark registration. Every domain name must be registered with an approved domain name registry before the name can be used as an Internet address. That's *domain name registration*. A business may also want to register its domain name as a trademark or service mark with the U.S. Patent and Trademark Office (USPTO). That's referred to as *trademark registration*.

But locking up the domain name for yourself isn't enough. To avoid legal problems, you should be confident that no one else has trademark rights in the domain name before you start using it. Someone who claims such rights can invoke an arbitration procedure or take you to court to stop your use of the name.

a. Preliminary check for trademark conflicts

You don't want to risk losing an inspired domain name by waiting too long. But at least make a cursory check for possible trademark conflicts. You can do a preliminary trademark check online in less than 15 minutes. First, look at the U.S. Patent and Trademark Office site, www.uspto.gov. The site contains clear instructions for conducting your search. After you've visited the USPTO site, you might enter your preferred domain name in a regular search engine like www.google.com. If someone else is already using the name as a trademark, you can abandon it at this early stage and save yourself the registration or reservation fee.

b.   Securing your domain name

You can secure your domain name by registering it with a domain name registry. For an alphabetical list of approved registries, go to www.internic.net or www.icann.org. Fees can vary a bit among the registries, and some offer extra services such as email, website hosting, Web page design, or longer registration periods.

To check on the availability of a name, go to any approved registry and look for the search feature. If the name is taken, you can learn who owns it by checking at www.whois.net. This is helpful in case you want to offer to buy the name.

Once you register your domain name, it's yours. Normally, no one can stop you from using that domain name as your Internet address. But be aware that there are some exceptions to this general rule. The primary ones are:

- You forget to pay your domain name fees. You need to renew your domain name and pay a fee, either yearly or every two years. If you fail to pay, someone else can grab the name.
- You're a cybersquatter. You can lose the name if you registered it in bad faith—for example, with the intention of selling it to a company with a similar domain name or trademark.
- You're infringing on someone's trademark. If customers will be confused because your domain name is too close to another business's trademark, you may be forced to give up the name.
- You're diluting someone else's famous trademark. You're not allowed to blur someone else's trademark or tarnish it.

3.   Domain Names as Trademarks

As a general rule, domain names qualify as trademarks if they are being used to market underlying products or services being offered on the website. Domain names probably will be treated like any other mark in that they will be considered an infringement of an existing mark if:

- they conflict with the mark in a way that creates the likelihood of customer confusion, or

- the existing mark is famous and the use of the domain name can be said to dilute its strength.

a. Registering your domain name as a trademark

You're the owner of a trademark if you're the first to use it to identify your goods and services. That principle also applies to a domain name that functions as your trademark. Whether or not you've registered the name with the U.S. Patent and Trademark Office, you can stop someone else's subsequent use of a similar mark on similar goods and service.

So why bother registering it as a trademark? For one thing, registering your trademark makes it easier for you to enforce your rights as a trademark owner because you'll be *presumed* to own the mark, and anyone who later uses it is presumed to know about it. This makes it a bit easier to convince a judge that the later user is intentionally infringing on your mark. If you are able to prove the infringement was intentional, it can put more money in your pocket. The possibility of suing for enhanced damages will make it easier to find a lawyer to take your case if someone infringes on your trademark.

Not All Domain Names Can Be Registered as Trademarks. The USPTO is particular about what can be registered as a domain name. For example, you will have a problem registering a generic name like drugs.com as a trademark. And you'd face an uphill struggle to register a domain name that you use solely as an address and not a signifier of services. For example, the law firm of Smith & Jones would have a hard time registering smith&jones.com as a trademark. It would have to prove that the domain is being used for some other purpose than for people to find and contact the law firm. For more information, review the USPTO publication, "Trademark Examination of Domain Names," available at www.uspto.gov/web/offices/tac/notices/guide299.htm.

Domain names are federally registered the same way as any other trademark. However, to complete the registration process, you have to actually be using the domain name on a website. But you can start the process if you intend to use name soon (an intent-to-use application). When you do start using the name and complete the registration process, the application date will be treated as the date you first used the mark. This will give you a priority claim over later users.

4. Disputes Involving Domain Names

The companies that assign and register domain names do not check to see if a requested domain name violates an existing trademark. They are only concerned with whether the name is already taken as a domain name. In short, whether or not you are assigned the domain name you request says nothing about whether it will conflict with an existing trademark—that is, whether it is the same or similar to a famous mark or is likely to cause customers to confuse your site with the business or products carrying the existing mark.

If you do pick a domain name that creates a trademark conflict, several outcomes are possible:

- If your domain name prevents the owner of a registered trademark from using its mark as its domain name, the owner of the registered mark may be able to cause your domain name to be deregistered (you can't use it anymore).
- If your domain name is the same or similar to an existing famous mark, the mark's owner may file a lawsuit preventing any further use of your domain name, even if customers wouldn't likely be confused by its use.

- If your domain name conflicts with any existing mark that is being used in a way that would likely lead to customer confusion between your business or products and those offered by the mark's owner, you may be forced to stop using the name and possibly be liable for large damages if your infringement is judged to be willful.

ICANN, the international nonprofit organization in charge of domain name registrations worldwide, manages a process called the Uniform Domain Name Dispute Resolution Policy or UDRP. This administrative procedure only works for cybersquatting disputes—that is, when someone has registered a domain name in a bad-faith attempt to profit from someone else's trademark. A person or company who wins under the UDRP gets the domain name transferred to it unless the loser files a lawsuit.

 For a detailed discussion of the UDRP, refer to *Domain Names: How to Choose & Protect a Great Name for Your Website*, by Stephen Elias and Patricia Gima (Nolo); and check out the following websites: www.icann.corm and www.DomainMagistrate.com. ∎

Software and Website Ownership

This chapter is about software and website ownership—that is, who owns the intellectual property rights in software or websites. It also covers transferring ownership rights.

What Do We Mean by a "Website"?

The word "website" is used in this chapter to include all the materials used to create and run a website, including text, graphics, photos, videos, music and other sounds, computer software, and—to the extent it's copyrightable—HTML code and similar forms of code.

A. Copyright Ownership

Software, websites, and other works of authorship that satisfy the criteria for copyright protection discussed in Chapter 3, are protected automatically upon creation and fixation in a tangible medium. At that same moment, the author or authors of the work become the initial owners of the copyright in the work. This section is about determining who these authors—and initial owners—are.

There are several basic ways to create software or a website and thereby become its initial owner.

- An individual may independently author the work.

- An employer may pay an employee to author the work, in which case the employer is the author under the work made for hire rule.
- A person or company may hire an independent contractor (not an employee) to create the work on its behalf, in which case the hiring party is the author, assuming the independent contractor signs a written agreement to this effect.
- Two or more individuals or entities may collaborate to become joint authors.

We discuss each of these types of authorship (and initial ownership) in turn.

1. Independent Authorship by an Individual

Software or a website created by a single self-employed individual is initially owned by that individual.

> **EXAMPLE:** Lucy is a self-employed freelance programmer. She writes a program that helps investors analyze stock market data. Lucy created the program on her own time—that is, not on anyone's behalf. Lucy owns all the copyright rights in the program.

> **EXAMPLE:** Lucy decides to create a website to market her stock market program. Lucy designs the site herself and creates all the text and other con-

tent it contains. Lucy owns all the copyright rights in her website.

Individual copyright owners may exercise any of their copyright rights themselves. For example, they may reproduce and sell their work themselves, or authorize others to do so. They may also transfer their ownership in whole or in part to others. (See Section C.) Individual copyright owners can do whatever they want with their copyright; they are accountable to no one.

2. Ownership of Works Created by Employees (Works Made for Hire)

Today, the majority of software programs and websites are created by employees or independent contractors, not self-employed programmers working on their own behalf. Copyrightable works created by an employee within the scope of employment are owned by the employer. Such works are called works made for hire. Not only is the employer the owner of the copyright in a work made for hire, it is considered to be the work's author for copyright purposes. This is so whether the owner is a human being or a business entity, such as a partnership or corporation. As the author, the employer is entitled to register the work with the Copyright Office, exercise its copyright rights in the work such as distributing it

to the public, permit others to exercise these rights, or sell all or part of its rights. The employee—the actual creator of the work—has no copyright rights at all. All he or she receives is whatever compensation the employer gives him or her.

This result is considered to be an obvious and natural consequence of the employer-employee relationship. It's assumed that an employee understands and agrees to this when he or she takes a job. Thus, an employer doesn't have to tell an employee that it will own copyrightable works she creates on the employer's behalf; the employee is supposed to know this without being told. Likewise, the employer need not have the employee sign an agreement relinquishing his copyright rights—he or she doesn't have any to relinquish.

> **EXAMPLE:** John is hired to work as a programmer for AcmeSoft, Inc. John is AcmeSoft's employee. He is assigned to a project to develop a new database program. All of John's work on the program will be work made for hire to which AcmeSoft owns all the copyright rights. AcmeSoft need not tell John this or have him sign a copyright transfer agreement.

At first glance, this all sounds very straightforward. It would seem that both the hiring firm and the worker should always know who owns any copyrightable works created by the worker. However, things are not always so simple. In fact, it can be very difficult to know for sure who owns software created by workers for hiring firms. This is because there are problems in determining:

- just who is an employee, for copyright ownership purposes, and
- when a work is created within the scope of employment.

a. Who is an employee?

A person is an employee for copyright ownership purposes if the person or entity on whose behalf the work is done has the right to control the manner and means by which the work is created. If the hiring firm does not have the right to control the worker, he or she is not an employee for copyright purposes; rather, the worker is an independent contractor and a whole other set of ownership rules apply, as discussed in Section A3 below.

It makes no difference what the parties call themselves or how they characterize their relationship. If the person or entity on whose behalf the work is done has the right of control, the person hired is an employee and any protectible work he creates within the scope of his employment is a work made for hire. It also makes no difference whether the control is actually exercised. All that matters is that the hiring firm has the right to exer-

cise such control. (*CCNV v. Reid*, 109 S.Ct. 2166 (1989).)

When a legal dispute arises as to whether the creator of a protectible work is an employee, the courts are supposed to examine a variety of factors to determine if the hiring firm has the right to control the worker. The rules are ambiguous and given to highly subjective interpretation. Thus, if a dispute later arises, it is always possible that a judge could decide the programmer an employer thought was an employee was actually an independent contractor. The consequences could be disastrous for the employer and quite surprising for the worker. (See Section A5 below.)

b. Factors considered in determining employee status

Here is a list of some of the factors the Supreme Court has said judges might consider in determining if a hiring firm has the right to control a worker. As stated above, if the right to control is present, the worker is an employee; if not, he is an independent contractor. This is not an exclusive list, and no single factor is determinative:

- the skill required to do the work (highly skilled workers are less likely to perform their work under a hirer's direct control)
- the source of tools and materials used to create the work (workers who sup-

ply their own equipment are less likely to be under a hirer's control)
- the duration of the relationship (long-term relationships indicate control by the hiring firm and employee status)
- whether the person who pays for the work has the right to assign additional projects to the creative party
- who determines when and how long the creative party works
- the method of payment (paying by the hour indicates an employment status, payment by the job indicates the worker is an independent contractor)
- who decides what assistants will be hired, and who pays them
- whether the work is in the ordinary line of business of the person who pays for the work (if yes, the hiring party will more likely control the worker)
- whether the creative party is in business for herself
- whether the creative party receives employee benefits from the person who pays for the work
- the tax treatment of the creative party.

However, legal decisions in recent years make clear that two of the factors of prime importance in determining whether a worker is an employee for copyright ownership purposes are:
- whether the hiring firm pays the worker's Social Security taxes, and

- whether the hiring firm provides the worker with employee benefits.

Obviously, if a company (or individual) hires someone and pays their Social Security taxes and gives him or her employee benefits, the company (and worker) must believe that the worker is an employee.

In one important decision, the court held that a part-time programmer employed by a swimming pool retailer was not the company's employee for copyright purposes and the programmer was therefore entitled to ownership of a program he wrote for the company. The court stated that the company's failure to provide the programmer with health, unemployment, or life insurance benefits, or to withhold Social Security, federal, or state taxes from his pay was a "virtual admission" that the programmer was an independent contractor. These factors were so important they outweighed other factors that indicated a right of control by the pool company, such as the fact that the company could assign the programmer additional projects. (*Aymes v. Bonelli*, 980 F.2d. 857 (2d Cir. 1992).)

Another reason the tax treatment of the worker is so important is fairness. It is manifestly unfair for a hiring firm to treat a worker like an independent contractor for tax purposes (and thereby avoid paying payroll taxes and employee benefits) and then turn around and claim he or she is an employee for copyright ownership purposes (and thereby claim that his or her copyrightable creations are works made for hire).

The moral for hiring firms: If a hiring firm doesn't pay a worker's Social Security taxes or provide him or her with benefits available to other employees, the firm should assume the worker is an independent contractor for copyright ownership purposes.

Results May Be Different for IRS and State Purposes

Not paying a worker's Social Security taxes will likely make him or her an independent contractor for copyright ownership purposes, but this does not necessarily mean he or she will be an independent contractor for IRS or state law purposes such as workers' compensation and state unemployment insurance. The IRS and state agencies look at a variety of factors to determine whether a worker is an employee or independent contractor. Whether Social Security taxes are paid for a worker is just one of these factors and is not determinative in and of itself. For a detailed discussion, refer to *Hiring Independent Contractors*, by Stephen Fishman (Nolo).

What should software and website development workers do? A worker should always clarify his or her employment status before beginning any job. If you're supposed to be an employee, you should be put on the hiring firm's payroll and be classified and treated as an employee for tax, salary, job benefit, and all other purposes. If you're going to be an independent contractor, you should have the firm sign a written independent contractor agreement that states what it is you're supposed to do, how and how much you will be paid, and who will own the copyright in your work. If you are going to transfer ownership of your work to the hiring firm, try to make the transfer contingent on payment as provided under the agreement.

c. When is a work created within the scope of employment?

Even when it is clear that an employment relationship exists, serious disputes can arise as to whether an employee who creates a copyrightable work did so within the scope of employment. For example, many people employed in the software and Web development industries are moonlighters—they create software, websites, or other copyrightable works on their own time, using their own equipment, alone or with others. If such work is closely related to an employee's job duties, the employer may claim an ownership interest in it, while the employee insists that he is the sole owner.

Where such a dispute arises, the courts look to the common law of agency relationships to determine whether a work was created within the scope of employment. Under these rules, an employee's work is created within the scope of employment if it:

- is the kind of work the employee is paid to perform
- occurs substantially within work hours at the work place, and
- is performed, at least in part, to serve the employer.

These rules are subject to inconsistent interpretations. Consider these real-life examples where opposite results were reached in cases involving similar fact situations:

> **EXAMPLE 1:** Miller was a supervisor who worked at CP Chemicals' quality control lab. He created a program for making mathematical computations needed for in-process adjustments to one of CP's products. Miller was paid by the hour and created the program primarily at home on his own computer during off hours, and without any overtime pay. Nevertheless, the court held that the program was created within the scope of Miller's employment and was therefore owned by CP Chemicals, not Miller. The court held that the first and third factors listed above favored CP Chemicals, while only the second favored Miller. The court reasoned that "the ultimate purpose of the development of the computer program was to benefit CP by maximizing the efficiency of the operation of the quality control lab." (*Miller v. CP Chemicals, Inc.,* 808 F. Supp. 1238 (D. S.C. 1992).)

> **EXAMPLE 2:** While employed by Avtec Systems, Pfeiffer created a computer program for managing and presenting satellite data. The court held that the program was not created within the scope of Pfeiffer's employment, and was therefore not a work for hire owned by Avtec. This was so even though the program performed many of the same functions found in other programs used by Avtec and by Pfeiffer during his employment by Avtec. The court found that the majority of Pfeiffer's work on the program was done on his own time and his own computer in furtherance of a personal hobby, and not to satisfy any specific work obligations for Avtec. (*Avtec Systems, Inc. v. Pfeiffer,* 805 F. Supp. 1312 (E.D. Va. 1992).)

The result of all this is that an employee (or ex-employee) might be able to legitimately claim that he or she should own the copyright in his contribution to a software or website project because he was not hired or paid to create that work. As you might expect, such disputes can get messy and very expensive, particularly if the software involved is quite valuable.

d. What employers should do

The best policy for companies and individuals who employ others to create software, websites, or any other copyrightable works is to have all creative (or potentially creative) employees sign employment agreements. Such an agreement should:

- make clear that the employee's job duties include creating, or contributing to the creation of, software, websites, and other copyrightable works
- provide that any software, websites, or other copyrightable works the employee creates as part of his job are works made for hire to which the company owns all the copyright rights, and
- provide that if for some reason such works are determined not to be works made for hire, the employee assigns in advance (transfers) to the employer all his copyright rights in such works.

A signed document like this will help convince a court that creating software or other copyrightable works was part of the employee's job. And the assignment provision will serve as a backup in case a court determines the work made for hire rule does not apply.

Not only should new employees assign their copyright rights to their employers, but existing employees should do so as well if they haven't already. (See Chapter 14 for a detailed discussion and sample employment agreements.)

e. Copyright concerns for moonlighting employees

Employees of companies who create software, websites, or other copyrightable works on their own time need to be very careful. As discussed above, an employer owns the intellectual property rights in software created by an employee within the scope of her employment. Moreover, an employer may even have certain rights over works created outside the scope of employment if the employee used the employer's resources (for example, did a substantial amount of the work during business hours or used the employer's equipment). If an employee creates a valuable work on his or her own time, an unscrupulous employer might try to assert ownership over it by claiming that the work was within the scope of employment or the employee used its resources.

To avoid potential problems, if you plan to do software- or website-related work on your own, make sure you inform your employer and obtain written acknowledgment that the employer will not have an ownership interest in such work. For obvious reasons, it's a lot easier to get that acknowledgment before you do the work than after.

EXAMPLE: Art Acres, a Java developer, is hired by World's End, a major mail order clothing retailer, to work on its extensive website. On his own time, Art decides to develop a computer game. Art's work on the game is in no way connected with his work for World's End, nor could the game be competitive with any of World's End's products. However, just to make sure there will be no problems, Art informs his boss about his plans and gets World's End to sign the following letter of agreement:

March 1, 200X

Bill Fates

President

World's End, Inc.

1000 Main St.

Seattle, WA 90002

Dear Bill:

This letter is to confirm the understanding we've reached regarding ownership of my computer game program, tentatively titled You Are What You Eat.

You acknowledge that my program will be written on my own time and shall not be written within the scope of my employment with World's End, Inc.

It is expressly agreed that I shall be the owner of all rights in the program, including the copyright. Furthermore, World's End, Inc., will sign all papers necessary for me to perfect my ownership of the entire copyright in the work.

If this agreement meets with your approval, please sign below to make this a binding contract between us. Please sign both copies and return one to me. The other signed copy is for your records.

Sincerely,

Art Acres

I agree with the above understanding and represent that I have authority to make this agreement and to sign this letter on behalf of World's End, Inc.

Bill Fates

Date:

---

3. Ownership of Works Created by Independent Contractors

Subject to the important exceptions discussed in this section, works created by independent contractors (nonemployees) are not works made for hire, that is, the independent contractor, not the hiring firm, owns the copyright in what he or she creates. This means that the hiring firm must always require independent contractors to sign written agreements assigning their copyright ownership to the hiring firm. To ensure that such an agreement will be effective, it should be signed *before* the independent contractor begins work on the project. (See Chapter 15 for sample independent contractor agreements.)

> **EXAMPLE 1:** AcmeSoft hires Dana, a freelance software engineer, to help create a new Web application. Dana is not AcmeSoft's employee. AcmeSoft has Dana sign an independent contractor agreement before commencing work. The agreement contains a provision whereby Dana assigns to AcmeSoft all his ownership rights in the work he will perform on the application. Dana completes his work and his relationship with AcmeSoft ends. Because of the signed agreement, AcmeSoft owns all the copyright in Dana's work.

> **EXAMPLE 2:** Assume instead that AcmeSoft hires Dana, but fails to have him sign an independent contractor agreement transferring his ownership rights. When Dana completes his work he, not AcmeSoft, will own the copyright in the work he created for AcmeSoft. This is so even though AcmeSoft paid for it! However, AcmeSoft would be at least entitled to use the work.

a. When works created by independent contractors are works made for hire

Certain types of works created by independent contractors are considered to be works made for hire to which the hiring party automatically owns all the copyright rights—provided that:

- the hiring party and independent contractor both sign an agreement before the work is created stating that the work shall be a work made for hire, and
- the work falls within one of the following categories:
  - ✓ a contribution to a collective work (a work created by more than one author such as an anthology)
  - ✓ a part of an audiovisual work
  - ✓ a translation
  - ✓ "supplementary works" such as forewords, afterwards, supplemen-

tal pictorial illustrations, maps, charts, editorial notes, bibliographies, appendixes, and indexes
✓ a compilation
✓ an instructional text
✓ a test and test answer materials
✓ an atlas.

Websites are ordinarily collective works or compilations. This means that such works can be works made for hire if the independent contractor signs an agreement to that effect before starting work.

> **EXAMPLE:** AcmeSoft, Inc., hires David, a freelance Web graphic designer, to create graphics for its website. AcmeSoft has David sign an agreement before he commences work stating that his work on the website shall be a work made for hire. When David finishes his work, the graphic will be considered a work made for hire to which AcmeSoft owns all the copyright rights. Indeed, AcmeSoft will be considered the author for copyright purposes. David will have no copyright ownership interest whatsoever in the graphics.

User manuals and other software documentation (whether printed or online) written by independent contractor technical writers may fall within the supplementary work or collective work categories.

> **EXAMPLE:** AcmeSoft, Inc., hires Alberta, a freelance technical writer, to write the user manual for its new small business accounting software. AcmeSoft has Alberta sign an agreement before she commences work stating that her work on the manual shall be a work made for hire. When Alberta finishes her work, the manual will be considered a work made for hire.

b. Does software fall within a work made for hire category?

Unfortunately for software companies, most of the work made for hire categories set out above don't seem to have much application to computer programs themselves (but merely to their written documentation). A computer program might arguably constitute a collective work, compilation, or even an audiovisual work, but no court has so ruled. Moreover, Copyright Office officials have stated that in their opinion none of the work made for hire categories applied to software. For this reason, until the question is conclusively resolved by court or congressional action, persons who hire independent contractors to create, or contribute to the creation of, computer programs should never rely on the work made for hire rule but rather should obtain an assignment of rights.

Work for Hire Agreements May Be Ineffective

Many software companies have independent contractors who work on software projects sign agreements stating that their work "shall be a work made for hire." Such an agreement will not make the contractor's work a work made for hire unless it falls within one of the categories listed above. (See the discussion in Section A2.)

---

4. Jointly Authored Works

A work is jointly authored automatically upon its creation if (1) two or more authors contributed material to the work; and (2) each of the authors prepared his or her contribution with the intention that it would be combined with the contributions of the other authors as part of a single unitary work. We'll refer to such works as "joint works."

The key to determining whether a work is a joint work is the authors' intent at the time the work is created. If the authors intended that their work be absorbed or combined with other contributions into an integrated unit, the work that results is a joint work. It is not necessary that the authors work together or work at the same time. Indeed, it is not even necessary that they know each other when they create their respective contributions.

EXAMPLE: Peter and Mary agree to create a new website to publicize their Web development company. Peter designs and codes the site and Mary creates the graphics and test. When the website is completed, it will be jointly owned by Peter and Mary because they intended that their respective contributions be combined to form one integrated work—a new website.

a. How much material must a person contribute to be a joint author?

The respective contributions made to a joint work by its authors need not be equal in terms of quantity or quality. But to be considered a joint author, a person must contribute more than a minimal amount of work to the finished product.

Most courts require that a person's contribution be separately copyrightable in its own right for him or her to be considered a joint author. A person who merely contributes ideas or other unprotectible items is not entitled to an ownership interest in the work's copyright unless the parties expressly agree to it, preferably in writing.

As the following real-life example illustrates, simply describing to a programmer what a program should do is not sufficient to become a joint author.

EXAMPLE: Ross and Wigginton decided to collaborate to develop a computer spreadsheet program. They agreed that Ross would write the computational component of the program (the engine) and Wigginton design the user interface. Ross provided Wigginton with a handwritten list of potential commands that should be incorporated in the user interface. The two later went their own ways and Wigginton's interface was combined with another engine component and marketed by Ashton-Tate. Ross filed suit, claiming that Wigginton's interface was a joint work. The court held that the interface was not a joint work because Ross's list of commands was not separately copyrightable. The court stated that the list was merely an unprotectible idea, telling Wigginton what tasks Ross believed the spreadsheet interface should perform. (*Ashton-Tate Corp. v. Ross*, 916 F.2d 516 (9th Cir. 1990).)

It is always a good idea for collaborators to have a written agreement setting forth their respective interests in the work to be written. This way, if one contributor is found not to be a joint owner of the work because he did not contribute protectible expression to it, he or she would still be entitled (as a matter of contract law) to the ownership interest stated in the collaboration agreement.

b. Employees are not joint authors

An employee who contributes copyrightable work to a joint work is not a joint author. As discussed above, copyrightable works created by employees within the scope of employment are owned by the employer—indeed the employer is deemed author of such a work made for hire. Thus, the employer would be the joint author, not the employee.

EXAMPLE: Simon and Sally agree to jointly create a shareware program. Simon hires Suzy, a skilled programmer, to aid him in coding the program. The code Suzy creates is a work made for hire owned by Simon, Suzy's employer. Suzy is not a joint author of the game, only Simon and Sally are.

c. Joint authors need not be human beings

A joint author doesn't have to be a human being. A corporation, partnership, or other business entity can also be a joint author. For example, two software companies can agree to jointly develop new software. This type of strategic partnering is common.

> **EXAMPLE:** Sunnydale Software, Inc., and AcmeSoft, Inc., agree to jointly develop a new software package designed to enable dairy farmers to automate milk production. Sunnydale and AcmeSoft employees work together to design, code, and test the new software. The software package, called Milkrun, is a joint work that is also a work made for hire. The joint authors are Sunnydale and AcmeSoft.

d. Joint authors' agreement

A written agreement is not legally required to create a joint work; an oral agreement is sufficient. However, as Samuel Goldwyn supposedly once said, "An oral agreement isn't worth the paper it's printed on." It is vital that joint authors draft and sign a written agreement spelling out their rights and responsibilities. This avoids innumerable headaches later on.

If you're collaborating with one or more people or companies to create software or websites, you're entering into a partnership or joint venture. You're in a partnership if you intend the collaboration to be open-ended—that is, to involve more than one software project. If you intend to collaborate only on a single

project, you're in a joint venture. Joint ventures are governed by the same laws as partnerships. The only legal difference between partnerships and joint ventures is that the latter are for a limited purpose.

You and your collaborators should sign a written partnership or joint venture agreement setting forth each person's ownership interests, rights, and duties. *The Partnership Book*, by Denis Clifford and Ralph Warner (Nolo), contains a partnership/joint venture agreement that may fill your needs.

e. Joint author's rights and duties in the absence of an agreement

The drafters of the Copyright Act realized that not all joint authors would be prudent enough to enter into a written (or even oral) agreement setting forth their ownership interests, rights, and duties. To avoid chaos, they made sure that the act contained provisions governing the most important aspects of the legal relationship between joint authors who fail to agree among themselves how their relationship should operate. You might think of these provisions as similar to a computer program's "default settings" that control the program when the user fails to make his own settings.

- *Ownership interests*: Unless they agree otherwise, joint authors each have an undivided interest in the entire work. This is basically the same as joint ownership of a house or other real estate. When a husband and wife jointly own their home they normally each own a 50% interest in the entire house; that is, they each have an undivided one-half interest. Similarly, joint authors share ownership of all five exclusive rights that make up the joint work's copyright.

- *Right to exploit copyright*: Unless they agree otherwise, each joint author has the right to exercise any or all of the five copyright rights inherent in the joint work: any of the authors may reproduce and distribute the work or prepare derivative works based upon it (or display or perform it). Each author may do so without the other joint authors' consent.
- *Right to license joint work*: Unless they agree otherwise, each joint author may grant third parties permission to exploit the work—on a non-exclusive basis—without the other joint authors' consent. This means that different authors may grant non-exclusive licenses of the same right to different persons!

Anyone who wishes to purchase an exclusive right in a joint work should require signatures by all the authors to ensure that they all agree to the transfer.

- *Right to transfer ownership*: Unless they agree otherwise, each author of a joint work may transfer her entire ownership interest to another person without the other joint authors' consent. Such person then co-owns the work with the remaining authors. But a joint author can only transfer her particular interest, not that of any other author.
- *Duty to account for profits*: Along with these rights, each joint author has the duty to account to the other joint authors for any profits received from his use or license of the joint work. All the joint authors are entitled to share in these profits. Unless they agree otherwise, the profits must be divided among the authors according to their proportionate interests in the joint work. (Note, however, that such profits do not include what one author gets for selling his or her share of the copyright.)

It may not seem fair that a joint author—who goes to the time and trouble of exploiting the copyright in the joint work by getting it published or creating derivative works based upon it—is required to share his profits equally with the other joint authors, who did nothing. This is still another reason why it's wise to enter into a written agreement.

- *When joint authors die*: When a joint author dies, his or her share in the joint work goes to the author's heirs.

If the author wrote a will, the share would go to whomever the will directs. If the author died without a will, the share would go to whomever state inheritance laws require—normally the author's closest living relatives. The other joint authors do not acquire a deceased owner's share unless, of course, the deceased author willed it to them, or the author died without a will and another joint author was related to her and inherited her interest under the state inheritance laws. However, joint authors can change this result by entering into a joint tenancy with right of survivorship agreement. Under such an agreement, a deceased joint author's share would automatically go to the remaining joint author(s).

5. What If a Hiring Firm Fails to Obtain Ownership of Works It Pays For?

The discussion above should make clear that it's quite possible for a company or person to hire another person to create or contribute to the creation of software or a website, pay for the work, and yet end up not owning the copyright in that person's work product. This can happen in a variety of ways:

- a worker the hiring firm thought was an employee turns out to be an independent contractor

- the work performed by the employee was outside his or her scope of employment
- the hiring firm fails to obtain a written assignment of copyright rights in advance from an independent contractor, or
- the hiring firm has an independent contractor sign a work for hire agreement, but the work does not fall within one of the work for hire categories enumerated in Section A3.

Whenever any of these things happen there are three possible consequences:

- the creator of the work will be considered the sole copyright owner
- the creator and hiring party will be considered to be joint authors and share ownership, or
- the hiring party will be considered the sole copyright owner.

a. The creator of the work owns the copyright

First of all, unless the hiring firm can obtain an ownership interest by claiming joint authorship or by virtue of some written document (see below), the worker will solely own all of the copyright rights in her work product.

EXAMPLE 1: The law firm of Dewey, Cheatum, and Howe hires Sally, a freelance website designer, to design and code custom case management software for the firm. Sally is not Dewey's employee and signs no document transferring her ownership rights in her work to Dewey. Sally completes the program and is paid in full. Sally is also the sole copyright owner of the case management software. This means that Sally may sell the software to others, reproduce it, create derivative works from it, or otherwise exercise her copyright rights in the software.

However, all will not be lost for the hiring firm. At the very least, a company or person who pays an author to create a protectible work has a nonexclusive license to use it as intended. (*Avtec Systems, Inc. v. Pfeiffer*, 805 F. Supp. 1312 (E.D. Va 1992).) This seems only fair, considering that the hiring party paid for the work. A person with a nonexclusive license in a work may use the work, but may not prevent others from using it as well. Nonexclusive licenses may be implied from the circumstances; no express agreement is required.

EXAMPLE 2: Since Dewey in Example 1 paid Sally to create the case management software, it would have a nonexclusive license to use the software. But this would not prevent Sally from allowing others to use the software as well.

b. Joint work created

The best thing that could happen from the hiring firm's point of view, would be for it to be considered a joint author of the work. This way, it would share ownership with the other creators. However, as discussed in Section A4, for a person or company to be considered a joint author, it must contribute actual copyrightable expression to the finished work. Simply describing how a program or website should function or contributing other ideas or suggestions is not sufficient.

EXAMPLE 3: Assume that Sally in the examples above was aided by Dewey's employees. The employees contributed not only ideas, but actually helped design the program, contributing work that was separately copyrightable in its own right (flowcharts, for example). In this event, the software would probably constitute a joint work and would be jointly owned by Sally and Dewey. (See Section A4 for a detailed discussion of joint works.)

c. Hiring party is sole copyright owner under work made for hire contract

Many companies use form agreements with independent contractors that state that the contractor's work will be a work made for hire. But such an agreement will be effective only if the contractor's work falls within one of the enumerated work for hire categories. Websites ordinarily fall into one or more of these categories, but software may not fall into any. In the case of software, this means that the contractor's work may not be deemed a work made for hire even though he signed the agreement.

EXAMPLE 4: Assume that Dewey in the example above had Sally sign a contract stating that the case management software would be a work made for hire. Unfortunately for Dewey, such software does not come within one of the nine categories of specially commissioned works. This means that regardless of what the contract said, the work is not a work made for hire and Sally is the author and initial owner of the copyright.

However, it is possible that a court would interpret the work made for hire contract as a transfer by Sally to Dewey of all her copyright rights in his work. Sally would still be the initial owner and author, but Dewey would still end up owning all the copyright rights in the work—that is, Dewey would have the exclusive right to use and reproduce it, create derivative works based upon it, and so on. But it's also possible that a judge would rule the contract unenforceable

and simply award Dewey a nonexclusive license.

6. Marriage, Divorce, and Copyright Ownership

This section is for individuals who already own software or website copyrights, or who may own them in the future. Like everybody else, individuals who own software copyrights get married and get divorced. A copyright is an item of personal property that must be given to one spouse or the other, or somehow shared, upon divorce. Every state has a set of laws about how property acquired or created by married persons is owned and divided upon divorce. These laws vary greatly from state to state. This section highlights some basic principles. You'll need to consult an attorney to answer specific questions about how the laws of your state operate.

a. Copyrights as community property

Nine states have community property laws: Arizona, California, Idaho, Louisiana, Nevada, New Mexico, Texas, Washington, and Wisconsin (in all but name). Under these state laws, unless they agree otherwise, a husband and wife automatically become joint owners of most types of property they acquire during their marriage. Property acquired before or after marriage is separately owned.

A court in the most populous community property state—California—has held that a copyright acquired by one spouse during marriage is community property jointly owned by both spouses. (*Marriage of Worth*, 195 Cal. App. 3d 768, 241 Cal. Rptr. 135 (1987).) This means that if you are married and reside in California (or later move there), any work you have created or will create automatically would be owned jointly by you and your spouse unless you agree otherwise in writing (see below).

> **EXAMPLE:** Emily and Robert are married and live in California. Emily writes a computer program. Under the federal Copyright Act, Emily becomes the sole owner of the program the moment it's created. But at that same moment, under California's community property law, Robert automatically acquires an undivided one-half interest in the copyright (unless they agree otherwise).

A court in Louisiana has held that copyrights are not community property in that state. (*Rodrigue v. Rodrigue*, 50 U.S.P.Q. 2d 1278 (E.D. La. 1999).) Courts in the other seven community property states have yet to consider whether copyrights are community property. No one knows whether they will follow California's lead. If you're married and reside in Arizona, Idaho, Nevada, New Mexico, Texas, Washington, or Wisconsin, the most prudent approach is to assume that the copyright in any protectible work you create during marriage is community property. However, check with a family law or copyright lawyer familiar with the laws of your state before taking any action such as entering into a prenuptial agreement dividing your and your spouse's property in advance in the event you later divorce.

The following discussion briefly highlights the effect of according copyrights community property status in California.

b. California: right to control copyrights

Normally, either spouse is entitled to sell community personal property (which would include a copyright) without the other's consent. But the profits from such a sale would themselves be community property (that is, jointly owned). The rule is different, however, as to gifts: neither spouse can give away community property without the other's consent. However, a special provision of California law (Civil Code § 5125(d)) provides that a spouse who operates a business has the primary management and control of that business and its assets. In most cases, a married freelance software programmer or Web developer would probably be considered to be operating a business and would therefore have primary management and control over any work he or she creates (the business's assets).

This means that a married freelance programmer or Web developer may transfer all or part of the copyright in a work he or she creates during marriage without his or her spouse's consent or signature on any contract. However, the programmer is legally required to give his or her spouse prior written notice of such transfers (but failure to do so only results in giving the nonauthor spouse the right to demand an accounting of the profits from the transfer).

c. California: when a spouse dies

Under California law (Probate Code § 201.5) each spouse may will a one-half interest in their community property to whomever they choose; this would include, of course, their interest in any community property copyright. If a spouse dies without a will, the surviving spouse acquires all the deceased spouse's community property.

d. California: division of copyrights at divorce

When a California couple gets divorced, they are legally entitled to arrange their own property settlement, jointly dividing their property as they wish. If, however, they can't reach an agreement and submit the dispute to the court, a judge will divide the community property equally.

e. California: changing marital ownership of copyrights by contract

Property acquired during marriage by California residents does not have to be community property. Spouses are free to agree either before or during marriage that all or part of their property will be separately owned. Such an agreement must be in writing and signed by the spouse giving up their community property interest. In some cases, it is desirable for the spouse giving up their community property interest to first consult a lawyer.

f. Equitable distribution states

All states other than the nine community property states listed above and Mississippi employ a doctrine known as equitable distribution when dividing property at divorce. Under the equitable distribution doctrine, assets (including copyrights) acquired during marriage are divided equitably (fairly) at divorce. In theory, equitable means equal, or nearly so. In some equitable distribution states, however, if a spouse is shown to be at fault in making the marriage fail, that spouse may receive less than an equal share of the marital property. Check with a family law attorney in your state for details.

B. Trade Secret and Patent Ownership

The rules for determining ownership of trade secrets and patentable inventions are essentially the same. Unless one of the very important exceptions discussed below applies, a patent or trade secret is initially owned by the person who creates or invents it.

1. Trade Secrets and Inventions Developed by Employees and Independent Contractors

Unlike copyright ownership, the basic rule for patents and trade secrets is that if you pay someone to invent or develop something, you own any patents or trade secrets developed in the course of the work.

a. Employees and independent contractors hired to invent specific items

When an employee or independent contractor is hired to develop or invent a specific product, device, or procedure, the employer owns the patent and trade secret rights to that item. In this situation, the employee or independent contractor is deemed to have sold whatever rights he may have had in the invention or trade secret to the employer in advance, in return for his salary or other compensation.

EXAMPLE: Abe, a programmer, is hired by TopSoft to develop an Internet security program. TopSoft owns the rights to any patentable inventions and trade secrets developed by Abe in the course of his assigned task.

b. Generally inventive employees or independent contractors

If, instead of being hired to invent or develop a specific item, the employee or independent contractor is hired to do research in a general area or is generally employed to design something, the employer will own the rights to any patentable inventions and trade secrets developed by the worker so long as they were created:

- during working hours, and
- within the scope of employment.

EXAMPLE: Assume that instead of being hired specifically to invent an Internet security program, Abe in the example above is hired by TopSoft simply to create new and useful programs. Abe decides to develop the security program and designs it during working hours. TopSoft owns the rights to any patents and trade secrets created by Abe in developing the program.

An employee who is not hired to invent or develop new products or technology owns the rights to any patentable inventions or trade secrets she creates. However, the employer will be entitled to use the invention and include it in the products it sells without the employee's permission and without paying the employee for the use if:

- the employee used the employer's resources in creating the invention (for example, did a substantial amount of the work during business hours or used the employer's equipment), or
- the employee allowed the employer to promote the invention with a reasonable expectation of royalty-free use by the employer.

This type of license is called a "shop right." It is nonexclusive (it does not prevent an employee-inventor from transferring her patent rights to others) and is nontransferable by the employer.

EXAMPLE 1: Ada is employed by Phoenix, Inc., a financial services company, as a webmaster. Her job duties do not include developing new Web applications or methods of doing business on the Web. Ada develops a new way for Phoenix's online customers to more easily manage their IRA accounts and creates software to implement the idea on the Web. Ada has created a new Internet business method that qualifies for a patent. Ada owns these patent rights because she is a noninventive employee—she was hired by Phoenix solely as a webmaster.

EXAMPLE 2: Assume that Ada developed her software and new business method during working hours on a Phoenix computer. Ada still owns the patentable inventions she developed, but Phoenix is entitled to use the method and software for free—it has a "shop right" in it. But Phoenix cannot sell it or use rights to others.

EXAMPLE 3: Assume that Ada develops her software and business method at home and then shows it to a Phoenix executive. She permits Phoenix to implement the new business method on its website. Ada does not ask to be compensated for the use. Phoenix subsequently licenses the software and method to other websites. Phoenix has a shop right in the method Ada let Phoenix use for free. By failing to ask for compensation, Ada led Phoenix reasonably to believe that they could use it without paying her.

2. Contracts Assigning Patentable Inventions and Trade Secrets to Hiring Party

Unless someone is clearly hired to develop a specific product, bitter and costly disputes can develop as to the ownership of patentable inventions or trade secrets developed by employees and independent contractors. High-technology companies avoid these types of disputes by having employees and independent contractors sign agreements transferring their ownership rights in advance to the hiring firm.

However, seven states, notably including California, have statutory restrictions on invention assignments in employment contracts. Employment contracts are discussed in detail in Chapter 14. Contracts with independent contractors are discussed in Chapter 15.

C. Transferring Software and Website Ownership and Use Rights

Like other forms of property, intellectual property can be sold or otherwise transferred to another party. There are two basic types of intellectual property transfers: exclusive licenses and assignments. Although these terms are often used interchangeably, there are some differences.

1. Licenses

A license is a grant of permission to do something. For example, when you get a driver's license the government gives you permission to drive a car. A copyright, patent, trade secret, or trademark owner can give others permission to exercise one or more of the owner's exclusive rights, while retaining overall ownership. Such a permission is usually called a license.

Today, most software is licensed to end-users rather than sold outright. Website materials—including text, graphics, photos, videos, music—are also frequently licensed. Software and website licenses are discussed in detail in Chapter 16.

2. Assignments

The word "assignment" means a transfer of all the rights a person owns in a piece of property. So whenever a person or entity transfers all the intellectual property rights it owns in a work of authorship, the transaction is usually called an "assignment" or sometimes an "all rights transfer." An assignment of a copyright or patent must be in writing to be valid.

Trade secrets are usually not assigned to others except when a business is being sold; they are licensed instead. A written agreement is not required for assignments of trade secrets, but it is always a good idea to use one anyway.

When such an assignment transaction is completed, the original intellectual property owner no longer has any ownership rights at all. The new owner—the assignee—has all the rights the transferor formerly held.

Unless the work involved has been patented (a rare situation), you'll normally use a copyright assignment to transfer ownership to others or obtain ownership of others' software or Web content. Such an assignment need not be a lengthy or complex document. Following is an example of a simple copyright assignment:

Copyright Assignment

[Name of copyright owner], for value received, grants to [name of person or entity receiving assignment] all right, title, and interest in the work described as follows: [List work's title and copyright registration number, if any].

[Name of Copyright Owner]

By:

Typed name

Date:

Address:

[Name of Person or Entity Receiving Assignment]

By:

Typed name

Date:

Address:

The text of this Copyright Assignment is on the CD-ROM forms disk.

Right to Terminate Copyright Transfers After 35 Years

There are many sad stories about authors or artists who sold their work for a pittance when they were young or unknown, only to have it become extremely valuable later in their lives or after their death. In an effort to protect copyright owners and their families from unfair exploitation, the Copyright Act gives individual authors or their heirs the right to terminate any transfer of their copyright rights 35 to 40 years after it was made. This special statutory termination right may be exercised only by individual authors or their heirs, and only as to transfers made after 1977. This termination right can never be waived or contracted away by an author. The owner of a work made for hire, whether an individual or a business entity such as a corporation or partnership, has no statutory termination rights.

Given the pace of development in the software industry, it is likely that little or no software will have any economic value 35 years after its creation. There are no similar termination rights for patents or trademarks.

3. Recording Copyright Transfers With the Copyright Office

The Copyright Office does not make or in any way participate in transfers of copyright ownership. But the office does record transfer documents after they have been signed by the parties. When a transfer document is recorded, a copy is placed in the Copyright Office files, indexed, and made available for public inspection.

The Difference Between Recordation and Registration

As described in detail in Chapter 4, copyright registration is a legal formality by which an author or other copyright owner fills out a registration application for a published or unpublished work and submits it to the Copyright Office along with one or two copies of the work. If the copyright examiner is satisfied that the work contains protected expression and the application is completed correctly, the work is registered—that is, assigned a registration number, indexed and filed in the Copyright Office's records, and the copies retained for five years.

Recordation does not involve submitting copies of a work. Recordation simply means that the Copyright Office files a document so that it is available for public inspection. As mentioned above, this can be any document relating to copyright. It can be for a work that is published, unpublished, or even not yet created. A good way to distinguish the two procedures is to remember that computer programs themselves are registered, while contracts or other documents relating to the copyright in a program are recorded.

---

a. Why record a copyright transfer?

Because a copyright is intangible and can be transferred simply by signing a piece of paper, it is possible for dishonest copyright owners to rip off copyright purchasers.

EXAMPLE: AcmeSoft signs a contract transferring the exclusive right to publish and distribute a new database program to Scrivener & Sons. Scrivener fails to record the transfer with the U.S. Copyright Office. Two months later, AcmeSoft sells the same rights in the program to MegaSoft. MegaSoft had no idea that AcmeSoft had already sold the same rights to Scrivener. AcmeSoft has sold the same property twice! As a result, if Scrivener and MegaSoft both publish the program, they'll be competing against each other (and they'll both probably be able to sue AcmeSoft for breach of contract, fraud, and other causes of action).

Recordation of transfer documents protects copyright transferees from these and other abuses by establishing the legal priorities between copyright transferees if the transferor makes overlapping or confusing grants. Recordation also establishes a public record of the contents of transfer documents.

Things would be much better for Scrivener & Sons in our example above if it had recorded the copyright transfer from AcmeSoft. In that event, the transfer to Scrivener would have priority over MegaSoft and would be deemed the only valid transfer. This would mean that as the sole copyright owner, only Scrivener would have the right to distribute the computer program.

b. What can be recorded?

Any document pertaining to a copyright can be recorded with the Copyright Office. Of course, this includes any document transferring all or part of a copyright—whether it be an exclusive license or assignment. It also includes nonexclusive licenses, wills, powers of attorney in which authors or other copyright owners give others the power to act for them, and other contracts dealing with a copyrighted work.

It's a very good idea to record any document that affects a transfer of copyright ownership. Also, record any document that contains information you want the world at large to be aware of—for example, a change of the copyright owner's name. Documents pledging a copyright as collateral or security for a loan should also be recorded.

c. How to record transfer documents

To record a document with the Copyright Office, you must complete and sign the Copyright Office Document Cover Sheet form and send it to the Copyright Office along with the document and recordation fee.

If the work involved hasn't already been registered with the Copyright Office, it should be at the same time the document is recorded. It's possible to record without registering, but important priority rights are obtained if the work is registered. (Of course, you can't register if the work is not yet in existence.) For more information on recording documents, download Circular 12, *Recordations of Transfers and Other Documents,* from the Copyright Office website.

 A copy of the Document Cover Sheet is on the CD-ROM forms disk at the end of this book. If you need further information on completing the Document Cover Sheet, see the accompanying instructions in the file.

Special Rules for California

California law provides that a person or business entity such as a corporation, partnership, or limited liability company that commissions a work made for hire is considered to be the employer of the creator of the work for purposes of the workers' compensation, unemployment insurance, and unemployment disability insurance laws. (Cal. Labor Code § 3351.5(c); Cal. Unemployment Insurance Code §§ 621, 686.) No one is entirely sure what impact this has on persons or entities who commission works made for hire. Neither the California courts nor state agencies have addressed the question. However, it may mean that the commissioning party has to obtain workers' compensation coverage for the creative party and might be liable for any injuries he or she sustains in the course of her work. It might also mean that special penalties could be assessed against a commissioning party who willfully fails to pay the creative party any monies due him or her after he or she is discharged or resigns.

These potential requirements and liabilities are one reason why it might be desirable for those commissioning work in California not to enter into work made for hire agreements, and instead have the creator assign the desired copyright rights to the commissioning party in advance. One theoretical disadvantage of using an assignment of rights as opposed to a work made for hire agreement is that an assignment can be terminated by the author or her heirs 35 to 40 years after it is made. However, this disadvantage is essentially meaningless because little or no software can be expected to have a useful economic life of more than 35 years. ■

Electronic Databases

A n electronic database (or "automated database" in Copyright Office parlance) is a body of facts, data, or other information assembled into an organized format suitable for use in a computer. Prior to the computer age, databases typically took the form of a list or a paper card system or file. With the advent of computer technology, traditional hard-copy databases have been eclipsed in importance by electronic databases. These may be accessed on the Internet, via online subscription services like LEXIS/NEXIS and Dialog, or are available on computer CD-ROMs.

For an electronic database to be constructed, a computer must be told (programmed) where the information is stored and how that information can be retrieved upon request. Accordingly, when an electronic database is actually constructed, it consists of:

- the data, and
- the database software—that is, the unique set of instructions that defines the way the data is to be organized, stored, and retrieved.

This chapter discusses legal protection for the data in electronic databases. The database software is protected in the same manner and to the same extent as any other computer software. Accordingly, protection for database software is covered throughout the rest of the book.

A. Types of Databases

The variety of information contained on electronic databases is nearly endless and growing rapidly. However, for our purposes they can be classified into two types: published databases and unpublished databases.

1. Published Databases

Published databases are those that are made available to the general public. Today, most of these are available on the Internet. Examples include large commercial online information services such as America Online, LEXIS/NEXIS, and Dialog. Online services such as these are actually collections of many databases provided by a variety of publishers and other sources. The services negotiate contracts with the owners of the databases for the right to distribute them, and pay royalties based primarily on how much the database is used. Costs to use such services are usually based on a subscription fee plus usage charges for actual use of particular databases.

Untold thousands of Internet databases are also maintained by universities, research institutions, government agencies, companies, and individuals.

EXAMPLE: Cynthia Powell, a romance novel fan in Michigan, created a website called the Romance Novel Database. Here she lists 244 romance novels and rates them by quality—five hearts is best, one heart is worst. Cynthia's website is a database consisting of 244 facts—the names of 244 romance novels. You can view the list at www.personal.si.umich.edu/~sooty/romance/rating.html.

Websites such as this qualify as "automated databases" for copyright registration purposes, which greatly decreases the costs of registration. (See Chapter 4.) Still other published electronic databases are available on CD-ROM disks or other magnetic storage media.

2. Unpublished Databases

As the name implies, unpublished databases are those not available to the general public. These include all types of electronic databases created and maintained by businesses—for example, a database containing customer ordering and payment information, or a computerized list of auto parts used by an auto parts store. Many individuals also have their own private databases; containing tax information, for example, or a list of personal property for identification and valuation purposes in the event of fire or theft.

B. Copyright Protection for Electronic Databases

Copyright law is the primary vehicle for legally protecting databases. However, not all databases are protected by copyright, and even those that are may enjoy very limited protection.

1. Databases Are Compilations or Collective Works

First, a little copyright law background. The individual bits of data contained in many databases are not entitled to copyright protection on their own. For example, names and addresses or numerical data may not qualify for copyright in their own right. But the way the database creator selected and arranged all these bits of data may constitute an original work of authorship protected by copyright. In other words, the individual materials contained in a database may not be entitled to copyright protection, but the selection and arrangement of the entire database may be. This type of database is called a fact compilation.

However, many databases contain items that qualify for copyright protection on their own—for example, a database containing the full text of copyrighted articles. This type of database is a collective work. A collective work is a special type of compilation. It is a work created by selecting and arranging into a single whole work preexisting materials that are separate and independent works entitled to copyright protection in their own right. Also, as with fact compilations, there may be copyright protection for the selection and arrangement of the materials making up a collective work.

Of course, some databases contain both protectible and unprotectible material, and are therefore both fact compilations and collective works.

2. Database Selection and Arrangement Constitutes Protected Expression

You may be wondering why any compilation should be protected by copyright. The author of a compilation does not really create anything new, he merely selects and arranges preexisting material; so what is there to protect? For example, say that you compile an electronic database listing the 1,000 baseball cards you consider most desirable for collectors listed in order of desirability. What makes such a database protectible is the creativity and judgment you would have to employ in deciding which of the thousands of baseball cards in existence belong on your list of the 1,000 most desirable cards and deciding in what order the names should appear on the list. It is this selection and arrangement of the material making up a compilation that constitutes protected expression.

The copyright in a protectible fact compilation or collective work as a whole extends only to this protected expression—that is, only to the compiler's selection and arrangement of the preexisting material, not to the preexisting material itself. Of course, the individual items in a collective work may be copyrightable themselves.

3. Minimal Creativity Required for Protection

A work must be the product of a minimal amount of creativity to be protected by copyright. This requirement applies to fact compilations as well as all other works. The data contained in a factual compilation need not be presented in an innovative or surprising way, but the selection or arrangement cannot be so mechanical or routine as to require no creativity whatsoever. If no creativity was employed in selecting or arranging the data, the compilation will not receive copyright protection.

In a landmark decision on fact compilations, the U.S. Supreme Court held that the selection and arrangement of white pages in a typical telephone directory fails to satisfy the creativity requirement and is therefore not protected by copyright. (*Feist Publications, Inc. v. Rural Telephone Service Co.*, 111 S.Ct. 1282 (1991).) There are doubtless many other types of compilations that are unprotectible for the same reason.

Copyright Does Not Protect Hard Work

In the past, some courts held that copyright protected databases and other works that lacked originality and/or creativity if a substantial amount of work was involved in their creation. These courts might have protected a telephone directory, for example, if the authors had personally verified every entry. However, the Supreme Court outlawed this "sweat of the brow" theory in the *Feist* decision. It is now clear that the amount of work done to create a database or other work has absolutely no bearing on the degree of copyright protection it will receive. As discussed in detail in Chapter 3, copyright protects original expression, not hard work. To tell if a database is sufficiently creative to be protected by copyright, you need to answer two questions:

1) Is the *arrangement* of the data minimally creative?
2) Is the *selection* of the data minimally creative?

A database is eligible for copyright protection if either the selection or arrangement is minimally creative. Of course, many databases satisfy both criteria.

a. Is the arrangement of the data creative?

Famed "information architect" Richard Saul Wurman in his book *Information Ar-chitects*, points out that there are only six ways to arrange data. You may use:

- location
- alphabet
- time
- number
- category, or
- hierarchy.

Common sense tells us that of these six methods only location, category, and hierarchy can require minimal creativity and can be protected by copyright. No creativity is involved in arranging a database by alphabet, time, or number. These types of organization are purely mechanical—that is, they require no exercise in judgment. You just have to know the alphabet, how to tell time, or count, to arrange a database by these methods.

b. Is the selection of the data creative?

The selection of the data in a database satisfies the minimal creativity test only if the compiler has:

- chosen less than all of the data in a given body of relevant material, regardless of whether it is taken from one or more sources, and
- the selection is based on the compiler's opinion about something.

For example, no selectivity is required to compile a directory of *all* the restaurants in New York City. The compiler of such a directory need not employ any judgment in deciding which restaurants belong in the directory.

But a list of the 100 "best" restaurants in New York City is minimally creative and protected by copyright. Here, the compiler must use selectivity and judgment to decide which 100 of the thousands of restaurants in New York City are "best."

c.   Examples of databases that lack creativity

Representatives of the Copyright Office have indicated that, in their view, the following types of databases will usually fail to satisfy the minimal creativity requirement. The Copyright Office's views don't have the force of law, but the courts likely would follow them.

- *Street address directories, alumni directories, membership lists, mailing lists, and subscriber lists:* Works such as these often require no more creativity to compile than the white pages in a phone book. This would be the case where (1) the material is arranged in alphabetical or numerical order, and (2) no judgment was needed to decide which names and addresses should be included.

    EXAMPLES: The following databases lack creativity: an alphabetical list of all Harvard alumni, all the members

of the ACLU, or all the subscribers to *Time* Magazine; a mailing list in numerical order according to zip code of all persons who have contributed more than $1,000 to the Republican Party.

- *Parts lists:* An alphabetical or numerical list of all the parts in a given inventory clearly fails the creativity test: If the list is exhaustive, no selectivity is required to compile it; if it is arranged in alphabetical or numerical order, no creativity is required to arrange it.
- *Genealogies:* A genealogy (that is, a table or diagram recording a person's or family's ancestry) consisting merely of transcriptions of public records, such as census or courthouse records, or transcriptions made from headstones in a few local cemeteries, are also deemed by the Copyright Office to lack minimal creativity. On the other hand, the creativity requirement may be satisfied where the creator of a genealogy compilation uses judgment in selecting material from a number of different sources.
- *De minimis compilations:* De minimis in Latin means trifling or insignificant. A de minimis compilation is one that contains only a few items. The Copyright Office considers a compilation of only three items to be clearly de minimis and not protected by copy-

right. Even if a de minimis compilation meets the minimal creativity requirement, the Copyright Office will refuse to register it. This means the compiler can't file a copyright infringement suit if anyone else uses their list of three or fewer things.

4. Using Raw Data From Protected Fact Compilation Databases

As discussed above, the copyright in a fact compilation extends only to the selection, coordination, and arrangement of the data contained in the compilation and to any new expression the database author adds—for instance, instructions on how to use the database. The raw data itself is not protected. This is sometimes called a thin copyright.

Since the copyright in a fact compilation extends only to the compiler's selection and arrangement of the facts, the raw facts or data themselves are not protected by copyright. The Supreme Court has stated that the raw facts may be copied at will and that a compiler is even free to use the facts contained in another's compilation to aid in preparing a competing compilation. *(Feist Publications, Inc. v. Rural Telephone Service Co.,* 111 S.Ct. 1282 (1991).)* But the competing work may not feature the exact same selection and arrangement as the earlier compilation—provided that this selection and arrangement passes the minimal creativity test as described in the previous section.

This means that a database user may extract the individual bits of data from a fact compilation database without incurring liability for copyright infringement, but may not copy the entire database, since this would involve copying the copyright owner's protected expression—that is, selection and arrangement (provided it is minimally creative).

EXAMPLE: A website called Who's Alive and Who's Dead contains the birth and—where applicable—death dates for over 1,700 celebrities, political figures, sports stars, and others. This information is organizing in a variety of interesting ways. For example, you look up your favorite television show and see when the cast members were born and if any are dead. This website is a simple database. The creators of this database are entitled to copyright protection for the way they have selected and arranged the material on their website. However, they do not have a copyright in the individual facts in their database—meaning they don't own the birth and death dates of celebrities. These facts are not protectible by copyright. Anyone can look up a birth date in the database and use that date without obtaining permission from the creators of the database. There is no need to go back to the original sources the database's creators used to compile their database, such as newspaper obituary records or government records of births and deaths.

It may seem unfair that the facts contained in a database gathered at great trouble and expense may be used by others without violating the copyright laws. However, the purpose of copyright is to advance the progress of knowledge, not to reward authors. If the first person to compile a group of raw facts acquired a monopoly over them, progress would be greatly impeded. This might not seem so serious if we were only talking about birth and death dates of celebrities. But many databases contain far more vital information that no one should be allowed to monopolize.

But, don't get the idea that raw facts in databases may always be freely copied. Database owners can use laws other than copyright to prevent the public from doing just that. (See Section D below.)

Copyright protection is greater where a database is a collective work—a work consisting of materials entitled to their own copyright protection. In this event, the database owner holds a thin copyright in the selection and arrangement of the entire database, and the items contained in the database may be protected

individually. For example, each article contained in a full-text bibliographic database may be protected by copyright, as well as the selection and arrangement of the database as a whole.

C. Registering Contents of Electronic Databases

If an electronic database is protected by copyright, it should be registered with the Copyright Office for all the reasons discussed in Chapter 4. Since most databases are frequently updated or revised, the Copyright Office has instituted a special group registration procedure whereby a database and all the updates or other revisions made within any three-month period may be registered in one application. This way, a database need only be registered a maximum of four times per year, rather than each time it is updated or revised.

Database Software Must Also Be Registered

The discussion below is only about how to register the selection and arrangement of the contents of an electronic database. It does not cover registration of computer software designed to be used with databases to facilitate retrieval of the data.

---

1. Qualifying for Group Registration

To qualify for group registration, a database must meet all of the following conditions:

- all of the updates or revisions must be fixed or published only in machine-readable copies
- all of the updates or revisions must have been created or published within a three-month period, all within the same calendar year
- all of the updates or revisions must be owned by the same copyright claimant (see Chapter 4 for more on copyright claimants)
- all of the updates or revisions must have the same general title, and
- the updates or revisions must be organized in a similar way.

For information on preparing the registration form (Form TX) and the deposit requirements for an automated database, Download Circular 65, *Copyright Registration for Automated Databases,* from the Copyright Office website at www.loc.gov/copyright.

 A digital copy of Form TX is on the Forms Disk at the end of this book. The forms are in Adobe Acrobat PDF format. You can complete these forms on your computer and then print them out; but before you do this, read the instructions in Chapter 4, Section B. You can also obtain the forms directly from the Copyright Office.

2. Nongroup Registration

If your database doesn't qualify for group registration, or for some reason you do not wish to use that procedure, simply complete Form TX in the same manner as for any other compilation. You should deposit the first and last 25 pages of a single-file database. If the database consists of separate and distinct data files, deposit one copy of 50 complete data records (not pages) from each file, or the entire file, whichever is less. You must also include a descriptive statement for a multiple-file database containing the same information described in Section C1 just above.

If the database is fixed in a CD-ROM, deposit one complete copy of the CD-ROM package, any instructional manual, and a printed version of the work which is fixed on the CD-ROM if such an exact print version exists. The deposit must also include any software that is included as part of the package. A printout of the first and last 25 pages of the software source code is acceptable. If the software contains trade secrets, other deposit arrangements can be made. See the discussion in Chapter 4, Section E.

D. Using Noncopyright Means to Protect Databases

Given the limitations on copyright protection for databases and the fact that many databases don't qualify for any protection at all, the owners of valuable databases often use other ways to protect their creations. These means are used not only to protect the selection and arrangement of the data, but the data itself.

1. Licenses

A database license is a contract restricting what a person can do with the data. These licenses are commonly used to protect databases that are not made freely available to the public. People who use the database must agree in advance to the terms of the license.

Database licenses take many forms. Some are form contracts, while others are negotiated agreements tailored to particular individuals or institutions. They may appear in traditional print form, under the shrink-wrapping of a computer disk or CD-ROM, on a computer screen as part of software, online, or in a combination of these formats.

The terms of database licenses also vary, but they generally restrict or limit how the database can be used. For example, an online license typically dictates when the database can be downloaded or disseminated to others. These restrictions put limits on a user's ability to use the contents of the database beyond what copyright law allows.

Licenses also usually establish enforcement procedures and remedies should the licensee violate the terms of the license. Such terms can include terminating a subscriber's access, suspending services, or suing the subscriber for damages. (See Chapter 16 for a detailed discussion of licenses.)

2. Trade Secrets

We've seen above that databases get extremely limited copyright protection or, in many cases, none at all. For this reason, database owners often use state trade secrecy laws to protect their works. For example, electronic databases that are maintained by companies on their internal—that is, nonpublic—computer networks are usually protected as trade secrets. This form of legal protection may be used to supplement copyright protection. If the database cannot be protected by copyright, it may be the owner's main line of defense against unauthorized use.

Not everything can be a trade secret. The database owner must take reasonable steps to keep the data in the database secret—for example, carefully restrict access by keeping it in a password-protected computer system. Databases that are published or otherwise made available to the public cannot be protected as trade secrets; nor can databases that contain information that is generally known in the industry involved. Data that everybody knows cannot provide anyone with a competitive advantage. However, the information in a database need not be novel or unique to qualify as a trade secret. All that is required is that the information not be generally known by people who could profit from its disclosure and use.

(See Chapters 7 and 8 for a detailed overview of trade secrets law.)

3. Encryption

Another form of protection for electronic databases is encryption—that is, encoding the data in an unreadable form that can be "unlocked" and read only with the proper key. This is not a legal protection, but it makes it difficult or impossible to obtain access to a database. The government has been encrypting its sensitive data for years. Powerful encryption technologies that can prevent unauthorized access to and changes in databases are now commercially available. Moreover, recent changes to the copyright laws generally make it illegal for anyone to obtain access to a database or other work by circumventing technological measures such as encryption. ■

Website and Software Permissions

This chapter covers the permissions problems that arise whenever a Web or software developer seeks to add content to a project. Sections A though E discuss the special copyright problems faced by developers. Section F covers publicity and privacy concerns.

A. Introduction

Most websites and software programs combine a variety of materials, including text, graphics, photos, videos, and sounds. Unfortunately, such projects can present difficult and expensive legal problems. These fall into two main categories:

- *Copyright permissions problems*: You may need to obtain permission to use materials protected by copyright, whether it be text, photos, video and film clips, software, or music. Obtaining permissions for a Web or software project can involve tracking down many different copyright owners and negotiating licenses to use their material. (This is discussed in detail in Section B, below.)
- *Publicity/privacy problems*: Use of photos, film or video footage, or audio recordings can constitute a breach of the privacy or publicity rights of the people whose likenesses are used. You'll need to consider whether you must obtain privacy releases from persons whose images or voices are used. (This is discussed in detail in Section F, below.)

Obtaining copyright permission and publicity/privacy releases can be a weighty task.

EXAMPLE: The University of the Midwest History Department decides to create a comprehensive website about Columbus's "discovery" of America. Midwest wants to incorporate into the website a variety of pre-existing materials about Columbus, including:

- text from various articles and books
- photos from books, magazines, and other sources
- video clips from several television programs
- film clips from two theatrical movies about Columbus
- music to be used as background to the images and text, and
- excerpts from a Broadway musical and Italian opera based on Columbus's life.

Midwest also plans to create an abbreviated version of the website on a CD-ROM for high school students.

All in all, Midwest intends to incorporate hundreds of separate items into its website and CD-ROM. This sounds like a fine idea for a website and CD-ROM. However, Midwest needs to address and resolve the copyright permissions problem and publicity/privacy problems before it can place its website online.

Other Intellectual Property Concerns

A Web or software developer's main concerns are with copyright and publicity/privacy problems. However, other intellectual property laws may come into play as well. For example:

- Third-party software may be patented, as may certain business methods used on the Web. A license must be obtained to use any material protected by a patent.

- The federal and state trademark laws may protect character names, physical appearance, and costumes; some titles; as well as product names, logos, slogans, and packaging. A developer may have to obtain permission to use a trademark on a website. (See Chapter 10 for an overview of trademarks.)

- Finally, trade secret problems may occur whenever a developer uses or is exposed to any material or information (even a mere idea) that is covered by a confidentiality agreement. A developer must be particularly vigilant about avoiding use of confidential information any employee obtained from a prior employer. (See Chapter 7 for a detailed discussion of trade secrets.)

There are ways to get around, or at least alleviate, permissions problems. First we'll discuss when a Web or software developer does and does not need to obtain permissions, and second, where and how to get them if they are needed. We'll then review the privacy and publicity issues that arise in Web and software projects.

B. When You Need to Obtain Permission

Whether or not a Web or software developer needs permission to include any given item in a project depends on:

- whether the item is protected by copyright or is in the public domain
- whether or not the material is created especially for the project
- who created it (employee, independent contractor, or third party), and
- the extent and nature of the intended use.

1. New Material Created for a Web or Software Project

No copyright permissions problems are normally presented when material is created especially for a Web or software project, whether by the developer's employees or independent contractors.

Under the copyright laws, a developer will automatically own the copyright in materials created in-house by its own employees. As a result, the developer need not obtain permission from its employees to use copyrighted works—the developer already owns those rights. For example, Midwest University would not need to obtain permission to use text or graphics created by an employee for its website on Columbus. It is wise, however, to have creative employees sign employment agreements transferring whatever ownership rights they might conceivably have to the developer. (See Chapter 14 for a detailed discussion and sample forms.)

When a developer hires an independent contractor to contribute to a Web or software project, it should require the contractor to assign copyright rights to the developer. For example, if Midwest hires a freelance artist to create drawings for its Columbus project, it should have the artist, before commencing work, sign an independent contractor agreement assigning her rights in the drawings to Midwest. (See Chapter 15 for a detailed discussion and sample forms.)

2. Preexisting Materials

The permissions problem raises its ugly head when a developer wishes to use preexisting materials—that is, materials previously created by nonemployees (or created by employees before they became employees). You can figure out whether permission is required by answering the following two questions:

- Is the material in the public domain?
- Does your intended use of the material constitute a "fair use?"

If your answer to both questions is "no," you need permission; otherwise you don't. To help you answer these questions, Section C discusses what is in the public domain and Section D examines the fair use rule.

3. Using Copyrighted Material Without Permission

You might be tempted to use copyrighted material without permission if you are unable to locate the copyright owner or simply don't have the time, money, or staff to obtain numerous permissions. If the copyright owner later discovers what you've done, at the very least you will be liable for the reasonable value of the use. If the material is not terribly valuable, this won't amount to much, and the owner will probably accept a small permission fee.

> **EXAMPLE:** Midwest University wants to quote two pages from an old magazine article about Columbus. The magazine is out of business and neither the author nor her heirs can be located. Midwest University decides to use the quotation anyway. One year later, Midwest University is

contacted by the article's copyright owner. The owner agrees to accept $250 from Midwest for retroactive permission to use the quotation.

On the other hand, if the material is valuable, you could find yourself in big trouble. At the very least, you'll be liable for a substantial permission fee, perhaps more than you'd be able or willing to pay. Instead of settling for a permission fee, the copyright owner might sue you for copyright infringement. In this event, you could face substantial damages. The copyright owner you've stolen from could ask the court for the reasonable value of the use and the amount of any economic loss caused by your theft; or, if the material has been registered with the U.S. Copyright Office, the copyright owner could ask for special statutory damages, which can range up to $150,000 (it's up to the judge or jury to decide how much). In some cases, you could even be subject to criminal prosecution. And don't forget, you'll be paying your attorney handsomely, regardless of how the case turns out.

EXAMPLE: Midwest University "borrows" several minutes from the video version of a recent theatrical movie about Columbus and uses it on its website. The film's copyright owners discover the theft and sue Midwest for copyright infringement. They obtain an injunction prohibiting Midwest University from using the pirated footage and ultimately obtain a court judgment against Midwest. They ask the judge to award statutory damages, and, because the judge finds that the infringement was willful and blatant, she awards $50,000 in damages against Midwest.

C. Works That Are in the Public Domain

The general nature of copyright protection is discussed in Chapter 3. If you haven't read that material, do so now. Copyright protects all original works of authorship. This includes, but is not limited to, writings of all kinds, music, sound recordings, paintings, sculptures and other works of art, photographs, software, film, and video.

Luckily for Web and software developers, however, not every work of authorship ever created is currently protected by copyright—not by a long shot. A work that is not protected by copyright is said to be in the "public domain"; in effect, it belongs to everybody. Anyone is free to use it without asking permission, but no one can ever own the work again. By using public domain materials, a developer can avoid going through the time, trouble, and expense involved in getting permission to use copyrighted materials.

Following is a brief description of the types of materials that are in the public domain. However, to determine whether a particular work is in the public domain, refer to *The Public Domain: How to Find & Use Copyright-Free Writings, Music, Art & More*, by Stephen Fishman (Nolo).

1. Things That Are Never Protected by Copyright

Certain works of authorship and other items are never protected by copyright and are therefore always in the public domain. These include:

- *Ideas and facts*: Because copyright only protects an author's expression, ideas and facts themselves are not protected.
- *Words, names, titles, slogans, and other short phrases*: Individual words are always in the public domain, even if they are invented by a particular person. However, these items may be protected under state and federal trademark laws if they are used to identify a product or service. (See Chapter 10.)
- *United States government works*: All works created by U.S. government employees as part of their jobs are in the public domain. This includes, for example, everything printed by the U.S. Printing Office, NASA photographs, the president's speeches and publications, and other works by federal agencies. But this rule does not apply to works by state and local government employees; those works may be protected by copyright.

2. Works Whose Copyright Has Expired

Another large category of public domain works are those whose copyright has expired. Every work published in the United States before 1923 is in the public domain in the U.S. Many works initially published in the U.S. during 1923-1963 are also in the public domain because their copyrights were never renewed.

3. Works Dedicated to the Public Domain

The owners of some works have decided they don't want them to be protected by copyright and dedicate them to the public domain. For example, some software has been dedicated to the public domain. There are no formal procedures for dedicating a work to the public domain. The author just has to indicate on the work that no copyright is claimed.

4. Public Domain Works Are Not Always Freely Available

The fact that a work is in the public domain does not necessarily mean that it is freely available for use by a developer.

Although the copyright in a work may have expired, the work itself may still be owned by someone, who may restrict or charge for access to it.

This is usually not a problem for written works, which can be found in bookstores and libraries, but it is a problem for other types of works. For example, all works of art published in the United States before 1923 are in the public domain, but recent photographs of them may not be. Museums and individual collectors usually control access to valuable works of art that are in the public domain and often own all available photographs of such works. Getting permission to use such photographs or to take new ones can be difficult and expensive.

Fees may also have to be paid to obtain access to and make use of public domain photographs, film, and music from collectors, private archives, and other sources.

D. The "Fair Use" Exception to Copyrighted Works

Even if the material you want to use is protected by copyright, you will not need permission if your intended use constitutes a "fair use." Under the fair use rule, an author is permitted to make limited use of preexisting protected works without asking permission. All copyright owners are deemed to give their automatic consent to the fair use of their work by others. The fair use rule is an important exception to a copyright owner's exclusive rights.

The fair use rule is designed to aid the advancement of knowledge, which is the reason for having a copyright law in the first place. If scholars, educators, and others were required to obtain permission every time they quoted or otherwise used brief portions of other authors' works, the progress of knowledge would be greatly impeded.

Determining whether the fair use privilege applies in any given situation is not an exact scientific process. Rather, it requires a delicate balancing of all the factors discussed below. Probably the best rule for fair use is the following variant of the Golden Rule: "Take not from others to such an extent and in such a manner that you would be resentful if they so took from you." (McDonald, "Non-infringing Uses," 9 *Bull. Copyright Society* 466 (1962).)

The following four factors must be considered to determine whether an intended use of an item constitutes a fair use:

- the purpose and character of the use
- the nature of the copyrighted work
- the effect of the use upon the potential market for or value of the copyrighted work, and
- the amount and substantiality of the portion used in relation to the copyrighted work as a whole (17 U.S.C. § 107).

Not all these factors are equally important in every case, but all are considered by the courts in deciding whether a use is "fair." You should consider them all in making your own fair use analysis. For a more detailed discussion of fair use principles and the fair use factors, see Chapter 6, Section B5.

If you're not sure whether an intended use is a fair use, seek legal advice or get permission.

Giving Credit Does Not Make a Use "Fair"

Some people have the mistaken idea that they can use any amount of material so long as they give the creator or copyright owner credit. This is simply not true. Providing credit will not in and of itself make a use "fair." Nevertheless, attribution should always be provided for any material obtained or copied from third parties. Passing yourself off as the creator of other people's work is a good way to get sued for copyright infringement, and is likely to make a judge or jury angry if you are sued. Quoting with attribution is a very good hedge against getting sued, or losing big if you are sued. Thus, you should always provide a credit line for any material you make fair use of.

E. Obtaining Permission to Use Copyrighted Materials

If you want to use material that is not in the public domain and your use doesn't qualify as a fair use, you need to get permission. With the notable exception of the music industry, which has had a system of rights collectives in place for many decades, obtaining permission to use copyrighted materials in a website or software project can be a difficult, time-consuming, and often chaotic process.

Obtaining permissions can be especially hard because, for a variety of reasons, many copyright owners are reluctant to grant any website or software permissions. Many owners are reluctant to permit their work to be reduced to digitized form for fear they will lose control over unauthorized copying. Still others intend to launch their own website or software ventures and don't want to help potential competitors. Some owners will grant permission, but only for exorbitant amounts of money (there are generally no standard rates for such permissions).

Securing a website or software permission, then, can require a good deal of persistence, salesmanship, and creative negotiating on a developer's part.

For a detailed explanation of how to go about getting permission and all the forms you may need, refer to *Getting Permission: How to License & Clear Copyrighted Materials Online & Off*, by Richard Stim (Nolo).

Expect permissions to take anywhere from one to three months to negotiate and obtain. The first step is to learn how much a particular work would cost to use. Depending on your budget for obtaining permissions, the cost might make your decision for you, if it is beyond your means. Often copyright owners have a sliding scale of fees for different uses. Commercial uses are usually more costly than nonprofit uses.

It is best to obtain written permission before you begin using the copyrighted work. But you should absolutely obtain it before your project is completed. It is sometimes more difficult and more expensive to obtain permission after a website or software program is completed. If the copyright owner becomes aware that you have a vested interest in obtaining permission (for example, your website is already online), the price may rise. In addition, if you can't obtain permission, you'll have to re-do the work, which can be expensive and time-consuming. The best policy is to start seeking all required permissions as soon as possible.

Clearance Firms

If you need to obtain many permissions, or simply don't want to bother getting them yourself, there are private companies and individuals who obtain permissions on an author or publisher's behalf. These permission specialists may have contacts with some publishers that enable them to get better and faster results than you can yourself. Clearance firms usually charge by the hour.

A comprehensive list of clearance firms can be found in the *Literary Market Place* (LMP), a directory for the publishing business, under "Permissions." The LMP can be accessed online at www.literarymarket place.com.

---

1. Written Materials (Text)

Obtaining permission to use any type of copyrighted written materials—excerpts from books, magazines, journals, and so forth—can be merely difficult or simply impossible. There is no single, centralized group or organization granting such permissions and there are no standard fees. You—or someone you hire—must track down the copyright owner of the material you want to use, or his or her representative (usually publisher or agent), and cut your own deal.

2. Photographs

If you need photographs, several sources are available:

- you can use commercially available clipmedia—materials that are typically published on websites or CD-ROM disks specifically for users to incorporate into websites, software, and other works. (Review the license agreement that comes with the clipmedia to make sure you can publicly distribute the material for commercial purposes.)
- you can try to get the rights to use photos that have appeared in magazines, books, and other publications
- you can directly contact photographers and try to get permission to use their work
- you can deal with stock photo agencies—companies that acquire the rights to photos and license them over and over again to magazines, advertising agencies, book publishers, and others.

The easiest way to find a stock photo house is to use the World Wide Web.

A good place to begin your search is the Yahoo Commercial Stock Photography Directory (www.yahoo.com/Business _and_Economy/Companies/Photography/ Stock_Photography).

3. Film and Video

A variety of film and video footage is available from stock houses—companies that acquire the right to license films and videos. A good place to begin a footage search is Footage.net (www.footage.net).

Image Sampling

With modern digital technology, it is very easy for website and software developers to take a photo or film or video footage and alter it to such an extent that it is no longer recognizable by its original creator. Is this copyright infringement? If the end result is not recognizable as coming from the original, it may not be. In the words of one court, "copying ... so disguised as to be unrecognizable is not copying" (*See v. Durang*, 711 F.2d 141 (9th Cir. 1983).) However, before the final result is reached, it may be necessary to create intermediate copies of the original work that are clearly recognizable. It is unclear whether this would constitute copyright infringement. The conservative approach is to obtain permission before using any copyrighted photo or footage.

---

4. Drawings and Other Artwork

Permission to use and reproduce drawings, paintings, and other works of art must be obtained from the owner, or sometimes the artist. Artists sometimes retain the reproduction rights to a particular piece while selling the piece itself and the right to display it. The person or entity controlling the reproduction rights must be tracked down—whether a museum, individual collector, artist, or artist's estate. Fees and terms for such rights vary widely.

5. Cartoons

The rights to cartoons are usually handled by distribution syndicates or agents. A flat fee is customarily charged for a limited-time use. You should be able to find out who to contact for permission by calling the publication in which the cartoon appeared.

6. Music

Although the music industry has in place a standardized process for obtaining permissions, the procedures and expenses can be formidable. Keep in mind that there are two distinct copyrights associated with recorded music: one for the musical composition and the other for the recording.

This means that to make a new recording of a song for inclusion in a website or computer program, a developer must obtain permission from the music publisher. But to use an existing recording, permission must be obtained from the music publisher and the recording company.

This discussion just scratches the surface of music licensing. For a detailed explanation of all the issues involved in music licensing, refer to *The Art of Music Licensing*, by Al and Bob Kohn (Prentice Hall Law & Business). This book is expensive—about $80—but it's well worth it.

a. Making new recordings of existing music for software

The music industry has developed a process for obtaining permission to make a new recording of existing copyrighted music and reproducing it in a multimedia program. The Harry Fox Agency—a subsidiary of the National Music Publishers' Association—issues licenses and collects and distributes royalties on behalf of music publishers who have entered into agreements with Fox for this service. The agency can be contacted at www.harry fox.com.

The Harry Fox Agency handles what are known as mechanical and synchronization licenses—licenses to record a song or other musical composition and use it in conjunction with still or moving images. This is sufficient for personal use of a multimedia program.

b. Using existing recordings for software

Obtaining permission to use an existing recording can be more difficult and expensive than making a new one. First, it is necessary to obtain the mechanical and synchronization rights to the music itself through the Harry Fox Agency, as outlined above. If the multimedia product is to be performed in public, a performance license must also be obtained through one of the appropriate performing rights societies, listed below:

- ASCAP (American Society of Composers, Authors & Publishers) (www .ascap.com)
- BMI (Broadcast Music, Inc.) (www .bmi.com)
- SESAC (Society of European State Authors and Composers) (www.sesac .com).

Permission must also be obtained to use the recording itself (termed "master recording rights") from the owner of the copyright in the recording.

The "special markets division" of the appropriate recording company must be contacted to obtain master recording rights. The recording contract must be examined to see who has the right to grant permission to reuse the recording. This may be the record company or the artist.

Recording companies are generally reluctant to permit their recordings to be reused, particularly if a well-known song is performed by a well-known artist. Where obtainable, permission to do so is usually very expensive. Musician union agreements may also require that reuse fees be paid to the musicians, vocalists, and others who worked on the recording.

Music Sampling

With modern digital audio technology, anyone with access to a digital synthesizer can capture all or part of a previous recording and reuse bits and pieces in new recordings. The unauthorized sampling of even a few seconds of a sound recording can constitute copyright infringement of both the sound recording from which the sample is taken and the underlying song. Particularly if the recording is well known, there is a real risk of being sued for illegal copying and having to pay substantial damages. This risk is reduced if the sampled sounds are so altered that their original source is not recognizable. But if the source of sampled music is recognizable, permission for the use should be obtained as outlined in this section. A good general rule is, "If you can name the tune, get permission."

c. Webcasting and audio streaming rights

There are two common ways to transmit music over the Internet: downloading and streaming. Audio streaming (and webcasting) is a process by which digital music is broadcast over the Internet, much like a radio station broadcasts music. The computer user hears the music simultaneously as it is being played by the website. Both webcasting and audio streaming are referred to as "digital audio transmissions."

- If you created the music and the recording, no permission is needed for digital audio transmissions.
- If you are using someone else's song but you have recorded your own version, you will need both performance and mechanical rights permissions from the music publisher.
- If you are streaming a song that is owned by a music publisher and a record company, you will need permission from both entities.

EXAMPLE: Larry develops a website for a perfume company He wants to stream a recording of "Addicted to Love" by Robert Palmer. He will need permission from the publisher of the song and from the record company that owns the Robert Palmer classic in order to permit downloading of that version.

Below we discuss each type of permission.

d. Music publisher permission for streaming website use

Before offering a song for streaming at a website, you'll need permission from the music publisher. The rules for how to pay the music publisher are evolving; music publishers currently are seeking to get paid in two ways (referred to as "double-dipping"): once for the reproduction of the sound file, and again for the transmission of the file over the Internet. Payments and permission are discussed below.

- **Payment to Music Publisher for Reproduction.** For songs previously recorded and released in the U.S., permission can be obtained by using what is known as a compulsory license. In terms of payments, music publishers consider downloads the same as compact discs or cassette recordings. You must pay the compulsory rate per copy.
- **Payment to Music Publisher for Transmission.** As of the writing of this book, a performance license and fee must be negotiated with the appropriate performing rights societies for the right to transmit a digital recording. Contact the performing rights society and request a license for

"digital phonorecord delivery." Before entering into one of these licenses, contact either ASCAP or BMI directly and inquire whether such a license is necessary for your use. For information on determining whether BMI or ASCAP represents a music publisher. Contact BMI at www.bmi.com and ASCAP at www.ascap.com.

e. Sound recording permission for streaming website use

You will need permission from the record company that owns the recording before streaming any songs. For example, if you were posting a recording by Blink 182, you would need permission from their record label.

f. Website downloads

To provide downloads (officially known as "digital phonorecord delivery" or DPDs) at a site, you'll need to obtain permission from the owner of the song (music publisher) and owner of the sound recording (record company). Of course, if you have self-produced the recording and created the music, there's no problem. But if not, you must get permission to permit downloads. Without permission, the owners can require that you remove the recording and perhaps make you pay financial damages. The same rules would

apply for downloads as well as for streaming.

g. Music clearance firms

Developers who do not wish to go to the time and trouble of obtaining music permissions themselves can retain the services of music clearance firms. For a fee, these companies will request, negotiate, and process music permissions. Using such firms will usually be cheaper than retaining a music attorney, and they are often more effective. These firms are located primarily in New York, Los Angeles, and Nashville, the centers of the music business. One of the best known firms is BZ Rights and Permissions, Inc. (www.bzrights.com). For more information on clearance firms, read *Getting Permission,* by Richard Stim (Nolo).

h. Production music libraries

Production Music Libraries ("PML"s) provide an inexpensive method of obtaining rights for original music and sound effects on a nonexclusive basis. PML music, which is primarily instrumental, is used in films, websites, slide shows, radio and television programming, commercials, software and multimedia, training videos, in-flight services, and similar applications.

Like stock photography, PML music is categorized by genre or mood (old time rock and roll, outer space, etc.) and is sold on compact disc collections on a royalty-free basis, for a blanket fee, or ooon a per use basis. A typical PML compact disc may contain ten to 15 original compositions, including a full-length version of each composition as well as shorter "tag" or "cue" version. Larger PMLs have hundreds of compact discs in their collection. Using the Internet, it is possible to search through these collections and hear samples.

7. Software

Websites and computer programs often include third-party software—software "engines"— that drive the program and application software programs to support graphics, sound, and animation. A license from the copyright owner must be obtained to distribute third-party software with a multimedia program. To obtain such a license, contact the software publisher.

F. Privacy and Publicity Problems

Privacy and publicity problems arise when a website or software work uses photographs, video, film, or other images of an individual's likeness or recordings of a person's voice. This is a complex area of the law and privacy/publicity rights vary from state to state. The following is a brief overview.

 The definitive work on these issues is *The Rights of Publicity and Privacy*, by J. Thomas McCarthy (Clark Boardman Callaghan).

1. Right to Privacy

The right to privacy is simply the right to be left alone. The law protects a person from humiliation, embarrassment, loss of self-esteem, or other injury to his or her sensibilities caused by the following types of activities:

- using a person's name, likeness, or voice for commercial purposes, without authorization—for example, in an advertisement

- entering or observing a private or secluded area without consent—for example, spying on a person's home or office without permission to take photographs

- publicly displaying an image which shows or implies something embarrassing and untrue about someone—for example, using a picture of an uninfected person in a work about sexually transmitted diseases in a way that implies that the person has such a disease, or

- publicly disclosing true, but private and embarrassing facts about a person that are of no legitimate public concern—for example, displaying film footage of a person hugging someone other than his or her spouse.

These privacy rights belong primarily to private individuals. Public officials (persons who hold important elective or appointed offices) and "public figures" have little or no right of privacy for acts relating to their public life. Determining if someone qualifies as a public figure can be difficult. Persons who are extremely influential and powerful, who frequently appear in the media, or who are in the forefront of public controversies all qualify as "public figures." This includes not only people we normally think of as "celebrities"—film and TV stars, rock stars, sports heroes, famous business tycoons, and so forth—but lesser-known individuals involved in public affairs—for example, the heads of the ACLU and NRA.

A person's privacy rights cease when he or she dies. Thus, there are no privacy issues presented in using old photos or archival or newsreel footage of people who are dead.

2. Right of Publicity

The right of publicity is the right to control when and how one's name, voice, or likeness may be used for purposes of advertising or trade—for example, to advertise or sell a product or service. Public figures—famous athletes or film stars, for example—can earn substantial sums by endorsing products and appearing in commercials. No one would pay for an endorsement if the right of publicity were not legally protected. Only human beings have a right of publicity; corporations, firms, and institutions do not.

Unlike the privacy rights discussed above, the right to publicity continues in some states for many years after a celebrity's death. For example, in California, the right to publicity lasts for 70 years after a person's death; in Oklahoma, 100 years. This means, for example, that it is illegal to use a photo of Marilyn Monroe or Elvis Presley for commercial purposes in California or Oklahoma without the consent of their estates. Because websites and most software programs are nationally distributed, permission must be obtained to use a deceased celebrity's name, likeness, or voice for commercial purposes. That is, a developer normally cannot restrict distribution only to those states not providing privacy rights after a person dies.

3. First Amendment Limitations on Privacy/Publicity Rights

The rights to privacy and publicity are not absolute. The First Amendment to the U.S. Constitution guarantees freedom of speech and of the press. The First Amendment gives priority to the public's right to know about newsworthy events of public significance. Courts have held that a person's name or likeness may be used without consent where it is done for educational or informational purposes. This enables the news media to publicly disclose a person's name, likeness, or other characteristics without permission for newsworthy and editorial purposes.

The First Amendment applies to software developers as well as to the news media. Under the First Amendment, a website or software developer has broad latitude to use a person's image, voice, or name for educational, cultural, and artistic purposes. This is particularly true where public figures are involved. But if your purpose is primarily to sell a product or service, the First Amendment will not protect the use. For example, film footage of General Norman Schwartzkopf could be used in a website history of the first Persian Gulf War without violating the General's privacy or publicity rights. Such a work has an educational purpose. However, the General's right to publicity would likely be violated if the same footage was used in a commercial website to help sell its products—for example, a website for gun dealers.

4. Releases of Privacy/Publicity Claims

A release is simply a contract by which a person consents to the use of his or her name, likeness, or other element of his persona for the purposes specified in the release. A release should be obtained from any individual whose likeness, voice, name, or other identifiable characteristics are used in recognizable form in a website or software work that has a purely commercial purpose. It may be difficult to determine whether a work is just commercial in nature or has an educational, artistic, or cultural purpose so as to be protected under the First Amendment (as discussed in Section F3). In this event, the conservative approach is to obtain privacy/publicity releases.

In most cases, you'll have to obtain any necessary releases yourself. Unless they happen to already have releases, it's unlikely that most copyright owners will be willing to get them for you. Stock photo and stock footage houses customarily do not provide releases, although some will do so for an additional fee.

Commercial photographers customarily obtain releases from their models, so you might be able to obtain releases from them when you deal directly with a photographer. If a photographer or other copyright owner has obtained a release for the material you wish to use, make sure to ask for a copy and review it. Here's what to look for:

- Make sure the release covers the material you want to use.
- The release should specify that the photographer may sell or assign the right to use the photos or other materials to third parties.

- If you intend to alter or otherwise change or distort the image, make sure the release allows this.
- A release should always be in writing. If the subject is a minor (under 18 years old), the release should be signed by his or her parent or legal guardian.
- Finally, the release should specify that it is irrevocable—otherwise the release could be terminated by the person giving it at any time.

If these requirements are not met, a new release must be obtained.

Below is a sample of a self-explanatory valid Publicity/Privacy Release, which may be used in connection with any kind of material.

 The full text of this release is on the CD-ROM forms disk.

Multimedia Publicity/Privacy Release

In consideration of [NAME OF DEVELOPER]'s ("Developer") agreement to incorporate some or all of the Materials identified below (the "Materials") in one or more of its multimedia works (the "Works"), and other good and valuable consideration, the receipt and sufficiency of which is hereby acknowledged, I hereby grant Developer permission to use, adapt, modify, reproduce, distribute, publicly perform, and display, in any form now known or later developed, the Materials specified in this release (as indicated by my initials) throughout the world, by incorporating them into one or more Works or advertising and promotional materials relating thereto.

This release is for the following Materials (initial appropriate lines):

_____ Name

_____ Voice

_____ Visual likeness (on photographs, video, film, etc.)

_____ Photographs, graphics, or other artwork as specified:

_____

_____ Film, videotape, or other audiovisual materials as specified:

_____

_____ Music or sound recordings as specified:

_____

_____ Other: _____

I warrant and represent that the Materials identified above are either owned by me, or are original to me, or that I have full authority from the owner of the Materials to grant this release.

I release Developer, its agents, employees, licensees, and assigns from any and all claims I may have now or in the future for invasion of privacy, right of publicity, copyright infringement, defamation, or any other cause of action arising out of the use, reproduction, adaptation, distribution, broadcast, performance, or display of the Works.

I waive any right to inspect or approve any Works that may be created containing the Materials.

I understand and agree that Developer is and shall be the exclusive owner of all right, title, and interest, including copyright, in the Works, and any advertising or promotional materials containing the Materials, except as to preexisting rights in any of the Materials released hereunder.

I am of full legal age and have read this release and am fully familiar with its contents.

_____

Signature

_____

Typed or Printed Name

_____

Date

Employment Agreements

This chapter is about agreements between website and software developers and their employees. Typically, the employer presents a predrafted employment agreement to the prospective employee when a job offer is made, or soon afterward. Part I, below, provides employers with guidance on drafting such an agreement. Part II discusses the prospective employee's concerns when presented with such an agreement

PART I. Employer's Guide to Drafting Employment Agreements

It is essential that a website or software developer enter into written agreements with its employees. This should always be done before the employees commence work. Current employees who have not already done so should be asked to sign appropriate agreements, as discussed in Section D, below.

This chapter only covers agreements between employers and employees. If you're not sure whether a worker qualifies as an employee or an independent contractor, review Chapter 15.

A. Why Use Employment Agreements?

Employment agreements are used by website and software developers to help accomplish the following goals:

- to make clear to employees that they are in a confidential relationship with the employer and have a duty not to disclose confidential information to outsiders without the employer's permission
- to identify as specifically as possible what information the employer regards as confidential
- to assign to the employer, in advance, all proprietary rights (copyright, trade secret, and patent) the employee may have in his or her work product, and
- where appropriate and legal, to impose reasonable restrictions on the employee's right to compete with the employer after the employment relationship ends.

B. Who Should Sign?

All employees who might have access to trade secrets should be required to sign an employment agreement. In order of priority, this includes:

- employees (website designers, graphic designers, Web and software programmers, software engineers, and other technical personnel) who play the key role in developing your website or software; in some companies, this is only a handful of employees

- other employees who help develop your Web or software projects, such as technical writers and product testers
- marketing people, and
- administrative and clerical staff who can be expected to come into meaningful contact with trade secret materials.

C. When New Employees Should Sign

A developer should be sure to give a new employee the agreement before he or she starts work—preferably, at the same time a job offer is made. This way, the hiree can take the agreement home and study it and even have his or her lawyer look at it. Don't wait until the employee has actually started work. At this point, after quitting his or her old job (and perhaps even moving), the employee may feel he or she has no choice but to sign the agreement as written. If you later need to enforce the agreement, a court may conclude that it was not a freely bargained contract and refuse to enforce it.

D. Agreements With Current Employees

To ensure that an employment agreement with a continuing employee will be legally enforceable, you should give the employee something of value in return for agreeing to abide by the agreement. The fact that you pay the employee a salary and benefits may not be sufficient, because the employee was receiving these before you asked him or her to sign the agreement.

Give the employee a small cash bonus, a pay raise that he wouldn't have gotten anyway, stock options, vacation time, or some other remuneration. This costs you something, but it ensures that the agreement will be enforceable. (It will also encourage the employee to sign the agreement.) The value of what you give a continuing employee for signing an employment agreement doesn't have to be enormous. But the greater the amount, the clearer it will be that there was a benefit to the employee and a binding contract was thereby created.

EXAMPLE: Burt has been working as a Web programmer for Elite Web Development since its earliest days. When he was first hired, Elite did not have him sign any type of employment agreement. A few years later,

Elite management realizes that Burt, a highly skilled programmer, has been exposed to valuable Elite trade secrets and has been intimately involved in the creation of some of Elite's most valuable products. Elite decides to ask Burt to sign an agreement containing nondisclosure and invention assignment clauses. To ensure that Burt receives something of value in exchange for his signing agreement Elite gives Burt a small pay raise.

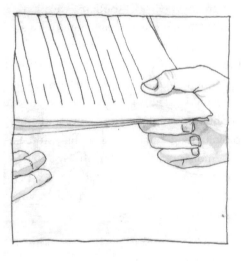

Getting Current Employees to Sign Employment Agreements

One big problem developers have with employment agreements is that they are usually not popular with employees, and some will refuse to sign them. Your employees may tell you that they know they can't divulge company trade secrets and view being asked to sign an agreement to that effect as unnecessary and an insult. This can be particularly true for small companies where the company owners and employees are (or view themselves as) friends.

Be sure to stress to any potentially offended employee that the use of such an agreement is no reflection on his character or trustworthiness. It is simply a standard legal precaution used by virtually all hi-tech businesses. Also, you may need to make the agreement as palatable as possible to the employee—for example, do not attempt to impose postemployment noncompetition restrictions on the employee, as discussed in Section G, below. When dealing with a truly key employee, consider offering substantial monetary or other benefits in return for signing the agreement.

E. Selecting Employment Agreements You Need

The following two sections contain two employment agreements:

- Employment Agreement for Nontechnical Employee (EMPLOY1 on disk), and
- Employment Agreement for Technical Employee (EMPLOY2 on disk).

Be sure to read the instructions and discussion to draft the forms; not all the provisions in the agreements may be appropriate for your situation.

F. Employment Agreement for Nontechnical Employees

This is an employment and nondisclosure agreement for use with nontechnical employees—that is, employees who are not expected to help develop websites or software. This includes clerical staff, production workers, personnel managers, marketing staff, sales staff, and so forth. This agreement does not contain a copyright and invention assignment clause, since such employees are not being paid to help develop copyrightable or patentable works.

The full text of the following agreement is on the CD-ROM forms disk.

[ALTERNATIVE 1 (FOR USE WITH NEW EMPLOYEE)] In consideration of the commencement of my employment with [NAME OF COMPANY] (the "Company") and the compensation hereafter paid to me, I agree as follows:

[ALTERNATIVE 2 (FOR USE WITH CONTINUING EMPLOYEE)] In consideration of my continued employment with [NAME OF COMPANY] (the "Company") and also in consideration of [CHOOSE ONE: "the amount of $[AMOUNT]" OR "stock options to purchase [NUMBER OF SHARES] shares of the Company's stock" OR LIST OTHER FORM OF CONSIDERATION], the receipt and sufficiency of which I hereby acknowledge, I agree as follows:

In the introductory paragraph, select Alternative 1 if a new employee will be signing the agreement, and fill in the name of the company. Select Alternative 2 if the agreement is with a current employee. Fill in the name of the company. To ensure that the agreement will be a legally binding contract, the employee should receive something of value over and above his or her normal salary and benefits for signing it—for example, cash or stock options. Specify the compensation to be provided.

1. Company's Trade Secrets

I understand that in performance of my job duties with the Company, I will be exposed to the Company's trade secrets. "Trade secrets" means information or material that is commercially valuable to the Company and not generally known in the industry. This includes, but is not limited to:

(a) any and all versions of the Company's proprietary computer software, hardware, firmware, and documentation;

(b) technical information concerning the Company's products and services, including product data and specifications, know-how, formulae, diagrams, flowcharts, drawings, source code, object code, program listings, test results, processes, inventions, research projects, and product development;

(c) information concerning the Company's business, including cost information, profits, sales information, accounting and unpublished financial information, business plans, markets and marketing methods, customer lists and customer information, purchasing techniques, supplier lists and supplier information, and advertising strategies;

(d) information concerning the Company's employees, including salaries, strengths, weaknesses, and skills;

(e) information submitted by the Company's customers, suppliers, employees, consultants, or coventurers with the Company for study, evaluation, or use; and

(f) any other information not generally known to the public which, if misused or disclosed, could reasonably be expected to adversely affect the Company's business.

As discussed in Chapter 7, an employee who learns trade secrets as a result of a confidential relationship with his or her employer has a legal duty not to disclose them to others without the employer's permission. This clause defines the company's trade secrets; the next clause addresses the employee's nondisclosure obligations.

Like all provisions in an employment agreement (or any other contract), this clause must be reasonable. It should not cover everything in the employee's brain. A clause that attempts to do so will likely be unenforceable in court, because it is unreasonable. You don't need to add anything to this clause; it sets out the types of information and material that should be considered to be trade secrets.

2. Nondisclosure of Trade Secrets

I will keep the Company's trade secrets, whether or not prepared or developed by me, in the strictest confidence. I will not use or disclose such secrets to others without the Company's written consent, except when necessary to perform my job. However, I shall have no obligation to treat as confidential any information which:

(a) was in my possession or known to me, without an obligation to keep it confidential, before such information was disclosed to me by the Company;

(b) is or becomes public knowledge through a source other than me and through no fault of mine; or

(c) is or becomes lawfully available to me from a source other than the Company.

This clause bars the employee from making unauthorized disclosures of the company's trade secrets. This makes clear to the employee that he or she has a duty to protect the employer's trade secrets. It also shows that the employer is serious about keeping trade secrets secret.

However, as explained in this clause, the employee's nondisclosure obligation does not extend to information the employee knew before coming to work for the company, information he learns from sources outside the company, and information that is not confidential because it is public knowledge (so long as the employee didn't make it public).

3. Confidential Information of Others

I will not disclose to the Company, use in the Company's business, or cause the Company to use, any information or material that is a trade secret of others.

It's a good idea to remind new employees that they have a duty not to disclose to the employer trade secrets learned from prior employers or others. Employers who take advantage of such information can easily end up being sued.

4. Return of Materials

When my employment with the Company ends, for whatever reason, I will promptly deliver to the Company all originals and copies of all documents, records, software programs, media, and other materials containing any of the Company's trade secrets. I will also return to the Company all equipment, files, software programs, and other personal property belonging to the Company.

It's important that employees understand their obligation to return all materials containing trade secrets when they leave the company. They should be reminded of this obligation in their employment agreement and before they leave.

5. Confidentiality Obligation Survives Employment

I understand that my obligation to maintain the confidentiality and security of the Company's trade secrets remains with me even after my employment with the Company ends and continues for so long as such material remains a trade secret.

It's important to make clear that the employee's duty not to disclose her employer's confidential information does not end when she leaves the company, but continues for as long as the material remains a trade secret.

6. Conflict of Interest

During my employment by the Company, I will not engage in any business activity competitive with the Company's business activities. Nor will I engage in any other activities that conflict with the Company's best interests.

This clause is intended to make clear to the employee that he shouldn't compete with the company while employed by it or engage in any activity that may harm the company.

7. Enforcement

I agree that in the event of a breach or threatened breach of this Agreement, money damages would be an inadequate remedy and extremely difficult to measure. I agree, therefore, that the Company shall be entitled to an injunction to restrain me from such breach or threatened breach. Nothing in this Agreement shall be construed as preventing the Company from pursuing any remedy at law or in equity for any breach or threatened breach.

This clause is intended to make it easier for the employer to obtain an injunction—a court order—to prevent the employee from breaching the agreement. For example, you may be able to obtain a court order preventing the employee from divulging your trade secrets to a competitor.

8. General Provisions

These general provisions are standard in many types of legal documents and are disused in detail in Chapter 17, Section B30.

9. Signatures

Although not absolutely necessary, it's a good idea to have the employee's signature witnessed by a company representative. This is intended to prevent the employee from later claiming her signature was forged.

 An example of a completed employment agreement for a nontechnical employee is on the CD-ROM forms disk.

G. Employment Agreement for Technical Employees

This agreement is for use with technical employees—Web and software programmers, Web designers, systems analysts, employees, who create documentation, software engineers, and others whose job is to help the company develop websites and/or software.

The full text of the following agreement is on the CD-ROM forms disk.

[ALTERNATIVE 1 (FOR USE WITH NEW EMPLOYEE)] In consideration of the commencement of my employment with [NAME OF COMPANY] (the "Company") and the compensation hereafter paid to me, I agree as follows:

[ALTERNATIVE 2 (FOR USE WITH CONTINUING EMPLOYEE)] In consideration of my continued employment with [NAME OF COMPANY] (the "Company") and also in consideration of [CHOOSE ONE: "the amount of $[AMOUNT]" or "stock options to purchase [NUMBER OF SHARES] shares of the Company's stock," OR list other form of consideration], the receipt and sufficiency of which I hereby acknowledge, I agree as follows:

In the introductory paragraph, select Alternative 1 if a new employee will be signing the agreement, and fill in the name of the company. Select Alternative 2 if the agreement is with a current employee. Fill in the name of the company. To ensure that the agreement will be a le-gally binding contract, the employee should receive something of value over and above his or her normal salary and benefits for signing it—for example, cash or stock options. Specify the compensation to be provided.

1. Company's Trade Secrets

I understand that in performance of my job duties with the Company, I will be exposed to the Company's trade secrets. "Trade secrets" means information or material that is commercially valuable to the Company and not generally known in the industry. This includes:

(a) any and all versions of the Company's proprietary computer software (including source code and object code), hardware, firmware, and documentation;

(b) technical information concerning the Company's products and services, including product data and specifications, diagrams, flowcharts, drawings, test results, know-how, processes, inventions, research projects, and product development;

(c) information concerning the Company's business, including cost information, profits, sales information, accounting and unpublished financial information, business plans, markets and marketing methods, customer lists and customer information, purchasing techniques, supplier lists and supplier information, and advertising strategies;

(d) information concerning the Company's employees, including their salaries, strengths, weaknesses, and skills;

(e) information submitted by the Company's customers, suppliers, employees, consultants, or co-venturers with the Company for study, evaluation, or use; and

(f) any other information not generally known to the public which, if misused or disclosed, could reasonably be expected to adversely affect the Company's business.

As discussed in Chapter 7, an employee who learns trade secrets as a result of a confidential relationship with his or her employer has a legal duty not to disclose them to others without the employer's permission. This clause defines the company's trade secrets; the next clause addresses the employee's nondisclosure obligations.

Like all provisions in an employment agreement (or any other contract), this clause must be reasonable. It should not cover everything in the employee's brain. A clause that attempts to do so will likely be unenforceable in court, because it is unreasonable. You don't need to add anything to this clause; it sets out the types of information and material that should be considered to be trade secrets.

2. **Nondisclosure of Trade Secrets**

I will keep the Company's trade secrets, whether or not prepared or developed by me, in the strictest confidence. I will not use or disclose such secrets to others without the Company's written consent, except when necessary to perform my job. However, I shall have no obligation to treat as confidential any information which:

(a) was in my possession or known to me, without an obligation to keep it confidential, before such information was disclosed to me by the Company;

(b) is or becomes public knowledge through a source other than me and through no fault of mine; or

(c) is or becomes lawfully available to me from a source other than the Company.

This clause bars the employee from making unauthorized disclosures of the company's trade secrets. There are several good reasons for an employer to include a nondisclosure clause in its employment agreements. As we discussed in Chapter 7, information qualifies as a trade secret only if reasonable precautions are taken to keep it secret. The use of nondisclosure clauses (or separate nondisclosure agreements; see Chapter 8) is perhaps the single most important reasonable precaution. Confidential information may not be deemed to be a trade secret where an employer does not use such agreements.

Including a nondisclosure clause in an employment agreement makes clear to the employee that he has a duty to protect the employer's trade secrets. It also shows that the employer is serious about keeping trade secrets secret.

This clause clearly defines employee obligations regarding trade secrets, which will also make it easier to obtain relief in court if an employee or ex-employee makes unauthorized disclosures.

However, as explained in this clause, the employee's nondisclosure obligation should not extend to information the employee knew before coming to work for the company, information he learns from sources outside the company, and information that is not confidential because it is public knowledge (so long as the employee didn't make it public).

3. Confidential Information of Others

> I will not disclose to the Company, use in the Company's business, or cause the Company to use, any information or material that is a trade secret of others. My performance of this Agreement will not breach any agreement to keep in confidence proprietary information acquired by me prior to my employment by the Company.

It's a good idea to remind new employees that they have a duty not to disclose to the employer trade secrets learned from prior employers or others. Employers who take advantage of such information can easily end up being sued.

4. No Conflicting Obligations

> I have no other current or prior agreements, relationships, or commitments that conflict with this Agreement or with my relationship other than the following: [SPECIFY; IF NONE, SO STATE].

Many workers in the Web and software development industries have previously signed employment agreements or consulting agreements that may conflict with their ability to work for you—for example, because they contain noncompetition restrictions or restrictions on disclosure of trade secrets that may touch upon the work the employee will perform for you. To make sure this isn't a problem, the agreement asks the employee to list any such prior agreements. If there are any, obtain copies and review them to make sure the employee isn't in any way barred from working for you.

5. Return of Materials

> When my employment with the Company ends, for whatever reason, I will promptly deliver to the Company all originals and copies of all documents, records, software programs, media, and other materials containing any of the Company's trade secrets. I will also return to the Company all equipment, files, software programs, and other personal property belonging to the Company.

It's important that employees understand their obligation to return all materials containing trade secrets when they leave the company. They should be reminded of this obligation in their employment agreement and before they leave.

6. Confidentiality Obligation Survives Employment

> I understand that my obligation to maintain the confidentiality and security of the Company's trade secrets remains with me even after my employment with the Company ends and continues for so long as such material remains a trade secret.

It's important to make clear that the employee's duty not to disclose her employer's confidential information does not end when she leaves the company, but continues for as long as the material remains a trade secret.

7. Intellectual Property Ownership

> I understand that as part of my job duties I may be asked to create, or contribute to the creation of, computer programs, documentation, and other copyrightable works. I agree that any and all computer programs, documentation, and other copyrightable materials that I am asked to prepare or work on as part of my employment with the Company shall be "works made for hire" and that the Company shall own all the copyright rights in such works. IF AND TO THE EXTENT ANY SUCH MATERIAL DOES NOT SATISFY THE LEGAL REQUIREMENTS TO CONSTITUTE A WORK MADE FOR HIRE, I HEREBY ASSIGN ALL MY COPYRIGHT RIGHTS IN THE WORK TO THE COMPANY.

Where technical employees are involved, clauses that assign intellectual property rights (transfer rights of ownership) to the employer are even more important than nondisclosure clauses. This clause covers assignment issues, as do these clauses discussed below:

- "Disclosure of Developments" clause
- "Assignment of Developments" clause, and
- "Post-Employment Assignment" clause.

Copyrightable works created by employees within the scope of their employment are "works made for hire" to which the employer is considered the "author" for copyright purposes. (See Chapter 15.) However, it is dangerous for employers to rely solely on the work made for hire rule. This is because of possible legal uncertainty regarding who is an "employee" for copyright purposes, and when copyrightable works are created within the scope of employment. Therefore, the employee should be required to assign, in advance, all copyright rights in work-related works to the employer.

This clause makes clear that the employee may create copyrightable works as part of his or her job and that such works will be works made for hire. But if for some reason the work for hire rule does not apply, the employee assigns all copyright rights in work-related works to the employer.

8. Disclosure of Developments

> While I am employed by the Company, I will promptly inform the Company of the full details of all my inventions, discoveries, improvements, innovations, and ideas (collectively called "Developments")—whether or not patentable, copyrightable, or otherwise protectible—that I conceive, complete, or reduce to practice (whether jointly or with others) and which:
>
> (a) relate to the Company's present or prospective business, or actual or demonstrably anticipated research and development; or
>
> (b) result from any work I do using any equipment, facilities, materials, trade secrets, or personnel of the Company; or
>
> (c) result from or are suggested by any work that I may do for the Company.
>
> [IN WASHINGTON STATE, ADD THE FOLLOWING: "The Company will maintain a written record of all such disclosures for at least five years."]

The employee must be required to disclose promptly to the employer any and all work-related inventions and other developments she creates. This clause complies with state restrictions on invention assignments discussed in the "Assignment of Developments" clause, below.

In the state of Washington you must include the paragraph on the disk that states that the Company will maintain a written record of all such disclosures for at least five years.

9. Assignment of Developments

I hereby assign to the Company or the Company's designee, my entire right, title, and interest in all of the following, that I conceive or make (whether alone or with others) while employed by the Company:

(a) all Developments;

(b) all copyrights, trade secrets, trademarks, and mask work rights in Developments; and

(c) all patent applications filed and patents granted on any Developments, including those in foreign countries.

Absent an assignment of rights to an employee's work-related inventions and other developments, the employer may not own what the employee creates. Or, at the very least, the employer may be subject to a costly and bitter legal fight over ownership rights. (See Chapter 11.)

An assignment is simply a transfer of ownership. An employee may transfer his ownership rights in any copyrights, trade secrets, patentable inventions, or "mask works" (semiconductor chip designs) he creates on the employer's behalf before he actually commences work. This is when an assignment ideally should be

made—before an employee begins his or her job. As discussed in Section D, above, if an assignment is executed long after an employee is hired, the employer must give the continuing employee a raise or other compensation to ensure that the assignment is enforceable.

10. Postemployment Assignment

I will disclose to the Company any and all computer programs, inventions, improvements, or discoveries actually made, or copyright registration or patent applications filed, within [NUMBER OF MONTHS; SIX TO 12 IS RECOMMENDED] months after my employment with the Company ends. I hereby assign to the Company my entire right, title, and interest in such programs, inventions, improvements, and discoveries, whether made individually or jointly, which relate to the subject matter of my employment with the Company during the [NUMBER OF MONTHS; SIX TO 12 IS RECOMMENDED] -month period immediately preceding the termination of my employment.

Unfortunately, not all employees are honest when it comes to intellectual property rights. Some might try to steal materials they create that belong to their employer. Consider this scenario:

> **EXAMPLE:** Josephine, a programmer employed by Miracle Systems, has

signed an enforceable, reasonable assignment agreement. While employed by Miracle, she develops a potentially valuable program that should be assigned to Miracle under the terms of the agreement. However, Josephine conceals her new program from Miracle. She leaves Miracle and two months later registers her program with the Copyright Office, listing herself as the sole owner. Does Miracle have any ownership rights in the program? Maybe, if it can convince a court she developed it while employed by Miracle. But a lengthy and expensive court battle would be required.

To help avoid these types of shenanigans, many hi-tech employers require inventive employees to agree to assign copyrightable or patentable works they create after the employment relationship ends. Such postemployment assignments are enforceable in most states if they are reasonable. To be reasonable, a postemployment assignment must:

- be for a limited time—probably no more than six months to one year after employment ends
- apply only to works that relate to the inventor's former employment, and
- apply only to works actually in existence, not to mere ideas or concepts in the employee's brain.

11. Notice Pursuant to State Law

[ALTERNATIVE 1 (CALIFORNIA EMPLOYEES)] I understand that this Agreement does not apply to any invention that qualifies fully under the provisions of California Labor Code Section 2870, the text of which is attached as Exhibit A. This section shall serve as written notice to me as required by California Labor Code Section 2872.

[ALTERNATIVE 2 (ILLINOIS EMPLOYEES)] I understand that this Agreement does not apply to any invention that qualifies fully under the provisions of Illinois Revised Statutes, Chapter 140, Sections 302(1) and (2), the text of which is attached as Exhibit A. This section shall serve as written notice to me as required by Illinois Revised Statutes, Chapter 140, Section 302(3).

[ALTERNATIVE 3 (KANSAS EMPLOYEES)] I understand that this Agreement does not apply to any invention that qualifies fully under the provisions of Kansas Statutes Annotated Sections 44-130(a) and (b), the text of which is attached as Exhibit A. This section shall serve as written notice to me as required by Kansas Statutes Annotated Section 44-130(c).

[ALTERNATIVE 4 (MINNESOTA EMPLOYEES)] I understand that this Agreement does not apply to any invention that qualifies fully under the provisions of Minnesota Statutes Annotated Sections 181.78(1) and (2), the text of which is attached as Exhibit A. This section shall serve as written notice to me as required by Minnesota Statutes Annotated Section 181.78(3).

[ALTERNATIVE 5 (WASHINGTON STATE EMPLOYEES)] I understand that this Agreement does not apply to any invention that qualifies fully under the provisions of Washington Revised Code Annotated Section 49.44.140(1), the text of which is attached as Exhibit A. This section shall serve as written notice to me as required by Washington Revised Code Annotated Section 49.44.140(3).

A prospective or continuing employee and his or her employer are usually in an unequal bargaining position—the employer generally has the upper hand. Some hi-tech employers have attempted to take advantage of their leverage by requiring their employees to agree to very broadly worded assignments that purport to transfer to the employer in advance ownership of everything the employee creates, whether related to the job or not. In the words of one court, these employers try to obtain "a mortgage on a man's brain." (*Aspinwall Mfg. Co. v. Gill*, 32 F. 697 (3d Cir. 1887).)

To protect employees, several states, including California, impose restrictions on the permissible scope of assignments of employee-created inventions. Note that these restrictions apply only to "inventions" an employee creates—that is, software, Internet business methods, or other items for which a patent is sought. The restrictions apply only to employees, not to independent contractors.

The California restrictions are typical. Under California law, an employee cannot be required to assign any of his or her rights in an invention he or she develops "entirely on his or her own time without using the employer's equipment, supplies, facilities, or trade secret information" unless:

- when the invention was conceived or "reduced to practice" (actually created or a patent application filed) it related to the employer's business or actual or "demonstrably anticipated" research or development, or
- the invention resulted from any work performed by the employee for the employer (California Labor Code, § 2870).

The following states impose similar restrictions:

- Delaware (Delaware Code Annotated, Title 19, § 805)
- Illinois (Illinois Compiled Statutes, Chapter 765, § 1060/2)
- Kansas (Kansas Statutes Annotated, Chapter 44, § 130)
- Minnesota (Minnesota Statutes Annotated, § 181.78)

- North Carolina (North Carolina General Statutes, §§ 66-57.1, 66-57.2)
- Utah (Utah Code Annotated, §§ 34-39-2, 34-39-3)
- Washington (Washington Revised Code Annotated, §§ 49.44.140, 49.44.150).

Invention Assignment Restrictions in Other States

Employers doing business in states that do not have laws restricting invention assignments like the eight states discussed above should nevertheless not attempt to impose unreasonable invention assignments on their employees. Even in the absence of a state law like California's, a court could well refuse to enforce an assignment agreement that it deemed unreasonable—that is, that tried to obtain a "mortgage on a man's brain." Assignments complying with California law would probably be deemed reasonable in these states.

Here are examples that illustrate how these types of restrictions operate in practice.

EXAMPLE 1: Jim is a programmer employed by Orchid Development Co. Orchid is located in Northern California and is in the business of developing and marketing computer databases for business use. Before he began working for Orchid, Jim signed an employment agreement containing an invention assignment, complying with California law. An active computer game player, Jim creates a computer adventure game for children that uses revolutionary new methods to animate its characters in a very lifelike way. Portions of this program could well constitute a patentable invention.

Assume that Jim wrote his program at home, completely on his own time. Who owns Jim's invention, Orchid or Jim? Probably Jim. Since Orchid is not in the business of creating computer games, Jim's invention probably doesn't relate to its business or research and development; nor did Jim's game result from any work he performed for Orchid.

EXAMPLE 2: Assume the same facts above. But what if Jim created his game during working hours? In this event, Orchid's invention assignment would probably be effective—that is, it would own any inventions contained in the game.

EXAMPLE 3: Again, assume the same facts. What if Jim created the game at home, but his new animation method was a spin-off from work he performed for Orchid? Orchid's invention assignment would probably be effective because Jim's invention resulted from work he performed for Orchid.

If the employee will work in California, Illinois, Kansas, Minnesota, or Washington State, state law requires that the employee be given written notice of state law restrictions on an employer's right to obtain an assignment of employee inventions. If this is not done, the assignment might be unenforceable. If the employee will work in any other state, delete this entire clause. Otherwise, include the appropriate state notice on the disk that states that an Exhibit A is attached, which sets forth written notice of state assignment restrictions. The applicable Exhibit A, setting forth the text of the state law, must also be attached to the agreement. (This is covered below.)

12. Execution of Documents

Both while employed by the Company and afterwards, I agree to execute and aid in the preparation of any papers that the Company may consider necessary or helpful to obtain or maintain any patents, copyrights, trademarks, or other proprietary rights at no charge to the Company, but at its expense.

If the Company is unable to secure my signature on any document necessary to obtain or maintain any patent, copyright, trademark, or other proprietary rights, whether due to my mental or physical capacity or any other cause, I hereby irrevocably designate and appoint the Company and its duly authorized officers and agents as my agents and attorneys-in-fact to execute and file such documents and do all other lawfully permitted acts to further the prosecution, issuance, and enforcement of patents, copyrights, and other proprietary rights with the same force and effect as if executed by me.

This clause simply requires the employee to execute any documents necessary to effect the assignment of intellectual property rights. If the employee is unable to do so because of sickness or for any reason, the company is appointed the employee's attorney-in-fact and may execute such documents on the employee's behalf.

13. Prior Developments

As a matter of record, I have identified all prior developments [IF MANY, ADD: "relevant to the subject matter of my employment by the Company"] ("Prior Developments") that have been conceived or reduced to practice or learned by me, alone or jointly with others, before my employment with the Company, which I desire to remove from the operation of this Agreement. The Prior Developments consist of: [LIST ALL PRIOR DEVELOPMENTS OR "None."]

I represent and warrant that this list is complete. If there is no such list, I represent that I have made no such Prior Developments at the time of signing this Agreement.

Unless the parties desire otherwise, the Agreement's assignment of intellectual property rights should not cover software, patents and other materials created and owned by the employee before commencing employment with the company. Since the employee wasn't working for the company when such items were created, the company shouldn't own them. This provision makes this clear and requires the employee to list all such prior developments.

14. Conflict of Interest

During my employment by the Company, I will not engage in any business activity competitive with the Company's business activities. Nor will I engage in any other activities that conflict with the Company's best interests.

This clause is intended to make clear to the employee that he shouldn't compete with the company while employed by it or engage in any activity that may harm the company.

15. Postemployment Noncompetition Agreement

[THIS "POST-EMPLOYMENT NONCOMPETITION AGREEMENT" CLAUSE CANNOT BE USED IN ALABAMA, CALIFORNIA, COLORADO, HAWAII, LOUISIANA, MONTANA, NEVADA, NORTH CAROLINA, NORTH DAKOTA, OKLAHOMA, OREGON, SOUTH DAKOTA, OR WISCONSIN. IN ALL OTHER STATES, THIS CLAUSE IS OPTIONAL.]

[ALTERNATIVE 1] I understand that during my employment by the Company I may become familiar with confidential information of the Company. Therefore, it is possible that I could gravely harm the Company if I worked for a competitor. Accordingly, I agree for [TIME PERIOD, USUALLY SIX MONTHS TO TWO YEARS] following the end of my employment with the Company not to compete, directly or indirectly, with the Company in any of its business. Competition includes the design, development, production, promotion, or sale of products or services competitive with those of the Company.

[ALTERNATIVE 2] I understand that during my employment by the Company I may become familiar with confidential information of the Company. Therefore, it is possible that I could gravely harm the Company if I worked for a competitor. Accordingly, I agree for [TIME PERIOD, USUALLY SIX MONTHS TO TWO YEARS] following the end of my employment with the Company not to compete, directly or indirectly, with the Company in any of its business if the duties of such competitive employment inherently require that I use or disclose any of the Company's confidential information. Competition includes the design, development, production, promotion, or sale of products or services competitive with those of the Company.

[ALTERNATIVE 3] I understand that during my employment by the Company I may become familiar with confidential information of the Company. Therefore, it is possible that I could cause grave harm to the Company if I worked for a competitor. Accordingly, I agree for [TIME PERIOD, USUALLY SIX MONTHS TO TWO YEARS] after the end of my employment with the company not to engage in, or contribute my knowledge to, any work that is competitive with or functionally similar to a product, process, apparatus, or service on which I worked while at the Company at any time during the period of [TIME PERIOD, USUALLY SIX MONTHS TO TWO YEARS] immediately before my employment ended.

(a) Diversion of Company Business: For a period of [TIME PERIOD, USUALLY SIX MONTHS TO TWO YEARS] months from the date my employment ends, I will not divert or attempt to divert from the Company any business the Company enjoyed or solicited from its customers during the [NUMBER OF MONTHS, USUALLY SIX TO 12] months prior to the termination of my employment.

(b) Geographic Restrictions: I acknowledge and agree that the software developed by the Company is, or is intended to be, distributed to customers nationally throughout the United States. According, I agree that these restrictions on my postemployment competitive activity shall apply throughout the entire United States.

A postemployment noncompetition agreement (also called a "covenant not to compete" or "noncompete clause") is designed to discourage a former employee from competing for a given period of time in the market in which the employer does business.

Alternatives to Noncompetition Restrictions

To put it mildly, noncompetition clauses are not popular with employees. Some potential (or continuing) employees will simply refuse to sign them. There are other, less drastic ways, to accomplish the same goals:

- *Deferred compensation*: Instead of forcing employees to sign an agreement with a noncompetition clause, many hi-tech companies give their employees stock options, pension benefits, or other benefits that fully vest only after several years of employment. This gives the employee a strong financial incentive to stay.

- *Employment contracts for a definite term*: Normally, employment is "at will"—meaning the employer can fire the employee for any reason or no reason at all. Likewise, the employee can quit at any time. However, this can be changed by either a written or oral contract. One way a developer can help assure a key employee will stay with the company is to have him or her sign an employment contract guaranteeing employment for a definite term—say two or three years. This means the employer can't fire the employee during that time and the employee can't quit. If he or she does, the employer can sue for breach of contract.

These types of agreements are common in some businesses, for example, the entertainment industry and professional sports; but they can have a real down side. If the employee doesn't work out, keeping him or her on can be a horrible burden for the company. Moreover, if an employee really wants to be somewhere else, the quality of his or her work will inevitably suffer. Obviously, both parties need to consider carefully before making such a long-term commitment.

a. States where postemployment noncompetition clauses are unenforceable or restricted

Noncompetition agreements can make it impossible for ex-employees to earn a living in their chosen line of work—a fundamental right. For this reason, some states will not enforce noncompetition agreements with employees or restrict how they may be used.

Summary of State Laws Affecting Noncompete Agreements

State	Code Section
Alabama	Ala. Code § 8-1-1
California	Cal. Bus. & Prof. Code §§ 16600-16602
Colorado	Colo. Rev. Stat. § 8-2-113
Florida	Fla. Stat. Ann. §§ 542.33; 542.335
Louisiana	La. Rev. Stat. Ann. § 23.921
Montana	Mont. Rev. Code Ann. § 28-2-703
Nevada	Nev. Rev. Stat. Ann. § 613.200
North Dakota	N.D. Cent. Code § 9-08-66
Oklahoma	Okla. Stat. Tit. 15, §§ 217-219
Oregon	Or. Rev. Stat. § 653.295
South Dakota	S.D. Codified Laws Ann. §§ 53-9-8 to -11
Texas	Tex. Bus. & Com. Code Ann. §§ 15.03, 15.05

Alabama

Alabama prohibits "professionals," such as doctors and lawyers, from entering into noncompete agreements. Since the state courts have had a tough time assessing what qualifies as a profession as opposed to a trade or business, we recommend that you seek the help of an attorney if you want to create an agreement.

California

California refuses to enforce noncompete agreements between employers and employees. Employers in California should not use such agreements. To protect trade secrets, rely on nondisclosure agreements, which are enforceable in California.

Colorado

Colorado prohibits anyone except "executive and management personnel and officers," as well as "employees who constitute professional staff to executive and management personnel," from entering into noncompete agreements with their employers. An employer in Colorado can enter into a noncompete agreement with any employee as long as the agreement provides only for the recovery of educational and training expenses if the employee violates the agreement. This recovery will be awarded only if the employee works for the employer for less than two years before switching to a competitor.

Florida

Florida law provides that a noncompete agreement can be used only to protect:
- trade secrets or valuable, confidential business or professional information
- relationships with specific prospective or existing customers, patients, or clients, or
- extraordinary or specialized training.

The law also imposes time limits on such agreements. A noncompete agreement with a duration of six months to two years is assumed to be reasonable and enforceable. However, a noncompete agreement written to protect trade secrets can last up to five years.

Montana, North Dakota, and Oklahoma

These states have statutes that appear to prohibit employee noncompete agreements. However, some courts in these states have indicated that, despite what the law says, noncompete agreements might be enforceable against employees if they are reasonable and necessary to prevent a former employee from disclosing trade secrets to a competitor. If you are located in one of these states, seek the help of an attorney to create an enforceable noncompetition agreement.

Oregon

Noncompete agreements are enforceable in Oregon if they:
- are entered into when employees are hired or promoted, or
- qualify as a "bonus restriction agreement," in which case they can be entered into at any time during employment.

A bonus restriction agreement forces an employee to forfeit any profit-sharing or bonus compensation if the employee competes against the employer after the employee leaves the company. Consult an Oregon attorney if you want to make this type of agreement.

South Dakota and Louisiana

South Dakota and Louisiana statutes allow noncompete agreements, but don't allow the agreements to last more than two years after an employee leaves the company.

Texas

Noncompetition agreements are usually enforceable against employees in Texas provided that the employer gives the employee a benefit in addition to the job itself as compensation for signing the noncompete agreement. The standards for such benefits are low—for example, granting the employee a 14-day notice period before the employee is terminated.

b. Why use postemployment noncompetition clauses?

From an employer's point of view, a noncompetition clause in an employment agreement can serve several highly useful functions:

- By making it difficult, if not impossible, for a key employee to leave the company, it helps ensure that the employer will receive full return on its investment in training the employee.

- It may help an employer maintain a competitive advantage by preventing key employees from working for— and thereby aiding—competitors.

- It can help keep the employer's valuable trade secrets out of the hands of competitors.

- Indeed, where enforceable, noncompetition clauses are far more effective in protecting trade secrets than nondisclosure clauses. It can be very difficult for an employer to know whether an ex-employee has disclosed trade secrets to a competitor. Moreover, even if the employer is sure trade secrets have been disclosed, it can be difficult to obtain court relief for violations of a nondisclosure clause. The ex-employer must prove that the employee actually disclosed confidential information or that there is an imminent threat of such an unauthorized disclosure. This can be an onerous task, especially where the ex-employee claims that the information allegedly disclosed didn't qualify as a trade secret.

These problems do not exist with noncompetition clauses. It's usually easy to discover whether an ex-employee has gone to work for a competitor. To enforce a noncompetition clause in court, the ex-employer need only show that the ex-employee went to work for a competitor in violation of the clause's terms.

The best part about a noncompetition clause from an employer's point of view is that it will deter both the employee from seeking employment with a competitor and the competitor from hiring him or her. This significantly reduces an employee's incentive and opportunity to divulge trade secrets.

Of course, noncompetition clauses can make it impossible for an employee to earn a living in her chosen line of work if he or she leaves his or her job. The right to earn a living is considered to be one of the most fundamental rights a person has. For this reason, courts generally look on such clauses with disfavor and will only enforce them if the terms are reasonable and enforcement serves a legitimate interest of the employer.

c. When to use postemployment noncompetition clauses

Don't try to use a postemployment noncompetition clause simply to chain an employee to his job or obtain an unfair advantage over your competitors. A noncompetition clause should be used only in states where it's allowed, when there is a legitimate business need for it. For example:

- **Protection of trade secrets.** An employer has a legitimate interest in preventing its trade secrets from being disclosed to competitors. Thus, a noncompetition clause may be called for where the employee has access to trade secrets.
- **Return on substantial investment in an employee.** Where an employer spends substantial time and money giving an employee special training, it has a legitimate interest in obtaining a fair return on its investment. Thus, an employer may legitimately insist that an employee sign an agreement with a noncompetition clause before making such an investment in him or her.
- **Key employees.** Particularly in the software industry, where highly valuable programs are often created by a few extremely talented individuals, an employer may have a legitimate interest in preventing employees with special, unique, or extraordinary skills from working for competitors.

d. Reasonableness requirement

To be enforceable in the states that permit them, noncompetition clauses must be reasonable. If such a clause is found to be unreasonable, courts in some states will refuse to enforce it at all; others will ignore the unreasonable provisions and apply what they deem to be reasonable restrictions.

To be reasonable, a noncompetition clause must be limited as to time, scope, and geographic region.

- **Time.** A noncompetition clause cannot last forever; it must have a definite time limit—the shorter the better. Such clauses typically last for no more than six months to two years. Some states have statutes that limit the time. In Louisiana and South Dakota, for example, noncompete agreements that last more than two years are presumed to be unreasonable. In New York, depending on the circumstances, restrictions from one to five years are considered reasonable. But even in states with mandated limits, courts can review and shorten noncompetition restrictions they deem unreasonable.

EXAMPLE: A federal court in New York ruled that a one-year restriction on competition by a former employee was unreasonable because, given the dynamic nature of the Internet advertising industry, the useful life of the employee's information was much shorter than a year. (*EarthWeb, Inc. v. Schlack,* 71 F. Supp. 2d 299 (S.D. N.Y. 1999).)

- **Scope.** A noncompetition clause should be no more restrictive than necessary to accomplish the employer's legitimate objectives. The clause should define as specifically as possible exactly what types of activities the employee cannot perform for a competitor. Generally, these activities ought to be similar to those currently being performed by the employee.

- **Geography.** A noncompetition clause must specify the geographic region in which it applies. It should be limited to the geographic area in which the company does business or in which it has made definite plans to do business in the immediate future. Of course, most website and software developers market their work to customers throughout the United States, so their noncompetition clauses can apply to the entire country.

e. Sample noncompetition clause

The more limited a noncompetition clause is in scope and time, the more likely it will be deemed reasonable and therefore enforceable in court. The clause provided here bars the employee from working for any other company if doing so would require the disclosure of the hiring firm's confidential information. It also prevents the employee from performing services for a competitor that are similar to his or her job duties for the hiring firm; this is so whether or not disclosure of confidential information would occur. You need to state how long the restrictions will last; six months to two years is the common time period.

Most Web development and software companies do business throughout the United States, so their noncompetition covenants should apply in every state as well. Section (a) of the clause makes this clear. However, if your business is restricted to one or a few states, delete this clause and add the following: "This noncompetition agreement shall apply in the following territory: _____." List the state or states where you do business.

16. Additional Postemployment Noncompetition Terms

[THIS ENTIRE "ADDITIONAL POSTEMPLOYMENT NONCOMPETITION TERMS" CLAUSE IS OP-
TIONAL AND MAY ONLY BE USED IN CONJUNCTION WITH "POSTEMPLOYMENT
NONCOMPETITION AGREEMENT" ABOVE.]

The following postemployment noncompetition term(s) shall apply:

(a) Written Consent: I understand that I will be permitted to engage in the work or activity described in this Agreement if I provide the Company with clear and convincing written evidence, including assurances from my new employer and me, that the contribution of my knowledge to that work or activity will not cause me to disclose, base judgment upon, or use any of
the Company's confidential information. The Company will furnish me a written consent to that effect if I provide the required written evidence. I agree not to engage in such work or activity until
I receive such written consent from the Company.

(b) Inability to Secure Employment: If, solely as a result of this noncompetition agreement, I am unable to secure employment appropriate to my abilities and training, despite my diligent efforts to
do so, the Company shall either: (1) release me from my noncompetition obligations to the extent
necessary to allow me to obtain such employment, or (2) pay me a periodic amount equal to my
monthly base pay at termination for the balance of the term of this noncompetition agreement.

If and while the Company elects to pay me the amounts described above, I promise to diligently
pursue other employment opportunities consistent with my general skills and interests. I understand
that the Company's obligation to make or continue the payments specified above will end upon my
obtaining employment, and I will promptly give the Company written notice of such employment.

If you completed the Postemployment Noncompetition Agreement clause above, you have the option to add any or all of the following:

- **Written Consent.** This lets the employee off the hook if he or she can convince the company that no confidential information will be disclosed to the new employer. It will help make the noncompete clause appear reasonable to a judge. This would be most appropriate where the employee's new duties wouldn't tempt him or her to disclose the prior employer's trade secrets.

- **Inability to Secure Employment.** An excellent way for an employer to make a noncompetition clause appear reasonable in the eyes of a court is for the employer to agree to pay all or part of the ex-employee's salary if the employee is unable to find work because of the noncompetition clause. This can be expensive, but it may be worth it to prevent a key employee from working for the competition and possibly divulging trade secrets.

17. Nonsolicitation

[OPTIONAL "NONINTERFERENCE WITH COMPANY EMPLOYEES" CLAUSE]

While employed by the Company and for [TIME PERIOD, USUALLY SIX MONTHS TO TWO YEARS] afterwards, I will not:

(a) induce, or attempt to induce, any Company employee to quit the Company's employ,

(b) recruit or hire away any Company employee, or

(c) hire or engage any Company employee or former employee whose employment with the Company ended less than one year before the date of such hiring or engagement.

It's pretty much impossible for an employee to quit and start a competitive business by himself or herself. He or she needs help, and will usually try to find it among co-workers. Indeed, it has been a common occurrence in the hi-tech field

for groups of employees to leave a company to start a competitive company. This clause tries to prevent this by barring the employee from persuading other employees to leave the company.

This simple provision can be almost as effective as a covenant not to compete, while not presenting the difficult enforcement problems that noncompetition restrictions do. (But, of course, this clause will not prevent an employee from joining an already-established competitor.) This optional clause may be used in any state, including those that prohibit post-employment noncompetition clauses.

18. Enforcement

I agree that in the event of a breach or threatened breach of this Agreement, money damages would be an inadequate remedy and extremely difficult to measure. I agree, therefore, that the Company shall be entitled to an injunction to restrain me from such breach or threatened breach. Nothing in this Agreement shall be construed as preventing the Company from pursuing any remedy at law or in equity for any breach or threatened breach.

If the employee breaches, or threatens to breach the Agreement, this clause gives the employer the automatic right to an injunction to prevent such a breach. This clause does not preclude the employer's right to seek additional remedies.

19. General Provisions

The general provisions in this agreement are standard in many types of legal documents and are disused in detail in Chapter 17, Section B30.

20. Signatures

Although not absolutely necessary, it's a good idea to have the employee's signature witnessed by a company representative. This is intended to prevent the employee from later claiming her signature was forged.

21. Exhibit A

To protect employees, several states impose restrictions on the permissible scope of assignments of employee-created inventions. If the employee will work in California, Illinois, Kansas, Minnesota, or Washington State, include the appropriate notice of state law provided on the disk. Delete all state law notices that don't apply.

PART II. Employment Agreements From the Employee's Viewpoint

This section covers employment agreements from the employee's point of view. Hi-tech employees are commonly asked to sign various agreements either before or after they begin work. They may be told that these merely are "standard forms" that everyone signs. These forms may be quite lengthy and filled with difficult to understand legalese. Before you sign any agreement, read it carefully and make sure you both understand it and are comfortable signing it.

Of course, the extent to which the employer will be willing to alter any of the provisions in an employment agreement depends largely on how badly it wants you as an employee. And, the extent to which you may be willing to demand significant changes depends on how much you want the job.

Be sure to ask any prospective employer if you will be required to sign an employment contract, and, if so, ask for a copy before you accept the job. You don't want to be presented with a harsh agreement after you've already started work. At this point, having quit your old job, you may feel you have no choice but to sign it as written; or, at the very least, you will be in a much worse bargaining position than you were before accepting the new job.

Following are some of the key items you should look for when reviewing an employment agreement:

- confidentiality of trade secrets
- intellectual property ownership rights, and
- postemployment noncompetition restrictions.

H. Confidentiality of Trade Secrets

The agreement may contain a clause requiring you to keep the company's trade secrets confidential. There is nothing to object to here. Even without such a clause, you have a legal duty not to disclose your employer's trade secrets if you're routinely exposed to them as a part of your job. (See Chapter 7 for a detailed discussion.) This duty applies not only to your new employer, but to all past employers as well. In other words, do not bring to your new job or disclose to your new employer your old employer's trade secrets.

Be Careful What You Take From Your Prior Employer

The best way to get your new employer and yourself involved in a trade secret suit is to take materials containing trade secrets belonging to your old employer when you leave for your new job. This includes not only documents but computer disks and even trade journal articles (you may have written valuable notes on these that belong to your old employer). The wisest policy is to ask your old employer's permission before taking any document, disk, or other item that could conceivably contain the employer's trade secrets. It's best to get such permission in writing.

I. Intellectual Property Ownership

If the employer knows what it is doing, the agreement should contain a provision by which you transfer your intellectual property ownership rights in copyrightable materials you create as part of your job duties. This is perfectly reasonable and unobjectionable. However, if you and your new employer are going to share ownership of any of your work product, make sure that the employment agreement (or perhaps another side agreement) spells out exactly what you've agreed to. The discussion of ownership of custom software in Chapter 17, Section B10, should be useful here as well. It discusses the various ways a developer and customer can parcel out ownership rights. Rights in employee-created software or Web materials can be handled in the same way.

1. Employee-Owned Materials

If you own any development tools (for example, code you've created and used in all your software), patents, or other valuable materials, and you want these items to remain your sole property, the agreement should make clear that your employer is not acquiring any ownership rights in them. Following is a sample clause for this; you'll need to type it yourself.

> The following Developments [if many, add: "relevant to the subject matter of my employment by the Company"] have been conceived or reduced to practice or learned by me, alone or jointly with others, before my employment with the Company and I desire that they be removed from the operation of this Agreement: [list all employee-owned materials].

2. Work Outside the Scope of Employment

You need to be very careful if you intend to create potentially valuable products on your own time. An employer owns the intellectual property rights in works created by an employee within the scope of employment. Moreover, an employer may even have certain rights over works created outside the scope of employment if the employee used the employer's resources—for example, did a substantial amount of the work during business hours or used the employer's equipment. If an employee creates a valuable work on his or her own time, an unscrupulous employer might try to assert ownership over it by claiming that the work was within the scope of employment or the employee used its resources.

To avoid potential problems, if you plan to do work on your own, make sure you inform your new employer and obtain its written acknowledgment that it has no ownership interest in such work. (See Chapter 11 for sample form.)

3. Postemployment Invention Assignments

Some employers seek to include a provision by which the employee agrees to assign to the employer copyrightable or patentable work the employee creates after the employment relationship ends. Such postemployment assignments are enforceable only if they are reasonable. From your point of view, a postemployment assignment provision is just as undesirable as a noncompetition clause. It can make it very difficult for you to get a new job, because your new employer may not be entitled to own anything you create during the period of the assignment provision.

Try to avoid signing agreements containing such provisions, or at least seek to keep the length of the restriction as short as possible. Also, make sure the assignment applies only to works actually in existence, not to mere ideas or concepts in your brain.

J. Postemployment Restrictions on Competition

Postemployment restrictions on competition (also called "covenants not to compete") are contractual provisions that attempt to prevent an employee from competing with the employer after the employment relationship ends. This is one area in which the interests of the employer and employee are diametrically opposed. Quite simply, you don't want to have any restrictions on your right to work for others if you leave the company. However, the more valuable your skills, the more likely it is that your employer will want to prevent you from working for the competition.

Fortunately for employees, postemployment noncompetition restrictions are highly disfavored by the courts. Moreover, several states, including California, have laws making employee covenants not to compete generally unenforceable. (See Section G15, above, for a list.) If you're in a state that doesn't have such a law, this doesn't mean the employer may impose

extremely harsh noncompetition restrictions on you. Covenants not to compete must be reasonable to be enforceable. A noncompetition clause that would prevent you from earning a living in your chosen occupation for a substantial time would likely be unenforceable in court. (See Section G15d, above, for detailed discussion.)

If your prospective employer absolutely insists on having a noncompetition clause, at least try to limit it as much as possible. Here are some pointers:

- **Time.** Seek to make the length of the restriction as short as possible. Try for six months or a year; anything over two years is probably unreasonable.
- **Scope.** Try to avoid promising not to work for any of the company's competitors or for certain named competitors. Rather, agree not to help develop products or services competitive with or similar to products you actually worked on for the company.
- **Geography.** The noncompete clause should apply only to the geographic areas in which the company does business or has definite plans to do business when you terminate your employment. However, if the company distributes its products throughout the United States (as most do), a noncompete clause can apply to the entire country.

See Section G15, above, for sample language incorporating these restrictions into a noncompetition clause. ∎

15

Consulting Agreements

This chapter is for people who hire independent contractors or consultants, those who work as independent contractors, and the many people who do both. The terms "independent contractor" and "consultant" are used interchangeably. (For agreements between employers and employees, see Chapter 14.)

- Part I is for people or companies who are hiring independent contractors or consultants.
- Part II is for people who work as independent contractors or consultants. You can skip to Part II if you're in the second category.

PART I. Hiring Independent Contractors

Part I explains all aspects of independent contractor agreements. A complete independent contractor agreement is contained in the forms disk at the back of this book. It is advisable, however, that you read the following discussion in conjunction with using the forms disk. The disk contains a number of options you'll have to choose from, and the rest of this chapter explains these options in detail.

A. Introduction

Software and website developers place heavy reliance on self-employed workers.

Whether they are called "independent consultants," "dailies," "vendors," or nothing at all, such workers routinely provide developers with a variety of services, including website design, Web and software programming, software development and design, technical advice, software and website maintenance, training, and technical writing. The general term for a self-employed individual who offers services to the public is "independent contractor."

Independent contractors are treated very differently from employees for tax, insurance, and other purposes. They must also be treated very differently from employees by the businesses that hire them. Significant savings can be realized by treating a worker as an independent contractor rather than as an employee. However, as we'll discuss below, there are significant risks as well. If the IRS or a state taxing authority concludes that a worker is really an employee and not an independent contractor, substantial penalties may be imposed on that worker's employer. There may also be significant and surprising consequences if an independent contractor creates a copyrightable work.

Various government agencies—the IRS, Department of Labor, state taxing authorities, and unemployment insurance and workers' compensation agencies—may decide, independently of each other, whether a worker is an employee or independent contractor. Where disputes arise over the ownership of a work product, the courts may have to determine employment status for copyright purposes.

For a complete discussion of all the legal issues involved in hiring independent contractors, see *Hiring Independent Contractors*, by Stephen Fishman (Nolo).

B. Benefits and Drawbacks of Using Independent Contractors

A hiring firm that classifies workers as independent contractors obtains many financial and other benefits, but may face serious risks and drawbacks as well. Let's look at these in detail.

1. Benefits of Using Independent Contractors

Perhaps the main reason any business uses independent contractors is that it can save a great deal of money. A business that hires an employee incurs a number of obligations in addition to paying that employee's salary, including:

- **Federal tax withholding.** The employer must withhold federal income tax from the wages paid to an em-

ployee and pay them to the IRS. Each year, the employer must send the employee a Form W-2 showing how much he or she earned and how much was withheld.

- **Social Security and Medicare taxes.** Social Security and Medicare taxes (FICA) are levied on both the employer and employee and must be paid together with the withheld federal income tax.
- **Federal unemployment taxes.** Employers must pay federal unemployment taxes (FUTA).
- **State taxes.** Employers must also pay state unemployment taxes and, in many states, also withhold state income taxes from employees' paychecks.
- **Workers' compensation insurance.** Employers must provide workers' compensation insurance coverage for employees in case they become injured on the job.
- **Employment benefits.** Although not legally required, most employers give their employees health insurance, sick leave, paid holidays, and vacations. More generous employers also provide pension benefits for their employees.
- **Office space and equipment.** An employer normally provides an employee with office space and whatever equipment he or she needs to do the job.

All of these items add enormously to the cost of hiring and keeping an employee. Typically, more than one-third of all employee payroll costs go for Social Security, unemployment insurance, health benefits, and vacation.

By hiring an independent contractor instead of an employee, a business incurs none of these obligations. It need not withhold or pay any taxes. Perhaps most importantly, an independent contractor need not be provided with health insurance, workers' compensation coverage, a pension plan, or any other employee benefits. The business need only report amounts paid to an independent contractor by filing a Form 1099-MISC with the IRS. (Even this form need not be filed if an independent contractor is incorporated or paid less than $600 in a calendar year.)

There is another important reason businesses often prefer to use independent contractors: It avoids making a long-term commitment to the worker. An independent contractor can be hired solely to accomplish a specific task, enabling a business to obtain specialized expertise only for a short time. The hiring firm need not go through the trauma, severance costs, and potential lawsuits brought on by laying off or firing an employee.

2. Drawbacks and Risks of Using Independent Contractors

You might now be thinking, "I'll never hire an employee again; I'll just use independent contractors." Before doing this, you should know that there are some substantial risks involved in classifying workers as independent contractors.

a. Adverse tax consequences

The IRS and most states want to see as many workers as possible classified as employees, not independent contractors. This way, the IRS and states can immediately collect taxes based on payroll withholding. It also makes it far more difficult for workers to underreport their income or otherwise evade taxes.

In the 1970s and '80s the IRS mounted an aggressive attack on employers who, in the view of the IRS, misclassified employees as independent contractors. One of the industries the IRS targeted was the software industry. Then, in the late 1990s, all IRS audit activity dramatically decreased due to budgetary and other problems. However, this trend is not expected to continue.

If the IRS concludes that an employer has misclassified an employee as an independent contractor, it may impose substantial assessments, penalties, and interest.

An employer's woes do not necessarily end with the IRS. The state version of the IRS and/or state unemployment or workers' compensation agency may also audit the employer and order that it pay back taxes and/or unemployment or workers' comp insurance.

Such assessments can easily put a small company out of business. Also, keep in mind that the owners of the business may be held personally liable for such assessments and penalties, even if the business is a corporate entity. If the business owners cannot pay the taxes or fees, other responsible company officials such as the controller or treasurer may be held personally liable for them.

b. Potential loss of intellectual property rights

Another potential drawback that may arise from using independent contractors instead of employees is that the hiring firm faces a possible loss of copyright ownership. Unless the hiring firm obtains a written assignment (transfer) of the contractor's copyright rights, the contractor may end up owning the copyright in the materials the contractor creates—even though the hiring firm paid the contractor to do the work. To avoid this consequence, hiring firms must obtain written assignments from independent contractors. (See Chapter 11 for a detailed discussion.)

c. Loss of control over workers

By using independent contractors, the hiring firm gives up control of its workers. Independent contractors legally may not be treated like employees. For instance, the hiring firm may not supervise an independent contractor. He or she must more or less be left alone to perform the agreed-upon services without substantial guidance or interference. If you want to control how a worker performs, classify the worker as an employee.

C. Which Workers Qualify as Independent Contractors

Given the risks involved in misclassifying an employee as an independent contractor, it is important for website and software developers to clearly understand whether a worker qualifies as an independent contractor or should be treated as an employee. Stated simply, an independent contractor is a person who is in business for himself or herself. Anyone with an independent business qualifies.

To decide whether a worker is an independent businessperson or a mere employee, the IRS and courts assess the degree of control the hiring party has over the worker. An independent contractor maintains personal control over the way he or she does the work contracted for, including the details of when, where, and how the work is done. The hiring party's control is limited to accepting or rejecting the final result of the independent contractor's work. An independent contractor is just that—independent.

If the person or company that hires a worker has the right to control the worker, that worker is an employee. This is so whether or not that right was actually exercised—that is, whether the worker was really controlled. If the right of control is present, the IRS will view the worker as an employee, even if you have a written agreement calling him or her an independent computer consultant, independent contractor, partner, or coventurer.

Part-Time Workers Can Be Employees

If the right to control the worker exists, it also makes no difference whether a person only works part-time. Even a part-time worker will be considered an employee if he or she is not operating an independent business.

1. IRS Factors for Measuring Control

To help determine whether a worker is an employee or independent contractor, the IRS has developed a set of factors it uses to measure how much control the hiring firm has the right to exercise over the worker. These factors are an attempt by the IRS to synthesize the results of court decisions on who is and is not an independent contractor. They are intended to serve as flexible guidelines for IRS auditors, not as a strict series of tests. Not all the factors may apply to a given worker, and some may be more important than others. The factors are summarized in the following chart:

IRS Control Factors

Behavioral Control

Factors that show whether a hiring firm has the right to control how a worker performs the specific tasks he or she has been hired to do:

A worker will more likely be considered an IC if you:

- do not give him or her instructions how to work

- do not provide training

- do not evaluate how the worker performs. A worker will more likely be considered an employee if you:

- provide instructions that the worker must follow about how to work

- give the worker detailed training

- evaluate how the worker does the job (as opposed to evaluating the results of his or her work).

Financial Control

Factors showing whether a hiring firm has a right to control a worker's financial life:

A worker will more likely be considered an IC if he or she:

- has a significant investment in equipment and facilities

- pays business or travel expenses himself or herself

- markets his or her services to the public

- is paid by the job, and

- has opportunity for profit or loss.

A worker will more likely be considered an employee if:

- you provide equipment and facilities free of charge

- you reimburse the worker's business or traveling expenses

- the worker makes no effort to market his or her services to the public

- you pay the worker by the hour or other unit of time

- the worker has no opportunity for profit or loss—for example, because you pay by the hour and reimburse all expenses.

Relationship of the Worker and Hiring Firm

Factors showing whether you and the worker believe he or she is an IC or employee:

A worker will more likely be considered an IC if:

- you don't provide employee benefits such as health insurance

- you sign an IC agreement with the worker

- the worker performs services that are not a part of your regular business activities.

A worker will more likely be considered an employee if:

- you provide employee benefits

- you have no written IC agreement

- the worker performs services that are part of your core business.

Microsoft Shows What Not to Do

A highly publicized case involving Microsoft shows how a software developer that uses ICs can get into trouble. Microsoft supplemented its core staff of employees with a pool of people it classified as ICs. These people worked as software testers, production editors, proofreaders, formatters, and indexers. They all signed independent contractor agreements, worked on specific projects, and submitted invoices for their services. But otherwise they were treated much the same as Microsoft's employees: they worked along with regular employees, sharing the same supervisors, performing identical functions, and working the same core hours. They also received admittance card keys, office equipment, and supplies from Microsoft. The IRS determined that the workers were really employees for Social Security and income tax purposes and Microsoft agreed to pay overdue employment and withholding taxes. To add insult to injury, several of the workers then sued Microsoft claiming that they were entitled to pension and stock ownership benefits Microsoft provided its employees. The court agreed, having been swayed by the IRS rulings and Microsoft's own admission that the workers should have been classified as employees all along. (*Vizcaino v. Microsoft*, 173 F.3d 713 (9th Cir. 1999).)

2. Section 530—The Employer's "Safe Harbor"

Applying the factors discussed just above is a highly subjective exercise, leading to a great deal of uncertainty. Moreover, many employers and tax experts believe that IRS examiners often arbitrarily interpret the facts in order to find an employment relationship.

In an attempt to make life a little easier for hiring firms, Congress added Section 530 to the Internal Revenue Code in 1978. Section 530 serves as a "Safe Harbor" for a firm that classifies a worker as an independent contractor. Section 530 prohibits the IRS from retroactively reclassifying a worker from independent contractor to employee if the hiring firm satisfies three requirements:

- it filed all required 1099-MISC forms reporting to the IRS the payments to the workers in question

- it consistently treated the workers involved and others doing similar work as ICs, and

- it had a reasonable basis—that is, a good reason—for treating the workers as ICs—for example, treating such workers as ICs is a common practice in the software industry or an attorney or accountant said the workers qualified as ICs.

When the IRS audits a hiring firm, it will first determine whether the Safe Harbor applies; if it does, the auditor won't bother to consider the control factors discussed in the previous section.

a. Safe Harbor cannot be claimed by brokers or consulting firms

It's very common for software and Web developers to obtain the services of temporary or highly specialized workers though brokers. In these situations, three parties are involved in the relationship: the client contracts with the broker who in turn contracts with the worker to provide services for the client. The broker is in effect a middleman. The client pays the broker who pays the worker after taking its own cut.

> **EXAMPLE:** Acme Technical Services is a broker that provides website programmers to others. Acme contracts with Burt, a freelance programmer, to perform programming services for the Old Reliable Insurance Company. Reliable pays Acme who in turn pays Burt after deducting a broker's fee.

Such brokers—also called technical services firms or consulting firms—may not use the Safe Harbor if they contract to provide third-party clients with:

- engineers
- designers
- drafters
- computer programmers
- systems analysts, or

- other similarly skilled workers.

The provision in the Safe Harbor rules setting forth this limitation is often referred to as Section 1706. Section 1706 has engendered a great deal of fear, often bordering upon paranoia, among hi-tech firms. Many such firms refuse to hire ICs or will deal only with brokers who treat the workers as their own employees.

This fear is largely misplaced. The fact is that Section 1706 does not make anyone an employee. It just means that the broker or consulting firm that serves as the middleman between them and their clients can't use the Safe Harbor. The workers may nevertheless be ICs under the IRS control test. (See Section C1.)

b. Section 1706 doesn't apply to clients

Moreover, Section 1706 applies only to the broker in the middle of a three-party relationship, not to the client. The client could use the Safe Harbor if it was audited by the IRS and the examiner claimed the worker was the client's employee under the control test.

> **EXAMPLE:** AcmeSoft, Inc., contracts with Quickhelp Technical Services to obtain the services of Burt, a freelance programmer. AcmeSoft is then audited by the IRS. The examiner claims that AcmeSoft has the right to exert sufficient control over Burt for

him to be AcmeSoft's employee under the control test. AcmeSoft can qualify for Safe Harbor protection if it meets the three requirements discussed above—reasonable basis, consistency, 1099s.

In addition, the Safe Harbor can always be used where a firm contracts directly with a technical services worker, rather than going through a broker or consulting firm.

> **EXAMPLE:** AcmeSoft, Inc., contracts with Burt directly to provide it with programming services—that is, it does not go through a broker. If

AcmeSoft is audited, it can obtain Safe Harbor protection, provided that it satisfies the requirements.

c. State audits

No state has a counterpart to the IRS Safe Harbor. A state unemployment compensation or workers' compensation auditor will not be impressed by the fact that you've obtained Safe Harbor protection from the IRS. You'll need to convince the state auditor that the workers involved qualify as ICs under the state rules. These can be stricter than the IRS rules.

Do's and Don'ts for Software Companies That Use Independent Contractors

Software firms that classify workers as independent contractors need to remember that the workers must be treated like independent businesspeople, not like employees. Treat the worker the same way you would the accountant who does your company's taxes or the lawyer who handles your legal work. This means:

- *Sign a written contract with the independent contractor before the work begins.* The contract should specify the work to be performed and make it clear that the worker is an independent contractor. The contract should be for a term of no longer than three to six months. Even where extensive projects are involved, this can be accomplished by narrowly defining the work to be done and then drawing up new contracts to cover additional tasks.

- *Don't provide ongoing instructions or training.* If the independent contractor needs special training, he or she should procure and pay for it himself or herself.

- *Don't supervise the independent contractor or establish working hours.* It's up to the independent contractor to control when and how to accomplish the job.

- *Don't require formal written reports.* An occasional phone call inquiring into the work's progress is acceptable, but requiring regular written status reports indicates the worker is an employee. However, contracts for specific projects can (and should) have benchmarks for show-and-tell demonstrations or reports.

- *Don't invite an independent contractor to employee functions.* The exception is where outside vendors will be there as well.

- *Don't ever fire an independent contractor.* Instead, terminate the contract if he or she fails to meet the specifications or standards set forth in it.

- *Don't ever refer to an independent contractor as an "employee."* This should not be done verbally or in writing.

- *Set up a separate vendor file for each independent contractor you hire.* Keep in this file the independent contractor's contract, invoices, copies of 1099 forms and any other information that shows the worker is operating an independent business. This may include the independent contractor's business card and stationery, and evidence that the independent contractor has workers' compensation insurance coverage for her employees. Don't keep independent contractor records with your employee personnel files.

- *Don't pay independent contractors on a weekly, biweekly, or monthly basis like you pay your employees.* Rather, require all independent contractors to submit invoices, which are paid the same time you pay other outside vendors, such as your office supply company.

D. Independent Contractor Agreement Favorable to Hiring Firm

A hiring firm should develop a form IC agreement it can use over and over again with all the ICs it hires. The agreement provided in this section favors the hiring firm—that is, when it comes to those issues where the interests of the hiring firm and IC diverge, the agreement favors the hiring firm. The agreement is self-explanatory, with the following clarifications.

 The full text of the Consulting Agreement is on the CD-ROM forms disk.

When completing the introductory paragraph, avoid referring to an IC as an employee or to yourself as an employer. Initially, it's best to refer to the IC by his or her full name. If an IC is incorporated, use the corporate name, not the IC's own name. For example: "John Smith Incorporated" instead of just "John Smith." If the IC is unincorporated but is doing business under a fictitious business name, use that name. A fictitious business name or assumed name is a name sole proprietors or partners use to identify their business other than their own names. For example, if Al Brodsky calls his one-man marketing computer consulting business "ABC Consulting," use that name. This shows

you're contracting with a business, not a single individual.

For sake of brevity, it is usual to identify yourself and the IC by shorter names in the remainder of the agreement. You can use an abbreviated version of the IC's full name—for example, "ABC" for "ABC Consulting." Or you can refer to the IC simply as "Consultant" or "Contractor."

Refer to yourself initially by your company name and subsequently by a short version of the name or as "Client" or "Firm."

Put the short names in quotes after the full names. Also include the address of the principal place of business of the IC and yourself. If you or the IC have more than one office or workplace, the principal place of business is the main office or workplace.

1. Services Performed by Consultant

[ALTERNATIVE 1 (SERVICES DESCRIBED IN AGREEMENT)] Consultant agrees to perform the following services for Client: [DESCRIBE SERVICES CONSULTANT WILL PERFORM, INCLUDING ANY AGREED-UPON WORK SCHEDULE]

[ALTERNATIVE 2 (SERVICES DESCRIBED ON ATTACHMENT)] Consultant agrees to perform the services described in Exhibit A, which is attached to and made part of this Agreement.

The agreement should describe, in as much detail as possible, what the consultant is expected to do. Make sure to cover everything the consultant should deliver.

It is often helpful to break the project down into discrete parts or stages—often called phases or "milestones." This makes it easier for the hiring firm to monitor the consultant's progress and may aid the consultant in budgeting her time. For ex-ample, the consultant's pay could be contingent upon the completion of each milestone. (Payment schedules are covered below, under "Consultant's Payment.")

You can include the description in the main body of the agreement. Or, if it's a lengthy explanation, put it on a separate document labeled "Exhibit A" and attach it to the agreement.

2. Consultant's Payment

[ALTERNATIVE 1 (FIXED FEE)] Consultant shall be paid $[STATE AMOUNT] upon completion of the work as detailed in Clause 1.

[ALTERNATIVE 2 (INSTALLMENT PAYMENTS)] Client shall pay Consultant a fixed fee of $[TOTAL AMOUNT], in [NUMBER OF INSTALLMENTS] installments as follows:

(a) $[FIRST INSTALLMENT AMOUNT] upon completion of the following services: [DESCRIBE].

(b) $[SECOND INSTALLMENT AMOUNT] upon completion of the following services: [DESCRIBE].

[THE PROJECT CAN BE DIVIDED INTO AS MANY PHASES AS DESIRED; ADD ADDITIONAL INSTALLMENT SCHEDULE CLAUSES AS NEEDED.]

(c) $[FINAL INSTALLMENT AMOUNT] upon completion of all the work to be performed and the services to be rendered in accordance with the schedule set forth in Clause 1 above, and written acceptance by Client.

[ALTERNATIVE 3 (PAYMENT BY THE HOUR/DAY/WEEK/MONTH)] Consultant shall be compensated at the rate of $[PAYMENT RATE] per [SPECIFY "hour," "day," "week," or "month"]. [OPTIONAL: "Unless otherwise agreed upon in writing by Client, Client's maximum liability for all services performed during the term of this Agreement shall not exceed $[MAXIMUM AMOUNT]."]

There are a number of ways a consultant may be paid; choose the alternative that suits your needs:

- **Alternative 1:** Fixed Fee. The simplest way for a consultant to be paid is to pay a fixed fee for the entire project. This way, you know exactly how much the work will cost you and the consultant won't have an incentive to pad the bill by working more hours.
- **Alternative 2:** Installment Payments. Paying a consultant a fixed fee for the entire job, rather than an hourly or daily rate, supports a finding of independent contractor status. However, this can pose problems for the consultant due to difficulties in accurately estimating how long the job will take. One way to deal with this problem is to break the job down into phases or "milestones" and pay the consultant a fixed fee upon completion of each phase. If you use this approach, you must describe in the agreement what work the consultant must complete to receive each payment.
- **Alternative 3:** Payment by the Hour/Day/Week/Month. If a fixed fee for the job is impractical, it doesn't make much difference for IRS purposes whether the consultant is paid by the hour, day, week, or month. It's generally a good idea to place a cap on the consultant's total compensation. This may be a particularly good idea if you're unsure how reliable or efficient the consultant is.

3. Expenses

[ALTERNATIVE 1 (NO EXPENSES)] Consultant shall be responsible for all expenses incurred while performing services under this Agreement.

[ALTERNATIVE 2 (EXPENSES PAID IF PRE-APPROVED)] Consultant will not be reimbursed for any expenses incurred in connection with the performance of services under this Agreement, unless those expenses are approved in advance in writing by Client.

The IRS considers the payment of a worker's business or traveling expenses to be a mild indicator of an employment relationship. It's best not to reimburse an IC for expenses; instead, pay the IC enough so that he or she can pay his or her own expenses.

Select one of the two alternatives. Alternative 1 provides you will not pay any of the consultant's expenses. Alternative 2 provides that you will pay only those expenses you agree in advance in writing to reimburse.

4. Invoices

Consultant shall submit invoices for all services rendered. Client shall pay Consultant within _____ [CHOOSE ONE: 30, 45, 60] days after receipt of each invoice.

An independent contractor should never be paid weekly, biweekly, or monthly the way an employee is. Instead, he or she should submit invoices, which should be paid at the same time and manner as you pay other vendors. You need to decide how long after you receive the invoice you will pay the consultant, 30 days is a common period.

5. Consultant an Independent Contractor

Consultant is an independent contractor, and neither Consultant nor Consultant's staff is, or shall be deemed, Client's employees. In its capacity as an independent contractor, Consultant agrees and represents, and Client agrees, as follows:

[INCLUDE ALL OF PROVISIONS 5a-j THAT APPLY]

(a) Consultant has the right to perform services for others during the term of this Agreement subject to noncompetition provisions set out in this Agreement, if any.

(b) Consultant has the sole right to control and direct the means, manner, and method by which the services required by this Agreement will be performed.

(c) Consultant has the right to perform the services required by this Agreement at any place or location and at such times as Consultant may determine.

(d) Consultant will furnish all equipment and materials used to provide the services required by this Agreement, except to the extent that Consultant's work must be performed on or with Client's computer or existing software.

(e) The services required by this Agreement shall be performed by Consultant, or Consultant's staff, and Client shall not be required to hire, supervise, or pay any assistants to help Consultant.

(f) Consultant is responsible for paying all ordinary and necessary expenses of its staff.

(g) Neither Consultant nor Consultant's staff shall receive any training from Client in the professional skills necessary to perform the services required by this Agreement.

(h) Neither Consultant nor Consultant's staff shall be required to devote full time to the performance of the services required by this Agreement.

(i) Client shall not provide insurance coverage of any kind for Consultant or Consultant's staff.

(j) Client shall not withhold from Consultant's compensation any amount that would normally be withheld from an employee's pay.

One of the most important functions of an agreement between a hiring firm and consultant is to help establish that the consultant is not the hiring firm's employee. In an audit of the hiring firm, an IRS examiner or similar official will almost surely want to see the firm's agreements with all workers classified as independent contractors. If the agreement indicates that the hiring firm has the right to control the worker, he or she will undoubtedly be viewed as an employee by the IRS. This will cause problems not only for the hiring firm, but for the consultant as well.

On the other hand, an agreement that indicates a lack of the right to control on the part of the hiring firm will contribute to a finding of independent contractor status. But such an agreement will not be determinative in and of itself. Simply signing a piece of paper will not make a worker an independent contractor. The agreement must reflect reality—that is, you must actually not have the right to control the worker.

The language in this clause addresses most of the factors the IRS and other agencies consider in measuring the degree of control of the hiring firm. (These factors are discussed in Section C.) All provisions show that the hiring firm lacks the right to control the manner and means by which the consultant will perform the agreed-upon services.

Include all of provisions a-j that apply to your particular situation. The more that apply, the more likely that the consultant will be viewed as an independent contractor.

6. Intellectual Property Ownership

[ALTERNATIVE 1 (CLIENT OWNS WORK PRODUCT)]

Work Product includes, but is not limited to, any computer code (in object code and source code form), programming code, data, specifications, work-up files, website content (including HTML script, designs, forms, text, music, graphics, photographs, and videos), and other materials, in whatever form, developed solely for Client under this Agreement.

Consultant hereby assigns to Client its entire right, title, and interest, including all patent, copyright, trade secret, trademark, and other proprietary rights, in the Work Product.

Consultant shall, at no charge to Client, execute and aid in the preparation of any papers that Client may consider necessary or helpful to obtain or maintain—at Client's expense—any patents, copyrights, trademarks, or other proprietary rights. Client shall reimburse Consultant for reasonable out-of-pocket expenses incurred under this provision.

[ALTERNATIVE 2 (CONSULTANT OWNS WORK PRODUCT)]

Work Product includes, but is not limited to, any computer code (in object code and source code form), programming code, data, specifications, work-up files, website content (including HTML script, designs, forms, text, music, graphics, photographs, and videos), and other materials, in whatever form, developed solely for Client under this Agreement.

Client agrees that Consultant shall retain any and all rights Consultant may have in the Work Product. Consultant hereby grants Client an unrestricted, nonexclusive, perpetual, fully paid-up, worldwide license to use and sublicense the use of the Work Product for the purpose of developing and marketing its products and services, but not for the purpose of marketing Work Product separate from its products and services.

Usually, you will want to obtain sole ownership of what the consultant creates. However, there is no rule that this has to be the case. Two different ownership alternatives are presented in the contract. Choose only one alternative and delete the other. Here's an explanation:

- **Alternative 1:** Client Owns Consultant's Work Product. Obtaining ownership of the consultant's work product presents many advantages: you can do anything you want with the material and the consultant is prevented from giving the same material to your competitors. If you and the consultant agree that you will own the consultant's work product, you should obtain a written assignment of the consultant's intellectual property rights in such work. Alternative 1 contains such an assignment. As discussed in detail in Chapter 11, a hiring firm can never be sure it owns what it pays an independent contractor to create unless it obtains such an assignment. Among the most important reasons to obtain an assignment from the IC is that otherwise the hiring firm may not have the right to create "derivative works" based on the original work product—for example, new versions of a program or website originally created by the consultant.

- **Alternative 2:** Consultant Owns Work Product. You and the consultant may agree that the consultant will retain his or her ownership rights in the work product (perhaps in return for receiving reduced monetary compensation). In this event, instead of assigning his or her rights to the client, the consultant will grant you a nonexclusive license to use the work product.

This clause grants the client a nonexclusive license to use the consultant's work product in any of its products or services, but prevents it from selling the consultant's work to others. This is a generous license grant.

7. Ownership of Consultant's Materials

"Consultant's Materials" means all copyrightable materials, that:

- do not constitute Work Product,

- are incorporated into the Work Product, and

- are owned solely by Consultant or licensed to Consultant with a right to sublicense.

Consultant's Materials include, but are not limited to, the following: [DESCRIBE]

Consultant shall retain any and all rights Consultant may have in Consultant's Materials. Consultant hereby grants Client an unrestricted, nonexclusive, perpetual, fully paid-up worldwide license to use and sublicense the use of Consultant's Materials for the purpose of developing and marketing its products and services.

A software or website consultant will often have various development tools, routines, subroutines, applets, and other programs, data, and materials that he or she brings to the job and that might end up in the final product. One term for these type of items is "Consultant's Materials."

You must make sure the consultant grants you a license to use these materials. This clause grants you a nonexclusive license to use such materials in any of your products. Try to have the consultant list in the agreement what these materials are. This avoids confusion later on.

8. Confidential Information

(a) Consultant agrees that the Work Product is Client's sole and exclusive property. Consultant shall treat the Work Product on a confidential basis and not disclose it to any third party without Client's written consent, except when reasonably necessary to perform the services under this Agreement.

(b) Consultant will not use or disclose to others without Client's written consent Client's confidential information, except when reasonably necessary to perform the services under this Agreement. "Confidential information" includes, but is not limited to:

- the written, printed, graphic, or electronically recorded materials furnished by Client for use by Contractor

- Client's business plans, customer lists, operating procedures, trade secrets, design formulas, know-how and processes, computer programs and inventories, discoveries and improvements of any kind

- any written or tangible information stamped "confidential," "proprietary," or with a similar legend, and

- any written or tangible information not marked with a confidentiality legend, or information disclosed orally to Consultant, that is treated as confidential when disclosed and later summarized sufficiently for identification purposes in a written memorandum marked "confidential" and delivered to Consultant within 30 days after the disclosure.

(c) Contractor shall not be restricted in the use of any material which is publicly available, already in Contractor's possession, or known to Contractor without restriction, or which is rightfully obtained by Contractor from sources other than Client.

(d) Contractor's obligations regarding proprietary or confidential information extend to information belonging to customers and suppliers of Client about whom Contractor may have gained knowledge as a result of Client's services to Client.

[OPTIONAL (PARTIES' RELATIONSHIP CONFIDENTIAL)] (e) All information concerning the existence of this Agreement and the existence of any business relationship between Consultant and Client shall be kept in confidence. [END OPTION]

(f) Consultant will not disclose to Client information or material that is a trade secret of any third party.

(g) The provisions of this clause shall survive any termination of this Agreement.

In the course of his or her work, the consultant may be exposed to your most valuable trade secrets. It is reasonable, therefore, for you to seek to include a nondisclosure provision in the agreement. Such a provision states that the consultant may not disclose the client's trade secrets to others without the client's permission.

These are the most important parts of the confidentiality provision in the agreement:

(a) This clause provides that the consultant has a duty not to disclose to others the work he or she creates for the hiring firm. This clause should be deleted from the agreement if the consultant retains ownership of her work product.

(b) This clause prevents the unauthorized disclosure by the consultant of any of your confidential information. Confidential information includes any written material you mark "confidential" or information disclosed orally that you later write down, mark as confidential, and deliver to the consultant.

(c) A consultant should have no duty to keep material confidential if it does not qualify as a trade secret, is lawfully learned from persons other than the client, or is independently developed by the consultant.

(e) If you don't want to permit the consultant to disclose your business relationship, include this clause.

9. Noncompetition

> Consultant agrees that during performance of the services required by this Agreement [OPTIONAL: "and for [SIX MONTHS TO TWO YEARS] after completion"], Consultant will not perform the same services for any competitor of Client in the specific field in which Consultant is performing services for Client.

A firm that hires a consultant naturally doesn't want the consultant to perform the same work for a competitor, thereby allowing the competitor to benefit from work originally paid for by the hiring firm. A hiring firm is protected from this problem to some extent where it obtains an assignment of all the consultant's rights in the work product. Theoretically, in this case the consultant can't use the work product on other projects because she doesn't own it. However, in practice it can be difficult to determine whether or not the consultant is using the client's work product on other projects.

A hiring firm obtains much greater protection by including a noncompetition clause in the independent contractor agreement. As discussed in Chapter 14, restrictions on competition are enforceable only if reasonable. To be viewed as reasonable by the courts, such restrictions must be drafted as narrowly as possible.

This optional clause only prevents the consultant from performing the exact same services for competitors that it performed for the hiring firm. This provision can be limited to the time the consultant is working for the client, or it can be extended for a limited period afterwards; no more than two years would be considered reasonable by most courts.

10. Term of Agreement

This Agreement will become effective when signed by both parties and will end no later than _____ [DATE].

An independent contractor agreement should last no more than one or two years at most. Anything longer makes the consultant look like an employee. Successive agreements can be used if the project can't be completed in the time frame set out in this agreement.

11. Termination of Agreement

(a) Each party has the right to terminate this Agreement if the other party has materially breached any obligation herein and such breach remains uncured for a period of 30 days after notice thereof is sent to the other party.

(b) If at any time after commencement of the services required by this Agreement, Client shall, in its sole reasonable judgment, determine that such services are inadequate, unsatisfactory, no longer needed, or substantially not conforming to the descriptions, warranties, or representations contained in this Agreement, Client may terminate this Agreement upon _____ [STATE NOTICE PERIOD—ANYTHING FROM 5 TO 30 DAYS] days' written notice to Consultant.

Many consultants and hiring firms want to have the right to terminate their agreements for any reason on two weeks' notice. Unfortunately, the IRS considers such an unfettered termination right to be an indicator of an employment relationship (an employee normally can quit or be fired at any time). This clause attempts to reach a compromise between the parties' desire to be able to get out of the agreement and at the same time satisfy the IRS and others that the consultant is an independent contractor. Of particular note are:

(a) This paragraph permits either party to terminate the agreement if the other has breached it and failed to remedy the breach within 30 days.

(b) Most software or website consulting agreements are basically contracts for personal services. If the client becomes dissatisfied with the service he or she is receiving and loses confidence in the consultant, the client should have the right to terminate the agreement. This paragraph permits the client to terminate the agreement only if in the client's "reasonable judgment" the consultant's performance is inadequate or unnecessary. This stops short of giving the client a completely unfettered right to fire the consultant at will.

12. Return of Materials

> Upon termination of this Agreement, each party shall promptly return to the other all data, materials, and other property of the other held by it.

This clause requires both you and the consultant to return each others' materials at the end of the agreement.

13. Warranties and Representations

> (a) Consultant has the authority to enter into this Agreement and to perform all obligations hereunder.
>
> (b) The Work Product and Consultant's Materials are and shall be free and clear of all encumbrances including security interests, licenses, liens, or other restrictions except as follows: _____ [LIST; IF NONE, STATE "NONE"]
>
> (c) The use, reproduction, distribution, or modification of the Work Product and Consultant's Materials does not and will not violate the copyright, patent, trade secret, or other property right of any former client, employer, or third party.
>
> (d) For a period of _____ days [STATE LENGTH OF WARRANTY PERIOD—ANYWHERE FROM 90 DAYS TO 1 YEAR OR MORE] following acceptance of the Work Product, the Work Product will be:
>
> - free from reproducible programming errors and defects in workmanship and materials under normal use, and
> - perform substantially in conformance with the specifications and functions set forth in this Agreement.

A warranty is a promise or statement regarding the quality, quantity, performance, or legal title of something being sold. Software and website consulting agreements typically contain several warranty provisions.

(a) This clause provides that the consultant has the authority to perform as promised. This means, for example, that the consultant is not prevented from working for you because he or she has previously signed a noncompetition agreement for a previous client.

(b) In this clause, the consultant promises that the client will obtain free and clear ownership or license rights to consultant's work product and material. If the consultant has licensed any materials from third parties that are to be included in the work product, the licenses should be listed here.

(c) The consultant promises in this clause that his or her work product and materials will not infringe on others' copyrights, patents, trade secrets, or other intellectual property rights.

(d) The consultant promises here that the work product will perform in substantial conformance with the specifications and will be free of reproducible programming errors. You need to state how long this warranty will last—it can be anywhere from 90 days to one year or longer.

14. Indemnification

Consultant agrees to indemnify and hold harmless Client against any claims, actions, or demands, including without limitation reasonable attorney and accounting fees, alleging or resulting from the breach of the warranties contained in this Agreement. Client shall provide notice to Consultant promptly of any such claim, suit, or proceeding and shall assist Consultant, at Consultant's expense, in defending any such claim, suit, or proceeding.

Indemnification is a fancy legal word that means a promise to repay someone for their losses or damages if a specified event occurs. This clause requires the consultant to indemnify you or your business if someone sues or threatens to sue because the consultant breached any of the warranties made in the agreement. For example, if the consultant copied code from a third party and sold it to you, and that third party sued for infringement, the consultant would be required to pay for your legal defense and any damages a court awarded.

15. Employment of Assistants

[ALTERNATIVE 1 (CONSULTANT MAY EMPLOY ASSISTANTS)] (a) Consultant may, at Consultant's own expense, employ such assistants or subcontractors as Consultant deems necessary to perform the services required by this Agreement. However, Client shall have the right to reject any of Consultant's assistants or subcontractors whose qualifications in Client's good faith and reasonable judgment are insufficient for the satisfactory performance of the services required by this Agreement.

[ALTERNATIVE 2 (NO ASSISTANTS WITHOUT CLIENT'S CONSENT)] (a) Consultant may neither subcontract nor hire persons to aid in the performance of the services required by this Agreement without Client's prior written consent.

(b) Consultant warrants and represents that the Work Product shall be created solely by Consultant, Consultant's employees during the course of their employment, or independent contractors who assigned all right, title, and interest in the work to Consultant.

Because independent contractor agreements are basically personal services contracts, it's often appropriate for you to have some control over who will do the work. If you've hired a consultant because of his or her particular skills, you may wish to have a say-so as to whether the consultant can get others to do the work you hired him or her to do. This is not exercising control over how the work will be done but rather agreeing on who will do the work.

a. Alternative clauses

Choose the alternative Paragraph (a) that best suits you:

- **Alternative 1:** Consultant May Employ Assistants. This clause leaves the issue up to the consultant.
- **Alternative 2:** No Assistants Without Client's Consent. This clause requires the client's prior approval.

b. Assignment of copyright by ICs used by your IC

The consultant promises in this clause that any independent contractors the consultant hires will assign their rights to the consultant so the consultant may in turn assign or license those rights to you. As discussed in detail in Chapter 14, the copyright in website content software and other creative works created by an employee will automatically be owned by the employer only if created within the scope of employment. Works created by an independent contractor will be owned by the hiring party only if assigned to it by the independent contractor.

16. Mediation and Arbitration

If a dispute arises under this Agreement, the parties agree to first try to resolve it with the help of a mutually agreed-upon mediator in the following location _____ [LIST CITY OR COUNTY WHERE MEDIATION WILL OCCUR]. Any costs and fees other than attorney fees associated with the mediation shall be shared equally by the parties.

If it proves impossible to arrive at a mutually satisfactory solution through mediation, the parties agree to submit the dispute to binding arbitration at the following location _____ [LIST CITY OR COUNTY WHERE ARBITRATION WILL OCCUR] under the rules of the American Arbitration Association. Judgment upon the award rendered by the arbitrator may be entered in any court with jurisdiction to do so.

As you doubtless know, court litigation can be very expensive. To avoid these costs, alternative forms of dispute resolution have been developed that don't involve going to court. These include mediation and arbitration. For a thorough discussion of mediation and arbitration, see Chapter 17, Section B27.

17. Attorney Fees

If any legal action is necessary to enforce this Agreement, the prevailing party shall be entitled to reasonable attorney fees, costs, and expenses.

If you have to sue the consultant in court or bring an arbitration proceeding to enforce the agreement and win, you normally will not be awarded the amount of your attorney fees unless your agreement requires it. Including such an attorney fees provision in the agreement can be in your interest. It can help make filing a lawsuit economically feasible. It will also give the consultant a strong incentive to negotiate with you if you have a good case.

On the other hand, an attorney fees provision can also work against you. It may help the consultant find an attorney to sue you and make you more anxious to settle. If you think it's more likely you'll violate the agreement than the consultant will, an attorney fees provision is probably not a good idea.

Under this provision, if either person has to sue the other in court or bring an arbitration proceeding to enforce the agreement and wins—that is, becomes the prevailing party—the loser is required to pay the other person's attorney fees and expenses.

18. General Provisions

(a) Sole agreement: This is the entire Agreement between Consultant and Client.

(b) Severability: If any part of this Agreement is held unenforceable, the rest of the Agreement will continue in full force and effect.

(c) Applicable law: This Agreement will be governed by the laws of the State of [LIST APPLICABLE STATE].

(d) Notices: All notices and other communications given in connection with this Agreement shall be in writing and shall be deemed given as follows:

- When delivered personally to the recipient's address as appearing in the introductory paragraph to this Agreement;
- Three days after being deposited in the United States mails, postage prepaid to the recipient's address as appearing in the introductory paragraph to this Agreement, or
- When sent by fax or electronic mail. Notice is effective upon receipt provided that a duplicate copy of the notice is promptly given by first-class or certified mail, or the recipient delivers a written confirmation of receipt.

Any party may change its address appearing in the introductory paragraph to this Agreement by giving notice of the change in accordance with this paragraph.

(e) No partnership: This Agreement does not create a partnership relationship. Consultant does not have authority to enter into contracts on Client's behalf.

(f) Assignment: Consultant may not assign its rights or obligations under this Agreement without Client's prior written consent. Client may freely assign its rights and obligations under this Agreement.

These general provisions are standard in many types of legal documents. We provide a detailed explanation of these provisions in Chapter 17, Section B30.

19. Signatures

It is not necessary for the parties to sign the agreement in the same room or on the same day. At least two copies should be signed, with each party retaining one. For more information on signing agreements, see Chapter 1.

PART II. Working as an Independent Contractor

Part II is for the huge number of people in the software and website development fields who work as independent contractors. It provides an overview of the benefits and drawbacks of this lifestyle and includes a detailed consulting agreement favorable to the independent contractor.

For a complete discussion of all the legal issues involved in working as an independent contractor, see *Working for Yourself*, by Stephen Fishman (Nolo).

E. Benefits and Drawbacks of Working as an Independent Contractor

Being an IC can give you more freedom than employees have and result in tax benefits. But there are also drawbacks.

1. Benefits of Being an Independent Contractor

- *You're your own boss*: When you're an IC you're your own boss, with all the risks and rewards that entails. This freedom from control is particu-larly appealing to many of the highly creative and independent people in the software industry.

- *You may earn more than employees*: You can often earn more as an IC than as an employee in someone else's business. According to *The Wall Street Journal*, ICs are usually paid at least 20% to 40% more per hour than employees performing the same work. This is because hiring firms don't have to pay half of ICs' Social Security taxes, pay unemployment compensation taxes, or provide work-ers' compensation coverage or em-ployee benefits like health insurance and sick leave. Of course, how much you're paid is a matter for negotiation between you and your clients. ICs whose skills are in great demand may receive far more than employees do-ing similar work.

- *Tax benefits*: Being an IC also provides you with many tax benefits that em-ployees don't have. For example, no federal or state taxes are withheld from your paychecks as they must be for employees. Instead, ICs normally pay estimated taxes directly to the IRS four times a year. Even more impor-tant, you can take advantage of many business-related tax deductions that are limited or not available at all for employees. This may include, for ex-ample, office expenses including those for home offices, travel expenses, entertainment and meal expenses, equipment and insurance costs, and more.

2. Drawbacks of IC Status

Despite the advantages, being an IC is no bed of roses. Following are some of the major drawbacks and pitfalls.

- *No job security*: As discussed above, one of the best things about being an IC is that you're on your own. But this can be one of the worst things about it as well. When you're an employee, you must be paid as long as you have your job, even if your employer's business is slow. This is not the case when you're an IC. If you don't have business, you don't make any money.

- *No employer-provided benefits*: Although not required to by law, employers usually provide their employees with health insurance, paid vacations, and paid sick leave. More generous employers may also provide retirement benefits, bonuses, and even employee profit sharing. When you're an IC, you get no such benefits.

- ICs also don't have the safety net provided by unemployment insurance. Nor do hiring firms provide them with workers' compensation coverage.

- *Risk of not being paid*: Some ICs have great difficulty getting their clients to pay them on time or at all. When

you're an IC, you bear the risk of loss from deadbeat clients.

- *Liability for business debts*: If like most ICs you're a sole proprietor or partner in a partnership, you are personally liable for your business debts. An IC whose business fails could lose most of what he or she owns.

- *More complex tax returns*: Finally, your tax returns will likely be far more complex when you work as an IC than they were when you worked as an employee. In addition, you'll have to pay your own income and Social Security taxes directly to the IRS in the form of quarterly estimated taxes. Your clients will not withhold any taxes from your compensation.

F. Consulting Agreement Favorable to Independent Contractor

You should always use a written agreement whenever you work as an independent contractor. This can avoid innumerable headaches later on. The agreement need not be long or complex. A simple letter stating the services you'll perform, your compensation, and the deadline for performance may be sufficient for small jobs.

However, for longer or more complex jobs, you'll probably want to use a more extensive agreement. The following agreement covers all the issues a software or website consultant may wish to include in a full-blown consulting agreement. This agreement is favorable to the consultant.

 The text of a Consultant Agreement is in the CD-ROM forms disk.

At the beginning of your contract, it's best to refer to yourself by your full business name. Later on in the contract, you can use an obvious abbreviation. For more information on completing the introductory paragraph, see Section E.

1. Services You'll Perform

[ALTERNATIVE 1 (SERVICES DESCRIBED IN AGREEMENT)] Consultant agrees to perform the following services for Client: DESCRIBE SERVICES CONSULTANT WILL PERFORM, INCLUDING ANY AGREED-UPON WORK SCHEDULE]

[ALTERNATIVE 2 (SERVICES DESCRIBED ON ATTACHMENT)] Consultant agrees to perform the services described in Exhibit A, which is attached to and made part of this Agreement.

The agreement should describe in as much detail as possible what you're expected to accomplish. Word the description carefully to emphasize the results you're expected to achieve. Don't describe the method by which you will achieve the results. As an IC, it should be up to you to decide how to do the work. The client's control should be limited to accepting or rejecting your final results. The more control the client exercises over how you work, the more you'll look like an employee.

It's perfectly okay for the agreement to establish very detailed specifications for your finished work product. But the specs should only describe the end results you must achieve, not how to obtain those results.

You can include the description in the main body of the Agreement. Or if it's a lengthy explanation, put it on a separate attachment.

2. Payment

[ALTERNATIVE 1 (FIXED FEE)] Consultant shall be paid $[STATE AMOUNT] upon execution of this agreement and $[STATE AMOUNT] upon completion of the work as detailed in Clause 1.

[ALTERNATIVE 2 (INSTALLMENT PAYMENTS)] Client shall pay Consultant a fixed fee of $[TOTAL AMOUNT], in [NUMBER OF INSTALLMENTS] installments according to the payment schedule described in Exhibit [A or B] which is attached to and made part of this Agreement.

[ALTERNATIVE 3 (PAYMENT BY THE HOUR/DAY/WEEK/MONTH)] Consultant shall be compensated at the rate of $[PAYMENT RATE] per [SPECIFY "hour," "day," "week," or "month"]. [OPTIONAL: "Unless otherwise agreed upon in writing by Client, Client's maximum liability for all services performed during the term of this Agreement shall not exceed $[MAXIMUM AMOUNT]."]

Software consultants can be paid in a variety of ways. Choose the alternative that suits your needs.

- **Alternative 1:** Fixed Fee. In a fixed fee agreement, you charge an agreed-upon amount for the entire project. This clause requires the client to pay you an initial sum when the work is commenced and the remainder when it's finished.

- **Alternative 2:** Installment Payments. If the project is long and complex, you may prefer to be paid in installments rather than waiting until the project is finished to receive the bulk of your payment. One way to do this is to break the job into phases or milestones and be paid a fixed fee when each phase is completed. Clients often like this pay-as-you-go arrangement too. To do this, draw up a schedule of installment payments tying each payment to your completion of specific services. It's usually easier to set forth the schedule in a separate document and attach it to the agreement as an exhibit. The main body of the agreement should simply refer to the attached payment schedule.

Following is an example of a schedule of payments. This schedule requires four payments: a down payment when the contract is signed and three installment payments. However, you and the client can have as many payments as you want.

Schedule of Payments

Client shall pay Contractor according to the following schedule of payments:

1) $[STATE SUM] when this Agreement is signed.

2) $[STATE SUM] when an invoice is submitted and the following services are completed:

[DESCRIBE FIRST STAGE OF SERVICES]

3) $[STATE SUM] when an invoice is submitted and the following services are completed:

[DESCRIBE SECOND STAGE OF SERVICES]

4) $[STATE SUM] when an invoice is submitted and the following services are completed:

[DESCRIBE THIRD STAGE OF SERVICES]

[ADD ANY ADDITIONAL PAYMENTS]

- **Alternative 3:** Payment by Unit of Time. Probably the majority of software and Web consultants charge by the hour or other unit of time. This is by far the safest way to be paid if it's difficult to estimate exactly how long a project will take. However, many clients will wish to place a cap on your total compensation because they're afraid you'll "pad" your bill. If this is the case, include the optional sentence providing for a cap, but make sure it's large enough to allow you to complete the job.

3. Invoices

Consultant shall submit invoices for all services rendered. Client shall pay the amounts due within ____ days of the date of each invoice.

You should always submit an invoice to be paid. You need to fill in the time the client has to pay you after you send your invoice; 30 days is common, but you can shorten this period if you wish.

4. Late Fees

Late payments by Client shall be subject to late penalty fees of _____% per month from the due date until the amount is paid.

Many consultants charge a late fee if the client doesn't pay within the time specified in the consulting agreement or invoice. Charging late fees for overdue payments can get clients to pay on time. The late fee is normally expressed as a monthly interest charge—for example, 1% per month.

If you wish to charge a late fee, make sure it's mentioned in your agreement. You should also clearly state what your late fee is on all your invoices.

5. Expenses

[ALTERNATIVE 1] Consultant shall be responsible for all expenses incurred while performing services under this Agreement.

[OPTIONAL: However, Client shall reimburse Consultant for all reasonable travel and living expenses necessarily incurred by Consultant while away from Consultant's regular place of business to perform services under this Agreement. Consultant shall submit an itemized statement of such expenses. Client shall pay Consultant within 30 days from the date of each statement.]

[ALTERNATIVE 2] Client shall reimburse Consultant for the following expenses that are directly attributable to work performed under this Agreement:

- travel expenses other than normal commuting, including airfares, rental vehicles, and highway mileage in company or personal vehicles at __ cents per mile
- telephone, facsimile (fax), online, and telegraph charges
- postage and courier services
- printing and reproduction
- computer services, and
- other expenses resulting from the work performed under this Agreement.

Consultant shall submit an itemized statement of Consultant's expenses. Client shall pay Consultant within 30 days from the date of each statement.]

Expenses means the costs you incur that are directly attributable to your work for a client. It would include, for example, the cost of phone calls or traveling done on the client's behalf. Expenses do not include your normal fixed overhead costs such as your office rent or the cost of commuting to and from your office. They also do not include materials the client provides you to do your work.

- **Alternative 1:** You Pay Your Own Expenses. Government agencies may consider payment of a worker's business or traveling expenses to be an indicator of an employment relationship. For this reason, it is usually best that you not be separately reimbursed for expenses. Instead, your compensation should be high enough to cover your expenses.

Setting your compensation at a level that covers your expenses has another advantage as well: It frees you from having to keep records of your expenses. Keeping track of the cost of every phone call or photocopy you make for a client can be a real chore and may be more trouble than it's worth.

However, if a project will involve expensive traveling, you may wish to separately bill the client for the cost. In this event, include the optional clause for this.

- **Alternative 2:** Expenses Reimbursed. The second clause requires the client to reimburse you for your expenses. You need to provide how many cents per mile you'll charge for travel time.

6. Materials

> Client shall make available to Consultant, at Client's expense, the following materials, facilities, and equipment:
>
> _____
>
> [LIST]. These items will be provided to Client by ____ [DATE].

If the client will provide you with any materials or equipment, list them in this clause. If you need these items by a specific date, specify the deadline as well.

7. Term of Agreement

> This Agreement will become effective when signed by both parties and will end no later than _____, 20__.

The term of the agreement means when it begins and ends. Unless the agreement provides a specific start date, it begins on the date it's signed. If you and the client sign on different dates, the agreement begins on the date the last party signed. You normally shouldn't begin work until the client signs the agreement, so it's usually best that the agreement not provide a specific start date that might be before the client signs.

An IC agreement should have a definite end date. This ordinarily will mark the final deadline for your completion of your services. A good outside time limit is one, or at most two, years. A longer term makes the agreement look like an employment agreement, not an IC agreement. If the work is not completed at the end of the term, you can negotiate and sign a new agreement.

8. Terminating the Agreement

> [ALTERNATIVE 1] With reasonable cause, either party may terminate this Agreement effective immediately by giving written notice of termination for cause. Reasonable cause includes:
>
> - a material violation of this agreement, or
> - nonpayment of Consultant's compensation after 20 days written demand for payment.
>
> Consultant shall be entitled to full payment for services performed prior to the effective date of termination.]
>
> [ALTERNATIVE 2] Either party may terminate this Agreement at any time by giving ____ [5, 10, 15, 30, 45, 60] days written notice of termination without cause. Consultant shall be entitled to full payment for services performed prior to the effective date of termination.]

When you sign a contract it doesn't mean you're irrevocably bound by it no matter what happens. Either you or the client can terminate a consulting agreement under certain circumstances. Termination means you cancel the agreement and you and the client go your separate ways. However, you could each still be liable to the other for any damages caused by failure to obey the contract before it was terminated.

It's important to clearly define the circumstances under which you or the client may terminate the agreement.

It's wise to place some limits on the client's right to terminate the contract. It's usually not in your best interest to give a client the right terminate you for any reason or no reason at all, since the client may unfairly abuse it.

Instead, both you and the client should be able to terminate the agreement without legal repercussions only if there is reasonable cause to do so; or, at most, only by giving written notice to the other.

- **Alternative 1:** Termination With Reasonable Cause. Termination with reasonable cause means either you or the client have a good reason to end the agreement. A material—that is, serious—violation of the agreement is reasonable cause to terminate the agreement. What constitutes a material violation depends on the particular facts and circumstances. A violation is material if it impairs the value of the contract as a whole to the other party.

A minor or technical contract violation is not serious enough to justify terminating the contract for cause. For example, a

slightly late payment by a client will normally be classified as minor and not justify terminating the agreement. However, if the client knows that you have cash flow problems, the late payment could constitute a material violation. Similarly, a minor delay in your performance wouldn't ordinarily be a material contract violation.

Unless your contract provides otherwise, a client's failure to pay you on time may not necessarily constitute reasonable cause for you to terminate the agreement. You may add a clause to your contract providing that late payments are always reasonable cause for terminating the contract. The following clause provides that you may terminate the agreement if the client doesn't pay you what you're owed within 20 days after you make a written demand for payment. For example, if you send a client an invoice due within 30 days and the client fails to pay within that time, you may terminate the agreement 20 days after you send the client a written demand to be paid what you're owed. This may help give clients incentive to pay you.

The clause also makes clear that the client must pay you for the services you performed before the contract was terminated.

- **Alternative 2:** Termination Without Cause. Sometimes you or the client just can't live with a limited termination right. Instead, you want to be able to get out of the agreement at any time without incurring liability.

For example, a client's business plans may change and it may no longer need your services. Or you may have too much work and need to lighten your load.

In this event, add a provision giving either party the right to terminate the agreement for any reason upon written notice. You need to provide at least a few days notice. Being able to terminate without notice tends to make you look like an employee. Thirty days is a common notice period, but less notice may be appropriate if the project is of short duration.

9. Independent Contractor Status

Consultant is an independent contractor, and neither Consultant nor Consultant's staff is, or shall be deemed, Client's employees. In its capacity as an independent contractor, Consultant agrees and represents, and Client agrees, as follows:

[INCLUDE ALL OF PROVISIONS 9a-j THAT APPLY]

(a) Consultant has the right to perform services for others during the term of this Agreement subject to noncompetition provisions set out in this Agreement, if any.

(b) Consultant has the sole right to control and direct the means, manner, and method by which the services required by this Agreement will be performed.

(c) Consultant has the right to perform the services required by this Agreement at any place or location and at such times as Consultant may determine.

(d) Consultant will furnish all equipment and materials used to provide the services required by this Agreement, except to the extent that Consultant's work must be performed on or with Client's computer or existing software.

(e) The services required by this Agreement shall be performed by Consultant, or Consultant's staff, and Client shall not be required to hire, supervise, or pay any assistants to help Consultant.

(f) Consultant is responsible for paying all ordinary and necessary expenses of its staff.

(g) Neither Consultant nor Consultant's staff shall receive any training from Client in the professional skills necessary to perform the services required by this Agreement.

(h) Neither Consultant nor Consultant's staff shall be required to devote full time to the performance of the services required by this Agreement.

(i) Client shall not provide insurance coverage of any kind for Consultant or Consultant's staff.

(j) Client shall not withhold from Consultant's compensation any amount that would normally be withheld from an employee's pay.

One of the most important functions of an agreement between a hiring firm and consultant is to help establish that you are not the hiring firm's employee. In an audit of the hiring firm, an IRS examiner or similar official will almost surely want to see the firm's agreements with all workers classified as independent contractors. If the agreement indicates that the hiring firm has the right to control you, you will undoubtedly be viewed as an employee by the IRS. This will cause problems not only for the hiring firm, but for you as well.

On the other hand, an agreement that indicates a lack of control on the part of the hiring firm will contribute to a finding of independent contractor status. But such an agreement will not be determinative in and of itself. Simply signing a piece of paper will not make you an independent contractor. The agreement must reflect reality—that is, you must actually not be controlled on the job by the hiring firm.

The language in this clause addresses most of the factors the IRS and other agencies consider in measuring the degree of control of the hiring firm. (These factors are discussed in Section C1.) All provisions show that the hiring firm lacks the right to control the manner and means by which you will perform the agreed-upon services.

Include all of provisions a-j that apply to your particular situation. The more that apply, the more likely that you will be viewed as an independent contractor.

10. Intellectual Property Ownership

[ALTERNATIVE 1: (CLIENT OWNS WORK PRODUCT)] Consultant assigns to Client its entire right, title, and interest in anything created or developed by Consultant for Client under this Agreement ("Work Product"), including all patents, copyrights, trade secrets, and other proprietary rights. This assignment is conditioned upon full payment of the compensation due Consultant under this Agreement.

Consultant shall, at no charge to Client, execute and aid in the preparation of any papers that Client may consider necessary or helpful to obtain or maintain—at Client's expense—any patents, copyrights, trademarks, or other proprietary rights. Client shall reimburse Consultant for reasonable out-of-pocket expenses incurred under this provision.

[OPTIONAL] Client grants to Consultant a nonexclusive, [CHOOSE ONE: "irrevocable license" OR "license for the term of [NUMBER OF YEARS] years"] to use the Work Product. [ADD ANY PAYMENT PROVISIONS OR OTHER RESTRICTIONS.]

[ALTERNATIVE 2: (CONSULTANT OWNS WORK PRODUCT)] Consultant shall retain all copyright, patent, trade secret, and other intellectual property rights Consultant may have in anything created or developed by Consultant for Client under this Agreement ("Work Product"). Consultant grants Client a nonexclusive worldwide license to use and sublicense the use of the Work Product for the purpose of developing and marketing its products and services but not for the purpose of marketing Work Product separate from its products and services. The license shall have a perpetual term and may not be transferred by Client. This license is conditioned upon full payment of the compensation due Consultant under this Agreement.

Usually, the client will want to obtain sole ownership of what you create, whether it be a software program, website code, design or graphics, or other material. However, there is no rule that this has to be the case. Two different ownership alternatives are presented in the contract. Choose only one alternative and delete the other. Here's an explanation:

- **Alternative 1:** Client Owns Consultant's Work Product. If it's agreed that the client will own your work product, you should assign your rights to the client. But this assignment is expressly conditioned upon receipt of all your compensation from the client.

Optional sentence: An assignment of all rights means that you may not use the work you performed for the client without permission—for example, you may not include it in a program written for someone else. If desired, such permission can be included in the independent contractor agreement. The optional sentence in this clause grants you a nonexclusive license to use the work product. The license can be limited in any way—for example, as to term or area of use. If the client decides to grant the consultant such a license, it must decide if it will be "irrevocable"—that is, last forever; or be limited to a specified time period—for example, one or two years. The appropriate language in the optional clause should be used.

- **Alternative 2:** Consultant Owns Work Product. In some cases, the consultant and client may agree that the consultant will retain his or her ownership rights in the work product (perhaps in return for receiving reduced monetary compensation). In this event, instead of assigning her rights to the client, the consultant will grant the client a nonexclusive license to use the work product.

This clause grants the client a nonexclusive license to use the consultant's work product in any of its products and services, but prevents it from selling the consultant's work to others. Such a license could be more restrictive—for example, it could limit the use to a particular product or service. If this is desired, modify the clause to indicate the restrictions.

11. Consultant's Materials

Consultant owns or holds a license to use and sublicense various materials in existence before the start date of this Agreement ("Consultant's Materials"). Consultant may, at its option, include Consultant's Materials in the work performed under this Agreement.

[ALTERNATIVE 1 (CLIENT'S LICENSE EXTENDS TO ALL PRODUCTS)] Consultant retains all right, title, and interest, including all copyright, patent rights, and trade secret rights in Consultant's Materials. Subject to full payment of the consulting fees due under this Agreement, Consultant grants Client a nonexclusive worldwide license to use and sublicense the use of Consultant's Materials for the purpose of developing and marketing its products and services, but not for the purpose of marketing Background Technology separate from its products and services. The license shall have a perpetual term and may not be transferred by Client. Client shall make no other commercial use of Consultant's Materials without Consultant's written consent.

[OPTIONAL] "This license is granted subject to the following terms:" [ADD ANY DESIRED PAYMENT OR ROYALTY PROVISIONS.]

[OPTIONAL] Consultant's Materials include, but are not limited to, those items identified in Exhibit __, attached to and made part of this Agreement.

[ALTERNATIVE 2 (CLIENT'S LICENSE LIMITED TO SPECIFIC PRODUCTS)] Consultant retains all right, title, and interest, including all copyright, patent rights, and trade secret rights in Consultant's Materials. Subject to full payment of the consulting fees due under this Agreement, Consultant grants Client a nonexclusive worldwide license to use the Background Technology in the following product(s) and services: [DESCRIBE—FOR EXAMPLE: "the website described in Clause 2 of this Agreement, and all updates and revisions thereto"]. The license shall have a perpetual term and may not be transferred by Client. Client shall make no other commercial use of the Background Technology without Consultant's written consent.

[OPTIONAL] Consultant's Materials include, but are not limited to, those items identified in Exhibit __, attached to and made part of this Agreement.

A software or Web consultant will often have various development tools, routines, subroutines, applets, and other programs, data, and materials that he or she brings to the job and that might end up in the final product. One term for these types of items is "Consultant's Materials."

Unless you want to transfer ownership of such materials to the hiring firm, you should make sure the independent contractor agreement provides that you retain all your ownership rights in this material. But, in this event, the agreement must also give the hiring firm a nonexclusive license to use the background technology that you include in your work product.

There are two clauses to choose from:

- **Alternative 1:** Client's License Extends to All Products. The client would probably prefer to have the right to use the consultant's technology in any of its products. In this event, some sort of payment or royalty provision may be appropriate; if so, include the optional sentence and describe the compensation.
- **Alternative 2:** Client's License Limited to Specific Products. This clause permits the hiring firm to use the background technology only in a particular product or products. Make sure you describe any such products in detail.

Optional Clause: *Identifying Materials.* If you know what such materials consist of in advance, it's a good idea to list them in an exhibit attached to the agreement. Include this optional clause if you do this.

If possible, identify your background technology in the source code copies of the programs you deliver to the client and in any printouts of code delivered to the client. You might include a notice like the following where such material appears: "[Your Company Name] CONFIDENTIAL AND PROPRIETARY."

12. Confidentiality

During the term of this Agreement and for _____ [6 MONTHS TO 5 YEARS] afterward, Consultant will use reasonable care to prevent the unauthorized use or dissemination of Client's confidential information. Reasonable care means at least the same degree of care Consultant uses to protect its own confidential information from unauthorized disclosure.

Confidential information is limited to information clearly marked as confidential, or disclosed orally and summarized and identified as confidential in a writing delivered to Consultant within 15 days of disclosure.

Confidential information does not include information that:

- the Consultant knew before Client disclosed it
- is or becomes public knowledge through no fault of Consultant
- Consultant obtains from sources other than Client who owe no duty of confidentiality to Client, or
- Consultant independently develops.

Since software and Web consultants often have access to their clients' valuable confidential information, hiring firms often seek to impose confidentiality restrictions on them. It's not unreasonable for a client to want you to keep its secrets away from the eyes and ears of competitors. Unfortunately, however, many of these provisions are worded so broadly that they can make it difficult for you to work for other clients without fear of violating your duty of confidentiality.

If, like most consultants, you make your living by performing similar services for many firms, insist on a confidentiality provision that is reasonable in scope and defines precisely what information you must keep confidential. Such a provision should last for only a limited time—five years at the most.

The optional confidentiality provision in this agreement prevents the unauthorized disclosure by you of any written material of the client marked confidential or information disclosed orally that the client later writes down, marks as confidential, and delivers to you within 15 days. This enables you to know for sure what material is, and is not, confidential.

13. Warranties

[ALTERNATIVE 1] Consultant warrants that all services performed under this Agreement shall be performed consistent with generally prevailing professional or industry standards. Client must report any deficiencies in Consultant's services to Consultant in writing within ____[30, 60, 90 OR MORE] days of performance to receive warranty remedies.

Client's exclusive remedy for any breach of the above warranty shall be the reperformance of Consultant's services. If Consultant is unable to reperform the services, Client shall be entitled to recover the fees paid to Consultant for the deficient services.

THIS WARRANTY IS EXCLUSIVE AND IN LIEU OF ALL OTHER WARRANTIES, WHETHER EXPRESS OR IMPLIED, INCLUDING ANY IMPLIED WARRANTIES OF MERCHANTABILITY OR FITNESS FOR A PARTICULAR PURPOSE AND ANY ORAL OR WRITTEN REPRESENTATIONS, PROPOSALS, OR STATEMENTS MADE PRIOR TO THIS AGREEMENT.

[ALTERNATIVE 2] THE GOODS OR SERVICES FURNISHED UNDER THIS AGREEMENT ARE PROVIDED AS IS, WITHOUT ANY EXPRESS OR IMPLIED WARRANTIES OR REPRESENTATIONS; INCLUDING, WITHOUT LIMITATION, ANY IMPLIED WARRANTIES OF MERCHANTABILITY OR FITNESS FOR A PARTICULAR PURPOSE.

A warranty is a promise or statement regarding the quality, quantity, performance, or legal title of something being sold. Everyone has some familiarity with warranties. Whenever you buy an expensive product such as a car, television, or computer, the seller normally warrants—promises—that the product will do what it is supposed to do for a specific or reasonable time period. If it doesn't, the seller will repair or replace it.

Clients often expect software or Web consultants to make some type of warranty regarding their services. If the product or service you provide fails to live up to your warranty, the client can sue you in court for breach of warranty and obtain damages. The client doesn't have to prove that you were negligent—that is, failed to do your work properly. All it has to show is that your goods or services didn't perform the way you said they would. This makes it much easier for the client to obtain damages.

- **Alternative 1:** Providing Work Product As Is. Many consultants don't want to provide any warranties at all. To do this, you must include a clause in your agreement stating that your goods or services are provided "as is." This means that if your goods or services are unsatisfactory, the client has no basis for a complaint.

The clause also disclaims—or disavows—certain implied warranties that can be assumed to be made even if no words are written or spoken. These are:

Implied warranty of merchantability. This warranty basically means that the seller promises that the goods are fit for their commonly intended use—in other words, they are of at least average quality. This warranty applies only to sales of new goods.

Implied warranty of fitness for a specific purpose. If a customer is relying on the seller's expertise to select suitable goods, and the seller is aware that the customer intends to use the goods for a particular purpose, the product becomes impliedly guaranteed for that purpose.

> **EXAMPLE:** A computer consultant is hired by a company to choose and install a new computer system. The consultant is told by the client that it needs the system to process new accounts within 12 hours. The system the consultant chooses and installs becomes impliedly guaranteed to do so.

However, this clause won't excuse you from failure to live up to the project specifications included in your written agreement. Nor will the clause protect you from charges of outright fraud if you lied to the client, or shield you from liability if your software is so defective it injures someone. To be effective, the as is clause should be printed in capitals so it won't be overlooked by the client.

- **Alternative 2:** Limited Warranty. Some clients may balk at having no warranty protection at all. In this event, you can use the following clause to give the client a limited warranty. It requires the client to report in writing any deficiencies in your work. You are then required to reperform your services; or, if you can't reperform, pay back the client what it paid you for your faulty work. The concluding paragraph states that this clause is the only warranty you're providing the client and disclaims the implied warranties discussed above. It's a good idea to print such a statement in capitals so the client won't overlook it.

14. Limited Liability

(a) In no event shall Consultant be liable to Client for lost profits of Client, or special, incidental, or consequential damages (even if Consultant has been advised of the possibility of such damages).

(b) Consultant's total liability under this Agreement for damages, costs, and expenses, regardless of cause, shall not exceed the total amount of fees paid to Consultant by Client under this Agreement [OPTIONAL: "or $[DOLLAR AMOUNT], whichever is greater"].

(c) Client shall indemnify Consultant against all claims, liabilities, and costs, including reasonable attorney fees, of defending any third-party claim or suit, other than for infringement of intellectual property rights, arising out of or in connection with Client's performance under this Agreement. Consultant shall promptly notify Client in writing of such claim or suit and Client shall have the right to fully control the defense and any settlement of the claim or suit.

Many consultants seek to include a provision in their agreements limiting their total liability to the client and/or third parties. Obviously, clients would prefer that there be no such clause, so we've included one only as an option. The clause contains four separate liability-limiting provisions, any of which may be included or excluded from the agreement; this is a matter for negotiation.

Under paragraph (a), the consultant is relieved from liability for any lost profits of the client, or special, incidental, or consequential damages arising from defects in the work furnished by the consultant. These types of damages—lost profits in particular—can far exceed the consul-tant's total compensation and could even send the consultant into bankruptcy.

Paragraph (b), which is perhaps the most important, limits the consultant's total liability to the client to the amount of money actually received from the client, or, if desired, a specific dollar amount.

Paragraph (c) requires the client to indemnify the consultant against third-party claims. These are claims brought by people or entities other than the client. Indemnification is a fancy legal word that means the client must pay attorney fees and other costs of defending such claims and any damages ultimately awarded against the consultant.

15. Taxes

> The charges included here do not include taxes. If Consultant is required to pay any federal, state, or local sales, use, property, or value added taxes based on the services provided under this Agreement, the taxes shall be separately billed to Client. Consultant shall not pay any interest or penalties incurred due to late payment or nonpayment of such taxes by Client.

A few states require independent contractors to pay sales taxes, even if they only provide their clients with services. These states include Hawaii, New Mexico, and South Dakota. Many other states require sales taxes to be collected and paid for certain specified services.

Whether or not you're required to collect sales taxes, include the following provision in your agreement making it clear that the client will have to pay these and similar taxes. States constantly change their sales tax laws, and more and more are beginning to look at services as a good source of sales tax revenue. So this provision could come in handy in the future even if you don't really need it now.

16. Contract Changes

Client and Consultant recognize that:

- Consultant's original cost and time estimates may be too low due to unforeseen events, or to factors unknown to Consultant when this Agreement was made
- Client may desire a midproject change in Consultant's services that would add time and cost to the project and possibly inconvenience Consultant, or
- Other provisions of this Agreement may be difficult to carry out due to unforeseen circumstances.

If any intended changes or any other events beyond the parties' control require adjustments to this Agreement, the parties shall make a good faith effort to agree on all necessary particulars. Such agreements shall be put in writing, signed by the parties, and added to this Agreement.

It's very common for clients and consultants to want to change the terms of an agreement after work has begun. For example, the client might want to make a change in the contract specifications which could require you to do more work for which you should be compensated. Or you might discover that you underestimated how much time the project will take and need to be paid more to complete it and avoid losing money.

This provision recognizes that the agreement may have to be changed. Although oral changes to contracts are enforceable, it's a very good idea to write them down. This provision states that you and the client must write down your changes and both sign the writing. Such a contract provision requiring modifications to be in writing is probably not legally enforceable—that is, both you and the client can still make changes without writing them down. However, it does stress the importance of documenting changes in writing.

Neither you nor the client is ever required to accept a proposed contract change. But because you are obligated to deal with each other fairly and in good faith, you can't simply refuse without attempting to reach a resolution. If you and the client can't agree on the changes, you're required to submit your dispute to mediation; and, if that doesn't work, to binding arbitration. This avoids expensive court litigation.

17. Disputes

If a dispute arises under this Agreement, the parties agree to first try to resolve the dispute with the help of a mutually agreed-upon mediator in the following location _____ [STATE, CITY, OR COUNTY WHERE MEDIATION WILL OCCUR]. Any costs and fees other than attorney fees associated with the mediation shall be shared equally by the parties.

If it proves impossible to arrive at a mutually satisfactory solution through mediation, the parties agree to submit the dispute to binding arbitration in the following location _____ [STATE, CITY, OR COUNTY WHERE ARBITRATION WILL OCCUR] under the rules of the American Arbitration Association. Judgment upon the award rendered by the arbitrator may be entered in any court with jurisdiction to do so.

As you doubtless know, court litigation can be very expensive. To avoid these costs, alternative forms of dispute resolution have been developed that don't involve going to court. These include mediation and arbitration. For a thorough discussion of mediation and arbitration, see Chapter 17, Section B27.

18. Attorney Fees

Attorney Fees: If any litigation or arbitration is necessary to enforce this Agreement, the prevailing party shall be entitled to reasonable attorney fees, costs, and expenses.

If you have to sue the client in court or conduct an arbitration to enforce the agreement and win, you normally will not be awarded the amount of your attorney fees unless your agreement requires it. Including such an attorney fees provision in the agreement can be in your interest. It can help make filing a lawsuit economically feasible. It will also give the client a strong incentive to negotiate with you if you have a good case.

Under this provision, if either person has to sue the other in court to enforce the agreement and wins—that is, becomes the prevailing party—the loser is required to pay the other person's attorney fees and expenses.

19. General Provisions

(a) Sole agreement: This is the entire Agreement between Consultant and Client.

(b) Severability: If any part of this Agreement is held unenforceable, the rest of the Agreement will continue in full force and effect.

(c) Applicable law: This Agreement will be governed by the laws of the State of [LIST APPLICABLE STATE].

(d) Notices: All notices and other communications given in connection with this Agreement shall be in writing and shall be deemed given as follows:

- When delivered personally to the recipient's address as appearing in the introductory paragraph to this Agreement;
- Three days after being deposited in the United States mails, postage prepaid to the recipient's address as appearing in the introductory paragraph to this Agreement, or
- When sent by fax or electronic mail. Notice is effective upon receipt provided that a duplicate copy of the notice is promptly given by first-class or certified mail, or the recipient delivers a written confirmation of receipt.

Any party may change its address appearing in the introductory paragraph to this Agreement by giving notice of the change in accordance with this paragraph.

(e) No partnership: This Agreement does not create a partnership relationship. Consultant does not have authority to enter into contracts on Client's behalf.

(f) Assignment: This Agreement is freely assignable.

These general provisions are standard in many types of legal documents. We provide a detailed explanation of these provisions in Chapter 17, Section B30.

the same day. At least two copies should be signed, with each party retaining one. For more information on signing agreements, see Chapter 1.

20. Signatures

It is not necessary for the parties to sign the agreement in the same room or on

 An example of a completed Consulting Agreement is provided on the CD-ROM forms disk. ∎

Software and Website Licenses

Many people sign and use licenses without really understanding what they are or why they are used. Don't be one of those people. This chapter is about software and website licenses. It includes several sample agreements that you can use.

A. What Is a License?

Computer software, website content (including text, photos, sounds, videos), and any other work of authorship is automatically protected by copyright law the moment it's created. Some software and Internet features are also protected by patent law, but copyright has always been and remains the primary legal vehicle by which software and website ownership and use rights are defined and transferred.

An author of software or website content automatically becomes the owner of a complete set of exclusive copyright rights in any protected work he or she creates. These include the right to:

- reproduce the protected work
- distribute copies of the work to the public by sale, rental, lease, or otherwise (but this right is limited by the first sale doctrine, which permits the owner of a particular copy of a work to sell, lend, or otherwise dispose of the copy without the copyright owner's permission; see Section B2 below)

- prepare derivative works using the work's protected expression (that is, adapt new works from the original work), and
- perform and display the work publicly.

These rights are exclusive because only the owner of one or more particular rights that together make up copyright ownership may exercise it or permit others to do so. For example, only the owner of the right to distribute a program may sell it to the public or permit others to do so.

A license is a grant of permission to do something. For example, when you get a driver's license the government gives you permission to drive a car. A copyright owner can give others permission to exercise one or more of the owner's exclusive rights listed above. Such a permission is also usually called a license. Licenses fall into two broad categories: exclusive and nonexclusive licenses.

1. Exclusive Licenses

When a copyright owner grants someone an exclusive license it means the recipient of the license becomes the only person entitled to exercise the rights covered by the license. The person or company granting a license is usually called the licensor, and the recipient is called the licensee.

Since the licensor is granting the licensee the exclusive right to exercise the rights covered by the license, an exclusive license is considered to be a transfer of copyright ownership. If you have the exclusive right to use something, you own it; that's what ownership is. Such an ownership transfer must be in writing to be legally valid.

EXAMPLE 1: AcmeSoft, a small software developer, creates a program designed to help websites show up accurately in Internet search engines such as Google. Since it lacks the resources to effectively market the program itself, AcmeSoft grants an exclusive license to distribute the program in the United States to Big Software, a large software distribution company. Granting such an exclusive license means that only Big may distribute the program in the U.S.; Big owns this right. But AcmeSoft retains all its other copyright rights not covered by the license. For example, it retains the right to market the program outside the U.S. and to create derivative works based upon it.

A software owner's exclusive rights can be divided and subdivided and transferred to others in just about any way imaginable: by geographical area, time, market segment, media, computer platform, operating system, hardware, or virtually any other way. Taking advantage of this sort of flexibility is often at the heart of a successful plan for getting a product distributed and sold in the marketplace.

EXAMPLE 2: AcmeSoft creates a program and gives Behemoth Distribution, Inc., a software distribution company, an exclusive license to distribute its program for use on PCs in the United States. AcmeSoft also gives CDS, Inc., another distributor, the right to bundle the program with personal computers in Europe. (This type of exclusive license is called an exclusive territorial license.) Finally, AcmeSoft grants an exclusive license to DigiTek, Inc., to create and distribute a Macintosh version of the program.

EXAMPLE 3: Jason creates an online computer game called *Kill or Die*. The game proves popular, so he creates version that can be played offline. He grants an exclusive license to sell the Windows version of the game in the United States for three years. He grants Nintendo an exclusive license to sell a version of the game on Nintendo dedicated game machines throughout the rest of the world. He licenses the right to create a movie from the game (a derivative work) to Repulsive Pictures. He retains all his other rights and produces and sells a Macintosh version of the game himself.

Exclusive Licensee's Rights

Again, the holder of an exclusive license—the "licensee"—becomes the owner of the transferred rights. As such, unless the exclusive license provides otherwise, he or she is entitled to sue anyone who infringes on that right while the licensee owns it, and is entitled to transfer her license to others. The licensee may also record the exclusive license with the Copyright Office; this provides many valuable benefits.

---

2. Nonexclusive Licenses

A nonexclusive license gives someone the right to exercise one or more of a copyright owner's rights, but does not prevent the owner from giving others permission to exercise the same right or rights at the same time. A nonexclusive license is not a transfer of ownership; it's a form of sharing.

Nonexclusive licenses (like all other licenses) can be restricted in all sorts of ways. Thus, you can grant a nonexclusive license to use (or sell a program for use) on one particular microcomputer in one country (or county) for a set period of time.

Except in cases where custom software is created for a single customer, software licenses with end-users normally take the form of nonexclusive licenses. This way, the software owner can give any number of end-users the right to use the software.

EXAMPLE 1: AcmeSoft creates a hot new program for identifying and locating lost cats. It grants nonexclusive licenses to dozens of fire departments and animal shelters throughout the country. These licenses give these end-users the right to copy and use the program. Since these licenses are nonexclusive, there is no limit on the number AcmeSoft can grant.

EXAMPLE 2: Elite Web Development grants a nonexclusive license to its client to use certain applets developed and owned by Elite. These licenses give Elite's clients the right to copy and use the applets on their websites. Since these licenses are nonexclusive, there is no limit on the number Elite can grant.

As with exclusive licenses, nonexclusive licenses may be limited as to time, geography, media, or in any other way. They can be granted orally or in writing. The much better practice, however, is to use some sort of writing.

3   How Licenses Are Formed

Software and website licenses are one type of contract, and the law generally applicable to contracts applies to them as well. There's no need for you to become an expert in contract law, but you should have a basic idea of how enforceable licenses are created.

A legally binding contract is created when one person agrees to do something for the other in exchange for something of value in return. To reach such an agreement, one person must offer to do something and the other must accept the offer. For example, a contract is formed when a software owner offers to license a program to a person or company for a specified price and the person or company accepts the offer—that is, promises to pay the license fee. All the elements for an enforceable contract are present in such a transaction:

- the software owner has promised to do something for the licensee—license the software to him, her, or it,
- the licensee has accepted the terms of the software owner's offer to license, and
- the licensee has promised to give the software owner something of value in return—a license fee.

However, negotiations aren't usually as simple as making an offer and having it immediately accepted. Often, there is some negotiation back and forth. For example, the prospective licensee will often accept part of the original offer but vary some important terms. An acceptance that varies the main terms of an offer serves as a rejection of the offer and becomes a counteroffer. The copyright owner then has the option of accepting or rejecting the counteroffer or making his or her own counteroffer. No contract is formed until one side's offer or counteroffer is fully accepted.

It's not necessary for a licensor and licensee to negotiate with each other face to face to form a contract. A license agreement can be formed over the phone, by fax, by email, snail mail, or by any other communications medium.

4. Do You Need It in Writing?

The Copyright Act requires that all exclusive licenses be in writing and be signed by the copyright owner to be valid.

The copyright law imposes no writing requirement for nonexclusive licenses. However, state laws governing the sale of goods require a writing for any sale involving goods worth more than $500. It's not entirely clear whether software constitutes "goods" under these laws or if a license is a "sale." But many courts have held that such licenses must be in writing.

Such a writing need not be a formal-looking contract printed on paper. Instead, it can consist of email that is printed out or saved on disk or other electronic transmissions stored in computer memory, faxes, or telexes.

5. Do You Need a Signature?

A license should be signed. The purpose of the signature is to authenticate the contents of the document. However, a "signature" need not consist of a handwritten ink signature on paper. A signature can also consist of symbols, codes, or letters so long as it can be demonstrated to be authentic. For example, a typewritten name on a telex has been construed to constitute a signature, as have faxed handwritten signatures.

Moreover, thanks to federal legislation signed into law in 2000, electronic and digital signatures are now just as legal and enforceable as traditional paper contracts signed in ink.

B. Why Use Licenses to Sell Software?

This section covers software licenses, including individually negotiated licenses, licenses for mass-marketed software, and shrink-wrap and click-wrap licenses.

Most works of authorship—such as books, magazines, records, photographs, and artwork—are sold outright, either directly to end-users or to middlemen such as bookstores, who in turn sell the works to end-users.

The transaction works like this: say you want to buy a book; you walk into a bookstore, pay your money, and you are sold a copy of the book. You now own the copy of the book. You don't have to sign a license agreement and the book doesn't contain any type of "shrink-wrap" license.

Software copyright owners are also free to simply sell copies of their software, that is, sell CD-ROMs or other media containing copies of the software to end-users; or to sell digital copies to users over the Internet and commercial online services such as America Online.

Today, however, virtually all software is licensed to end-users rather than sold outright like books are. Instead of owning the copy of the software they pay for, end-users merely acquire permission to use it. A written license agreement—a contract—carefully defines and restricts the nature and extent of that permission.

Why should this be so? The answer is simple: Money. Software owners believe that license agreements help them preserve their market share, obtain the maximum return on each transaction, and help safeguard their intellectual property rights. All of this adds up, at least in theory, to greater profits.

To understand why software owners prefer to license their work to end-users, you must first understand what rights the purchaser of a copy of a copyrighted work has. Software licenses are used to take away most of these rights.

Note carefully that a software user doesn't have any of the ownership rights discussed below unless the software license grants him or her such rights or the license turns out to be legally invalid.

1. What Is a Copy?

For copyright purposes, a "copy" is defined as any material object in which a work of authorship is "fixed." Software transferred to CD-ROMs, floppy disks, hard disks, and other media certainly qualifiy as a "copy." Thus, a person who downloads a program to a hard disk from the Internet, receives a "copy" of the program, just as person who buys the same program on a CD-ROM does.

Software contained in computer RAM may also qualify as a copy, so long as it stays in RAM for at least several minutes. Thus, copying occurs where a person downloads a program to RAM and uses it, even if it is never saved to a permanent storage medium such as a hard disk.

However, simply transmitting a computer program over the Internet probably doesn't involve making copies, even though temporary copies are stored in the RAM of various node computers on the Internet. These RAM copies likely exist for too short a time to be copies for copyright purposes. However, this is not a settled question.

2. Sales of Copies Do Not Transfer Copyright Ownership

Ownership of a copyright and ownership of a material object in which the copyrighted work is embodied—such as a computer disk—are entirely separate things. This means the sale or gift of a copy or copies of a program or other protected work does not operate to transfer the copyright owner's exclusive rights in the work. A copyright owner's exclusive rights can only be transferred by a written agreement. For example, a person who buys a CD-ROM containing a computer program owns the CD-ROM and the copy of the software it contains, but acquires no copyright rights in the program. Likewise, a person who downloads a program from the Internet to his or her hard disk, owns the copy on his or her disk, but obtains no copyright rights in the program.

3. Rights of Owners of Software Copies

The fact that a person who purchases a copy of a computer program acquires no copyright rights does not mean, however, that the purchaser has no rights at all. On the contrary, there are a number of things the purchaser can do with his or her copy.

a. Unlimited use rights

First, a software copy purchaser can use the program copy any way he wants. He can run it on any single computer he chooses, in any location, for any purpose. If he so chooses, a purchaser is free to use a program copy to operate a service bureau and perform data processing for third parties. Or, he can permit third parties to use the software on a time-sharing basis. This is so even though these third parties might otherwise buy the program themselves from the copyright owner.

b.   Right to copy the program into computer RAM

Of course, to utilize a program on a computer it is necessary to copy it from a permanent storage medium such as a CD-ROM into the computer's memory (also known as RAM or random access memory). Such copying is specifically permitted by Section 117 of the Copyright Act, which provides that "the owner of a copy of a computer program... [may] make or authorize the making of another copy ... of that computer program provided that such new copy ... is created as an essential step in the utilization of the computer program in conjunction with a machine and that it is used in no other manner." But courts have held that this provision does not permit permanent copies to be made on computer disks or other permanent storage mediums. (*Allen-Myland, Inc. v. IBM Corp.*, 746 F. Supp. 520 (E.D. Pa. 1990).)

Of course, in the real world, end-users usually copy the original copy of a program onto their computer's hard disk. This hard disk copy is what is then loaded into computer RAM. Section 117 apparently does not allow this copying onto a hard disk. But making one copy of a lawfully possessed program onto a hard disk for use on one computer almost certainly constitutes a fair use of the original copy and is almost certainly permissible. (See Chapter 6, Section B5.)

c.   Right to make archival copies

Because the magnetic media upon which computer programs are frequently stored can easily be damaged and the program rendered unusable, it is highly advisable to make a back-up or archival copy of a program. Section 117 of the Copyright Act provides that program owners may make permanent copies of their programs "for archival purposes only." This means they can only be used internally and cannot be made accessible to third parties. If the original copy is transferred, the copy must also be transferred with it or destroyed.

d.   Right to sell or give away the program

A software copy purchaser also has the right to sell his copy of the program to anyone he chooses, for any price he desires, without getting the copyright owner's permission. Or, the purchaser may give away his copy.

e. Adaptation right

Section 117 of the Copyright Act also gives the lawful owner of a program copy the right to create an adaptation of the program provided that it is "created as an essential step in the utilization of the computer program in conjunction with the [owner's] machine and in no other manner." (*Foresight Resource Corp. v. Pfortmiller,* 719 F. Supp. 1006 (D. Kans. 1989).)

Under this adaptation right, the lawful owner of a program copy is entitled to create enhancements or otherwise alter the program from the one he or she lawfully purchased. For example, the owner can perform his or her own upgrades and thereby avoid having to purchase upgrades from the software publisher or other copyright owner. The owner is completely within his or her legal rights, as long as he or she doesn't:

- Copy, distribute, display, or perform the work itself for commercial purposes, or
- Sell the adapted copy or give it away.

EXAMPLE: The large accounting firm Gray & Grim buys one copy of a tax accounting program. Firm employees rewrite two program modules to improve the package's processing speed. So long as Gray & Grim uses this adapted work solely to improve the copies that it has legitimately purchased and uses it in-house, no infringement of the copyright owner's exclusive right to prepare derivative works has occurred. However, if Gray & Grim distributes the software to other accounting firms without the copyright owner's permission, the owner's copyright in the original work, which includes the exclusive right to make adaptations (also called "derivative works"), would be infringed.

Software Licensee's Adaptation Rights

One question that has arisen is whether a software licensee has the right to make archival copies and adaptations as provided in Section 117 of the Copyright Act. By its own terms, Section 117 applies only to "the owner of a copy of a computer program." Most courts have interpreted this language literally and held that Section 117's back-up and adaptation rights apply only to program owners, not licensees. In other words, a person who purchases a program copy outright may make back-ups and adaptations, but a person who licenses a copy may not exercise such rights unless they are granted in the license agreement. (*S.O.S., Inc. v. Payday, Inc.,* 886 F.2d 1081 (9th Cir. 1988).) However, a few courts have held that Section 117 really applies to any rightful possessor of a program copy, and thus applies to licensees as well to purchasers. (For example, see *Foresight Resources Corp. v. Pfortmiller,* 719 F .Supp.1006 (D. Kan. 1989).)

f. Reverse engineering

Finally, a software purchaser is free to reverse engineer the program. That is, figure out how it works. Reverse engineering can take many forms. One form of reverse engineering is decompiling a program's unreadable object code into readable code. Whether or not such decompilation is permissible or is a copyright infringement has been hotly debated. But some courts have held that decompilation is permissible under some circumstances when the information is used to create a noncompeting product.

In any event, a purchaser of a software copy can use the information gained from reverse engineering not involving decompilation in any way he wishes. For example, he might create a competing program and go into competition with the seller of the original program.

4. Things Owners of Software Copies Can't Do

Since the purchaser of a copy of a program acquires no copyright rights, he can't exercise any of the copyright owner's exclusive rights listed at the beginning of this chapter.

a. No copies other than back-up and RAM copy

As mentioned above, a purchaser can't make any copies of the program other than archival copies, a copy loaded into a single computer's RAM, and a permanent copy contained on the computer's hard disk. If the purchaser sells or gives away the program, he or she must destroy these copies or give the permanent archival copies to the new owner.

Of course a purchaser can't make copies of a program and sell them, give them away, or otherwise distribute them.

b. Copy can only be used on a single computer at a time

A single program copy can only be used on a single computer at a time. This means, for example, that if a purchaser owns a desktop computer and a laptop, and wants to use his or her program on both, legally he or she must buy two copies. Similarly, a purchaser cannot load a program onto his or her hard disk and then give his or her CD-ROM containing the program to someone else to run simultaneously on another computer.

Nor is it permissible for a program owner to make RAM copies for use in more than one machine simultaneously. For example, it would be impermissible for a user to insert a CD-ROM in his computer, load a program into RAM, and then hand the disk to another user who would load the program into RAM on another computer.

c. No running the software on computer networks

Without permission from the copyright owner, the purchaser of a copy of a computer program may not use the program on a network. Remember, the purchaser may load a program into the RAM of only a single computer at a time. The multiple copies typically used in networks, although located only in volatile RAM, are not permissible without the copyright owner's permission. Persons or companies that want to use software on a network usually obtain a network/multiuser license from the copyright owner (see Section C); or, in the case of mass-marketed software intended to be used in networks, such licenses are already included in the package.

d. No software rentals or lending

Software developers and publishers have long feared that letting users lend or lease their software to the public would cause software piracy to increase (a potential pirate could simply rent a software package and copy it). After years of lobbying by the software industry, Congress added a special provision to the Copyright Act in 1990 expressly forbidding the owner of a copy of a computer program from renting, leasing, or lending the copy to the public for "direct or indirect commercial advantage." (17 U.S.C. § 109.)

However, there are four exceptions to this rental and lending prohibition:

- First, nonprofit libraries may lend software to the public for nonprofit purposes provided that the library affixes a copyright warning to the packaging of each copy lent.
- The rental prohibition also doesn't apply to "a computer program embodied in or used in conjunction with a limited purpose computer that is designed for playing video games." In other words, it is permissible to rent video game cartridges.
- The prohibition does not apply to "a computer program ... embodied in a machine or product" that "cannot be copied during ordinary operation or use." For example, it is permissible to rent a car that contains onboard computer programs.
- Finally, the transfer of possession of a lawfully made copy of a computer program from one nonprofit educational institution to another or to faculty, staff, and students does not constitute "rental, lease, or lending for direct or indirect commercial purposes" and thus is not prohibited.

e. No derivative works

Other than making an adaptation for her personal use, the purchaser of a copy of a program may not make any derivative works based on the copy without the copyright owner's permission.

5. How Licenses Restrict Users' Rights

Because they don't want users to have the rights outlined in Section B3 above, software owners typically license their software rather that sell copies of it. The user does not acquire ownership of a copy of the software. Instead, he or she just obtains a license—permission—to use a copy of it. The user has only those rights provided in the license agreement. The license agreement normally includes provisions that effectively take away most of the rights that a purchaser of a copy would have. Such licenses typically include one or more of these restrictions:

- limiting use of the software to a particular computer with a particular serial number
- limiting use of the software to a particular model of computer
- limiting use of the software to computers with a particular processing capacity
- limiting use of the software to computers at a particular physical location
- limiting use of the software to a specified number of concurrent users
- limiting use of the software to a particular application within the licensee's business

- prohibiting use of the software to perform processing for third parties or even for other divisions of the licensee's business
- prohibiting transfer or sublicensing of the license without the licensor's prior written consent
- prohibiting the use of the software on a computer network
- prohibiting copying of the software for all but adaptation and archival purposes
- prohibiting modification of the software, and
- prohibiting the licensee from reverse engineering, disassembling, or decom-piling the software.

C. Types of Software Licenses

Software licenses take a variety of forms:

- *Single user/CPU licenses*: This is a license giving permission to use the software on a single CPU/computer by a single user. The software may only be run on the computer designated in the license. Most single user licenses are for mass-marketed software. However, negotiated licenses are drafted and signed for some high-end programs.
- The other types of licenses discussed below all allow the user to make multiple copies of the software.

- *Site licenses*: As the name implies, a site license is a grant of permission to use software at a particular location. The location can be a single office address or an entire corporate division.
- *Enterprise licenses*: Rather than defining the scope of the licensee's use in terms of a physical location, enterprise licenses are based on the licensee's identity and the types of uses the licensee intends to make with the software. This approach leads to great flexibility regarding pricing. For example, the license price can be linked to the licensee's overall computing capacity or indexed to any other measure, such as the user's annual revenues. Many of the major software companies are experimenting with enterprise licenses.
- *Network/multiuser licenses*: These licenses permit the licensee to use the software on a computer network. Such licenses typically identify a series of computer/operating system combinations on which the software may be installed. The hardware platforms must be owned, leased to, or under the sole control of the licensee. Such licenses do not limit the number of computers on which the software may be installed, but may limit the number of users of the programs.

D. Licenses for Mass-Marketed Software

Of course it's not practical to negotiate individual license agreements for mass-marketed software that is purchased and used by thousands or even millions of end-users. Software developers and publishers typically have no contact in advance with the people who purchase their products from computer stores, mail-order houses, bookstores, and other retail outlets. Nor is it possible to negotiate individual licenses when thousands or even millions of end-users purchase a software product over the Internet and commercial online services.

This would seem to mean that copies of mass-marketed software must be sold—rather than licensed—to the public. However, software publishers really want to license their software, not sell it. So they developed the shrink-wrap license agreement. If you've ever bought a mass-marketed software package, you've probably seen a shrink-wrap license. They may be printed on an envelope inside the package in which the program disks are sealed or, in rare cases, printed in bold type on the outside of the software package under the clear plastic shrink-wrap. Some shrink-wrap licenses appear on the computer screen when the software is first installed. Their purpose is to turn what would otherwise be a simple consumer purchase of a copy of a computer program into a licensing transaction.

1. Are Shrink-Wrap Licenses Enforceable?

For years, copyright experts have questioned whether shrink-wrap licenses are legally enforceable. One of the requirements for an enforceable contract is a meeting of the minds. That is, the parties must knowingly agree on all the material terms of the contract. There would appear to be no meeting of the minds between most consumers of mass-marketed software and software publishers. Most consumers don't bother to read the shrink-wrap licenses before buying and opening the package. The vast majority undoubtedly assume that when they buy a software package in a store they own it, just as when they buy a book in a bookstore.

Because of such doubts, the software industry lobbied state legislatures in the mid-1980s to change existing state contract laws to permit enforcement of such licenses. Only two states ultimately enacted such laws—Illinois and Louisiana. The Illinois law was repealed in 1988 and a federal court held that most of the key provisions of the Louisiana law were invalid because they were preempted (superseded) by the federal copyright law. (*Vault Corp. v. Quaid Software Ltd.*, 847 F.2d 255 (5th Cir. 1988).)

However, shrink-wrap licenses received a huge shot in the arm in 1996, when for the first time a federal court ruled they were enforceable. This all happened when Matthew Zeidenberg bought a CD-ROM containing 95 million business telephone listings from ProCD. He downloaded the listings into his computer from the CD-ROM and made them available on his website, averaging over 20,000 "hits" per day. Zeidenberg did not commit copyright infringement because phone listings are in the public domain. However, he did violate the terms of the shrink-wrap license that came with the CD-ROM. The license barred purchasers from copying, adapting, or modifying the work. The license was contained in written form inside the box the CD-ROM came in. It was also splashed on the computer screen when the user started up the software. Zeidenberg had to agree to the license terms by clicking on an "I agree" box before he could access the data on the CD-ROM.

The court held that the license was an enforceable contract. ProCD had offered to form a contract with Zeidenberg—ProCD would allow him to use the CD-ROM subject to the terms of the enclosed license agreement in return for his payment. ProCD had invited Zeidenberg to accept the terms of the contract by conduct—clicking on the "I agree" icon and using the software after having had an opportunity to read the license agreement.

Zeidenberg had accepted and a valid contract was formed. Since Zeidenberg violated the terms of license, he was liable to ProCD for damages. (*ProCD v. Zeidenberg*, 86 F.3d 1447 (7th Cir. 1996).) Since, the *ProCD* case was decided, the majority of courts have gone along with its reasoning and enforced shrink-wrap licenses.

For a shrink-wrap license to be enforceable, however, the software licensor should take the following steps to alert the purchaser-licensee to the existence of the license prior to the sale:

- place a prominent notice on the outside packaging of the software stating that the purchaser will be bound by a shrink-wrap license
- when the purchaser first starts up the software, include an "I agree" routine in which the purchaser is required to scroll through the license terms and must then click on an "I agree" box or type in the words "I agree" before the software can be used, and
- give the purchaser the right to return the software and receive a full refund of the purchase price if he or she doesn't agree to the terms of the license.

2. Contents of Shrink-Wrap Licenses

As with negotiated end-user licenses, shrink-wrap licenses take away or restrict most of the rights a purchaser of a software copy would have.

 The full text of the Shrink-Wrap License Agreement is on the CD-ROM forms disk. Call up the agreement on your computer and read it along with the following discussion, which explains the wording of the form and describes what information you'll need to insert.

a. Notice provision

The first paragraph of the agreement is designed to alert the user that the software is being licensed, rather than sold. It is written in capitals to help ensure the user will read it. Two alternatives are provided; use the one that applies.

Alternative 1: This paragraph is used where the software includes an "I agree" routine in which the purchaser is required to scroll through the license terms and must then click on an "I agree" box or type in the words "I agree" before the software can be used. If the user doesn't agree to the license, he or she may return the software for a full refund.

Alternative 2: This paragraph should be used if there is no "I agree" routine. It provides that by opening the software package or the envelope containing the program diskettes, the user agrees to the terms of the license. If the user doesn't want to agree to the license, he is told to return the software for a full refund before opening the package.

b. License grant

The main purpose of using the shrink-wrap license is for the publisher to retain ownership of the copy of the software stored on the disk. The user just gets a nonexclusive license to use the program, subject to various restrictions. This means the user does not have any of the rights of a software copy owner discussed in Section B3 above.

This license permits the user to load and use the software only on one computer at a time. An optional provision allows the purchaser to use the software on a portable or home computer if the software is permanently installed on the hard disk or other storage device of a computer (other than a network server) and one person uses that computer more than 80% of the time. A provision of this type is commonly included in shrink-wrap licenses, but there is no legal requirement that you include it.

c. Title

This clause make clear that you retain all intellectual property rights in the software.

d. Back-up copies

This provision allows the user to make back-up or archival copies. As discussed in Section B3, it's unclear whether licens-ees have this right unless the license gives it to them.

e. Things you may not do

This provision outlines all the things the licensee may not do with the software, including reverse engineering, decompiling, or translating the software. The user is also not permitted to modify or adapt the software in any way, even for his or her own personal use. This is a right a software purchaser has. This means that if the user wants an upgrade he or she has to get it from the publisher.

Shrink-wrap licenses almost always contain a provision prohibiting the user from renting or leasing the software to the public, and one is included here. But, as discussed in Section B4 above, this is already prohibited by the Copyright Act.

The user is also barred from selling, sublicensing, lending, or giving away his or her copy of the software to any other person.

f. Limited warranty

The licensor promises in this clause that the program diskettes will be free from defects and the software will perform in substantial conformance with the documentation. The licensor makes no other warranties of any kind. You need to decide how long this warranty will last; 90 days is a common warranty period.

g. Limited remedy

If the software doesn't perform as promised, this clause gives the user the right to receive a replacement copy. If you can't provide a properly functioning copy, the user may return the software and receive a full refund.

The material in capitals is designed to limit your liability. It provides that you won't be liable for any damages arising from the licensee's use of the software.

h. Term and termination

The license automatically terminates if the licensee violates any of its terms. Upon termination, the licensee must return or destroy all copies of the software and documentation.

i. General provisions

These provisions are self-explanatory. You must fill in the state whose law will govern the agreement. This should be the state in which you have your principal place of business.

3. Contents of Click-Wrap Licenses

"Click-Wrap" licenses serve the exact same function as shrink-wrap licenses except they are used for software that is distributed to end-users over the Internet

and commercial online services. The user downloads the software directly into his or her computer over phone lines, so there is no package or physical written license agreement the user can read. Instead, the user is asked to read the terms of the license on the computer screen and then click on an "accept" button to initiate the software download.

A click-wrap license may be easier to legally enforce than a shrink-wrap license, because the user must take an active step—clicking on an accept button—to accept the license terms.

Moreover, the customer can be required to agree to the license before paying for the software. This avoids one of the principal legal objections to shrink-wraps: that they are not supported by consideration. Consideration is the value or quid pro quo that each party to a contract is supposed to receive from the other party in exchange for entering into the contract. Unless a contract provides some consideration for each party, the law will not usually recognize it as binding.

When a software consumer buys a software package containing a shrink-wrap license in a store or by mail order he or she gives consideration—the purchase price—and receives consideration in return—the software. The consumer assumes at this point that he or she owns the software copy. When the consumer then opens the software package he or she is supposed to enter into what seems a new agreement with the developer—the shrink-wrap license. The consumer is asked to provide consideration by giving up some of the ownership rights he or she would otherwise have, but gets no new consideration from the developer in return, since he or she already has the software. This can be avoided in an online transaction where the consumer must read and agree to the click-wrap license before purchasing the software.

However, one court held that a click-wrap license could not be enforced by a website that invited its users to download free software. The license attempted to restrict how the software could be used but it was visible to users of the site only if they scrolled down the screen. Under these circumstances, the court held that users could not be deemed to have agreed to the license merely by downloading the purportedly free software. (*Specht v. Netscape Communs. Corp.*, 306 F.3d 17 (2d Cir. 2002).)

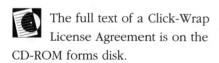 The full text of a Click-Wrap License Agreement is on the CD-ROM forms disk.

The Click-Wrap license is virtually identical to the Shrink-Wrap license discussed in Section D2 above, except for some alterations to the first paragraph. The user is not asked to return the package if the license is unacceptable—obviously, there is no package.

E. Negotiated License Agreements

Negotiated license agreements are those individually agreed upon and signed by the user after negotiations between the user and software owner. Such agreements are not used for software sold online, in stores, or by mail order. Rather, they are used when a software developer or owner deals personally with the end-user.

EXAMPLE: The Old Reliable Insurance Company wants to use a complex actuarial program developed by AcmeSoft, Inc. It contacts AcmeSoft and negotiates a deal: AcmeSoft agrees to license the program to Old Reliable for $10,000 per year for five years. AcmeSoft draws up a license agreement that is signed by both parties.

Negotiated end-user licenses are normally nonexclusive licenses. As discussed in Section A2 above, the holder of a nonexclusive license acquires none of the licensor's exclusive copyright rights. All he or she has are the use rights granted in the license agreement. The licensor is free to enter into other nonexclusive licenses with as many other customers as it chooses.

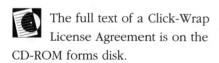 The full text of a Negotiated License Agreement is on the CD-ROM forms disk. Call up the agreement on your computer and read it along with the following discussion, which explains the wording of the form and describes what information you'll need to insert.

Start by listing the names and addresses of the software owner and the customer. In the rest of the agreement, the owner will be called the licensor and the customer the licensee. Be sure to precisely name the licensee. For example, if you're licensing the software to a particular division within a large corporation, be sure to identify the division correctly.

1. Definitions

This section defines some key terms in the license. Subsection (a) requires that you identify the software you're licensing in a separate schedule and attach it to the license agreement.

2. Rights Granted Licensee

Several alternatives are provided as to how the licensee may use the software.

- **Alternative 1—single user license:** The first alternative allows the licensee to use the software only on one computer at a time. This type of license is more common for mass-marketed software than for negotiated license agreements.
- **Alternative 2—multiple stand-alone computers:** The second alternative allows the licensee to use the software on a stated number of separate stand-alone computers. You need to state the number of computers allowed.

- **Alternative 3—site license:** This alternative permits the licensee to use the software on any number of computers at a given site. You need to provide the address or other identifying information for the site.
- **Alternative 4—network license:** This alternative permits the licensee to use the software on a network. You have the option of limiting the total number of computers that can use the software at one time.

3. License Term

The license term means how long the license will last.

- **Alternative 1—perpetual term:** The first alternative provides a perpetual license term. That is, the license lasts as long as the licensee continues to use the software and complies with the terms of the license—for example, continues to pay the license fee.
- **Alternative 2—term of years:** The second alternative provides an initial term of a stated number of years. You need to provide how long the term will last. When the initial term expires, the license is automatically renewed unless the licensee discontinues it by sending you a notice of nonrenewal. This favors the licensor, because the licensee must keep paying the licensors unless he or she takes an affirmative step to end the license when the term ends.

4. License Fee

You can set forth the license fee in the main body of the license or in a separate schedule attached to the agreement. Do whatever is most convenient.

5. Termination

This clause gives you the right to terminate the license if the licensee breaches any of its terms—for example, fails to pay you—or if the licensee goes bankrupt or becomes insolvent.

6. Return or Destruction of Software Upon Termination

When the license terminates, you don't want the licensee to keep any copies of the software. This provision requires the licensee to destroy all copies or return them to you. You have the right to inspect the licensee's premises to make sure all copies have been disposed of.

7. Title to Software

This provision makes clear that you retain all your intellectual property rights in the software.

8. Modifications and Enhancements

This provision bars the licensee from reverse engineering or modifying the software without the licensor's written consent.

9. Warranty

Licensors often provide some sort of guarantee for the software they license. However, there is no legal requirement that you do so. Two alternative warranty provisions are provided. These provisions are written in capital letters so the licensee can't later claim he or she overlooked them

- **Alternative 1—software provided "as is":** Under the first alternative, you provide the software "as is"—that is, you make no guaranties or warranties about its performance.
- **Alternative 2—limited warranty:** Alternative 2 provides a limited warranty. You promise that the software will function in substantial accordance with the documentation and specifications for a given time period. You need to state the period—for example, 90 days is a common period. If the software fails to perform adequately, you have the option of repairing or replacing it, or returning the licensee license fee.

10. Confidentiality

This provision requires the licensee to maintain the software in confidence. This will help ensure that you won't lose any trade secret protection for the software. (See Chapter 7.)

11. Arbitration

Arbitration is a relatively low-cost alternative to expensive court litigation, in which an informal hearing is held before one or more arbitrators (usually attorneys or retired judges) who decide the merits of the issues and render a decision, which may or not be binding depending on the arbitration agreement. There are a number of professional arbitrators' organizations which conduct arbitrations, notably the American Arbitration Association, which has offices in most major cities. This clause requires you and the client to submit any dispute over the agreement to arbitration.

12. Attorney Fees

If you have to sue the licensee in court to enforce the agreement, and win, you normally will not be awarded the amount of your attorney fees unless your agreement requires it. Including such an attorney fees provision in the agreement can be in your interest. It can help make filing a lawsuit economically feasible. It will also give the licensee a strong incentive to negotiate with you if you have a good case.

Under this provision, if either party has to sue the other in court to enforce the agreement and wins—that is, becomes the prevailing party—the loser is required to pay the other party's attorney fees and expenses.

13. General Provisions

Following are several provisions that are customarily lumped together at the end of a license agreement. This does not mean they are unimportant. You can find an explanation for these provisions in Chapter 17, Section B30.

F. Open Source Licenses

One of the most significant developments in the software and Web development community in the past few years has been the increased use of "open source" software. Open source software provides users and developers with many benefits, including the right to examine, modify, and reuse source code. However, when it comes to redistributing the software, certain conditions may apply depending on the license. It's vital for any programmer, Web designer, or other software or computer professional to understand these rights and responsibilities—preferably before work is begun on an open source project or software is distributed under an open source license.

1. What Is Open Source Software?

Many developers think software should be freely useable by the entire community of software developers and end-users. In the early days of computers, this practice was the norm. One of these developers was the famed programmer Richard Stallman, the father of the Free Software movement. Back in the 1980s, Stallman enunciated four key freedoms he wanted to preserve for all people who used software:

- the freedom to run the program for any purpose
- the freedom to study how the program works and adapt it to the user's needs
- the freedom to redistribute copies, and
- the freedom to improve the program and release the improvements to the public.

These developers realized that they could not achieve their goals simply by placing their software, including the source code, in the public domain—that is, giving up all their copyright and other legal rights to their software. This is because anyone may use public domain software any way they want. Thus, there is no way to be sure that modifications people make to software in the public domain remain freely available. For example, a person or company could modify a public domain program, distribute it to the public with a proprietary license, and refuse to provide the source code for the modifications to others.

The Proprietary Software Model

Proprietary software companies typically make their money by charging a license fee. In return for this fee, the customer receives a license to use the software with the following restrictions:

- End-users of commercial software are usually only provided with the object code version of the program, not the source code. This way it is almost impossible for them to change or modify the code themselves.

- In addition, users are required to agree to licenses restricting how they may use the software. As discussed in previous sections of this chapter, these software licenses typically bar reverse engineering, prohibit modifications, prohibit new works to be created based on the software, bar users from reselling or otherwise redistributing the software, and establish how many times the program may be installed.

By keeping the source code to themselves and using restrictive proprietary licenses, software developers and companies keep end-users dependent on them for new improved versions. And, of course, the end-user typically pays for maintenance and modification. The classic, and most profitable, example of this proprietary model for software development and distribution is Microsoft.

Stallman and the other pioneers of the open source movement came up with an ingenious solution to the problem. Instead of placing their software in the public domain, developers would retain their copyright rights and license their software to the public with mass-market licenses, just like Microsoft does. But they would use a radical new type of license—one that would require all users to preserve the four freedoms outlined above. Anyone who refused to abide by the license terms could be sued for breach of the license. Thus, the Free Software movement would use the power of the legal system to give away rights, not keep them, and make the giveaway stick. In the 1980s, after experimenting with several "copyleft" licenses, Stallman and Eben Moglen created the GNU General Public License (GPL). The GPL remains the most important Free Software license today.

2. The Open Source Definition

There is no single open source license. To help establish some degree of uniformity, the Open Source Initiative, a nonprofit corporation that promotes open source software, created the Open Source Definition to help classify open source licenses. To date, over 30 licenses have been certified. The Open Source Definition is not itself a software license. It is a specification of what is permissible in a license in order for the software to be called open source.

Licenses that meet the definition may contain the legend "OSI Certified" or use the OSI Certified logo. If you see either of these marks on software, it is being distributed under a license that conforms to the open source Definition. In other words, it is an open source license.

However, it is important to understand that these are minimum requirements. Licensors are free to use licenses that provide additional rights beyond the minimums. Thus, OSI certified licenses are not all the same (see Section F3 below).

To meet the Open Source Definition, a license must meet the ten requirements described below.

a. Free redistribution

First, the license must permit anyone who obtains and uses the covered software to sell or give it away it to others without having to pay a royalty or other fee to the original copyright owner(s). From now on, we'll refer to such users as licensees.

Open source software is not necessarily free—that is, without financial cost. Users may sell copies to others, and are free to charge whatever they want (and can get). In the open source universe, "free" refers to freedom, not price. Or, in Richard Stallman's famous words: "free as in free speech, not free beer." Thus, some open source software is sold and some is given away; in all cases, the recipients are free to redistribute the software.

Why would anyone pay for open source software? There are many possible reasons:

- they may be willing to pay a small fee to cover the cost of media or manuals
- they may pay for support and maintenance of the software or for training on how to use it
- they may be willing to pay to obtain the software from a trusted distributor with a well-known brand name, such as Red Hat, which distributes a version of the Linux operating system, or
- they may pool their resources in a consortium to fund the creation of software that will subsequently be available for everyone to use.

As a general rule, however, open source software is far less expensive than proprietary software, and most open source programs are typically available for free download in some form from the Internet.

b. Source code

Open source licenses require everyone who distributes the software to provide unfettered access to the program source code—the version of the program written in a computer language like C, Java, or Basic, that is intended to be read and un-

derstood by humans and debugged, modified, or adapted by them. Hence the name "Open Source." "Source" refers to the source code, and "open" means such code is freely available to users. (In contrast, proprietary software is ordinarily "closed." Users are only provided with the object code version of the program, which is not intended to be read.)

Although not required in an open source arrangement, the source code is usually provided along with the object code form of the program. Many copyleft licenses require that source code be made available to recipients of the program for free via download from the Internet, or on magnetic media for which a small fee may be charged.

The source code must be the preferred form in which a programmer would modify the program. Deliberately obfuscated source code is insufficient. Intermediate forms such as the output of a preprocessor or translator are also insufficient. The goal is to make it as easy for downstream recipients to make changes as it was for the original developer.

c. Derivative works

The license must allow users to modify the software, and to create new works based upon it. In legal parlance, such new works are called "derivative works" (see Chapter 6, Section A2, for an overview of derivative works). The license must permit such modifications and derivative works to be distributed under the same terms as the original software. Copyleft licenses actually *require* this, while all other open source licenses merely permit it.

It is this provision, coupled with the requirement that the source code be provided, that allows open source software to evolve so quickly. Programmers are free to modify and adapt the software—thereby hopefully improving it—and release the modifications to the world to be built upon even further by other programmers. However, you are not required to release your changes or enhancements to the world. If you wish, you can use them in-house and never let anyone else have access to them.

d. Integrity of the author's source code

Open source software is typically updated, debugged, modified, or otherwise altered by programmers other than the original creators. Since the software is open source and must be distributed along with the source code, these programmers need not obtain permission to make their changes.

However, in the typical open source project, someone acts as a "maintainer." This is a person, committee, or other body that works to maintain the integrity and usefulness of the software. Usually, the maintainer is the person or entity that be-

gan the open source project; but the task can be handed off to others. The maintainer's job, which is performed on a volunteer basis, is to accept or reject changes to the source code submitted by other programmers, apply patches, and monitor defects. By far the most famous maintainer is Linus Torvalds, creator of the Linux kernel (a "kernel" is the innermost portion of a computer operating system).

If a programmer's changes are rejected by the maintainer, they do not become part of the software's official source code tree. But the programmer may still distribute the changes. The original author(s) of the software can't prevent such distribution, but their license may require that the original source code be distributed unmodified, with modifications in a separate patch file. The original code is then combined with the patch file at build time to create a new working version of the software.

The open source license may also require that such "unofficial" code be identified with a name or version number different from the original software. This way, if the new code is buggy or poorly crafted, the programmer who's at fault will get the blame. If it is good, he or she will get the credit—an important incentive for many programmers who work without other compensation to improve open source software.

In most cases, those who disagree with the maintainer can create a "fork" and start an alternative project derived from the original source code base. This can happen without the maintainer's permission, and the new project may compete with the original project. No open source license may prohibit this. However, there is generally a good deal of community pressure to create incentives to avoid forking, so it generally persists only in extreme cases, where there is strong disagreement or sharply divergent needs related to the future of the project.

Although not mandated by the Open Source Definition, most open source licenses also require users who redistribute the software to include the copyright notice giving credit for authorship to the original author.

e. No discrimination against persons or groups

The license must not discriminate against any person or group of persons—in other words, anybody may use open source software so long as they abide by the open source license.

Some countries, including the United States, have export restrictions for certain types of software. An OSD-conformant license may warn licensees of applicable restrictions and remind them that they are obliged to obey the law; however, it may not incorporate such restrictions itself.

f. No discrimination against fields of endeavor

The license may not restrict anyone from using the software in a specific field of endeavor. For example, it may not restrict the program from being used in a business, or from being used for genetic research. This provision permits commercial users to join the open source community.

g. Distribution of license

When software is distributed under an open source license, that license must be a complete grant of rights and restrictions. For example, users cannot be required by the license to sign nondisclosure agreements, patent licenses, or any other agreements governing how the software may be used. This prevents closing up the software through indirect means.

h. License must not be specific to a product

The license may not restrict the software to a specific product or products. For example, open source software cannot be limited to use with Linux.

i. License must not restrict other software

The license may not place restrictions on other non-open source software that is distributed along with the open source software. For example, the license must not insist that all other programs distributed on the same CD-ROM or other media must be open source software. Thus, a company may distribute both open source and proprietary software in the same package. However, many copyleft licenses, notably the GPL (GNU General Public License) require that if a software package was derived from any GPL code, then it, too, must be released under the terms of the GPL.

Disclaiming Warranties in Open Source Licenses

Although not specifically required by the Open Source Definition, virtually all open source licenses contain a provision disclaiming (or disavowing) all warranties. In other words, open source software is provided "as is." For example, the GPL states:

BECAUSE THE PROGRAM IS LICENSED FREE OF CHARGE, THERE IS NO WARRANTY FOR THE PROGRAM, TO THE EXTENT PERMITTED BY APPLICABLE LAW. EXCEPT WHEN OTHERWISE STATED IN WRITING THE COPYRIGHT HOLDERS AND/OR OTHER PARTIES PROVIDE THE PROGRAM "AS IS" WITHOUT WARRANTY OF ANY KIND, EITHER EXPRESSED OR IMPLIED, INCLUDING, BUT NOT LIMITED TO, THE IMPLIED WARRANTIES OF MERCHANTABILITY AND FITNESS FOR A PARTICULAR PURPOSE. THE ENTIRE RISK AS TO THE QUALITY AND PERFORMANCE OF THE PROGRAM IS WITH YOU. SHOULD THE PROGRAM PROVE DEFECTIVE, YOU ASSUME THE COST OF ALL NECESSARY SERVICING, REPAIR, OR CORRECTION.

This is similar to the warranty disclaimer provision contained in the custom software development agreement in Chapter 18, Section B. The rationale for this is simple: Since open source developers generally receive little or no money from each individual user, they should not have to pay anyone who uses it and has problems. But, the fact that open source software is provided as-is doesn't necessarily mean it's unreliable—quite the opposite (see Section F5 below).

3. Comparing the Open Source Licenses

As stated above, there is no single open source license. To date, over 30 licenses are in use that are certified by the OSI to satisfy the Open Source Definition. (In addition, many licenses qualify that aren't certified.) You can find a list of, and links to, all the OSI certified open source licenses at the OSI website at www.open source.org/licenses/.

Anyone is free to create their own open source license; they don't have to use an existing license. New licenses may be submitted to the Open Source Initiative for certification. However, you probably don't need to go to the time and trouble of creating your own open source license. One of the existing licenses should meet your needs.

Keep in mind that using a new, non-standard open source license creates a feeling of uncertainty among users about the rights and restrictions that come with it. Also, if you contribute to an existing open source project, it will typically be aligned with a specific license and you should release your software under that license for compatibility's sake.

For conceptual convenience, the many open source licenses can be grouped into four broad categories or families:

- Strong copyleft licenses
- Weak copyleft licenses
- Non-copyleft licenses (including "BSD-style" and "MIT-style" licenses), and
- Other open source licenses.

a. Strong Copyleft licenses: GPL (GNU General Public License)

The notion of "copyleft" (a play on the word copyright) is the key concept that differentiates the various open software licenses. Copyleft is a category of license requirements that govern how modifications to the original open source software must be legally treated when they are publicly distributed. If a license contains a strong copyleft provision, anyone who modifies the software and distributes it to the public must license the resulting work back to the public under the same terms as the original software.

One of the first and most widely used implementations of copyleft was in the GPL (GNU General Public License). The GPL was created by Richard Stallman (along with Eben Moglen, his legal counsel), who also formed the Free Software Foundation. The Foundation's website (www.fsf.org) contains much useful information on the GPL, as well as a downloadable copy of the license itself.

The GPL's copyleft provision only comes into play when a programmer modifies a program licensed under a GPL and wishes to release the modified version to the public. In other words, a programmer may not combine GPL-licensed program code with any other code and then release the combination to the public under non-GPL terms. This prevents improved versions of GPL software from being delivered to the public on a proprietary basis. The intended result is that GPL-licensed software remains freely useable. We'll explore the significant practical effects of copyleft in Section F4.

b. Weak copyleft licenses

Some programmers who create or contribute to open source software don't want to give up all their ownership rights in their modifications. To meet their needs, several licenses have been created that contain bounded or "weak" copyleft provisions.

- **Mozilla Public License:** The Mozilla Public License (MPL) is the most popular open source license that contains a weak copyleft provision. It was first created to distribute the Mozilla Web browser (the open source version of the Netscape Web browser). It requires that the source code for all modifications that are publicly distributed either be included with the modified software itself, or made available for download under the terms of the MPL for a period of one year or six months, depending on the situation.

However the MPL's copyleft provision only applies to changes to files subject to the MPL, or new files into which MPL-licensed code is copied. New files that don't contain MPL-licensed code are not covered by the MPL. In other words, the MPL's value is weakened because it's copylefting per file and not copylefting the entire work.

One well-known example of this is the Netscape browser. It contains (and Netscape makes source code available for) many files from the Mozilla project, which are under the MPL. But it also contains proprietary code, for example to integrate with the AOL Instant Messenger service. An annotated version of the MPL, containing detailed explanations of its provisions, is available for review at www.mozilla.org/MPL/MPL-1.0-anno-tated-fs.html.

- **Lesser General Public License (LGPL):** The LGPL is another license created by the Free Software Foundation. It is similar to the GPL, but weakens the GPL's copyleft requirements. The LGPL permits programmers to link their software libraries to "non-free" software without forcing that software to be released under the GPL or LGPL. The license is only useful for software libraries; it was once called the GNU Library General Public License.

Today, the Free Software Foundation discourages the LGPL from being used. Instead, it urges users who don't want full strength copyleft, to add the following special clause to the GPL: "As a special exception, if you link this library with other files to produce an executable, this library does not by itself cause the resulting executable to be covered by the GNU General Public License. This exception does not however invalidate any other reasons why the executable file might be covered by the GNU General Public License."

c. No copyleft licenses

The Open Source Definition does not require that software be copylefted at all, and many open source licenses don't contain any copyleft provisions at all. A whole family of licenses contain no copyleft and few other restrictions on users. The best-known of these no-copyleft licenses is the Berkeley Software Distribution License (BSD).

This license, one of the earliest non-proprietary licenses, permits redistribution of verbatim or modified versions, with or without source code. Thus, developers of derivative works may choose whether or not to provide source code to those derivative works; they are not required to license their modifications under the BSD license, or to provide source code for their modifications. Because of this, some people say that BSD-licensed code may be "taken proprietary."

Indeed, there is little to distinguish BSD-license software from public domain software, except that the original software author technically retains copyright ownership in the code, and users are required to include a copy of the license and a copyright notice in publicly distributed versions of the software. Many no-copyleft licenses also contain warranty disclaimers. Two other well-known licenses, the Apache Software License and the MIT license, are very similar to the BSD License. Historically, some of these licenses have had clauses requiring that credit be given in advertisements for products based on the software.

d. Other licenses

Various other licenses are in use that combine elements from the other license families and contain additional provisions as well. Examples include the Artistic License, and the Academic Free License.

4. Considerations for Developers Who Use Open Source Software

Software developers frequently use open source software to develop new software, especially for the Internet. Why should you consider using open source software for your development work? There are several reasons:

- **Cost:** Open source software is usually cheaper than proprietary software (often, it's free or nearly free).

- **Reliability:** Open source software is often more reliable and less buggy than proprietary software because it can be tested, debugged, and upgraded by thousands of programmers all over the world, working independently of the original author of the software. Proprietary software is very different. Only the programmers employed by a developer that created the software, or others who obtain permission, can "get under the hood" of the software and work on its source code.
- **Independence:** When you use open source software, you are not dependent on the original developer for upgrades or modifications. You may create them yourself or use modifications created by others.
- **Freedom:** None of the many restrictions typically included in proprietary software licenses apply to open source licenses. For example, you don't have to pay extra to use it on more than one computer, on a network, or on more than one operating system. You don't have to worry about anyone coming to your company to conduct a "software audit" to determine if you are using pirated software.

However, before you make up your mind about open source licenses, you need to be aware of the practical implica-tions of using, modifying, and distributing open source software.

a. Using an Open Source program

Simply using an open source program on a day-to-day basis ordinarily does not have any legal implications for the user.

> **EXAMPLE:** Ralph, a freelance programmer, is hired by the Acme Power Corporation to create a program to help measure the pollution created by its coal-fired power plants. He uses the GNU Emacs text editor to write the program and the GNU Compiler to transform it into object code. Both programs are governed by the GPL, but Ralph's program need not be unless it includes code from the GPL-licensed programs he used.

In addition, you may include proprietary programs along with open source software on a storage or distribution medium without bringing the propriety software under the open source license.

> **EXAMPLE:** Ralph independently creates a database program that can be used with the Linux operating system, which is licensed under the GPL. Ralph may keep his database program proprietary and distribute it with a copy of Linux, since his program does not contain any Linux or other open source code. The two

programs are completely separate works—placing them on a single hard drive or CD-ROM does not change this. Thus, Ralph may require users to agree to a restrictive proprietary license to use his database program, but not Linux.

b. Modifying an open source program and not distributing it

Anyone who uses open source software has the freedom to modify the program, or to incorporate it into other programs. This is the reason the source code is provided to users. However, so long as the new work is only used internally, the open source license will not affect you.

EXAMPLE: Assume that Ralph from the above example doesn't want to go to the time and trouble of creating an entirely new program for Acme; and he does not want to have to pay to obtain the right to use an existing proprietary program. So, Ralph decides to use an open source program called Coal Source that accomplishes most of the tasks his client needs done. Ralph obtains the source code for the program for free from the Internet. Coal Source, like most open source software, is governed by the GPL. He makes several modifications to the program's source code so that it will better meet his client's needs. The resulting program is used by Acme to help monitor its power plants. But the program is never made available to the public, either through commercial distribution or by publishing it on the Internet. Since the program is not publicly distributed, the copyleft provisions contained in Coal Source's GPL have no affect on Ralph or Acme.

Open source software may also be used to provide services to the public without any copyleft provisions applying. For example, you can modify open source e-commerce software and place it on a server to help operate a commercial website. The modified software is not being published or distributed to the public, so your modifications need not be copylefted. In the future, this may change.

c. Distributing a modified open source program

The copyleft provisions of the GPL and other open source licenses are designed to apply when a user creates a derivative work from open source code and publicly distributes it. In this event, the new code must be distributed under the same open source license as the original code. This means the program must be licensed as a whole at no charge to all third parties under the terms of the GPL.

EXAMPLE: Assume that Ralph from the above example decides to market a commercial version of his modified Coal Source program. Since the original Coal Source was distributed under the GPL, Ralph's modified version of the program must be distributed under the GPL as well. The GPL requires that Ralph:

- "conspicuously and appropriately" publish on each copy an appropriate copyright notice and disclaimer of warranty
- keep intact all the notices that refer to this GPL and to the absence of any warranty
- give any other recipients of the program a copy of the GPL along with the program
- include prominent notices in the modified files stating that Ralph changed the files and the date of any change, and
- provide a complete machine-readable copy of the source code for the program either: (1) with the executable form of the program, or (2) downloadable from the Internet, or (3) made available at cost on CD-ROM or other medium for at least three years.

Ralph cannot require people who use his program to agree to additional restrictions of the sort that are typically used in proprietary licenses—for example, he cannot forbid users from modifying the program.

5. Considerations for Developers Who Create Open Source Software

Developers who create new software and wish to distribute it to the public have the option of doing so under an open source license.

a. Why develop open source software

There are many reasons you might want to develop open source software:

- you want other programmers to be able to easily access and modify or improve your software
- you want to become known in the open source community
- you want to contribute to the open source movement
- you want your software to be as widely used as possible, or
- you don't care about making money from your software.

Although open source software is usually provided for free or at very low cost, money can be, and is, made from it. For example, you can provide installation, services, and support for users of open source software, or sell open source software with value-added customizations.

In addition, many companies now sponsor open source software development—directly or indirectly. For example, a company may pay an employee or contractor to develop the core functionality of an open source software program, or contribute modifications or patches on a regular basis.

b. Choosing an open source license

If you want to release your software with an open source license, you must choose which license to use. This can seem like a daunting task since there are so many licenses to choose from. However, it needn't be too difficult. Here are some factors you should consider:

- You should almost certainly stick with one of the well known open source licenses such as the GPL, MPL, or BSD licenses. Others may be discouraged from using or working on your software if you use an unfamiliar license.
- If you're developing an application that falls within a family of preexisting open source software, you should choose the license that is commonly used for that software. For example, you should ordinarily use the GPL for Linux kernel code, since Linux is licensed under the GPL.
- If you want to prevent end-users from taking their modifications pri-

vate, use a strong copyleft license such as the GPL.
- If you don't care if users take their modifications private, use a no-copyleft license such as the BSD license.
- If you want copyleft protection for some core functionality, but are willing to grant broader latitude to others integrating your work into third-party systems, choose a weak copyleft license, such as the MPL.

Whatever license you choose, be sure to read it and understand it. Detailed explanations of the various licenses can be found on the Internet and a good starting point is www.opensource.org/licenses.

c. Dual licensing

All open source licenses are nonexclusive licenses (see Section A2). This means you can license the same software with an open source license and with a nonexclusive proprietary license for which royalties or other fees must be paid. This is called dual licensing. Why would a customer want to pay for a proprietary license when an open source version of your software is available for free or at low cost? One reason is that they don't want the software they use to be subject to copyleft provisions. A proprietary license can give the customer, you, or both the right to modify the software and release the modified version on a proprietary basis.

You can also use different licenses for different elements of your software. For example, you could distribute client software under a GPL license, and simultaneously distribute server software under a proprietary license. By providing the client version of the software for free to individual end-users you can build a large customer base. For example, this would encourage corporate and other large end-users to pay for your server software.

There are a few things to keep in mind when using dual licenses. Much dual licensing involves multiple open source licenses. Since some works involve shared authorship, written consent (or written copyright transfers or disclaimers) should be acquired from all persons with any copyright interest before dual licensing the work.

Also, some people use dual licensing as a business strategy, but copyleft is not readily compatible with this strategy while accepting community collaborations. Finally, remember that you have to have actual copyright in something to dual license it—an obstacle to people who aren't sole copyright holders of a work because the work contains contributions from the community.

6. Potential Problems With Open Source Software

The open source arena is one of the most exciting and dynamic areas in today's software industry. But there are potential legal problems with the open source concept.

a. Ownership problems

Open source software is not in the public domain, so somebody owns the copyright. The question is who. Some creators of open source software have assigned their copyrights to the Free Software Foundation, or to a project manager for the application. However, most open source software has many copyright owners—the original creator(s) and all the programmers who have modified or added to the original software. Do all the owners have to join in a legal action to enforce the open source license? The answer is unclear.

Moreover, ownership disputes can easily arise. For example, claims can be made that code added to an open source application was copied from a copyrighted program; or a company that employs a programmer could claim that it is the legal owner of contributions to an open source program created by its employee under the work for hire rule (see Chapter 11.) The Free Software Foundation has long suggested that proper written documentation can minimize the chance of either kind of ownership dispute. For example, contributors to open source programs may wish to obtain written clearance from their employers to avoid any future certainty.

SCO vs. the Linux Community

In 2003, the SCO Group, a small software company that claims to have inherited intellectual property relating to the original Unix operating system, brought a lawsuit against IBM seeking billions of dollars of damages. SCO alleged that IBM had copied UNIX code into Linux and that the copying violated contracts IBM entered into with SCO's predecessors in Unix ownership. SCO also attempted to require large corporate Linux users to enter into proprietary license agreements with it to continue to use Linux. The lawsuit is being vigorously opposed by IBM and the other defendants and many legal experts believe that the suit is without merit. However, this litigation demonstrates that regardless of the intentions of the developers, open source software can be the subject of legal attack. Some fear that SCO has opened the floodgates to more lawsuits against popular open source applications by opportunistic intellectual property attorneys and the companies they represent. For detailed information about the SCO litigation, see http://sco.iwethey.org/ and www.groklaw.com. Of course, these disputes aren't specific to open source software and proprietary software publishers routinely sue one another for alleged copyright infringement.

b. The software patent threat

Many legal experts believe that the greatest legal threat to open source software is not the SCO litigation (see "SCO vs. the Linux Community," above), but software patents. Many thousands of software patents have been issued since the early 1990s, most owned by large companies. Any of these patent owners could claim that an open source application violates one or more of its patents. Even if the claims are meritless, the cost of defending such patent infringement claims can be enormous. Some open source licenses contain patent retaliation provisions—for example, the GPL provides that if, as a result of a patent infringement lawsuit, the software cannot be freely distributed, then it cannot be distributed at all. These retaliation provisions have also not been tested in court.

Other licenses now contain patent-related provisions, usually intended to provide disincentives for patent holders who might threaten patent lawsuits against developers of open source software. For example, a license may demand that a licensee of open source software not assert certain patent claims. For example, if a company asserts patent rights over some functionality of the Linux kernel, GPL would require the company shut down all Linux server/database servers and so forth; and it would lose the right to use the software.

c. Termination of open source licenses

One legal issue few in the open source community have considered is the legal right of all copyright owners to terminate their licenses. The Copyright Act provides that any copyright license made by an individual, including an open source license, may be terminated by the copyright owner or his or her heirs 35 to 40 years after it was made. If the license is terminated, all copyright rights in the licensed work revert to the copyright owners. The copyright owners need not pay anything to get back their rights. (See Chapter 11, Section B2.)

Thus, it is possible that 35 years from now the creator of an open source application (or his or her heirs) could decide the program should no longer be open source and terminate the open source license. Everyone could then be required to pay royalties to continue to use the software. Of course, it's likely that not much software in use today will still be used 35 years from now; but the problem still exists.

Confusion About Open Source Terminology

There is a good deal of confusion about the terminology used to describe open source software. Below are the definitions of some basic terms. (For a thorough explanation of the terminology, check out www.fsf.org/philosophy/catgeories.html):

Open source software: This is software licensed to the public under a license that falls within the Open Software Definition; over 30 licenses have been certified by OSI.

Free software: This term is generally used to describe free software that provides the Four Freedoms identified by Richard Stallman under the GPL (GNU General Public License).

Copyleft software: Copyrighted software that contains a license provision requiring users who publicly distribute modifications to license them as open source software.

Freeware: Copyrighted software that is not open source, but is distributed to users at no cost.

Public domain software: Software for which all copyright and other intellectual property rights have been abandoned.

Shareware: Copyrighted non-open source software that is made available to users for free or at low cost for a trial period.

Proprietary software: Copyrighted non-open source software distributed under a typical software license agreement.

Closed software: Copyrighted software whose source code is not made available to users; usually distributed with a proprietary license.

G. Website Content License

Website developers often need to obtain content from others for use on the websites they create. Such content may include graphics, applets, text, photos and videos, or other works of authorship. Permission to obtain such content should always be obtained in writing. The website content license provided here may be used for this purpose.

 The full text of a Website Content License Agreement is on the CD-ROM forms disk. Call up the agreement on your computer and read it along with the following discussion, which explains the wording of the form and describes what information you'll need to insert.

1. Licensed Content

In the introductory paragraph, insert the names of the licensor (the party who owns the material) and the licensee (you or the person who is seeking permission). If you want to specify in what form the Licensed Content will be delivered, use the optional sentence.

2. Grant of Rights

In the "Grant of Rights" section, complete the grant to reflect the rights that you have negotiated. More information on the rights associated with grants is provided in Chapter 11.

3. Limitations on License

This section sets forth certain limitations on the license. Include all that apply.

4. Sublicensing

"Sublicensing" occurs when the developer licenses the licensed content to others. Some content owners will allow this without their permission; some won't. Include the provision that applies.

5. Fees

In the "Fees" section, indicate what type of fee has been negotiated. The fees for website use are evolving, which is another way of saying that nobody is sure how much to charge for such uses. The fees are affected by:

- the extent of advertising at the website
- whether the site is intended primarily to provide information to the public (sometimes referred to as an "editorial" purpose). The rights holder may want to know whether the purpose of the site is to provide information or sell products or services
- whether the organization sponsoring the site is nonprofit

- number of visitors to the site per day
- whether the text will be used in a print publication as well as a related website—for example, whether you will use the text in a magazine and the magazine's website.

For example, a national magazine may charge between $100 to $500 for posting an article at a website, with the higher fees being charged for popular commercial sites—for example, posting a review of a movie at a high-traffic Hollywood studio website. Because website uses are in their infancy, many copyright owners limit the length of time for these permissions to one year or less.

6. Delivery of Content

Indicate here when the content will be delivered to the developer (licensee) by the owner (licensor). This can either be a specified number of days after the license fee is paid or a specific date.

7. Term

This section provides when the license will begin and how long it will last. It provides for automatic renewal after the initial term ends. You need to indicate how many months the initial and renewal terms will last. These terms don't have to be the same.

8. Warranty

A warranty is a contractual promise made by the licensor. Some licensors do not want to make promises, particularly a promise that the work does not infringe any third parties' copyright or other rights. You may have to modify the warranty or strike it entirely if the licensor objects.

If you have the bargaining power, you may want to include an indemnity provision in the agreement. Indemnity is a financial punishment if the licensor breaks its promises. We have not included any indemnity provisions here. If you wish to add such a provision, samples and explanations are provided in Chapter 18.

9. Miscellaneous

Explanations for the Miscellaneous or "boilerplate" provisions are provided in Chapter 17, Section B30. If you have the bargaining power, you may want to include an attorney fees or an arbitration provision.

10. Signing Instructions

Follow the instructions for signing found in Chapter 1.

H. Website Linking Agreement

Typically, linking to another site isn't the subject of major negotiations. The site that's being linked to usually is happy to get the exposure and usually won't object —although it might do so if it feels that the site linking to it is offensive or otherwise unacceptable. Still, linking to another site without permission may result in a conflict, so it's generally a good idea to ask permission via a simple emailed note. If you want a more formal linking agreement you can use the one we provide below.

Our linking agreement gives the linking site (the Source Site) permission to use the trademarked, copyrighted, or other protected material owned by the site being linked to (the Destination Site) for the purposes of the link itself. For instance, when a site offers a link such as the following: "Click to the Microsoft site," it's using a trademark of the Microsoft company, which Microsoft can prevent others from using. Most sites are usually happy to have other sites link to them, but play it safe: get permission before using anyone else's trademarked or copyrighted material.

 The full text of the Linking Agreement is on the CD-ROM forms disk.

Linking Agreement

1. Names

This Agreement is made by Trout.com (Source Site) and Bass.com (Destination Site).

2. The Link

Source Site will provide a link to Destination Site's website. The Link will appear on the Source Site at the following URL(s): www.trout.com/index1.htm.

The Link will appear as follows:

The text at the Source Site that includes the link to the Destination Site website will read as follows: "For all your bass fishing needs visit bass.com, the best fishing site on the Web" with the words trout.com highlighted and underlined to constitute the actual Hypertext link.

The Link to the Destination URL, or to any other page at the Destination Site, will not be framed.

3. Grant of Rights

Destination Site grants to Source Site the nonexclusive rights, including all trademark, copyright, and other intellectual property rights, to display the Link at the Source Site website, if the specifications of Section 2 of this Agreement are met and if Source Site maintains the integrity of the Link. Destination Site reserves the right to revoke this Grant of Rights at any time for any reason.

4. Standard and Notifications

Source Site will maintain its website in accordance with industry standards. Upon notice from Destination Site, Source Site will promptly remove the Link if requested. Source Site will promptly notify Destination Site of any changes to the Link or to the Source Site affecting the Link.

Dated: Aug. 15, 20XX
Source Site: Trout.com   Destination Site: Bass.com

By: _____

Name: Brooke Trout
Title: President
Address: 100 Main Street, Marred Vista, CA 9000
Date: Aug. 15, 20XX

By: _____

Name: Ben Bass
Title: President
Address: 123 Dolphin Way, Orlando, FL 12345
Date: Aug. 3, 20XX

The following instructions explain how to put together a simple Linking Agreement.

1. Names

Enter the required identifying information for the Source Site and the Destination Site. For recommended ways to enter names in a contract, see Chapter 1.

2. The Link

Enter the URL of the Source Site page where the link will appear. Next, choose the option for how the link will appear, either as a text link, an image link, or both. For the options you choose, fill in the required information, including the sentence in which the link will appear, the actual words that constitute the link, and a description of the image that makes up the link, depending on what type of link you'll use.

Next, enter the URL of the Destination Site where the link will connect.

Our agreement prohibits framing, which is a method of linking that loads the information from the Destination Site into a window at the Source Site, rather than simply going to the the Destination Site. Most sites don't like to be framed, and would rather have a regular link to their site. If you don't want to prohibit framed links, you can remove this language.

3. Grant of Rights

This section allows the Source Site to use protected intellectual property of the Destination Site, such as trademarked or copyrighted information, for purposes of the link. It also establishes that the Destination Site may revoke permission at any time for any reason.

4. Standards and Notifications

This clause establishes that the Source Site must maintain its site to reasonable standards, must remove the link if required, and must notify the Destination Site of any changes to the link or the Source Site that will affect the link.

5. Signing Instructions

Follow the instructions for signing found in Chapter 1. ■

Website Development Agreement

f you're performing website development, get the agreement in writing. There are too many legal issues involved to leave it to a handshake. For example:

- **Specifications and timelines.** You'll need to reach agreement on the details of the website and when work should be completed.
- **Warranties and indemnity.** Both parties will need assurances that the work will not create legal problems such as claims of copyright infringement or libel.
- **Who owns the work.** You'll need to determine who claims copyright ownership of the site's design and appearance.
- **Assigning the contract.** If you want the right to assign the work to someone else, you'll need to include the ability to assign the agreement.
- **Objections and approvals.** You'll want a simple system for approving (or objecting) to the work.
- **Termination.** Both parties will want an escape hatch in case things turn sour during the development process.

In this chapter we provide a section-by-section analysis of a website development agreement. Explanations of each provision are provided after each section of the agreement.

 The full text of a Website Development Agreement is on the CD-ROM forms disk.

A. Identifying the Parties to the Agreement

Before analyzing the contract you will need to properly identify the parties. The sample agreement includes an opening section as follows:

> This Agreement is made between _____ [NAME OF CLIENT] (the "Client") with a principal place of business at _____ [ADDRESS] and _____ [NAME OF WEBSITE DEVELOPER] (the "Developer") with a principal place of business at _____ [ADDRESS].

Both parties should list their full business names. Later on in the contract, you can use obvious abbreviations.

If you're a sole proprietor, use the full name you use for your business. This can be your own name or a fictitious business name or assumed name you use to identify your business. For example, if Jane Adams calls her Web development business "ABC Web Development," she would use that name on the contract. Using a fictitious business name helps show you're a business, not an employee.

If your business is incorporated, use your corporate name, not your own name—for example: "John Smith, Incorporated" instead of "John Smith."

If you're a limited liability company, use the name of your company—for example, "John Smith, LLC," instead of just "John Smith."

If you're a partner in a partnership, use your partnership name—for example, "The Smith Partnership" instead of "John Smith."

Refer to the client initially by its company name and subsequently by a short version of the name or as Client.

B. Contents of Website Development Agreements

The sample form contains a number of blank spaces to fill in and several alternative provisions you must choose from. The following section explains each section of the agreement and provides guidance on how to complete it. (Refer to Chapter 1 for information about how to assemble and finalize the agreement together.)

1. Definitions

The Site means a series of linked Web pages under common control and developed by Developer for Client under this Agreement.

Client Content means all data, code, trademarks, and copyrighted content provided by Client for use by Developer on the Site.

Developer Content means all data, code, trade secrets, patents, designs, drawings, text created by Developer for use on the Site, including any modifications or enhancements provided by Developer.

The definitions establish the meanings for key terms in the agreement. The definitions for Client Content and Developer Content help to establish ownership rights. The Client Content includes materials that the client will supply for use on the site such as photos or trademarks. Later in the agreement, the client makes assurances that it has the legal right to use this material.

2. Developer Services

Developer will perform the development services described in Attachment 1. There are four stages of development services: Concept, Design, Initial Development, and Final Development. Developer will complete the four stages on or before the dates listed in Attachment 1. Before delivering the Site to Client, Developer will test its components to make sure the Site and its components work as intended.

We've divided the development process into four stages: concept, design, initial development, and final development. Many developer agreements have variations—for example, using only two stages: initial and final development. We've used four to break the project into bite-sized pieces and allow changes in course at various checkpoints.

In the preliminary stage, you and the client simply work on specifications and concepts. This is a good way to determine whether the client's ideas for the site are workable.

After that, we've established a design stage that should allow you and the client to have a good idea what the site will be. That's followed by the initial and final stages.

3. Evaluation and Acceptance

As Developer completes each stage, Developer will submit the completed materials to Client for approval. Client will have __ days to approve the completed materials or provide corrections and comments.

Developer will have __ days after receiving Client's comments and corrections to submit a revised version of the materials to Client. Client will review the revised version within __ days of receipt and either approve the corrected version or make further changes.

If Client determines, in its reasonable discretion, that the materials are not acceptable after two attempts at correction by Developer, Client can terminate this Agreement. If Client fails to provide approval or comments during any of the approval periods, those materials will be considered to be approved.

If Client terminates this Agreement under this provision, Developer shall be entitled to compensation on a time and materials basis at an hourly rate of $[HOURLY RATE] plus expenses to the date of termination. Developer shall submit an invoice detailing its time and expenses. If the invoice amount is less than the amounts paid to Developer prior to termination, Developer shall promptly return the excess to Client. If the invoice amount exceeds the amounts paid to Developer prior to termination, Client shall pay Developer the difference within 30 days of the date of the invoice.

Once the project is underway, the client will want a chance at various points to review what's been done and to accept or reject it. This clause requires the client to sign off on each phase of the project as it is completed. You need to indicate how many days the client will have to accept or reject your work after it is received. If the client rejects your work, you have a given number of days to revise it. You need to indicate how many days. The client will then have a certain number of days to review your changes—you need to indicate how many in this clause.

If the client feels you've failed to correct the deficiencies after two attempts, it has the right to terminate the agreement. But, in this event, the client must pay you at an hourly rate for the work you've already done. You must indicate your hourly rate in this clause.

Also, note that the clause provides that if the client fails to provide approval or comments during any of the approval periods, those materials will be deemed to be approved.

4. Compensation

There are two basic ways to pay a developer for creating a website:

- a fixed price agreement, or
- a pay per hour ("time and materials") agreement.

a. Alternative 1: fixed price agreements

Client shall pay, upon completion of each of the following Milestones, the following amounts to Developer:

Fee	Due Date
$_____	Within ___ days of the effective date
$_____	Upon approval of the Design Stage
$_____	Upon approval of the Initial Development Stage
$_____	Upon approval of the Final Development Stage

One payment option is for the client to pay the developer a fixed price for the entire project. In theory, this payment scheme favors the client by giving the client certainty as to what the project will cost. Moreover, if payments are tied to the progress of the developer's work, it gives the client substantial leverage to insist on timely and successful completion of the project.

At first glance, fixed-price agreements would seem to be risky for developers: If the project takes much longer than originally anticipated, the developer could end up losing money. However, as a practical matter, fixed-price agreements usually do not end up favoring the client as much as one would think. If it turns out that the fixed price originally agreed upon will not provide the developer with fair compensation because the project ends up taking too long, the client will probably end up agreeing to pay the developer more money. Otherwise the developer may quit or end up delivering a hastily completed and shoddy product.

Fixed-price contracts are normally paid in installments, with payment of each installment tied to completion and acceptance of a phase of the project. This clause requires you and the client to agree on the amounts to be paid after approval of each phase. In addition, an initial down payment is made when the contract is signed.

The amount of the down payment is often a point of contention in fixed-price contracts. Naturally, the developer should obtain as large a down payment as possible.

b. Alternative 2: "time and materials" agreements

Developer shall be compensated at the rate of $[RATE] per hour [OR "day," "week," "month"]. Payment will be made within [NUMBER OF DAYS] days of the date of Developer's invoice for work completed. [OPTIONAL: "Unless otherwise agreed upon in writing by Client, Client's maximum liability for all services performed during the term of this Agreement shall not exceed $[MAXIMUM AMOUNT]."]

Under a "time and materials" agreement, the developer charges the client by the hour, day, or month at a flat hourly cost. This is by far the safest way to be paid if it's difficult to estimate exactly how long a project will take. However, many clients will wish to place a cap on your total compensation because they're afraid you'll "pad" your bill. If this is the case, include the optional sentence providing for a cap, but make sure it's large enough to allow you to complete the job.

5. Payment of Developer's Expenses

Expenses are the costs you incur that you can attribute directly to your work for a client. They include, for example, the cost of phone calls or traveling done on the client's behalf. Expenses do not include your normal fixed overhead costs such as your office rent, the cost of commuting to and from your office, or the wear and tear on your equipment. They also do not include materials the client provides you to do your work.

Whether or not you are reimbursed for expenses and the extent of such reimbursement is a matter for negotiation.

WEBSITE DEVELOPMENT AGREEMENT   **17/7**

a. **Alternative 1: full reimbursement**

Client shall reimburse Developer for all out-of-pocket expenses incurred by Developer in performing services under this Agreement. Such expenses include, but are not limited, to

(a) all communications charges

(b) travel expenses other than normal commuting, including airfares, rental vehicles, and highway mileage in company or personal vehicles at _____ cents per mile; and

(c) other expenses resulting from the work performed under this Agreement.

Developer shall submit an itemized statement of Developer's expenses. Client shall pay Developer within 30 days from the date of each statement. The first alternative calls for payment of all the devel-oper's out-of-pocket expenses; this may include items like communications charges (telephone, fax, postage, etc.).

b. **Alternative 2: you pay expenses**

Developer shall be responsible for all expenses incurred while performing services under this Agreement

Setting your compensation at a level high enough to cover your expenses is simple and safe. On the practical side, it frees you from having to keep records of your expenses. Keeping track of the cost of every phone call or photocopy you make for a client can be a real chore and may be more trouble than it's worth. However, if a project will involve expensive traveling, you may wish to separately bill the client for the cost.

Covering your own expenses will also help bolster your status as an IC. In the recent past, the IRS viewed the payment of a worker's expenses by a client as a sign of employee status. Although the agency now downgrades the importance of this factor, it's not entirely gone. You'll be on solid ground if you don't ask the client to reimburse you for expenses.

Choose Alternative 2 if you are responsible for expenses.

6. **Late Fees**

Late payments by Client shall be subject to late penalty fees of _____% per month or the maximum allowed under state law from the due date until the amount is paid.

Many developers charge a late fee if the client doesn't pay within the time specified in the development agreement or invoice. Charging late fees for overdue payments can get clients to pay on time. The late fee is normally expressed as a monthly interest charge—for example, 1% per month.

If you wish to charge a late fee, make sure it's mentioned in your agreement. You should also clearly state what your late fee is on all your invoices.

7. Materials

Client shall make available to Developer, at Client's expense, the following materials, facilities, and equipment: _____ [LIST]. These items will be provided to Client by _____ [DATE].

If the client will provide you with any materials or equipment, list them in this optional clause. If you need these items by a specific date, specify the deadline as well.

8. Changes in Project Scope

If Client wishes to implement major revisions after Client has already accepted Developer's work product following completion of any stage of development, Client shall submit to Developer a written proposal specifying the desired changes.

Developer will evaluate each such proposal at its standard rates and charges. Developer shall submit to Client a written response to each such proposal within ten working days following receipt thereof. Developer's written response shall include a statement of the availability of Developer's personnel and resources, as well as any impact the proposed changes will have on the contract price, delivery dates, or warranty provisions of this Agreement.

Client shall have ten business days from receipt of Developer's response to its proposal to accept or reject it in writing. If Client accepts Developer's response, Developer shall draft a written Contract Amendment Agreement to reflect the desired changes and acknowledge any effect of such changes on the provisions of this Agreement. The Contract Amendment Agreement shall be signed by authorized representatives of Client and Developer, whereupon Developer shall commence performance in accordance with it.

Should Client reject Developer's response to its proposal, Client will so notify Developer within ten working days of Client's receipt of the response. Developer will not be obligated to perform any services beyond those called for in this original Agreement.

It's quite common in the course of website development for the client to wish to make changes—adding new features and/or deleting others. Of course, any changes to the specifications or any other provision of the contract should be in writing and signed by both parties to be effective. (This is required by Section 30(b), below.)

Major changes in the scope of the project may greatly increase—or decrease—the amount of work the developer has to do. If the developer is paid a fixed fee, it is only fair that its compensation should be increased or decreased to reflect the change in the workload. This usually is not an issue where the developer is paid by the hour; but if there is a cap on the total hourly compensation to be paid, the cap may have to be increased.

Changes in the scope of the project may also require changes in proposed delivery dates, and perhaps in the contract's warranty provisions. (Warranties are discussed in Section 18.)

This provision sets forth a procedure for the parties to follow if the client wants to change the specifications or other parts of the development plan. First, the client must submit a written proposal to the developer showing the desired changes. The developer then responds to this proposal in writing, stating, among other things, what impact the desired changes will have on the contract price and delivery schedule. If the client wants to go ahead with the changes, it submits a "Development Plan Modification Agreement" specifying all the agreed-upon changes and their effect on the provisions of the Agreement. The developer has ten days to accept or reject the Development Plan Modification Agreement.

In many instances, the developer, not the client, will wish to alter the specifications. This may be because the specifications contain an error, do not accurately reflect the client's true needs, or the project as originally agreed upon proves commercially unfeasible for a developer being paid a fixed fee. All such changes should be in writing and signed by both parties as required by the clause dealing with modifications to the agreement. (See Section 30(b) below.)

9. Delays

Developer shall use all reasonable efforts to meet the delivery schedule set forth in Attachment 1. However, at its option, Developer can extend the due date for any deliverable by giving written notice to Client. The total of all such extensions shall not exceed ___ [NUMBER OF] days.

Any delay or nonperformance of any provision of this Agreement caused by conditions beyond the reasonable control of the performing party shall not constitute a breach of this Agreement, provided that the delayed party has taken reasonable measures to notify the other of the delay in writing. The delayed party's time for performance shall be deemed to be extended for a period equal to the duration of the conditions beyond its control.

Conditions beyond a party's reasonable control include, but are not limited to, natural disasters, acts of government after the date of the Agreement, power failure, fire, flood, acts of God, labor disputes, riots, acts of war or terrorism, and epidemics. Failure of subcontractors and inability to obtain materials shall not be considered a condition beyond a party's reasonable control.

It is common for creation of new websites to take longer than originally anticipated. There are many reasons for this. Estimating how long it will take to create a new website is an uncertain art at best. Delays may also result if the developer

has staffing changes or increased demands on existing staff.

The first paragraph of this section is designed to give the developer some leeway in the delivery schedule. Any deadline can be extended by the developer by giving the client written notice. However, a cap is placed on the total of all the extensions. You need to decide how many days this cap should be.

Sometimes a project is delayed due to circumstances beyond the developer's control—for example, where an earthquake, fire, or other act of God or acts of war or terrorism destroy or severely damage the developer's office and equipment. In this event, it is only fair that the developer's delay be excused. A special provision (often called a "force majeure" clause) is commonly included in development contracts to excuse a party's nonperformance due to circumstances beyond its control. The second and third paragraphs of this section contain such a provision.

10. Ownership of Developer Content

Many website developers and clients harbor the misapprehension that, since the developer is being paid to create the site by the client, the client will automatically own all rights to it. This is not the case. Absent a written contract transferring ownership from the developer to the Client, the developer will most likely own the copyright in anything it creates for the client (unless the developer is considered the client's employee; see Chapter 11).

One of the most important functions of a website development agreement is to establish exactly who will own the intellectual property rights to content to be created. This is often one of the most hotly contested issues between the developer and client. Ownership rules for intellectual property are covered in detail in Chapter 11. This section focuses on how to handle these issues in a website development agreement.

Two ownership alternatives are provided:

- sole ownership by the client, and
- ownership by developer with a nonexclusive license to client.

a. Alternative 1: ownership by client

Developer assigns to Client all right, title, and interest in the copyrights in Developer Content, including copyright in the Site's compilation or collective work and in the derivative copyrights of such works. Developer will sign any further documents reasonably requested by Client to put into effect the assignment of these rights.

Because they are paying the developer to create the website, some clients insist on receiving sole ownership of what the developer creates. The following clause grants all ownership rights in the Developer Content to the client, with no restrictions.

b. Alternative 2: ownership by developer

Developer shall retain all copyright, patent, trade secret, and other intellectual property rights Developer may have in Developer Content. Subject to payment of all compensation due under this Agreement, Developer grants Client a nonexclusive, nontransferable, royalty-free license to use Developer Content. This license shall authorize Client to:

- operate the Site on its host server
- update, revise, or republish the Site, and
- advertise and promote the Site.

Under this alternative, the developer retains ownership of all the Developer Content and gives the client only a nonexclusive license to use it. This means that the developer is free to license the content to anyone else, including the client's competitors. This is the most favorable ownership arrangement for the developer.

11. Ownership of Developer Tools

Client acknowledges that Developer owns or holds a license to use and sublicense various development or authoring tools it uses to create websites for its clients. By way of example, such tools may include, but are not limited to, such items as: HTML code, Java code, Java applets, subroutines, search engines, and toolbars for maneuvering between pages. Such material shall be referred to as "Developer's Tools." Developer Tools include, but are not limited to, those items identified in Exhibit __, attached to and made a part of this Agreement.

Developer retains all right, title, and interest, including all copyright, patent rights, and trade secret rights in Developer Tools. Subject to full payment of the fees due under this Agreement, Developer grants Client a nonexclusive, perpetual worldwide license to use the Developer Tools to operate the Site and for all updates and revisions thereto. However, Client shall make no other commercial use of Developer Tools without Developer's written consent.

A website developer will normally bring to the project various development tools, programs, subroutines, and other programs, data, and materials. One term for these items is "Developer Tools." It's quite possible that Developer Tools may end up in the final product. For example, this may include HTML code, Java code, Java applets, subroutines, search engines, and toolbars for maneuvering between pages.

If the developer transfers complete ownership of the website to the client, the client also may end up owning Developer Tools. Such an arrangement would prohibit the developer from using these materials in other projects without obtaining the client's permission (and perhaps paying a fee). A developer is usually well advised to avoid this problem by making sure the agreement provides that the developer retain all ownership rights in Developer Tools. In this event, the agreement also should give the client a nonexclusive license to use the Developer Tools included in the client's website.

This provision permits the client to use the Developer Tools to operate and update the site, but keeps ownership in the hands of the developer. The developer should prepare a separate exhibit that identifies the Developer Tools in as much detail as possible.

12. Website Credits and Links

Developer can:

[ ] state on the Site that Developer developed the Site

[ ] place hypertext links on Client's Site to Developer's website

[ ] place hypertext links on Developer's website to Client's Site as an example of Developer's services.

Most website developers obtain some form of credit on the completed site. Obviously, this type of exposure could lead to more jobs for the developer. The developer can even have the client provide a link from its site to the developer's own site. Our form includes three credit and link options you can obtain from the client. Simply check the boxes for the ones that you agree on.

13. Site Hosting

Client has selected an Internet service provider to host its completed Site. While the Site is under construction and until final payment is received by Developer, Developer will host the Site pages as they are constructed in a special directory on its Web space at: _____ [URL]. If the Site is not completed by the completion date set forth in Attachment 1, and if the cause of the delay is not attributable to Developer, Client agrees to pay Developer $____ per month for hosting the Site on Developer's Web space. Client will continue to pay Developer for hosting the Site at this rate until the Site is installed on Client's own Web space. This monthly rate shall be prorated if the Site is installed on Client's Web space before the end of any monthly period.

This Agreement contemplates that the Client will find its own ISP to host the completed website. This clause provides that you will host the site on your own website while it's being developed. However, if the site is not completed by the date provided in the agreement, and the delay is not yours, the client will pay you each month for hosting the site until it's completed and moved to the client's chosen ISP. You must state in this clause how much you will charge the client per month for hosting the site.

14. Domain Name

Developer has no legal or financial interest in the domain name chosen by Client for the site.

[OPTIONAL:] If requested by Client, Developer will cooperate with Client in registering the domain name with a domain name registry chosen by Client. Client shall bear all expenses incurred in registering the domain name.

This clause provides that the developer will have no ownership or other interest in the Site domain name. The optional clause provides that the developer will help the client register the domain name—but at the client's expense.

15. Developer Representations and Warranties

Warranties and representations are statements and promises that you make regarding your services. They give the client a legal basis for suing you if something goes wrong after your services are completed. For example, if you warrant (promise) that the website will meet all the contract specifications and operate as intended, and it doesn't, you'll be responsible for fixing it or paying the cost of getting it fixed. If you don't, the client can sue you for breach of warranty.

Clients usually expect website developers to warrant their work. However, it's in the developer's best interest to provide as few warranties as possible or even no warranties at all. Remember, the more promises you make about your services the more grounds the client will have to sue you for breach of warranty if something goes wrong.

a. Alternative 1: disclaimer of all warranties

THE DEVELOPER CONTENT FURNISHED UNDER THIS AGREEMENT IS PROVIDED ON AN "AS IS" BASIS, WITHOUT ANY WARRANTIES OR REPRESENTATIONS EXPRESS, IMPLIED, OR STATUTORY; INCLUDING, WITHOUT LIMITATION, WARRANTIES OF QUALITY, PERFORMANCE, NONINFRINGEMENT, MERCHANTABILITY, ,OR FITNESS FOR A PARTICULAR PURPOSE. NOR ARE THERE ANY WARRANTIES CREATED BY A COURSE OF DEALING, COURSE OF PERFORMANCE, OR TRADE USAGE. DEVELOPER DOES NOT WARRANT THAT THE OPERATION OF THE SITE WILL BE CONTINUAL, UNINTERRUPTED, OR ERROR-FREE. THE FOREGOING EXCLUSIONS AND DISCLAIMERS ARE AN ESSENTIAL PART OF THIS AGREEMENT AND FORMED THE BASIS FOR DETERMINING THE PRICE CHARGED FOR DEVELOPER CONTENT.

There is no requirement in most states that you provide any warranties at all. Your services may be provided "as is"—meaning you make no warranties at all. While an "as is" statement will protect you from many types of claims, it won't protect you from charges of outright fraud (if you actually lied to the client). To be effective, "as is" statements must be "conspicuous"—for instance, printed in boldface capitals and large type—so they won't be overlooked by the client (no proverbial "fine print").

b. Alternative 2: providing express warranties

> Developer represents and warrants to Client that:
>
> - Developer Content will substantially conform to all specifications set forth in this Agreement and its attachments upon delivery and for a period of _____ after delivery.
>   Developer has obtained or will obtain all necessary and appropriate rights and licenses to use Developer Content for the Site. Upon request, Developer will provide Client with copies of clearances for any intellectual rights obtained from third parties in connection with the website.
> - Developer will not engage in any defamatory, deceptive, misleading, or unethical practices that are or might be detrimental to Client or the Site.
>
> THE WARRANTIES SET FORTH IN THIS AGREEMENT ARE THE ONLY WARRANTIES GRANTED BY DEVELOPER. DEVELOPER DISCLAIMS ALL OTHER WARRANTIES EXPRESS OR IMPLIED, INCLUDING, BUT NOT LIMITED TO, ANY IMPLIED WARRANTIES OF MERCHANTABILITY OR FITNESS FOR A PARTICULAR PURPOSE. [END ALTERNATIVE 2]

It is reasonable for the client to expect the developer to stand behind its work. Website developers typically give the client certain express warranties and disclaim any other warranties. The parties need to negotiate exactly what type of express warranties the developer will make. Naturally, the client wants the developer's warranties to be as expansive as possible, while the developer wishes them to be narrowly drawn. A compromise must be reached.

Alternative 2 contains the following express warranties commonly found in website development agreements. Include whichever warranties are desired.

- **Warranty of Performance:** Under this warranty, the developer guarantees that the Developer Content will substantially conform to all the contract specifications. "Substantial conformance" means that trivial variations from the specifications will not violate the warranty.

This warranty is usually limited in time, to anywhere from 90 days to one year. During the warranty term, the developer is required to correct any substantial deviations from the specifications and modify the Developer Content as necessary, free of charge.

- **Rights and clearances:** This warranty provides that you'll obtain all necessary rights and licenses to use the material you provide for the Site. Upon request, you must give the client copies of these clearances.
- **Unethical practices:** This warranty provides that you will not engage in any defamatory, deceptive, mislead-

ing, or unethical practices that are or might be detrimental to the client or the site.

16. Intellectual Property Infringement Claims

"Intellectual property" is a catch-all term that includes copyrights, patents, trade secrets, and trademarks. (See Chapter 2 for a detailed discussion.) Most website development agreements contain some kind of warranty against intellectual property infringement. The extent of such a warranty is subject to negotiation.

In this highly litigious world, intellectual property infringement is an issue the developer must think about carefully. In some cases, the developer may even choose to lower its price or make other concessions to the client to avoid making a broad warranty of noninfringement. Three alternative warranty provisions are provided in the agreement.

a.   Alternative 1: limited warranty against infringement

Developer warrants that Developer will not knowingly infringe on the copyright or trade secrets of any third party in performing services under this Agreement. To the extent any material used by Developer contains matter proprietary to a third party, Developer shall obtain a license from the owner permitting the use of such matter and granting Developer the right to sublicense its use. Developer will not knowingly infringe upon any existing patents of third parties in the performance of services required by this Agreement, but Developer MAKES NO WARRANTY OF NONINFRINGEMENT of any United States or foreign patent.

[OPTIONAL—INDEMNIFICATION FOR CLAIMS:] If any third party brings a lawsuit or proceeding against Client based upon a claim that the Developer Content breaches the third party's patent, copyright, or trade secrets rights, and it is determined that such infringement has occurred, Developer shall hold Client harmless against any loss, damage, expense, or cost, including reasonable attorney fees, arising from the claim.

This indemnification obligation shall be effective only if:

- the third-party intellectual property rights involved were known to Developer prior to delivery of the Developer Content
- Client has made all payments required by this Agreement
- Client has given prompt notice of the claim and permitted Developer to defend, and
- the claim does not result from Client's modification of Developer Content.

To reduce or mitigate damages, Developer may at its own expense replace the Developer Content with noninfringing content.

In this clause the developer warrants that it will not knowingly violate the copyright or trade secrets rights of any third party. However, no warranty is made as to patent infringement. This is because it is very difficult for a developer to know for sure whether its content might violate a patent, primarily because many pending patent applications are kept secret. Instead, the developer simply promises that to the best of the developer's knowledge the Developer Content will not infringe any existing patent.

Some clients absolutely insist that the developer indemnify (repay) them if a third party brings a lawsuit claiming the Developer Content infringed on the party's intellectual property rights. An optional indemnification provision is provided here. It is as narrowly drafted as possible. The developer must indemnify the client only if the third-party intellectual property rights involved were known to the developer prior to delivery of the content.

b. Alternative 2: "no-knowledge" representation

Developer represents, BUT DOES NOT WARRANT, that to the best of its knowledge the Developer Content delivered to Client under this Agreement will not infringe any valid and existing intellectual property right of any third party.

Even better for the developer is to provide no warranty of noninfringement at all, and instead extend the "no-knowledge representation" to copyrights and trade secrets as well as patents.

c. Alternative 3: no warranties or representations

THE DEVELOPER CONTENT FURNISHED UNDER THIS AGREEMENT IS PROVIDED WITHOUT ANY EXPRESS OR IMPLIED WARRANTIES OR REPRESENTATIONS AGAINST INFRINGEMENT, AND DEVELOPER SHALL NOT INDEMNIFY CLIENT AGAINST INFRINGEMENT OF ANY PATENTS, COPYRIGHTS, TRADE SECRETS, OR OTHER PROPRIETARY RIGHTS.

Best of all, from the developer's point of view, is a provision in which the developer states that it makes no warranties or representations of any kind regarding intellectual property infringement and will not indemnify the client if an infringement claim is made (see discussion of indemnification below). If you use this clause, it should be printed in boldfaced, capital letters.

17. Limits on Developer's Liability

Limitation of Developer's Liability to Client:

(a) In no event shall Developer be liable to Client for lost profits of Client, or special or consequential damages, even if Developer has been advised of the possibility of such damages.

(b) Developer's total liability under this Agreement for damages, costs, and expenses, regardless of cause, shall not exceed the total amount of fees paid to Developer by Client under this Agreement [OPTIONAL: "or $[AMOUNT], whichever is greater"].

(c) Developer shall not be liable for any claim or demand made against Client by any third party except to the extent such claim or demand relates to copyright, trade secret, or other proprietary rights, and then only as provided in the section of this Agreement entitled Intellectual Property Infringement Claims.

(d) Client shall indemnify Developer against all claims, liabilities, and costs, including reasonable attorney fees, of defending any third-party claim or suit arising out of the use of the Developer Content provided under this Agreement, other than for infringement of intellectual property rights. Developer shall promptly notify Client in writing of any third-party claim or suit and Client shall have the right to fully control the defense and any settlement of such claim or suit.

This provision, which is optional, limits the developer's total liability to the client if something goes wrong with the developer's work.

a. No liability for consequential damages

Incidental or consequential damages include lost profits or other economic damages arising from a malfunction where the developer had reason to know that such losses could occur if the website malfunctioned. This could include, for example, the value of online sales lost if a client's website breaks down. Such damages can be substantial. This clause eliminates liability for such damages.

b. Limit on developer's liability to client

This clause limits the developer's potential liability to the client to a specified amount. A typical liability limit is the amount paid the developer by the client. This amounts to a money-back guarantee for the client, while getting the developer off the hook for a potentially much larger liability. If desired, a liability standard not based on the contract price can be set. Obviously, such a provision highly favors the developer.

c. Developer's liability for third-party claims

A third party is a person or company other than the client. It is possible that the developer could end up getting sued by a third party.

> **EXAMPLE:** Charlie Client hires the Acme Stock Photo Agency to provide Dave Developer with photos for the website Developer is creating for Client. Client fails to pay Acme. Acme sues both Client and Developer for payment.

This clause provides that the developer is not liable for any claim made against the client by any third party (other than for intellectual property infringement if it is providing a warranty against infringement).

d. Indemnification of developer for third-party claims

This clause requires the client to indemnify you if you are sued by a third party (someone other than the client). This means the client must pay your legal expenses and any damages awarded against you

18. Client Representations and Warranties

Client represents and warrants to Developer as follows:

- Client has the authority to enter into and perform its obligations under this Agreement

- Client has or will obtain all necessary and appropriate rights and licenses to grant the license to Developer to use Client Content for the Site, and

- Client has or will obtain any authorizations necessary for hypertext links from the Site to any other third-party websites.

Client will indemnify Developer from any third-party claims resulting in losses, damages, liabilities, costs, charges, and expenses, including reasonable attorney fees, arising out of any breach of any of Client's representations and warranties contained in this Agreement. For such indemnification to be effective, however, Developer must give Client prompt written notice of any such claim and provide Client such reasonable cooperation and assistance as Client may request in the defense of such suit. Client will have sole control over any such suit or proceeding.

The client should provide the developer with certain warranties. This clause provides that:

- The client has the authority to enter into and perform its obligations under this Agreement—this means the person who signs the Agreement has the legal authority to do so on the client's behalf
- The client has or will obtain all necessary rights and licenses for any content it provides the developer for the site, and
- the client has or will obtain any authorizations necessary for hypertext links from the site to any other third-party websites.

The clause also requires the client to indemnify the developer if any of these warranties are breached.

19. Confidentiality

Confidentiality: During the term of this Agreement and for ____ [6 months to 5 years] afterward, Developer will use reasonable care to prevent the unauthorized use or dissemination of Client's confidential information. Reasonable care means at least the same degree of care Developer uses to protect its own confidential information from unauthorized disclosure.

Confidential information is limited to information clearly marked as confidential, or disclosed orally that is treated as confidential when disclosed and summarized and identified as confidential in a writing delivered to Developer within 15 days of disclosure.

Confidential information does not include information that:

- the Developer knew before Client disclosed it
- is or becomes public knowledge through no fault of Developer
- Developer obtains from sources other than Client who owe no duty of confidentiality to Client, or
- Developer develops independently.

Since website developers often have access to their clients' valuable confidential information, clients often seek to impose confidentiality restrictions on them. It's not unreasonable for a client to want you to keep its secrets away from the eyes and ears of competitors. Unfortunately, however, many of these provisions are worded so broadly that they can make it difficult for you to work for other clients without fear of violating your duty of confidentiality.

If, like most Web developers, you make your living by performing similar services for many firms that may compete with each other, insist on a confidentiality provision that is reasonable in scope and defines precisely what information you must keep confidential. Such a provision should last for only a limited time—five years at the most.

The confidentiality provision in this agreement prevents the unauthorized disclosure by the developer of any written material of the client marked confidential or information disclosed orally that the client later writes down, marks as confidential, and delivers to you within 15 days. This enables the developer to know for sure what material is, and is not, confidential.

The clause also makes clear that the developer does not have any duty to

keep confidential material that does not qualify as a trade secret, is legitimately learned from persons other than the client, or is independently developed.

20. Term of Agreement

This Agreement commences on the date it is executed and shall continue until full performance by both parties, or until earlier terminated by one party under the terms of this Agreement.

This clause provides that the term of the Agreement runs from the date it is executed (signed by both parties) until full performance or earlier termination or cancellation.

21. Termination of Agreement

Each party shall have the right to terminate this Agreement by written notice to the other if a party has materially breached any obligation herein and such breach remains uncured for a period of 30 days after written notice of such breach is sent to the other party.

If Developer terminates this Agreement because of Client's default, all of the following shall apply:

(a) Client shall immediately cease use of the Developer Content.

(b) Client shall, within ten days of such termination, deliver to Developer all copies and portions of the Developer Content and related materials and documentation in its possession furnished by Developer under this Agreement.

(c) All amounts payable or accrued to Developer under this Agreement shall become immediately due and payable.

(d) All rights and licenses granted to Client under this Agreement shall immediately terminate.

[OPTIONAL:] This Agreement may be terminated by Client for its convenience upon thirty (30) days' prior written notice to Developer. Upon such termination, all amounts owed to Developer under this Agreement for accepted work shall immediately become due and payable and all rights and licenses granted by Developer to Client under this Agreement shall immediately terminate.

The language governing how the agreement may end is very important to both parties. The provision in this agreement is fairly standard. It permits either party to terminate the agreement if the other materially breaches any of its contractual obligations and fails to remedy the breach within 30 days. A "material" breach means a breach that is serious, rather than minor or trivial. Missing a deadline by one day is not "material"; missing it by three months is. For developers, the material breach most likely to result in termination is the client's failure to pay the developer in a timely fashion. If the developer terminates the agreement because of the client's default (usually because the client has failed to pay the developer), the client should return any Developer Content or other materials received from the eveloper and should pay the developer for the work it has done.

Optional provision—early client termination: The client may want the option to terminate the agreement at its convenience if it decides for some reason it doesn't want to go through with the project. In this event, the client should have to pay the developer all amounts due for accepted work and relinquish any rights in the developer content.

22. Taxes

The charges included here do not include taxes. If Developer is required to pay any federal, state, or local sales, use, property, or value added taxes based on the services provided under this Agreement, the taxes shall be separately billed to Client. Developer shall not pay any interest or penalties incurred due to late payment or nonpayment of such taxes by Client.

Whether or not the developer is required to collect sales or other taxes, the following provision should be included in the agreement making it clear that the client will have to pay these and similar taxes. States constantly change their sales tax laws and more and more are beginning to look at services as a good source of sales tax revenue. So this provision could come in handy in the future even if the developer doesn't really need it now.

23. Developer an Independent Contractor

Developer is an independent contractor, and neither Developer nor Developer's staff is, or shall be deemed, Client's employees. In its capacity as an independent contractor, Developer agrees and represents, and Client agrees, as follows:

[INCLUDE ALL PROVISIONS THAT APPLY]

(a) Developer has the right to perform services for others during the term of this Agreement subject to noncompetition provisions set out in this Agreement, if any.

(b) Developer has the sole right to control and direct the means, manner, and method by which the services required by this Agreement will be performed.

(c) Developer has the right to perform the services required by this Agreement at any place or location and at such times as Developer may determine.

(d) Developer will furnish all equipment and materials used to provide the services required by this Agreement.

(e) The services required by this Agreement shall be performed by Developer, or Developer's staff, and Client shall not be required to hire, supervise, or pay any assistants to help Developer.

(f) Developer is responsible for paying all ordinary and necessary expenses of its staff.

(g) Neither Developer nor Developer's staff shall receive any training from Client in the professional skills necessary to perform the services required by this Agreement.

(h) Neither Developer nor Developer's staff shall be required to devote full-time to the performance of the services required by this Agreement.

(i) Client shall not provide insurance coverage of any kind for Developer or Developer's staff.

(j) Client shall not withhold from Developer's compensation any amount that would normally be withheld from an employee's pay.

One of the most important functions of the agreement is to help establish that the developer is not the client's employee. A developer will be considered the client's employee if the client has the right to control the developer. This will cause problems not only for the client, but for the developer as well.

A development agreement that indicates a lack of control on the part of the hiring firm will contribute to a finding of independent contractor status. But such an agreement will not be determinative in and of itself. Simply signing a piece of paper will not make a developer an independent contractor. The agreement must reflect reality—that is, the developer must actually not be controlled on the job by the client.

The language in this clause addresses most of the factors the IRS and other agencies consider in measuring the degree of control of the hiring firm. All provisions show that the hiring firm lacks the right to control the manner and means by which the developer will perform the agreed-upon services.

Include all of provisions a-j that apply. The more that apply, the more likely that the developer will be viewed as an independent contractor.

24. Optional Provision: Nonsolicitation of Developer's Employees

> Client agrees not to knowingly hire or solicit Developer's employees during performance of this Agreement and for a period of [TIME PERIOD, USUALLY SIX MONTHS TO TWO YEARS] after termination of this Agreement without Developer's written consent.

Some Web developers fear that the client will hire away a star design or other key employee and do future work on website updates and enhancements in-house. This optional provision is designed to prevent this. It may give the developer some peace of mind.

25. Designated Representatives

> Each party will designate a representative to receive and send materials, approvals, comments, invoices, and other materials discussed in this agreement.
>
> Developer's Representative will be _____, who can be contacted by email at _____ and by telephone at _____.
>
> Client's Representative will be _____, who can be contacted by email at _____ and by telephone at _____.

Insert the name and contact information for each party's designated representative.

26. Website Maintenance and New Development

> Developer will maintain the Site or provide additional development after its launch according to the terms stated in Attachment 2.

If the client is not tech savvy or doesn't have the time or inclination to do it itself, it will need a person or firm on tap to keep the site running properly and to assist in keeping it up to date. One obvious option is to make the developer responsible for these ongoing chores. If so, you can include these arrangements in your development contract. We've provided an optional contract clause here for you and the client to consider.

27. Disputes

Arbitration and mediation are referred to as alternative dispute resolution (ADR) procedures because they offer ways to end squabbles without litigation. These ADR procedures have become popular over the last decade because they avoid the court system and can save time and money. However, taking a dispute out of the court system may not always be the right decision for you. In arbitration, for example, you'll be bound by a decision

from which there is no means of appeal. Our agreement gives you three alternatives on how to resolve disputes; you must choose one:

a. Alternative 1: litigation

> If a dispute arises, either party may take the matter to court.
>
> Mediation and Possible Litigation. If a dispute arises, the parties will try in good faith to settle it through mediation conducted by: _____ [NAME] OR a mediator to be mutually selected.

The first alternative calls for court litigation—meaning there will be no mediation or arbitration unless the parties change their minds and agree to it later.

b. Alternative 2: Mediation

> Each party will cooperate fully and fairly with the mediator and will attempt to reach a mutually satisfactory compromise to the dispute. If the dispute is not resolved within 30 days after it is referred to the mediator, either party may take the matter to court.

The second alternative requires mediation, with the costs of the mediator to be borne equally by developer and client. If the mediation fails, the matter may be taken to court.

c. Alternative 3: Mediation and arbitration

> If a dispute arises, the parties will try in good faith to settle it through mediation conducted by: _____ [NAME] OR a mediator to be mutually selected.
>
> The parties will share the costs of the mediator equally. Each party will cooperate fully and fairly with the mediator and will attempt to reach a mutually satisfactory compromise to the dispute.
>
> If the dispute is not resolved within 30 days after it is referred to the mediator, it will be arbitrated by: _____ [NAME] OR an arbitrator to be mutually selected. Judgment on the arbitration award may be entered in any court that has jurisdiction over the matter. The arbitrator will allocate costs of arbitration, including attorney fees.

The third alternative calls first for mediation, with the costs to be borne equally. If the mediation fails, the parties must take the matter to binding arbitration. You give up your right to go to court under this alternative.

Mediation and Arbitration Primer

Mediation and arbitration are not the same. It's important to understand the differences.

Mediation. In mediation, a neutral facilitator (the mediator) helps the parties resolve their dispute. Both sides sit down with the mediator and tell their stories. The mediator sorts out the issues and may suggest ways to resolve the dispute. If the two parties agree to a solution, they sign a settlement agreement. Because it's not binding and because it's less expensive than litigation or arbitration, some businesses prefer mediation, at least as a first step.

Mediation is the most inexpensive and peaceable method of solving problems. You can arrive at a settlement rather than being told how to resolve the dispute by an arbitrator or judge. It's less likely to exacerbate bad feelings between the parties, as lawsuits inevitably do.

By itself, however, mediation may not be enough because it doesn't force the parties to end the dispute. If you can't resolve the dispute with mediation, you must find some binding method of ending the battle, either arbitration or litigation.

Arbitration. Arbitration is like going to court, but with less formality and expense. Instead of filing a lawsuit, the parties hire one or more arbitrators to evaluate the dispute and make a determination. The arbitration process can be relatively simple, although it usually requires some document preparation and a hearing. You don't need a lawyer to represent you, but many businesses do prefer a lawyer's help in presenting the strongest legal arguments.

Occasionally, the parties may agree that an arbitrator's determination will be advisory (in which case either party can disregard it and file a lawsuit). Much more often, however, it's binding. A binding decision can be enforced by a court and can't be overturned unless something especially unfair happened—for example, the arbitrator ruled against you and you later learn that the arbitrator owned stock in your client's company.

To arbitrate a dispute, both parties must consent. Unfortunately, when you are in the midst of a dispute, it's hard to get the parties to agree to anything. So, the best method of guaranteeing arbitration is to include an arbitration provision in your contracts.

Arbitration is not, however, always preferable to litigation. Even though arbitration is quicker than going through a trial, it may take several weeks to initiate proceedings. By contrast, if a developer goes to court, it may obtain some relief—like a temporary restraining order—in less time than it takes to initiate arbitration. For this reason, you need to weigh the potential cost of litigation versus the speed of obtaining relief. For a small developer with limited resources, arbitration is usually the preferable route.

Finding a Mediator or Arbitrator. Many associations and companies offer mediation and arbitration services. The best-known organization is the American Arbitration Association (AAA). The AAA has offices in every state and can provide mediators and arbitrators in most areas. If you'd like to check the availability of AAA arbitrators or mediators in your area before using one of these clauses, visit www.adr.org.

Nolo's *How to Mediate Your Dispute: Find a Solution Quickly and Cheaply Outside the Courtroom*, by Peter Lovenheim, provides more information on mediation and arbitration.

28. Attorney Fees and Expenses

> If there is litigation, the prevailing party may collect from the other party its reasonable costs and attorney fees incurred in enforcing this Agreement.

What if the other party breaches the agreement and you're forced to sue? The rate for business lawyers is $200 to $400 an hour. The a lawsuit can cost $5,000 to $50,000 and even more, depending on the length of the suit and the subject matter. The amount you pay lawyers could quickly overshadow any amount you might win.

In the United States (unlike many other countries), the loser of a lawsuit isn't required to pay the winner's attorney fees. In other words, each party has to pay its own lawyer, regardless of how the suit turns out. There are two exceptions to this rule:

- a court may award fees if a specific law permits it; and
- a court must award attorney fees if a contract provides for it.

In most situations, you only get your attorney fees paid if you use a provision like the one in our agreement. Because lawyers are so expensive, having an attorney fee provision—that is, having each side afraid it will get stuck paying someone's attorney fees—can prove crucial to ending a dispute.

This attorney fees provision is mutual—that is, whoever wins the lawsuit is awarded attorney fees. This is fair, and encourages the quick resolution of lawsuits. We discourage a provision that allows only one party to receive attorney fees. No matter which side they favor, one-sided provisions create an uneven playing field for resolving disputes. One state (California) recognizes this unfairness and automatically converts a one-way attorney fees contract provision into a mutual one.

29. Survival

> The provisions of Sections 16 through 18 will survive any termination of this Agreement.

This clause ensures that Sections 16-18 dealing with the developer's liability and the client's warranties will survive any early termination of the agreement.

30. General Provisions

Following are several provisions that are customarily lumped together at the end of a development agreement. This does not mean they are unimportant.

a. Complete agreement

> This Agreement together with all exhibits, appendices, or other attachments, which are incorporated herein by reference, is the sole and entire Agreement between the parties. This Agreement supersedes all prior understandings, agreements, and documentation relating to such subject matter. In the event of a conflict between the provisions of the main body of the Agreement and any attached exhibits, appendices, or other materials, the Agreement shall take precedence.

This clause helps make it clear to a court or arbitrator that the parties intended the contract to be their final agreement. A clause such as this helps avoid claims that promises not contained in the written contract were made and broken. The developer should make sure that all documents containing any of the client's representations upon which the developer is relying are attached to the agreement as exhibits. If they aren't attached, they likely won't be considered to be part of the agreement.

b. Modifications

> Modifications and amendments to this Agreement, including any exhibit or appendix hereto, shall be enforceable only if they are in writing and are signed by authorized representatives of both parties.

This clause, which is very important, provides that any changes to the agreement must be in writing and agreed to by both parties to be effective. This provision protects both parties; reducing all modifications to writing lessens the possibility of misunderstandings. In addition, oral modifications may not be legally binding.

Contract Changes in the Real World

In the real world, people make changes to their contracts all the time and never write them down. If the changes are very minor, this might not pose a problem. But be aware that a contract alteration might not be legally binding if it is not written down. And, of course, if a dispute develops, the lack of a writing will make it difficult to prove what you actually agreed to.

If you agree to a minor contract change (over the phone, for example) and don't want to go to the trouble of dealing with a formal signed contract modification, at least send a confirming letter to the other party setting forth the gist of what you've agreed to. This isn't as good as a signed contract modification, but it will be helpful if a dispute later develops.

c. Applicable law

> This Agreement will be governed by the laws of the State of [LIST APPLICABLE STATE]

This clause specifies which state law governs the contract. This should be the state in which the developer does business or is incorporated.

d. Notices

All notices and other communications given in connection with this Agreement shall be in writing and shall be deemed given as follows:

- When delivered personally to the recipient's address as appearing in the introductory paragraph to this Agreement;
- Three days after being deposited in the United States mails, postage prepaid to the recipient's address as appearing in the introductory paragraph to this Agreement, or
- When sent by fax or electronic mail. Notice is effective upon receipt provided that a duplicate copy of the notice is promptly given by first-class or certified mail, or the recipient delivers a written confirmation of receipt.

When you want to do something important involving the agreement—terminate it, for example—you need to tell the client about it. This is called giving notice. This provision gives you several options for providing the client with notice: by personal delivery, by mail, or by fax or electronic mail followed by a confirming letter.

If you give notice by mail, it is not effective until three days after it's sent. For example, if you want to end the agreement on 30 days notice and mail, your notice of termination to the consultant, the agreement will not end until 33 days after you mailed the notice.

e. No agency

Nothing contained herein will be construed as creating any agency, partnership, joint venture, or other form of joint enterprise between the parties.

This clause helps you to make sure that the developer and client are separate legal entities, not partners or coventurers. If a client is viewed as a developer's partner, the developer will be liable for its debts and the client will have the power to make contracts that obligate the developer to others without the developer's consent.

f. Assignment

The rights and obligations under this Agreement are freely assignable by either party. Client shall retain the obligation to pay if the assignee fails to pay as required by this Agreement.

An assignment is the process by which rights or duties under a contract are transferred to someone else. For example, you may assign your duty to perform services for the client to someone else. This clause gives both parties an unfettered right to assign their rights or obligations.

g. Successors and assigns

This agreement binds and benefits the heirs, successors, and assigns of the parties.

It's possible that either party will be succeeded by someone else. For example, a sole proprietor's heirs may inherit the business. In that case, you'd want to make sure that the heirs are bound by all the requirements of the agreement—such as confidentiality requirements. In other cases, a party may assign its rights to another company. For example, the other business may be sold to another company. Our clause says that in either case, the new parties will get the benefits of the agreement—and will be bound by its requirements. If that's not what you want to happen, you can customize the agreement.

h. Severability

If a court finds any provision of this Agreement invalid or unenforceable, the remainder of this Agreement will be interpreted so as best to carry out the parties' intent.

This clause—which lawyers call a severability clause—provides that if you wind up in a lawsuit over the agreement and a court rules that one part of the agreement is invalid, that part can be cut out but the rest of the agreement will remain valid. If you don't include a clause like this and some portion of your agreement is deemed invalid, then the whole agreement may be canceled.

31. Signatures

Each party represents and warrants that on this date they are duly authorized to bind their respective principals by their signatures below.

The end of the main body of the agreement should contain spaces for the parties to sign. See Chapter 1 for a detailed discussion of how to sign agreements.

32. Attachments

Make sure that all the attachments are attached to all copies of the agreement. Each attachment should be consecutively numbered or lettered ("A,B,C" or "1,2,3"). Also, the references to the attachments in the main body of the agreement should match the actual attachments. The attachments to the agreement will include:

a. Attachment 1: development stages and due dates

ATTACHMENT 1: DEVELOPMENT STAGES AND DUE DATES

Development Services shall consist of four stages:

Stage	Services	Due Date
Concept	The parties will discuss and agree upon the basic concept for the Client website and Developer shall prepare a written summary of the basic elements of the website's functionality and appearance.	Within ____ days of the effective date.
Design	The parties will discuss and agree upon the design of the Client website and Developer shall prepare a detailed summary of the proposed appearance, operation, and functionality including a list of all necessary software and materials necessary to launch the Site.	Within ____ days of the approval of the Concept Stage.
Initial Development	During Initial Development, Developer shall prepare the following Web pages for the Site _____ _____ and demonstrate the following functionality for the Site _____	Within ____ days of the approval of the Design Stage.
Final Development	Developer will complete all requirements for the Site and host it in a manner that Client can view it for a period of at least ____ days.	Within ____ days of the approval of the Initial Development Stage.

For information on completing this attachment, see Section 2, above.

b. Attachment 2: optional maintenance and new development agreement

---

Maintenance and New Development

Following launch of the Site, Developer will provide the following services at the following rates:

Service	Rate
Technical support necessary to maintain reliable performance of the features and functionality of the Site	_____ per month
Consulting and new development services	_____ per hour

Client will pay Developer within 30 days of receiving Developer's invoice. Client grants to Developer a license to reproduce and modify the Site content to provide these services.

---

c. Attachment 3: developer's list of developer tools

Developer Tools include, but are not limited to, the following:

_____

_____

_____

_____

For information on completing this attachment, see Section 11, above. ■

Custom Software Development Agreement

This chapter covers contracts for the developer of custom software. It is written primarily from the developer's point of view, but contains much useful information for custom software customers as well. There is no standard definition of "custom" software. In this chapter, the term is used to mean software—usually an entire system—created specially for a particular customer. But custom software need not be created entirely from scratch. Many of the components of the system may have been used by the developer before (and may be used again for other customers). As long as the system as a whole is unique, it fits the custom software definition.

A. Introduction

Contrary to conventional wisdom, a developer does not benefit by starting work immediately on the basis of a handshake or a brief letter that sets forth the contract price and a vague description of the project. Unfortunately, many development projects are handled in just this way. However, this approach is a recipe for disaster. If problems later develop—particularly if the customer had unrealistic expectations or failed to understand exactly what the developer agreed to do—the developer will have no contract to fall back on for help. That piece of paper—the development contract—is the developer's lifeline. If properly drafted, it will help prevent disputes by making it clear exactly what's been agreed to. If problems develop, the agreement will provide ways to solve them. If the parties end up in court, the agreement will establish their legal duties to each other.

Negotiating a contract can take some time and effort, but by using the phased approach advocated in Section A1, below, the delay should be minimized. Under this approach, the contract can be signed on the basis of a simple functional specification, without going to the time and effort of creating final detailed specifications or a delivery and payment schedule—usually the most time-consuming parts of a development agreement. These are created later as part of the first phase of the project.

1. Phased Agreements Work Best

It's almost always advisable to break down a custom software development project into discrete parts or stages, often called phases or "milestones." At the end of each stage, the developer delivers an acceptable product. Having the customer sign off on each phase of the project avoids claims of unsatisfactory performance by the customer at the conclusion of the project.

The phased approach also allows the developer an opportunity to deal with the customer's changing needs and wants. Few software projects ever completely follow the original specifications. The project usually grows as the work is done and the developer and customer get ideas for a better (and usually more complex) project. Moreover, continuous operating system improvements often guarantee major changes in the course of development, especially if the project takes more than a year. At the very least, a custom software development project should consist of two phases:

- **Specification phase.** The developer prepares a detailed design specification and proposes a completion schedule. In the model development agreement, the developer includes these items as part of a development plan to be provided to the customer. (See Section B3 below.)
- **Development phase.** If the customer is satisfied with the detailed specifications, the customer typically pays a specified sum and the developer commences to create the software.

If the customer is not satisfied with the detailed specifications, the developer either revises them or the contract is canceled. It's usually best for the parties to go their separate ways if they can't reach some sort of agreement up front on detailed project specifications. If the contract is canceled, the developer is still entitled to be paid for the time and expense involved in creating the development plan.

Most custom software projects are too lengthy and complex to be divided into only two phases. After the initial specifications phase is completed, the customer will want the developer to deliver specified portions of the system as they are completed. In some cases, these system portions can run independently of each other so they can be tested as soon as they are completed.

2. Who Writes the Contract?

We recommend that a developer present the customer with a form agreement to review. The initial draft may undergo many changes, but it serves as the basis for the final contract.

 The full text of a Custom Software Development Agreement is on the CD-ROM forms disk.

B. Contents of Custom Software Development Agreements

Open the file now. The sample form contains a number of blank spaces to fill in and several alternative provisions you must choose from. The following section explains each section of the agreement and provides guidance on how to complete it.

1. Identification of the Parties

This Agreement is made between _____ [NAME OF CUSTOMER] (the "Customer") with a principal place of business at _____ [ADDRESS] and _____ [NAME OF SOFTWARE DEVELOPER] (the "Developer") with a principal place of business at _____ [ADDRESS].

Here at the beginning of the contract, both parties should list their full business names. Later on in the contract, you can use obvious abbreviations. For detailed information on identifying the parties, see Chapter 17, Section A.

2. Purpose of Agreement

Customer desires to retain Developer as an independent contractor to develop the computer software (the "Software") described in the Functional Specifications contained in Exhibit ___ attached to and made part of this Agreement. Developer is ready, willing, and able to undertake the development of the Software and agrees to do so under the terms and conditions set forth in this Agreement. Accordingly, the parties agree as follows:

It is customary to briefly state at the beginning the reason for the contract. This helps establish the parties' intent to create a legally binding contract, and may be helpful if the contract has to be interpreted and enforced by a judge or arbitrator, perhaps years after it was written. Note that the functional specifications, which describe the software in detail, should be attached to the agreement as an exhibit. (Functional specifications are discussed in Section A1, above.)

3. Preparation of Development Plan

Developer shall prepare a development plan ("Development Plan") for the Software, satisfying the requirements set forth in the Functional Specifications. The Development Plan shall include:

(a) detailed Specifications for the Software;

(b) a listing of all items to be delivered to Customer under this Agreement ("Deliverables");

(c) a delivery schedule containing a delivery date for each Deliverable; and

[OPTIONAL: INCLUDE IF DEVELOPER IS PAID FIXED PRICE FOR PROJECT] (d) a payment schedule setting forth the amount and time of Developer's compensation.

Developer shall deliver the Development Plan to Customer by [DEVELOPMENT PLAN DEADLINE]. Customer shall have [NUMBER OF DAYS TO REVIEW] days to review the Development Plan. Upon approval of the Development Plan by Customer, it will be marked as Exhibit __ and will be deemed by both parties to have become a part of this Agreement and will be incorporated by reference. Developer shall then commence development of Software that will substantially conform to the requirements set forth in the Development Plan.

If the Development Plan is in Customer's reasonable judgment unsatisfactory in any material respect, Customer shall prepare a detailed written description of the objections. Customer shall deliver such objections to Developer within [NUMBER OF DAYS TO OBJECT] days of receipt of the Development Plan. Developer shall then have [NUMBER OF DAYS TO MODIFY] days to modify the Development Plan to respond to Customer's objections. Customer shall have [NUMBER OF DAYS TO RE-REVIEW] days to review the modified Development Plan. If Customer deems the modified Development Plan to be unacceptable, Customer has the option of terminating this Agreement upon written notice to Developer or permitting Developer to modify the Development Plan again under the procedure outlined in this paragraph. If this Agreement is terminated, the obligations of both parties under it shall end except for Customer's obligation to pay Developer all sums due for preparing the Development Plan and the ongoing obligations of confidentiality set forth in the provision of this Agreement entitled "Confidentiality."

[OPTIONAL; FOR USE IF DEVELOPER IS NOT PAID ON HOURLY BASIS] Payment for Development Plan: If the Development Plan is not accepted by Customer and Customer terminates this Agreement, Developer shall be entitled to compensation on a time and materials basis at an hourly rate of $[HOURLY RATE] plus expenses to the date of termination. Developer shall submit an invoice detailing its time and expenses preparing the Development Plan. If the invoice amount is less than the amounts paid to Developer prior to termination, Developer shall promptly return the excess to Customer. If the invoice amount exceeds the amounts paid to Developer prior to termination, Customer shall promptly pay Developer the difference. [OPTIONAL: "However, Developer's total compensation for preparing the Development Plan shall not exceed $[AMOUNT]."]

The first phase of the project is the developer's preparation of a software development plan. The development plan should show the customer what the developer intends to do and how long it will take. In this clause, the customer's commitment to proceed with the project is contingent upon its acceptance of the development plan. This protects both the customer and developer. The customer's financial exposure is minimized: If the design fails to meet its original expectation, it can terminate the contract and seek a new developer without much loss. The developer is protected by having the customer agree in writing to the detailed specifications and delivery schedule before it actually starts to create the software. This prevents later claims that the finished product doesn't meet the customer's requirements.

This provision also gives the developer time to cure any deficiencies in the plan before the customer may terminate the contract. This seems only fair given the substantial investment of time and effort the developer will usually expend to create a development plan.

Following are the key points the agreement addresses:

a. Specifications

Before the development agreement is signed, the customer (often with the aid of a computer consultant), or the developer, should create a functional specification describing the software in general terms. The developer will use the functional specifications as a guide in creating a far more technical detailed specification. The detailed specifications serve as the final project blueprint. They describe the project in a very precise technical manner and should provide the developer with all the information it needs to actually create the software.

It can be difficult or impossible for a technically unsophisticated customer to get a feel for how the proposed software will function from written specifications. For this reason, the developer may be asked to create a prototype of the actual system. The prototype should include a complete set of proposed report formats, screen displays, and menus so that the customer can review the program's customer interface. The prototype can be done either by hand on "storyboards," or on computer, using readily available software.

b. Deliverables

The development plan should list all deliverables—that is, every item the customer wants the developer to provide. This includes not only the software itself, but the program and customer documentation as well.

Following is a checklist of deliverables for a typical software project:

- final specifications for the completed software, showing any changes from the specifications contained in the Development Plan
- complete customer documentation, including a description of how to access and use each application, screen prints of menus and input/output screens, data input descriptions, sample output/report forms, error code descriptions and solutions where appropriate, and explanations of all necessary disks and data used by the software
- complete program/technical documentation, including technical information about files and their locations, file names, file/database structure, record structure, and layout and data elements
- if the customer will receive a copy of the source code, program source code listings with comments
- description of backup and recovery procedures, including process, medium for backup, and number of diskettes or tapes to do a complete backup, and
- master copy of software on magnetic media, including all programs, online documentation, and any documentation developed on computer.

c. Delivery schedule

The development plan should also include a schedule showing when each deliverable will be completed. The developer must take care that the delivery schedule provides sufficient time to complete the project. Developers tend to be incorrigible optimists, so they constantly underestimate how long development projects will take. It's best for the developer to be realistic up front, and not promise the customer what it can't deliver. Since delays are so common, the development agreement should state how delays will be dealt with. (See Section 9, below.)

d. Payment for development plan

Drafting a development plan—particularly the specifications—is difficult and time-consuming. Thus, the developer should be compensated for its efforts fairly. Where the developer is being paid a fixed price, it normally receives a portion as a down payment upon execution of the contract. If the plan is not accepted and the contract is canceled, the down payment may provide the developer with too little or too much money for the work it did on the plan.

This clause deals with this problem by providing that the developer will be paid on a "time and materials" basis for the development plan if the plan is not accepted and the contract is canceled. ("Time and materials" means the developer is paid for its time and actual costs.) If this amount is less than the down payment, the developer must return the excess to the customer. This paragraph need not be included in contracts in which the developer is to be paid on an ongoing hourly basis (see Section 4a, below). It would merely be redundant.

4. Payment

There are two basic ways to pay a developer for creating custom software:

- a pay per hour ("time and materials") agreement, or
- a fixed price agreement.

a. Alternative 1: "time and materials" agreements

Developer shall be compensated at the rate of $[RATE] per hour [OR "day," "week," "month"]. Payment will be made within [NUMBER OF DAYS] days of Developer's submission of an invoice for work completed. [OPTIONAL: "Unless otherwise agreed upon in writing by Customer, Customer's maximum liability for all services performed during the term of this Agreement shall not exceed $[MAXIMUM AMOUNT]."]

Under a "time and materials" agreement, the developer charges the customer by the hour, day, or month at a flat hourly cost. This is by far the safest way to be paid if it's difficult to estimate exactly how long a project will take. However, many clients will wish to place a cap on your total compensation because they're afraid you'll "pad" your bill. If this is the case, include the optional sentence providing for a cap, but make sure it's large enough to allow you to complete the job.

b. Alternative 2: fixed price agreements

The total contract price shall be set forth in the Development Plan. Customer shall pay the Developer the sum of $[INITIAL AMOUNT] upon execution of this Agreement and the sum of $[AMOUNT IF PLAN APPROVED] upon Customer's approval of the Development Plan. The remainder of the contract price shall be payable in installments according to the payment schedule to be included in the Development Plan.

Each installment shall be payable upon completion of each project phase by Developer and acceptance by Customer in accordance with the provision of this Agreement entitled "Acceptance Testing of Software."

The other payment option is for the customer to pay the developer a fixed price for the entire project. In theory, this payment scheme favors the customer by giving the customer certainty as to what the project will cost. Moreover, if payments are tied to the progress of the developer's work, it gives the customer substantial leverage to insist on timely and successful completion of the project.

At first glance, fixed-price agreements would seem to be risky for developers: If the project takes much longer than originally anticipated, the developer could end up losing money. However, as a practical matter, fixed-price agreements usually do not end up favoring the customer as much as one would think. If it turns out that the fixed-price originally agreed upon will not provide the developer with fair compensation, because the project ends up taking too long, the customer will probably end up agreeing to pay the developer more money. Otherwise the developer may quit or end up delivering a hastily completed and shoddy product.

The developer's fixed-price quote should be included in the Development Plan, which will also contain the detailed specifications, deliverables list, and delivery schedule. Obviously, the developer should complete these last three items, particularly the detailed specification, be-

fore deciding how much to charge for the entire project. Only at this point can the developer have a reasonably accurate idea of how much time the project will require.

Fixed-price contracts are normally paid in installments, with payment of each installment tied to completion and acceptance of a phase of the project. In addition, an initial down payment is usually made when the contract is signed. This provision requires that a payment schedule be included as part of the development plan, which will be attached to the contract as an exhibit. The developer should make sure that the schedule requires the customer to make regular periodic payments so that the developer can meet its own financial obligations.

The amount of the down payment is often a point of contention in fixed-price contracts. Naturally, the developer should obtain as large a down payment as possible.

5. Payment of Developer's Costs

Whether a fixed-price or time and materials payment arrangement is used, the developer is usually reimbursed by the customer for at least some out-of-pocket expenses incurred in performing its duties under the contract. The extent of such reimbursement is a matter for negotiation.

a. Alternative 1: full reimbursement:

Customer shall reimburse Developer for all out-of-pocket expenses incurred by Developer in performing services under this Agreement. Such expenses include, but are not limited, to:

(a) all communications charges;

(b) costs for providing conversion services for converting Customer's database;

(c) media costs;

(d) travel expenses other than normal commuting, including airfares, rental vehicles, and highway mileage in company or personal vehicles at __ cents per mile; and

(e) other expenses resulting from the work performed under this Agreement.

Developer shall submit an itemized statement of Developer's expenses. Customer shall pay Developer within 30 days from the date of each statement.

The first alternative calls for payment of all the developer's out-of-pocket expenses; this may include items like communications charges (telephone, fax, postage, etc.).

Alternative 2—Partial reimbursement: One problem with the first alternative is that many government agencies consider payment of a worker's ordinary business expenses to be a mild indicator of an employment relationship.

b. Alternative 2: partial reimbursement

Customer shall reimburse Developer for all reasonable travel and living expenses necessarily incurred by Developer while away from Developer's regular place of business and engaged in the performance of services under this Agreement.

The second alternative clause limits reimbursement to extraordinary expenses, such as nonlocal travel, and will not be viewed as indicative of an employee-employer relationship.

6. Late Fees

Late payments by Customer shall be subject to late penalty fees of _____% per month from the due date until the amount is paid.

Many developers charge a late fee if the customer doesn't pay within the time specified in the development agreement or invoice. Charging late fees for overdue payments can get customers to pay on time. The late fee is normally expressed as a monthly interest charge—for example, 1% per month.

If you wish to charge a late fee, make sure it's mentioned in your agreement. You should also clearly state what your late fee is on all your invoices.

7. Materials

Customer shall make available to Developer, at Customer's expense, the following materials, facilities, and equipment:

_____

[LIST]. These items will be provided to Customer by _____ [DATE].

8. Changes in Project Scope

If at any time following acceptance of the Development Plan by Customer, Customer should desire a change in Developer's performance under this Agreement that will alter or amend the Specifications or other elements of the Development Plan, Customer shall submit to Developer a written proposal specifying the desired changes.

Developer will evaluate each such proposal at its standard rates and charges. Developer shall submit to Customer a written response to each such proposal within ten working days following receipt thereof. Developer's written response shall include a statement of the availability of Developer's personnel and resources, as well as any impact the proposed changes will have on the contract price, delivery dates, or warranty provisions of this Agreement.

Changes to the Development Plan shall be evidenced by a "Development Plan Modification Agreement." The Development Plan Modification Agreement shall amend the Development Plan appropriately to incorporate the desired changes and acknowledge any effect of such changes on the provisions of this Agreement. The Development Plan Modification Agreement shall be signed by authorized representatives of Customer and Developer, whereupon Developer shall commence performance in accordance with it.

Should Developer not approve the Development Plan Modification Agreement as written, Developer will so notify Customer within ten working days of Developer's receipt of the Development Plan Modification Agreement. Developer shall not be obligated to perform any services beyond those called for in the Development Plan prior to its approval of the Development Plan Modification Agreement.

For purposes of this Agreement, each Development Plan Modification Agreement duly authorized in writing by Customer and Developer shall be deemed incorporated into and made part of this Agreement. Each such Development Plan Modification Agreement shall constitute a formal change to this Agreement adjusting fees and completion dates as finally agreed upon.

If the client will provide you with any materials or equipment, list them in this optional clause. If you need these items by a specific date, specify the deadline as well.

It's quite common in the course of software development for the customer to wish to make changes—adding new features and/or deleting others. Of course, any changes to the specifications or any other provision of the contract should be in writing and signed by both parties to be effective. (This is required by Section 27(b) in the agreement.)

Major changes in the scope of the project may greatly increase—or decrease—the amount of work the developer has to do. If the developer is paid a fixed fee, it is only fair that its compensation should be increased or decreased to reflect the change in the workload. This usually is not an issue where the developer is paid by the hour; but if there is a cap on the total hourly compensation to be paid, the cap may have to be increased.

Changes in the scope of the project may also require changes in proposed delivery dates, and perhaps in the contract's warranty provisions. (Warranties are discussed in Section 16.)

This provision sets forth a procedure for the parties to follow if the customer wants to change the specifications or other parts of the development plan. First, the customer must submit a written proposal to the developer showing the desired changes. The developer then responds to this proposal in writing, stating, among other things, what impact the desired changes will have on the contract price and delivery schedule. If the customer wants to go ahead with the changes, it submits a "Development Plan Modification Agreement" specifying all the agreed-upon changes and their effect on the provisions of the Agreement. The developer has ten days to accept or reject the Development Plan Modification Agreement.

In many instances, the developer, not the customer, will wish to alter the specifications. This may be because the specifications contain an error, do not accurately reflect the customer's true needs, or the project as originally agreed upon proves commercially unfeasible for a developer being paid a fixed fee. All such changes should be in writing and signed by both parties as required by the clause dealing with modifications to the agreement.

9. Delays

Developer shall use all reasonable efforts to deliver the Software on schedule. However, at its option, Developer can extend the due date for any Deliverable by giving written notice to Customer. The total of all such extensions shall not exceed ___ [NUMBER] of days.

Any delay or nonperformance of any provision of this Agreement caused by conditions beyond the reasonable control of the performing party shall not constitute a breach of this Agreement, provided that the delayed party has taken reasonable measures to notify the other of the delay in writing. The delayed party's time for performance shall be deemed to be extended for a period equal to the duration of the conditions beyond its control.

Conditions beyond a party's reasonable control include, but are not limited to, natural disasters, acts of government after the date of the Agreement, power failure, fire, flood, acts of God, labor disputes, riots, acts of war, and epidemics. Failure of subcontractors and inability to obtain materials shall not be considered a condition beyond a party's reasonable control.

It is rare for custom software to be completed and delivered by the developer exactly on schedule. There are many reasons for this. Estimating how long it will take to create new software is an uncertain art at best (exacerbated by the fact that most programmers are incorrigible optimists and many customers are terminally impatient). Delays may also result if the developer has staffing changes or increased demands on existing staff.

The first paragraph of this section is designed to give the developer some leeway in the delivery schedule. Any deadline can be extended by the developer by giving the customer written notice. However, a cap is placed on the total of all the extensions. You need to decide how many days this cap should be.

Sometimes a project is delayed due to circumstances beyond the developer's control—for example, where an earthquake, fire, or other act of God destroys or severely damages the developer's office and equipment. In this event, it is only fair that the developer's delay be excused. A special provision (often called a "force majeure" clause) is commonly included in development contracts to excuse a party's nonperformance due to circumstances beyond its control. The second and third paragraphs of this section contain such a provision.

10. Acceptance Testing of Software

"Acceptance testing" is a procedure by which the software is tested to see if it satisfies the detailed specifications set forth in the Development Plan. Acceptance testing is one of the most important phases of the software development process. The purpose is to determine whether the software does what it is supposed to do and is reliable. Particularly where safety is involved (for example, software implemented in a "911" service or designed to run an elevator), the software should be tested as thoroughly as possible.

The acceptance testing should force the software to perform repeatedly, without failure, on a variety of the customer's actual data, with speed and accuracy to match the specifications. It is also a good idea to stress-test a system—that is, try to break it—to see how it recovers. Each section of the software should be tested independently and in combination with other sections.

The nature of the tests to be performed, the data to be used, and the procedure to be followed should be defined by the parties before the testing begins. In many cases, the acceptance tests cannot be well defined until the final specifications are agreed upon or even until the software is completed. The specifications for acceptance testing should be included as part of the development plan. Of course, these specifications may be subsequently modified by the parties.

Unfortunately, many bugs will not be discovered during acceptance testing. Some bugs appear only after many hundreds or thousands of customer hours. For this reason, it's common for the developer to agree to fix bugs free of charge for a stated period after the software is accepted—usually 90 days to a year. (See Section 12, below, for a detailed discussion.)

Trivial Bugs

No software is absolutely perfect. It is impossible for a developer to create software of any complexity that is completely bug-free. However, there is a big difference between true bugs—defects that prevent the software from performing the customer's required tasks satisfactorily—and interface and peripheral glitches and other minor irritants that don't materially affect the software's performance. A developer should never promise that its software will be completely bug-free. (See the discussion in Section 16, below.) Moreover, the acceptance criteria should be designed so as to overlook trivial bugs that can simply be ignored.

a. Alternative 1: acceptance testing provision for multiphase projects

Immediately upon completion of each development phase set forth in the Development Plan's delivery schedule, Developer shall deliver and install the Software and shall deliver all documentation and other materials required to be provided in accordance with the delivery schedule. Customer shall have [NUMBER OF TESTING DAYS] days from the delivery of the Software to inspect, test, and evaluate it to determine whether the Software satisfies the acceptance criteria in accordance with procedures set forth in the Development Plan, or as established by Developer and approved by Customer prior to testing.

If the Software does not satisfy the acceptance criteria, Customer shall give Developer written notice stating why the Software is unacceptable. Developer shall have 30 days from the receipt of such notice to correct the deficiencies. Customer shall then have 30 days to inspect, test, and reevaluate the Software. If the Software still does not satisfy the acceptance criteria, Customer shall have the option of either: (1) repeating the procedure set forth above, or (2) terminating this Agreement pursuant to the section of this Agreement entitled "Termination." If Customer does not give written notice to Developer within the initial 30-day inspection, testing, and evaluation period or any extension of that period, that the Software does not satisfy the acceptance criteria, Customer shall be deemed to have accepted the Software upon expiration of such period.

Upon completion of the final development phase set out in the Development Plan, acceptance testing shall be performed on the Software in its entirety to determine whether the Software satisfies the acceptance criteria and operates with internal consistency. Customer shall have [NUMBER OF TESTING DAYS FOR FINAL PRODUCT] days to perform such tests. If the completed Software does not satisfy the acceptance criteria, the parties shall follow the acceptance procedures described in the preceding paragraph [OPTIONAL: except that the time periods for corrections, inspection, reevaluation, and notice shall be increased to ___ [NUMBER] days] [END OF OPTION].

[INCLUDE IN FIXED PRICE CONTRACTS: If and when the acceptance tests establish that the Software delivered upon completion of any phase of development complies with the acceptance criteria, Customer shall promptly notify Developer that it accepts the delivered Software.] [END ALTERNATIVE 1]

Complex software systems often consist of a number of independent units or "modules" that can be tested when completed. This way, the customer doesn't have to wait until the entire project is finished to test the software and see how the work is progressing. Of course, the schedule for delivery of each portion of the system should be set forth in detail in the development plan's delivery schedule.

If the software does not satisfy the acceptance criteria, the customer should explain the problems to the developer and then give it an opportunity to correct them. Developers are typically given 30 days to make corrections, but more time may be required if the software is extremely complex. If the developer cannot make the corrections, or redelivers software that is still nonconforming, the customer should have the option of giving the developer more time or terminating the contract.

When all phases of development are completed, the software should be tested in its entirety. The same acceptance procedure is used as for testing each phase, except that optional language allows the time periods for the developer's corrections and the customer's review and reevaluation to be increased beyond the 30 days allowed for acceptance of each phase; 30 days may simply not be enough time to test and evaluate the entire program.

b. Alternative 2: testing when project completed

> Customer shall have 30 days from the date of delivery of the Software in final form to inspect, test, and evaluate it to determine whether the Software satisfies the acceptance criteria in accordance with procedures set forth in the Development Plan, or as established by Developer and approved by Customer prior to testing.
>
> If the Software does not satisfy the acceptance criteria, Customer shall give Developer written notice stating why the Software is unacceptable. Developer shall have 30 days from the receipt of such notice to correct the deficiencies. Customer shall then have 30 days to inspect, test, and evaluate the Software. If the Software still does not satisfy the acceptance criteria, Customer shall have the option of either (1) repeating the procedure set forth above, or (2) terminating this Agreement pursuant to the section of this Agreement entitled "Termination." If Customer does not give written notice to Developer within the initial 30-day inspection, testing, and evaluation period or any extension of that period, that the Software does not satisfy the acceptance criteria, Customer shall be deemed to have accepted the Software upon expiration of such period.

Some types of software really can't be tested until the entire system is completed and running, except perhaps the print and display functions. This clause is a simpler acceptance testing provision designed to be used where serious testing won't be conducted until the software is delivered in final form. This provision should also be used for projects where the entire program will be delivered at one time, rather than in phases.

11. Training

Developer shall provide [NUMBER OF TRAINING DAYS] days of training in the use of the Software by at least one (but not more than [MAXIMUM NUMBER OF TRAINERS]) qualified Developer personnel ("trainers"). The training will be conducted on such dates and locations as the parties may agree.

Customer will be responsible for all costs and expenses of all Customer's trainees, including room, board, transportation, salary, insurance and other benefits, and other expenses while attending the training.

[OPTIONAL:] Customer shall pay Developer the sum of $[AMOUNT] for each [HOUR/ DAY] of training by each trainer, plus each trainer's travel expenses. [END OPTION 2]

The customer and/or its employees will usually have to be trained how to use the software. This provision requires the developer to conduct training. Where the developer is paid a fixed fee, the cost of training can be included in the overall fee. However, where the developer is paid on an hourly basis, it will have to be paid extra for training. In either event, the customer should be responsible for its own costs associated with such training.

12. Maintenance of Software

Beginning on the first day of the first month following expiration of the warranty period set forth in the section of this Agreement entitled "Warranties," Developer shall provide the following error-correction and support services:

(a) telephone hot-line support during Developer's normal days and hours of business operation. Such support shall include consultation on the operation and utilization of the Software. Customer shall be responsible for all telephone equipment and communication charges related to such support; and

(b) error-correction services, consisting of Developer using all reasonable efforts to design, code, and implement programming changes to the Software, and modifications to the documentation, to correct reproducible errors therein so that the Software is brought into substantial conformance with the Specifications.

Payment for Maintenance: Customer shall pay Developer for error-correction and support services the annual sum of $[MAINTENANCE AMOUNT], payable in quarterly installments beginning on the first day of the first month following expiration of any warranty period. Three years after the date of Customer's final acceptance of the Software, Developer shall be entitled to increases in the maintenance fee upon at least ten days' prior written notice to Customer.

Customer's Role in Maintenance: The provision of the error-correction and support services described above shall be expressly contingent upon Customer promptly reporting any errors in the Software or related documentation to Developer in writing and not modifying the Software without Developer's written consent.

Term of Support: Subject to timely payment by Customer of the maintenance fees, Developer shall offer the maintenance described above for a minimum of [NUMBER OF YEARS] years after completion of the development work under this Agreement.

Customer Termination of Maintenance: Customer may discontinue the maintenance services described above upon not less than 90 days' written notice to Developer.

"Maintenance" is a term used for upkeep of software after it has been put into operation. There are two types of maintenance:

- fixing bugs (sometimes called "remedial maintenance"), and
- modifying and/or enhancing software because the customer's needs have changed (sometimes called "adaptive maintenance").

It can cost far more to maintain software than to develop it in the first place. Many developers consider maintenance to be a nuisance and would prefer to use their resources on other new development projects. Such developers want to terminate their work for the customer upon delivery and acceptance of the software. The customer, on the other hand, needs someone to maintain the software. It is often most efficient for the persons who originally create a piece of software to maintain it. Their familiarity with the original software's design should enable them to do a better job than someone who is completely new to the software.

Typically, custom software development agreements contain a warranty in which the developer promises to fix any bugs for free for a limited time—usually 90 days to a year. (See Section 16, below, for a detailed discussion.) The following provision addresses post-warranty remedial maintenance (bug correction) only. Adaptive maintenance (enhancements

and modifications) should be handled in a separate agreement.

This provision requires the developer to perform remedial maintenance and provide telephone hotline support after the warranty expires. The customer pays the developer an annual fee for this service. Note that the provision applies only to "reproducible errors ... so that the Software is brought into substantial conformance with the Specifications." This protects the developer from committing to fix trivial errors or errors that may occur only once in many thousands of hours of operation and that cannot be readily reproduced.

13. Ownership of Software

The moment computer code is written, it is protected by copyright and someone becomes the owner of that copyright. Similarly, patent and trade secret ownership rights may come into existence. Many software developers and customers harbor the misapprehension that, since the developer is being paid to create the software by the customer, the customer will automatically own all rights to it. This is not the case. Absent a written contract transferring ownership from the developer to the customer, the developer will most likely own the copyright in the software (unless the developer is considered the customer's employee or, perhaps, if it was part of a larger work and was prepared under a written work for hire agreement).

One of the most important functions of a software development agreement is to establish exactly who will own the intellectual property rights to the software to be created. This is often one of the most hotly contested issues between the developer and customer, and can easily become a "deal breaker." Ownership rules for intellectual property are covered in detail in Chapter 11. This section focuses on how to handle these issues in a custom software development agreement.

⚠ Ownership Isn't Intellectual Property Ownership. Owning the material object in which software is embodied—whether a CD-ROM, hard disk, or other medium—is separate and distinct from intellectual property ownership. When a customer is given a disk containing a software program written by the developer, the customer owns that disk—no one can legally take it away from him—but the customer cannot exercise any of the developer's exclusive copyright rights in the software contained on that disk absent a transfer (license or sale) of such rights from the developer to the customer.

This means that the customer could not legally make more than one archival copy of the software, could not distribute it to the public, and could not create derivative works based upon it—modified versions, for example. This is what we're talking about when we discuss software

ownership—ownership of intangible intellectual property rights—not ownership of disks or other media.

Ownership issues are critically important for the developer. If a developer signs a contract with a customer transferring its ownership of the intellectual property rights in the software, the developer can never use, sell, or license that software again. A developer who signs such a contract may end up giving up far more than it actually realized or intended—it may lose the ability to do similar work for other customers in the future.

We emphasized the "may" above because no one knows exactly to what extent computer software is protected by the law. It is clear that copyright protects source code, so a developer who relinquishes copyright ownership in a program may not use that same source code again unless provisions for such use are made as part of the transaction (or in a later license). But copyright protection might go beyond a program's literal source code—for instance, to the structure, sequence and organization of the code.

The potential problems do not end here. Copyright does not protect ideas, concepts, know-how, techniques, formulae, or algorithms. However, these items may be protected by trade secrecy or, in some instances, patents. Thus, a developer that relinquishes all its intellectual property rights in the software it creates for a customer could conceivably be barred by trade secrecy or patent law from using similar ideas, techniques, and so forth in other programs.

The moral is this: A developer should make sure that it either retains enough ownership rights in what it creates to allow it to continue to do similar development work for other customers, or obtains enough money from the customer to compensate it for the possible lost future business.

One way a developer can protect its future business is to obtain a nonexclusive license to use the software. Another is to retain ownership of the software and provide the customer with a license to use the software. Both these options are discussed below. In addition, the developer should be careful to retain ownership of its "background technology." That includes the programs and materials that the developer uses over and over again in most or all of its projects—such as routines for displaying menus, document assembly, and printing. (See Section 14 for a detailed discussion.)

Four ownership alternatives are provided:

- sole ownership by the customer
- ownership by developer with an exclusive license to customer
- ownership by developer with a nonexclusive license to customer, and
- joint ownership.

a. Alternative 1: ownership by customer

Developer assigns to Customer its entire right, title, and interest in anything created or developed by Developer for Customer under this Agreement ("Work Product") including all patents, copyrights, trade secrets, and other proprietary rights. This assignment is conditioned upon full payment of the compensation due Developer under this Agreement.

Developer shall execute and aid in the preparation of any documents necessary to secure any copyright, patent, or other intellectual property rights in the Work Product at no charge to client. However, Customer shall reimburse Developer for reasonable out-of-pocket expenses.

[OPTIONAL:] Customer grants to Developer a nonexclusive, [CHOOSE ONE: "irrevocable license" OR "license for the term of [NUMBER OF YEARS] years"] to use the Work Product. [ADD ANY PAYMENT PROVISIONS OR OTHER RESTRICTIONS] [END ALTERNATIVE 1]

Because they are paying the developer to create the software, some customers insist on receiving sole ownership. The following clause grants all ownership rights in the software to the customer, with no restrictions. Typically, a developer that relinquishes all its ownership rights will demand more payment than if it were allowed to retain at least some ownership and profit from the software by licensing it to others.

As mentioned above, an assignment of all of the developer's rights means that the developer may not use the software created for the customer, for example, by including part of it in a program created for someone else. This can work a substantial hardship on the developer, especially one that regularly works on similar types of software.

One way a developer can make such an ownership transfer more palatable is to have the customer grant the developer back a nonexclusive license to use the software. A nonexclusive license gives someone the right to use software or other copyrighted work, but does not prevent the copyright owners from granting others the same rights at the same time.

The license can be limited in any way—such as in duration, or in the type of software in which it can be used. For example, the developer can be barred from using the software to help the customer's named competitors or from developing similar types of products. The optional provision granting a license to the developer would be used in addition to the assignment from developer to customer.

b. Alternative 2: ownership by developer with exclusive license to customer

> Developer shall retain all copyright, patent, trade secret, and other intellectual property rights Developer may have in anything created or developed by Developer for Customer under this Agreement ("Work Product"). Developer grants Customer a nontransferable license to use the Work Product. The license is conditioned upon full payment of the compensation due Developer under this Agreement.
>
> The license shall be exclusive in [NAME TERRITORIES, SUCH AS "the United States"] for a period of [TIME PERIOD] following acceptance by Customer of the Software as set forth in this Agreement. The license shall automatically revert to a perpetual nonexclusive license following the period of exclusivity.
>
> The license shall authorize Customer to:
>
> (a) install the Software on computer systems owned, leased, or otherwise controlled by Customer;
>
> (b) utilize the Software for its internal data-processing purposes (but not for time-sharing or service bureau purposes); and
>
> (c) copy the Software only as necessary to exercise the rights granted in this Agreement.

Another option is for the developer to retain ownership of the software and give the customer an exclusive license to use it. (Nonexclusive licenses are covered below, in Alternative 3.)

With an exclusive license, only the customer has the right to use it—within the scope of the license. If an exclusive license gives the customer the right to use the software in every possible context at every possible location, it would be the functional equivalent of ownership. In practice, however, the parties usually agree to limit the customer's use rights. For example, the customer's right to use the software may be limited as to duration, area (worldwide or domestic), market, or hardware (the customer could be permitted to use the software only on a particular platform). Under this type of license, the developer would have the exclusive right to modify the software and could sell or license it to others outside the customer's area of exclusivity.

This type of arrangement often benefits both the customer and developer: The customer is assured that the developer will not sell or license the software to competitors during the term of the exclusive license. At the same time, the developer retains control over the software and will have the opportunity to earn income by licensing it to others outside the area of the customer's exclusivity and/or after the exclusive license expires.

This provision grants an exclusive license that is limited as to time. When the exclusive license expires, the customer receives a perpetual nonexclusive license, meaning that the developer is free to li-cense the software to others. This license is nontransferable—it does not permit the customer to sublicense the software to others, but this can be permitted if the parties desire. The license permits the customer to use the software on any number of computers for internal purposes and to make as many backup copies as it needs.

c. Alternative 3: ownership by developer with nonexclusive license to customer

Developer shall retain all copyright, patent, trade secret, and other intellectual property rights Developer may have in anything created or developed by Developer for Customer under this Agreement ("Work Product"). Subject to payment of all compensation due under this Agreement, Developer grants Customer a nonexclusive, nontransferable, royalty-free license to use the Work Product.

The license shall authorize Customer to:

(a) install the Software on computer systems owned, leased, or otherwise controlled by Customer;

(b) utilize the Software for its internal data-processing purposes (but not for time-sharing or service bureau purposes); and

(c) copy the Software only as necessary to exercise the rights granted in this Agreement.

The most favorable ownership arrangement for the developer may be for the customer to be given only a nonexclusive license to use the software. This means that the developer is free to license the software to anyone else, including the developer's competitors. This type of ownership arrangement would likely result in the lowest possible price to the customer, because the developer may earn additional income by licensing the software to others.

d. Alternative 4: joint ownership

> Developer hereby grants Customer an undivided one-half interest in the Software and associated documentation. The Software may be freely used by either party without accounting to the other party. Customer and Developer agree to execute all documents reasonably necessary to legally establish their joint ownership of the Software.

Yet another option is for the customer and developer to jointly own the software. Under a joint ownership arrangement, each party is free to use the software or grant nonexclusive licenses to third parties without the other's permission (unless they agree to restrict this right). Normally, joint owners must account for and share with each other any monies they earn from granting such licenses. This is probably not desirable in the developer-customer situation, so this provision specifically provides that neither party need account to the other—in other words, they need not share any money they earn from the software.

14. Ownership of Background Technology

> Customer acknowledges that Developer owns or holds a license to use and sublicense various preexisting development tools, routines, subroutines, and other programs, data, and materials that Developer may include in the Software developed under this Agreement. This material shall be referred to as "Background Technology." Developer's Background Technology includes, but is not limited to, those items identified in Exhibit __, attached to and made a part of this Agreement.
>
> Developer retains all right, title, and interest, including all copyright, patent rights, and trade secret rights in the Background Technology. Subject to full payment of the consulting fees due under this Agreement, Developer grants Customer a nonexclusive, perpetual worldwide license to use the Background Technology in the Software developed for and delivered to Customer under this Agreement, and all updates and revisions thereto. However, Customer shall make no other commercial use of the Background Technology without Developer's written consent.

A software developer will normally bring to the project various development tools, routines, subroutines, and other programs, data, and materials. One term for these items is "background technology." It's quite possible that background technology may end up in the final product. For example, this may include code used for installation, window manipulation, displaying menus, data searching, data storing, and printing.

If the developer transfers complete ownership of the software to the customer, the customer also may end up owning this background technology. Such an arrangement would prohibit the developer from using the background technology in other projects without obtaining the customer's permission (and perhaps paying a fee). A developer is usually well advised to avoid this problem by making sure the agreement provides that the developer retain all ownership rights in background technology. In this event, the agreement also should give the customer a nonexclusive license to use the background technology that's included in the customer's software.

This provision permits the customer to use the background technology as included in the software, but keeps ownership in the hands of the developer. The developer should prepare a separate exhibit that identifies in as much detail as possible the background technology to be included in the software.

This provision need not be included in a contract in which the developer retains ownership of the software.

Identify Background Technology

If possible, identify your background technology in the source code copies of the programs in any printouts of code you deliver to the customer. You might include a notice like the following where such material appears: "[Your Company Name] CONFIDENTIAL AND PROPRIETARY."

15. Source Code Access

Customer agrees that the Software developed under this Agreement shall be delivered to Customer in object code form only. Developer agrees that one copy of the source code version of the Software and associated documentation shall be deposited with an escrow agent specializing in software escrows to be mutually agreed upon in writing by Developer and Customer after good faith negotiation. Customer and Developer shall enter into a supplementary escrow agreement with the escrow agent.

The source code shall be delivered to the escrow agent within [NUMBER OF DAYS] days after delivery of the object code to Customer. Thereafter, the source code version of all updates, enhancements, and modifications of the Software created by Developer on Customer's behalf, as well as associated documentation, shall be deposited by Developer with the escrow agent. Customer shall pay all fees necessary to establish and maintain the escrow.

Developer hereby grants to Customer a contingent license to receive the source code from the escrow agent and to use the source code to support its use of the Software in machine-readable form if one or more of the following conditions occurs:

(a) Developer, whether directly or through a successor or affiliate, ceases to be in the software business.

(b) Developer fails to fulfill its obligations to maintain the Software as provided in this Agreement.

(c) Developer becomes insolvent or admits insolvency or a general inability to pay its debts as they become due.

(d) Developer files a petition for protection under the U.S. Bankruptcy Code, or an involuntary petition is filed against it and is not dismissed within 60 days.

[OPTIONAL:] (e) Developer comes under the control of a competitor of Customer. [END OPTION]

The source code shall be used solely by Customer to maintain the Software and shall be subject to every restriction on use set forth in this Agreement. Customer agrees not to disclose the source code to third parties except on a need-to-know basis under an appropriate duty of confidentiality.

If the customer obtains ownership of the software, it should receive the source code and system/program documentation created by the developer. But if the developer retains ownership and merely grants the customer a license to use the software, source code access can become an important issue.

Some clients insist on having access to the developer's source code. They're afraid the original developer won't be around months or years down the line when the software needs to be maintained, modified, or enhanced. They're afraid it will be difficult or impossible to do such work without the source code. However, as a practical matter, access to the source code is greatly overrated as a benefit for a software customer. The fact is, even with decent documentation, the expense involved in picking up somebody else's code is often greater than programming from scratch.

Software developers are understandably reluctant to give a customer a copy of their proprietary source code. A software developer's most important asset is usually its source code, which may contain highly valuable trade secrets. One way for a developer to deal with a client who demands access to the source code is to agree to a source code escrow.

Under a source code escrow agreement, the developer gives a copy of the source code and documentation to a neutral third party for safekeeping. The third party will release the source code to the customer only upon the occurrence of specified conditions, such as the developer's bankruptcy or failure to maintain the software. This keeps the developer's source code confidential while, in theory, assuring the customer access to it should it become necessary.

So long as the customer pays for the escrow and the conditions for its release are reasonable, this arrangement works well for the developer. It avoids giving the customer the source code outright.

Literally anybody can serve as the escrow agent. In the past, attorneys, accountants, and bank escrow departments have frequently been used. In recent years, though, a number of houses specializing in software escrows have been established. You can find a list of these on the Yahoo.com Internet directory at http:// dir.yahoo.com/Business_and_Economy/ Business_to_Business/Computers/Services/ Source_Code_Escrow. You may be able to find others by doing an Internet search.

Using an escrow firm that specializes in software affords several advantages. First, these companies provide a carefully controlled environment for storage of magnetic media, assuring that the deposited material is undamaged. In addition, some software escrow houses also provide a verification service. This may consist of simply making sure the materials deposited match the requirements of the escrow agreement. However, for an additional charge, some escrows will take the source code provided by the developer and compile it (turn it into object code) to see if it is identical to the object code given to the customer. Software escrow companies normally supply detailed form escrow agreements for the parties to sign. These agreements attempt to evenly balance the interests of both parties.

Since there is no guarantee when a development project is commenced that the software will be satisfactorily completed, it makes sense to delay spending the time and money involved in setting up a source code escrow until the software is actually written. This optional clause obliges the parties to set up an escrow with a software escrow house to be determined later. The escrow agreement is also to be negotiated later. This clause makes clear that the customer will pay for the escrow. This is fair because the escrow is really for the customer's benefit. It also sets forth the circumstances under which the escrowed materials will be released to the customer by the escrow company; this should also, of course, be spelled out in detail in the escrow agreement.

16. Warranties

A warranty is a promise or statement regarding the quality, quantity, performance, or legal title of something being sold. We all have some familiarity with warranties. Whenever we buy an expensive product from a car, to a television, to a computer,

the seller normally warrants that the product will do what it is supposed to do for a specific or reasonable time period, otherwise the seller will fix or replace it.

When goods are sold in the course of business, they generally are warranted. If the goods later prove defective and the seller fails to repair or replace them in accordance with the warranty, it is called a "breach of warranty" and the buyer can seek relief in the courts. In many states, hefty damages can be obtained against sellers who fail to live up to their warranties. These may include not only the cost of replacing the defective software, but any economic losses suffered by the customer as a result of the defect, such as lost profits.

Custom software developers are naturally hesitant about giving a warranty for something that is not yet in existence when the warranty is made. However, some customers usually demand assurance that the product will work.

Because this is an area of active bargaining between the developer and customer, warranty provisions vary widely. Before we discuss sample warranty provisions for custom software development contracts, let's take a quick look at the various types of warranties.

a. Express warranties

When a developer makes an actual promise about how the software will work, whether orally or in writing, it is making an "express warranty." An express warranty can be created by using formal words such as "guarantee," "affirm," or "warrant." However, it is important to understand that no magic words are necessary to create an express warranty. Representations make by salespeople, sales literature, statements at product demonstrations, proposals, manuals, or contractual specifications can all constitute express warranties. And this can even be true where the developer did not intend to create a warranty. Express warranties can last for any period of time, ranging from a few months to the lifetime of the software.

Customers often seek an express warranty from software developers guaranteeing that the software is free from defects and will meet the functional and design specifications set forth in the development plan. (See Subsection d, below.) Another common express warranty is a guarantee that the software will not infringe any third party's copyright, patent, or trade secret rights.

b. Implied warranties

In every commercial transaction involving the sale of movable goods, certain representations by the seller are assumed to be made, even if no words are written or spoken. These representations are implied by state laws based on the Uniform Commercial Code ("U.C.C."), a set of model laws designed by legal scholars that have been adopted by every state but Louisiana. The U.C.C. establishes uniform rules governing the sale of goods and other commercial transactions. In the past, a number of courts have disagreed on whether custom software qualifies as a "good" governed by these state U.C.C. laws, but today the trend appears to be that these laws apply to custom software sales transactions. (There is no question that the U.C.C. applies when software is bundled with hardware, or when standard off-the-shelf software is customized.)

This book can't provide a whole course on the U.C.C., but you should be aware that there are four implied warranties that automatically exist in contracts for the sale of goods unless they are expressly disclaimed (disavowed). These are:

- **Implied warranty of title.** All sellers warrant that they are transferring good legal title to the goods; that they have the right to make the transfer; and, as far as they know, the goods are not subject to any liens, encumbrances, or security interests. This warranty is particularly important for software development agreements because the software often contains elements that have been licensed from or to third parties.

- **Implied warranty against infringement.** The seller warrants that the product will be delivered free of any rightful claim by any third party that the product infringes such person's patent, copyright, trade secret, or other proprietary rights.

- **Implied warranty of fitness for a specific purpose.** If a customer is relying on the seller's expertise to select suitable goods, and the seller is aware that the customer intends to use the goods for a particular purpose, the product becomes impliedly guaranteed for that purpose. For example, if a developer knows that the customer needs software to operate an assembly line at a particular speed, and agrees to develop software for that purpose, there is an implied warranty that the software will operate the line at the proper speed even if this specification isn't made a part of the contract. This warranty almost always applies in custom software transactions.

- **Implied warranty of merchantability.** The seller promises that the goods are fit for their commonly intended use—in other words, they are of at least average quality. This means that software must perform so as to satisfy most customers' expectations. The software need only perform in a minimally acceptable manner to satisfy this warranty; it need not satisfy the highest function, speed, or other performance criteria.

c. Alternative 1: disclaimer of all warranties

> [DISCLAIMER OF ALL WARRANTIES] THE SOFTWARE FURNISHED UNDER THIS AGREEMENT IS PROVIDED ON AN "AS IS" BASIS, WITHOUT ANY WARRANTIES OR REPRESENTATIONS EXPRESS, IMPLIED, OR STATUTORY; INCLUDING, WITHOUT LIMITATION, WARRANTIES OF QUALITY, PERFORMANCE, NONINFRINGEMENT, MERCHANTABILITY, OR FITNESS FOR A PARTICULAR PURPOSE. NOR ARE THERE ANY WARRANTIES CREATED BY A COURSE OF DEALING, COURSE OF PERFORMANCE, OR TRADE USAGE. DEVELOPER DOES NOT WARRANT THAT THE SOFTWARE WILL MEET CUSTOMER'S NEEDS OR BE FREE FROM ERRORS, OR THAT THE OPERATION OF THE SOFTWARE WILL BE UNINTERRUPTED. THE FOREGOING EXCLUSIONS AND DISCLAIMERS ARE AN ESSENTIAL PART OF THIS AGREEMENT AND FORMED THE BASIS FOR DETERMINING THE PRICE CHARGED FOR THE SOFTWARE.

There is no requirement in most states that the seller of goods provide any warranties at all. The implied warranties discussed above (and any express warranties) may be expressly disclaimed by the seller. This means that the goods are sold "as is." While an "as is" statement will protect a seller from many types of claims, it won't protect it from charges of outright fraud (if it lied about the goods in question). To be effective, "as is" statements must be "conspicuous"—for instance, printed in boldface capitals and large type—so they won't be overlooked by the customer (no proverbial "fine print").

d. Alternative 2: providing express warranties

(a) Warranty of Software Performance: Developer warrants that for [WARRANTY PERIOD] following acceptance of the Software by Customer, the Software will be free from material reproducible programming errors and defects in workmanship and materials, and will substantially conform to the Specifications in the Development Plan when maintained and operated in accordance with Developer's instructions. If material reproducible programming errors are discovered during the warranty period, Developer shall promptly remedy them at no additional expense to Customer. This warranty to Customer shall be null and void if Customer is in default under this Agreement or if the nonconformance is due to:

(1) hardware failures due to defects, power problems, environmental problems, or any cause other than the Software itself;

(2) modification of the Software operating systems or computer hardware by any party other than Developer; or

(3) misuse, errors, or negligence of Customer, its employees or agents in operating the Software.

Developer shall not be obligated to cure any defect unless Customer notifies it of the existence and nature of such defect promptly upon discovery.

(b) Warranty of Title: Developer owns and has the right to license or convey title to the Software and documentation covered by this Agreement. Developer will not grant any rights or licenses to any intellectual property or technology that would conflict with Developer's obligations under this Agreement.

(c) Warranty Against Disablement: Developer expressly warrants that no portion of the Software contains or will contain any protection feature designed to prevent its use. This includes, without limitation, any computer virus, worm, software lock, drop-dead device, Trojan-horse routine, trap door, time bomb, or any other codes or instructions that may be used to access, modify, delete, damage, or disable Customer's Software or computer system. Developer further warrants that it will not impair the operation of the Software in any way other than by order of a court of law.

(d) Warranty of Compatibility: Developer warrants that the Software shall be compatible with the Customer's hardware and software as set forth in the Development Plan Specifications.

THE WARRANTIES SET FORTH IN THIS AGREEMENT ARE THE ONLY WARRANTIES GRANTED BY DEVELOPER. DEVELOPER DISCLAIMS ALL OTHER WARRANTIES EXPRESS OR IMPLIED, INCLUDING, BUT NOT LIMITED TO, ANY IMPLIED WARRANTIES OF MERCHANTABILITY OR FITNESS FOR A PARTICULAR PURPOSE. [END ALTERNATIVE 2]

Although creating custom software is a difficult and often uncertain process, it is reasonable for the customer to expect the developer to stand behind its product. In a custom software development agreement, the developer typically gives the customer certain express warranties and disclaims any and all implied warranties. The parties need to negotiate exactly what type of express warranties the developer will make. Naturally, the customer wants the developer's warranties to be as expansive as possible, while the developer wishes them to be narrowly drawn. A compromise must be reached.

Alternative 2 contains the following express warranties commonly found in custom development agreements. Include whichever warranties are desired.

- **Warranty of software performance.** Under a warranty of software performance, the developer guarantees that the software will function properly. The developer promises that the software is free from material defects (but not absolutely perfect) and will perform in substantial conformance with the specifications.

This warranty is usually limited in time, to anywhere from 90 days to one year. During the warranty term, the developer is required to correct any defects and modify the software as necessary, free of charge. Normally excluded from coverage are any defects caused by the customer's misuse of the software or from causes beyond the developer's control, such as a power failure.

- **Warranty of title.** The developer warrants that it has the legal right to grant the customer all rights specified in the contract. This normally means that no intellectual property rights to the software have been licensed to others on an exclusive basis. In addition, if the developer has used any code covered by another's copyright, patent or trade secret protections, it has the legal right to do so.

- **Warranty against disablement.** Developers who are concerned that they might not be paid fully or that the customer may breach the terms of the development contract have been known to include "computer viruses" and disabling devices in their software. These devices are intended to disable the software, either automatically with the passage of time or under the developer's control. The purpose, obviously, is to prevent the customer from using the software if the customer fails to uphold its end of the agreement.

Is this legal? One court has indicated it might be, but only if the developer tells the customer in advance that disabling devices will be included in the software and the customer agrees. (*Frank & Sons v. Information Solutions*, (N.D. Okla. No. 88C1474E), *Computer Indus. Lit. Rep.*, Jan. 23, 1989, at 8927-35.) In the absence of such notice and consent, a developer who disables a customer's software could be liable for all the customer's resulting damages. These could be substantial, especially if the customer's entire computer system is affected.

In one well-known case, a developer included a disabling device in an inventory control system it created for cosmetics manufacture for Revlon, Inc. When Revlon stopped paying the developer because it was dissatisfied with the system's performance, the developer sent Revlon a letter warning that it would disable the software if payment was not forthcoming. The developer then activated the disabling device by dialing into Revlon's computer system. As a result, two of Revlon's distribution centers were completely shut down for several days. Revlon estimated its losses at $20 million. Revlon sued the developer, who settled for an undisclosed amount. (*Revlon, Inc. v. Logisticon, Inc.*, No. 705933 (Cal. Super. Ct., Santa Clara Cty., complaint filed Oct. 22, 1990).) The lesson is clear: A developer should absolutely never include any disabling device in software without informing the customer and obtaining its consent in advance. Even then, the developer should think twice if a customer does consent—the customer might sue the developer anyway if activation of a disablement device causes it substantial losses.

Not only will most customers refuse to allow inclusion of a disabling device in their software, they will often demand that the developer expressly guarantee that none has or will be included.

- **Warranty of compatibility.** The warranty of compatibility provides that the software will be compatible with the hardware on which it will run and with any noncustom software included in the customer's system. This warranty is particularly important where a customer is acquiring a system from multiple vendors—that is, hardware from one or more vendors, and software from others.

- **Disclaiming warranties not in agreement.** In return for the express warranties included in the contract, the customer typically agrees to allow the developer to disclaim any and all other warranties, whether express or implied. Such a disclaimer should be typed in capitals, preferably boldface, to be enforceable.

Warranties a Developer Should Not Make

A developer should only provide a warranty as to those matters within its control. This is a matter of fairness and common sense. Matters beyond a developer's control include:

- *Error-free software.* A developer cannot realistically warrant that the software will be completely bug-free. All software, particularly custom software, inevitably contains some bugs. But there is a big difference between true bugs—defects that prevent the software from performing the customer's required tasks satisfactorily—and interface and peripheral glitches and other minor irritants that don't materially affect the software's performance. The most a developer should promise is that the software will not contain "material" defects. A developer should never promise to fix trivial bugs free of charge. Fixing minor bugs can be just as difficult and expensive as fixing major ones. Moreover, the customer really doesn't need to have trivial bugs fixed at all. All the customer needs is stable software that performs satisfactorily. Trivial bugs that don't prevent the software from performing satisfactorily can simply be ignored.

- *Software will be free from defects in materials and workmanship.* This type of warranty is commonly found in contracts for machinery, including computer hardware. However, it does not belong in software development contracts. Again, no developer can safely guarantee that custom software will be perfect.

- *Software will perform in exact conformance with specifications.* Developers shouldn't promise this unless they're absolutely sure it will be true. It's far better for the developer to warrant that the software will perform "in substantial conformance" with the specifications, meaning that trivial variations will not violate the warranty.

17. Intellectual Property Infringement Claims

"Intellectual property" is a catch-all term that includes copyrights, patents, trade secrets, and trademarks. (See Chapter 2 for a detailed discussion.) Most software development agreements contain some kind of express warranty against intellectual property infringement. The extent of such a warranty is subject to negotiation.

In this highly litigious world, intellectual property infringement is an issue the developer must think about carefully. In some cases, the developer may even choose to lower its price or make other concessions to the customer to avoid making a broad warranty of noninfringement. Three alternative warranty provisions are provided in the agreement.

Insurance Coverage for Infringement Claims

Your business may be insured for intellectual property infringement claims and you may not even know it. The Comprehensive General Liability Insurance ("CGL") policies typically obtained by businesses may provide such coverage. Several courts have held that the "advertising injury" provision included in many CGL policies covers infringement claims. However, not all CGL policies provide such coverage. Ask your insurance broker whether your policy covers infringement claims. If the broker doesn't know, you may need to consult with an insurance attorney who represents policyholders. If your CGL policy doesn't cover infringement claims, you may be able to obtain such coverage by purchasing umbrella or excess policy coverage from your insurer.

a. Alternative 1: limited warranty against infringement

Developer warrants that Developer will not knowingly infringe on the copyright or trade secrets of any third party in performing services under this Agreement. To the extent any material used by Developer contains matter proprietary to a third party, Developer shall obtain a license from the owner permitting the use of such matter and granting Developer the right to sublicense its use. Developer will not knowingly infringe upon any existing patents of third parties in the performance of services required by this Agreement, but Developer MAKES NO WARRANTY OF NONINFRINGEMENT of any United States or foreign patent.

[OPTIONAL—INDEMNIFICATION FOR CLAIMS:] If any third party brings a lawsuit or proceeding against Customer based upon a claim that the Software breaches the third party's patent, copyright, or trade secrets rights, and it is determined that such infringement has occurred, Developer shall hold Customer harmless against any loss, damage, expense, or cost, including reasonable attorney fees, arising from the claim.

This indemnification obligation shall be effective only if:

- the third-party intellectual property rights involved were known to Developer prior to delivery of the Software
- Customer has make all payments required by this Agreement
- Customer has given prompt notice of the claim and permitted Developer to defend, and
- the claim does not result from Customer's modification of the Software.

To reduce or mitigate damages, Developer may at its own expense replace the Software with a noninfringing product.

In this clause the developer warrants that it will not knowingly violate the copyright or trade secret rights of any third party. However, no warranty is made as to patent infringement. This is because it is very difficult for a developer to know for sure whether its software might violate a patent, primarily because many pending patent applications are kept secret. In-stead, the developer simply promises that to the best of the developer's knowledge the software will not infringe any existing patent.

Some customers absolutely insist that the developer indemnify (repay) them if a third party brings a lawsuit claiming the software infringed on the party's intellectual property rights. An optional indemnification provision is provided here. It is as narrowly drafted as possible. The developer must indemnify the customer only if the third-party intellectual property rights involved were known to the developer prior to delivery of the software. This means, for example, the developer won't be liable if a patent issued covering some element contained in the software after the software was delivered.

b. Alternative 2: "no-knowledge" representation

> Developer represents, BUT DOES NOT WARRANT, that to the best of its knowledge the Software delivered to Customer under this Agreement will not infringe any valid and existing intellectual property right of any third party.

Even better for the developer is to provide no warranty of noninfringement at all, and instead extend the "no-knowledge representation" to copyrights and trade secrets as well as patents. Because there are no uniform national rules, it remains far from clear exactly how far copyright protection for software extends. As a result, it can be difficult or impossible to know for sure if custom software violates the copyright in any similar pre-existing programs. In fact, there have

been many instances in which a developer's employees have included software elements belonging to a prior employer; as a practical matter, it can be impossible for a developer to know about or prevent this.

c. Alternative 3: no warranties or representations

> THE SOFTWARE FURNISHED UNDER THIS AGREEMENT IS PROVIDED WITHOUT ANY EXPRESS OR IMPLIED WARRANTIES OR REPRESENTATIONS AGAINST INFRINGEMENT, AND DEVELOPER SHALL NOT INDEMNIFY CUSTOMER AGAINST INFRINGEMENT OF ANY PATENTS, COPYRIGHTS, TRADE SECRETS, OR OTHER PROPRIETARY RIGHTS.

Best of all, from the developer's point of view, is a provision in which the developer states that it makes no warranties or representations of any kind regarding intellectual property infringement and will not indemnify the customer if an infringement claim is made (see discussion of indemnification below). This alternative is most logical when the developer retains ownership of the software; it's unlikely a customer who is to obtain ownership of the software would agree to it. If you use this clause, it should be printed in bold-faced, capital letters.

18. Limits on Developer's Liability

(a) In no event shall Developer be liable to Customer for lost profits of Customer, or special or consequential damages, even if Developer has been advised of the possibility of such damages.

(b) Developer's total liability under this Agreement for damages, costs, and expenses, regardless of cause, shall not exceed the total amount of fees paid to Developer by Customer under this Agreement [OPTIONAL: "or $[AMOUNT], whichever is greater"].

(c) Developer shall not be liable for any claim or demand made against Customer by any third party except to the extent such claim or demand relates to copyright, trade secret, or other proprietary rights, and then only as provided in the section of this Agreement entitled Intellectual Property Infringement Claims.

(d) Customer shall indemnify Developer against all claims, liabilities, and costs, including reasonable attorney fees, of defending any third-party claim or suit arising out of the use of the Software provided under this Agreement, other than for infringement of intellectual property rights. Developer shall promptly notify Customer in writing of any third-party claim or suit and Customer shall have the right to fully control the defense and any settlement of such claim or suit.

Although it may be rather frightening and depressing to think about, custom software developers face potentially enormous liabilities. Improperly designed or bug-ridden software can cause the customer serious financial losses for which the customer may look to the developer to make good.

> **EXAMPLE:** BioWorkware creates a custom software system designed to automate a biotechnology laboratory. A few weeks after installation, the system crashes. While BioWorkware tries to find out went wrong, the lab is forced to purchase software from another vendor to get the lab up and running. As a result of all this, the lab is shut down for a week and loses several experiments potentially worth hundreds of thousands of dollars. The lab demands that BioWorkware repay the losses caused by the crash. To pay this amount, BioWorkware would have to liquidate its business. BioWorkware refuses to pay, and the lab sues.

To prevent a nightmarish scenario of this type from driving them out of business, developers are wise to insist on the following provisions limiting their liability to the customer. These provisions are optional, but can be very helpful for developers.

a. No liability for consequential damages

The consequential damages arising out of even a modest problem can easily bankrupt a developer. At the very least, the developer should insist that the agreement include a provision excluding it from any liability for incidental or consequential damages arising out of the agreement. Such damages include lost profits or other economic damages arising from a malfunction where the developer had reason to know that such losses could occur if the software malfunctioned. This could include, for example, the value of the experiments lost by the biotech lab in the example above.

b. Limit on developer's liability to customer

Another way to limit the developer's potential liability is to limit the total liability to the customer to a specified amount. A typical liability limit is the amount paid by the customer for the software. This amounts to a money-back guarantee for the customer, while getting the developer off the hook for a potentially much larger liability. If desired, a liability standard not based on the contract price can be set. Obviously, such a provision highly favors the developer.

c. Developer's liability for third-party claims

The harm caused by malfunctioning software is not necessarily limited to the customer; it may economically or even physically damage third parties as well.

> **EXAMPLE:** SafeSoft writes a custom software package designed to operate a chemical factory. The software crashes and so does the factory, resulting in a chemical spill costing hundreds of thousands of dollars to clean up. Dozens of suits are brought against the chemical company by property owners affected by the spill. The chemical company demands that SafeSoft pay off these claims.

To avoid this type of scenario, the developer may seek to include in the development agreement a clause providing that it is not liable for any claim made against the customer by any third party (other than for intellectual property infringement if it is providing a warranty against infringement).

d. Indemnification of developer for third-party claims

If third parties are harmed by malfunctioning software, they'll likely sue everyone involved, including the developer. Both the customer and the developer may be liable for the full amount of such claims. Indemnification provisions are used to require one party to pay the other's attorney fees and damages arising from such claims. Indemnification provisions don't affect the third-party claimant. They simply straighten out liability between the developer and the customer.

In the example above, property owners affected by the chemical spill would undoubtedly sue not only the chemical factory, but SafeSoft as well, claiming that it negligently designed the software. A developer in this situation could find itself faced with defending itself against suits brought by persons and entities it never heard of. Its attorney fees alone could far exceed what it was paid to create the software.

Ideally, the developer would like the customer to agree to indemnify the developer against such third-party claims. Realizing that their software may adversely affect many people they never contracted with, more and more developers are seeking provisions like this which, of course, highly favor the developer. A developer of software that poses an obvious risk of potential financial and/or physical damage to third parties—for example, software implemented in banking hardware or airline radar—should seriously consider seeking such a provision in the development agreement.

19. Confidentiality

During the term of this Agreement and for _____ [6 months to 5 years] afterward, Developer will use reasonable care to prevent the unauthorized use or dissemination of Customer's confidential information. Reasonable care means at least the same degree of care Developer uses to protect its own confidential information from unauthorized disclosure.

Confidential information is limited to information clearly marked as confidential, or disclosed orally that is treated as confidential when disclosed and summarized and identified as confidential in a writing delivered to Consultant within 15 days of disclosure.

Confidential information does not include information that:

- the Developer knew before Customer disclosed it
- is or becomes public knowledge through no fault of Consultant
- Developer obtains from sources other than Customer who owe no duty of confidentiality to Customer, or
- Developer independently develops.

[OPTIONAL—USE WHERE DEVELOPER OWNS SOFTWARE] Customer acknowledges that the Software is Developer's sole and exclusive property. Customer shall treat the Software on a confidential basis and shall not, at any time, disclose the trade secrets embodied in the Software or supporting documentation to any other person, firm, organization, or employee who does not need to obtain access thereto consistent with Customer's rights under this Agreement. Under no circumstances may Customer modify, reverse compile, or reverse assemble the object code contained in the Software. Customer shall devote its reasonable best efforts to ensure that all persons afforded access to the Software and supporting documentation protect Developer's trade secrets against unauthorized use, dissemination, or disclosure.

Since software developers often have access to their customers' valuable confidential information, customers often seek to impose confidentiality restrictions on them. It's not unreasonable for a customer to want you to keep its secrets away from the eyes and ears of competitors. Unfortunately, however, many of these provisions are worded so broadly that they can make it difficult for you to work for other clients without fear of violating your duty of confidentiality.

If, like most software developers, you make your living by performing similar services for many firms within the computer industry, insist on a confidentiality provision that is reasonable in scope and defines precisely what information you must keep confidential. Such a provision should last for only a limited time—five years at the most.

The confidentiality provision in this agreement prevents the unauthorized disclosure by the developer of any written material of the customer marked confidential or information disclosed orally that the customer later writes down, marks as confidential, and delivers to you within 15 days. This enables the developer to know for sure what material is, and is not, confidential.

The clause also makes clear that the developer does not have any duty to keep as confidential material that does not qualify as a trade secret, is legitimately learned from persons other than the customer, or is independently developed.

Optional provision—Software confidentiality: If the developer retains ownership of the software, it wants to make sure that the customer treats it as confidential. In this event, this optional clause should be included in the development agreement.

20. Term of Agreement

> This Agreement commences on the date it is executed and shall continue until full performance by both parties, or until earlier terminated by one party under the terms of this Agreement.

The term of a software development should run from the date it is executed (signed by both parties) until full performance or earlier termination or cancellation.

21. Termination of Agreement

> Each party shall have the right to terminate this Agreement by written notice to the other if a party has materially breached any obligation herein and such breach remains uncured for a period of 30 days after written notice of such breach is sent to the other party.
>
> If Developer terminates this Agreement because of Customer's default, all of the following shall apply:
>
> (a) Customer shall immediately cease use of the Software.
>
> (b) Customer shall, within ten days of such termination, deliver to Developer all copies and portions of the Software and related materials and documentation in its possession furnished by Developer under this Agreement.
>
> (c) All amounts payable or accrued to Developer under this Agreement shall become immediately due and payable.
>
> (d) All rights and licenses granted to Customer under this Agreement shall immediately terminate.
>
> [OPTIONAL:] This Agreement may be terminated by Customer for its convenience upon thirty (30) days' prior written notice to Developer. Upon such termination, all amounts owed to Developer under this Agreement for accepted work shall immediately become due and payable and all rights and licenses granted by Developer to Customer under this Agreement shall immediately terminate.

The language governing how the contract may end is very important to both parties. The provision in this agreement is fairly standard. It permits either party to terminate the agreement if the other materially breaches any of its contractual obligations and fails to remedy the breach within 30 days. A "material" breach means a breach that is serious, rather than minor or trivial. Missing a deadline by one day is not "material"; missing it by three months is. For developers, the material breach most likely to result in termination is the customer's failure to pay the developer in a timely fashion. If the developer terminates the agreement because of the customer's default (usually because the customer has failed to pay the developer), the customer should return any software or other materials received from the developer and should pay the developer for the work it has done.

Optional provision—early customer termination: The customer may want the option to terminate the agreement at its convenience if it decides for some reason it doesn't want to go through with the project. In this event, the customer should have to pay the developer all amounts due for accepted work and relinquish any rights in the software.

22. **Taxes**

> The charges included here do not include taxes. If Developer is required to pay any federal, state, or local sales, use, property, or value added taxes based on the services provided under this Agreement, the taxes shall be separately billed to Customer. Developer shall not pay any interest or penalties incurred due to late payment or nonpayment of such taxes by Customer.

It is customary in custom software development agreements for the customer to pay any required state and local sales, use or property taxes. Whether or not the developer is required to collect sales taxes, the following provision should be included in the agreement making it clear that the customer will have to pay these and similar taxes. States constantly change their sales tax laws and more and more are beginning to look at services as a good source of sales tax revenue. So this provision could come in handy in the future even if the developer doesn't really need it now.

23. Developer an Independent Contractor

Developer is an independent contractor, and neither Developer nor Developer's staff is, or shall be deemed, Client's employees. In its capacity as an independent contractor, Developer agrees and represents, and Customer agrees, as follows:

[INCLUDE ALL OF PROVISIONS 23a-j THAT APPLY]

(a) Developer has the right to perform services for others during the term of this Agreement subject to noncompetition provisions set out in this Agreement, if any.

(b) Developer has the sole right to control and direct the means, manner, and method by which the services required by this Agreement will be performed.

(c) Developer has the right to perform the services required by this Agreement at any place or location and at such times as Developer may determine.

(d) Developer will furnish all equipment and materials used to provide the services required by this Agreement, except to the extent that Consultant's work must be performed on or with Customer's computer or existing software.

(e) The services required by this Agreement shall be performed by Developer, or Developer's staff, and Customer shall not be required to hire, supervise, or pay any assistants to help Developer.

(f) Developer is responsible for paying all ordinary and necessary expenses of its staff.

(g) Neither Developer nor Developer's staff shall receive any training from Customer in the professional skills necessary to perform the services required by this Agreement.

(h) Neither Developer nor Developer's staff shall be required to devote full time to the performance of the services required by this Agreement.

(i) Customer shall not provide insurance coverage of any kind for Developer or Developer's staff.

(j) Customer shall not withhold from Developer's compensation any amount that would normally be withheld from an employee's pay.

One of the most important functions of the agreement is to help establish that the developer is not the customer's employee. A developer will be considered the customer's employee if the customer has the right to control the developer. This will cause problems not only for the customer, but for the developer as well.

A development agreement that indicates a lack of control on the part of the hiring firm will contribute to a finding of independent contractor status. But such an agreement will not be determinative in and of itself. Simply signing a piece of paper will not make a developer an independent contractor. The agreement must reflect reality—that is, the developer must actually not be controlled on the job by the customer.

The language in this clause addresses most of the factors the IRS and other agencies consider in measuring the degree of control of the hiring firm. All provisions show that the hiring firm lacks the right to control the manner and means by which the developer will perform the agreed-upon services.

Include all of provisions a-j that apply. The more that apply, the more likely that the developer will be viewed as an independent contractor.

24. Optional Provision: Nonsolicitation of Developer's Employees

Customer agrees not to knowingly hire or solicit Developer's employees during performance of this Agreement and for a period of [TIME PERIOD, USUALLY SIX MONTHS TO TWO YEARS] after termination of this Agreement without Developer's written consent.

One of a software developer's fears is that a customer will hire away a star programmer or other key employee and do future work on program enhancements and modifications in-house. This optional provision is designed to prevent this. It may give the developer some peace of mind.

25. Disputes

[ALTERNATIVE 1—LITIGATION]

If a dispute arises, either party may take the matter to court.

Mediation and Possible Litigation. If a dispute arises, the parties will try in good faith to settle it through mediation conducted by: _____[NAME] OR a mediator to be mutually selected. [END ALTERNATIVE 1]

[ALTERNATIVE 2—PARTIES EQUALLY SHARE COSTS OF MEDIATOR]

Each party will cooperate fully and fairly with the mediator and will attempt to reach a mutually satisfactory compromise to the dispute. If the dispute is not resolved within 30 days after it is referred to the mediator, either party may take the matter to court. [END ALTERNATIVE 2]

[ALTERNATIVE 3—MEDIATION AND POSSIBLE ARBITRATION]

If a dispute arises, the parties will try in good faith to settle it through mediation conducted by:_____[NAME] OR a mediator to be mutually selected.

The parties will share the costs of the mediator equally. Each party will cooperate fully and fairly with the mediator and will attempt to reach a mutually satisfactory compromise to the dispute.

If the dispute is not resolved within 30 days after it is referred to the mediator, it will be arbitrated by: _____[NAME] OR an arbitrator to be mutually selected. Judgment on the arbitration award may be entered in any court that has jurisdiction over the matter. The arbitrator will allocate costs of arbitration, including attorney fees. [END ALTERNATIVE 3]

For an explanation of the dispute provision alternatives, see Chapter 17, Section B27.

26. Attorney Fees

If any legal action is necessary to enforce this Agreement, the prevailing party shall be entitled to reasonable attorney fees, costs, and expenses.

If you have to sue the client in court to enforce the agreement, and win, you normally will not be awarded the amount of your attorney fees unless your agreement requires it. Including such an attorney fees provision in the agreement can be in your interest. It can help make filing a lawsuit economically feasible. It will also give the customer a strong incentive to negotiate with you if you have a good case.

Under this provision, if either person has to sue the other in court to enforce the agreement and wins—that is, be- comes the prevailing party—the loser is required to pay the other person's attor- ney fees and expenses.

27. General Provisions

(a) Complete Agreement: This Agreement together with all exhibits, appendices, or other attachments, which are incorporated herein by reference, is the sole and entire Agreement between the parties. This Agreement supersedes all prior understandings, agreements, and documentation relating to such subject matter. In the event of a conflict between the provisions of the main body of the Agreement and any attached exhibits, appendices, or other materials, the Agreement shall take precedence.

(b) Modifications to Agreement: Modifications and amendments to this Agreement, including any ex- hibit or appendix hereto, shall be enforceable only if they are in writing and are signed by autho- rized representatives of both parties.

(c) Applicable law: This Agreement will be governed by the laws of the State of [LIST APPLICABLE STATE]

(d) Notices: All notices and other communications given in connection with this Agreement shall be in writing and shall be deemed given as follows:

• When delivered personally to the recipient's address as appearing in the introductory paragraph to this Agreement;
• Three days after being deposited in the United States mails, postage prepaid to the recipient's address as appearing in the introductory paragraph to this Agreement, or
• When sent by fax or electronic mail. Notice is effective upon receipt provided that a duplicate copy of the notice is promptly given by first-class or certified mail, or the recipient delivers a writ- ten confirmation of receipt.

(e) No Agency: Nothing contained herein will be construed as creating any agency, partnership, joint venture, or other form of joint enterprise between the parties.

(f) Assignment: The rights and obligations under this Agreement are freely assignable by either party. Client shall retain the obligation to pay if the assignee fails to pay as required by this Agreement.

(g) Successors and Assigns: This agreement binds and benefits the heirs, successors, and assigns of the parties.

(h) Severability: If a court finds any provision of this Agreement invalid or unenforceable, the remain- der of this Agreement will be interpreted so as best to carry out the parties' intent.

For an explanation of these provisions, see Chapter 17, Section B30.

28. Signatures

The end of the main body of the agreement should contain spaces for the parties to sign.

29. Exhibits

Make sure that all exhibits are attached to all copies of the agreement and that the references to the exhibits in the agreement match the actual exhibits. The exhibits to the agreement will include:

- the Functional Specification (see Section 3, above)
- the Development Plan (see Section 3, above), and
- the developer's list of Background Technology (see Section 14, above). ■

Help Beyond This Book

Hopefully, this book provides you with most of the information you need about software and website law and agreements. But you may need additional help, either in the form of more advanced legal resources or an attorney's advice.

Section A introduces you to resources that contain comprehensive information on each area of intellectual property law. Section B gives some tips for finding a lawyer.

A. Further Information on Intellectual Property Law

If you have any questions about intellectual property law (copyright, trade secret, patent, or trademark law) that have not been answered by this book, a two-step process is suggested.

- Check one or more of the websites listed below to see if there is an article or other discussion answering your question.
- If you need more in-depth information, take a look at one or more discussions by experts in the field to get a background and overview of the topic being researched. You will already have obtained a basic background from this book and will be looking for additional details on a particular topic. You'll probably need to go to a law library to find these materials.

Nolo's Legal Encyclopedia

Nolo.com's website at www.nolo.com offers an extensive Legal Encyclopedia which includes a section on intellectual property. You'll find answers to frequently asked questions about patents, copyrights, trademarks, and other related topics, as well as sample chapters of Nolo books and a wide range of articles. Simply click on "Legal Encyclopedia" and then on "Patents, Copyright, & Trademark."

---

1. Copyright Law

The first place to go for more information on copyright law is *The Copyright Handbook: How to Protect & Use Written Works*, by Stephen Fishman (Nolo). This book discusses copyright protection for writings, but the principles are applicable to software as well. It also has a chapter on copyright on the Internet. For information on acquiring rights to use copyrighted materials consult *Getting Permission*, by Richard Stim (Nolo).

a. Internet resources

You can find valuable information about copyright by using any of the following websites:

- The U.S. Copyright Office at www.copyright.gov: This site offers regulations, guidelines, forms, and links to other helpful copyright sites.

- Findlaw at www.findlaw.com: This search engine offers a comprehensive list of copyright resources on the Web. Click intellectual property under the topic heading on the home page and click copyright from the subcategory list on the intellectual property page. In addition, a number of articles dealing with copyright are listed on the Findlaw site.

b. Legal treatises

Copyright is discussed in many outstanding legal treatises.

- *Nimmer on Copyright*, by Melville and David Nimmer (Matthew Bender), is the leading treatise on all aspects of copyright law. This four-volume work covers virtually every legal issue concerning U.S. and foreign copyright law. Its coverage of computer software has recently been expanded, but it is not concerned exclusively with software.
- *The Law and Business of Computer Software*, edited by D.C. Toedt III (Clark Boardman Callaghan), contains a useful guide to copyright protection for software and discusses Web issues as well.

- *Scott on Computer Law*, by Michael D. Scott (Prentice Hall Law & Business). This two-volume treatise contains a detailed discussion of copyright protection for software, including copyright protection in foreign countries.
- *Law of the Internet*, by George B. Delta and Jeffrey H. Matsuura (Prentice Hall Law & Business) covers Internet legal issues, including copyright.
- *International Copyright Protection*, edited by Paul Geller and Melville Nimmer (Matthew Bender), provides exhaustive coverage of copyright protection in other countries.

c. Statutes

The primary law governing all copyrights in the United States is the Copyright Act of 1976. The Copyright Act is located in Title 17 of the United States Code. A complete copy is available for free at the Copyright Office website at www.copyright.gov.

2. Patent Law

Two sources to consult if you have any questions about patent law are Nolo's *Patents for Beginners,* by David Pressman and Richard Stim, and *Patent It Yourself,* by David Pressman.

a. Internet resources

You can find valuable information about patent law on the Internet by using any of the following sites:

- The U.S. Patent and Trademark Office at www.uspto.gov. This is the place to go for recent policy and statutory changes and transcripts of hearings on various patent law issues. You may also use this site to conduct a search of the first pages of patents (that include the patent abstracts) for patents issued since 1976.
- Another software patent resource is the Source Translation and Optimization patent website (www.bustpatents.com). The STO is directed by Gregory Aharonian, one of the PTO's most vocal critics. The site provides critiques, legal reviews, CAFC rulings, file wrappers, and infringement lawsuits relating to software patents. The STO also offers a free newsletter.
- Software Patent Institute at www.spi .org. This site lets you search for previous software developments that may affect whether a particular software item qualifies for a patent.

b. Legal treatises

Legal treatises on patents include:

- *Patent Law Fundamentals*, by Peter Rosenberg (Clark Boardman Callaghan), the best legal treatise for patent law. This publication is generally considered by patent attorneys to be the bible of patent law. Because it is written for attorneys, it might be somewhat difficult sledding for the nonlawyer. However, if you first obtain an overview of your topic from the Pressman book, you should do fine.
- *Patent Law Handbook*, by C. Bruce Hamburg (Clark Boardman Callaghan), another useful book. A new edition of this book is issued every year.

c. Statutes

The basic U.S. Patent Law is located in Title 35, United States Code, Section 101 and following. This can be found in the United States Code Annotated (U.S.C.A.) or United States Code Service, Lawyers Edition (U.S.C.S.). A copy of the complete Patent Law is located on the World Wide Web at wwwfindlaw.com/casecode/ uscodes/.

3. Trade Secret Law

The first source to consult if you have any questions about trade secret law is *Nondisclosure Agreements: Protect Your Trade Secrets & More,* by Richard Stim and Stephen Fishman (Nolo).

a. Internet resources

If you have access to the Internet's World Wide Web you can find valuable information about trade secrets by using the Trade Secret Home Page (www.rmark halligan2.com/tshp). This site provides discussions of recent developments and general background information on trade secrets.

b. Treatises

Treatises on trade secret law include:

* *Milgrim on Trade Secrets*, a comprehensive treatment of trade secret law published by Matthew Bender as Volume 12 of its Business Organizations series, is probably the most complete resource regarding trade secret issues, especially if you have a specific or detailed question.
* *Trade Secret Law Handbook*, by Melvin F. Jager (Clark Boardman Callaghan), contains mini-discussions of most trade-secret-related concepts, a number of sample agreements and licenses, as well as references to cases and statutes where appropriate.

c. Statutes

Most states have based their trade secret laws on something called the Uniform Trade Secrets Act, a model law drafted by legal scholars. Reviewing the Uniform Trade Secrets Act will help give you an idea what state trade secret laws are like. You can find the Uniform Trade Secrets Act on the Internet at www.nsi.org/Library/Espionage/usta.htm.

4. Trademark Law

Before consulting any of the resources cited below, first read *Trademark: Legal Care for Your Business & Product Name*, by Stephen Elias (Nolo). This guide provides an overview of trademark law and explains how to select and register a trademark and conduct trademark searches.

a. Internet resources

You can find valuable information about trademarks by using any of the following websites:

* Nolo at www.nolo.com: Nolo offers self-help information about a wide variety of legal topics, including trademark law. (See the Intellectual Property topic in the Legal Encyclopedia, which incidentally includes selected entries from this part of the book.)
* GGMARK at www.ggmark.com: This site, maintained by a trademark lawyer, provides basic trademark information and a fine collection of links to other trademark resources.

- Sunnyvale Center for Invention, Innovation, and Ideas at www.sci3.com: This site, maintained by the Sunnyvale Center for Innovation, Invention, and Ideas (a Patent and Depository Library), provides information about their excellent, low-cost trademark search service conducted by the Center's librarians.
- U.S. Patent and Trademark Office at www.uspto.gov: The U.S. Patent and Trademark Office is the place to go for recent policy and statutory changes and transcripts of hearings on various trademark law issues.

b. Treatises

For truly in-depth information on trademarks, consult the following treatises:

- *Trademarks and Unfair Competition*, by J. Thomas McCarthy (Clark Boardman Callaghan), the most authoritative book on trademark law. This multivolume treatise discusses virtually every legal issue that has arisen regarding trademarks.
- *Trademark Registration Practice*, by James E. Hawes (Clark Boardman Callaghan), provides a detailed guide to trademark registration.
- *Trademark Law—A Practitioner's Guide*, by Siegrun D. Kane (Practicing Law Institute), contains practical

advice about trademark disputes and litigation.

c. Statutes

The main law governing trademarks in the United States is the Lanham Act, also known as the Federal Trademark Act of 1946 (as amended in 1988). It is codified at Title 15, Chapters 1051 through 1127, of the United States Code. A copy of the complete Lanham Act is located on the World Wide Web at www4.law.cornell.edu/uscode/15/ch22.html.

B. Finding a Lawyer

If you're faced with a problem you cannot or do not want to handle yourself, you may need to see a lawyer. A lawyer with a solid background either working for or advising software or dotcom businesses is probably your best bet if you need help with contract drafting. But if you need help filing a patent application or (God forbid) with patent litigation, be aware that patent law is a separate legal specialty. Only lawyers admitted to the federal patent bar can practice patent law. Many patent lawyers specialize in a particular industry; be sure to ask any patent lawyer you consider hiring whether he or she has experience handling software patent applications or litigation.

1. What Not to Do

Don't expect to locate a good software or hi-tech lawyer by simply looking in the phone book, consulting a law directory, or reading an advertisement. There's not enough information in these sources to help you make a valid judgment. Almost as useless are lawyer referral services operated by bar associations. Generally, these services make little attempt to evaluate a lawyer's skill and experience. They simply supply the names of lawyers who have signed up with the service, often accepting the lawyer's own word about skills and experience.

2. Compiling a List of Prospects

A better approach is to talk to developers in your community who own or operate successful businesses. Ask them about other lawyers they've used and what led them to make a change. If you talk to half a dozen developers, chances are you'll come away with several good leads.

Other people who provide services to the business community can also help you. Ask them specifically about lawyers who have experience working for Web and software developers. Here are a few other sources you can turn to for possible candidates:

- The director of your state or local chamber of commerce.

- A law librarian can help identify authors in your state who have written books or articles on online business law.
- The director of your state's continuing legal education (CLE) program—usually run by a bar association, a law school, or both—can identify lawyers who lecture or write on Internet business law for other lawyers. Someone who's a "lawyer's lawyer" presumably has the depth of knowledge and experience to do a superior job for you—but may charge accordingly.

Once you have the names of several lawyers, a good source of more information about them is the *Martindale-Hubbell Law Directory*, available online at most law libraries and some local public libraries. This resource contains biographical sketches of most practicing lawyers and information about their experience, specialties, education, and the professional organizations they belong to. Many firms also list their major clients in the directory—an excellent indication of the types of practice the firm is engaged in.

In addition, almost every lawyer listed in the directory is rated "AV," "BV," or "CV." These ratings come from confidential opinions that Martindale-Hubbell solicits from lawyers and judges. The first letter is for "Legal Ability," which is rated as follows:

- "A"—Very High to Preeminent
- "B"—High to Very High
- "C"—Fair to High

The "V" part stands for "Very High General Recommendation," meaning that the rated lawyer adheres to professional standards of conduct and ethics. But it's practically meaningless because lawyers who don't qualify for it aren't rated at all.

(Martindale-Hubbell prudently cautions that the absence of a rating shouldn't be construed as a reflection on the lawyer; some lawyers ask that their rating not be published, and there may be other reasons for the absence of a rating.)

The rating system works remarkably well. Don't make it your sole criterion for deciding on a potential lawyer for your business, but be reasonably confident that a lawyer who gets high marks from other business clients and an "AV" rating from Martindale-Hubbell knows what he or she is doing.

You can reach Martindale-Hubbell online at www.martindale.com. The online listings contain everything except the ratings. The hardcover books are available at many law libraries.

Another source of information about lawyers is the *West Legal Directory* at www.lawoffice.com. This online service allows users to search by legal specialty, law firm, lawyer name, or by city.

3. Shopping Around

After you get the names of several good prospects, shop around. If you announce your intentions in advance, most lawyers will be willing to speak to you for a half hour or so at no charge so that you can size them up and make an informed decision. Look for experience, personal rapport, and accessibility. Some of these characteristics will be apparent almost immediately. Others may take longer to discover. So even after you've hired a lawyer who seems right for you, keep open the possibility that you may have to make a change later.

Pay particular attention to the rapport between you and your lawyer. No matter how experienced and well-recommended a lawyer is, if you feel uncomfortable during your first meeting or two, you may never achieve a good lawyer-client relationship. Trust your instincts and seek a lawyer whose personality is compatible with your own.

Your lawyer should be accessible when you need legal services. Unfortunately, probably the most common complaint about lawyers is that they don't return clients' phone calls quickly enough. If every time you have a problem there's a delay of several days before you can talk to your lawyer on the phone or get an appointment, you'll lose precious time, not to mention sleep. And almost nothing is more aggravating to a client than to leave a legal project in a lawyer's hands and then have weeks or even months go by without anything happening. You want a lawyer who will work hard on your behalf and follow through promptly on all assignments.

Try to find a lawyer who seems interested in your business and either already knows a lot about your field or who seems genuinely eager to learn more about it. Avoid the lawyer who's aloof and doesn't want to get involved in learning the nitty-gritty details of what you do.

Some lawyers are nitpickers who get unnecessarily bogged down in legal minutiae while a valuable business opportunity slips away. You want a lawyer who blends sound legal advice with a practical approach—someone who figures out a way to do something, not one who only offers reasons why it can't be done. ■

Appendix

How to Use the CD-ROM

The forms discussed in this book are included on a CD-ROM in the back of the book. This CD-ROM, which can be used with Windows computers, installs files that can be opened, printed, and edited using a word processor or other software. It is *not* a stand-alone software program. Please read this Appendix and the README.TXT file included on the CD-ROM for instructions on using the Forms CD.

Note to Mac users: This CD-ROM and its files should also work on Macintosh computers. Please note, however, that Nolo cannot provide technical support for non-Windows users.

How to View the README File

If you do not know how to view the file README.TXT, insert the Forms CD-ROM into your computer's CD-ROM drive and follow these instructions:

- Windows 9x, 2000, Me, and XP: (1) On your PC's desktop, double click the My Computer icon; (2) double click the icon for the CD-ROM drive into which the Forms CD-ROM was inserted; (3) double click the file README.TXT.
- Macintosh: (1) On your Mac desktop, double click the icon for the CD-ROM that you inserted; (2) double click on the file README.TXT.

While the README file is open, print it out by using the Print command in the File menu.

Two different kinds of forms are contained on the CD-ROM:

- Word processing (RTF) forms that you can open, complete, print, and save with your word processing program (see Section B, below), and
- Forms from the United States Copyright Office (PDF) that can be viewed only with Adobe Acrobat Reader 4.0 or higher. You can install Acrobat Reader from the Forms CD (see Section C below). These forms have "fill-in" text fields and can be completed using your computer. You will not, however, be able to save the completed forms with the filled-in data.

See Section D, below, for a list of forms, their file names, and file formats.

A. Installing the Form Files Onto Your Computer

Before you can do anything with the files on the CD-ROM, you need to install them onto your hard disk. In accordance with U.S. copyright laws, remember that copies of the CD-ROM and its files are for your personal use only.

Insert the Forms CD and do the following:

1. Windows 9x, 2000, Me, and XP Users

Follow the instructions that appear on the screen. (If nothing happens when you insert the Forms CD-ROM, then (1) double click the My Computer icon; (2) double click the icon for the CD-ROM drive into which the Forms CD-ROM was inserted; and (3) double click the file WELCOME .EXE.)

By default, all the files are installed to the \Software Development Forms folder in the \Program Files folder of your computer. A folder called "Software Development Forms" is added to the "Programs" folder of the Start menu.

2. Macintosh Users

Step 1: If the "Software Development CD" window is not open, open it by double clicking the "Software Development CD" icon.

Step 2: Select the "Software Development Forms" folder icon.

Step 3: Drag and drop the folder icon onto the icon of your hard disk.

B. Using the Word Processing Files to Create Documents

This section concerns the files for forms that can be opened and edited with your word processing program.

All word processing forms come in rich text format. These files have the extension ".RTF." For example, the form for the Software Beta Tester Nondisclosure Agreement discussed in Chapter 8 is on the file BetaTester.rtf.RTF. All forms, their file names, and file formats are listed in Section D, below.

RTF files can be read by most recent word processing programs including all versions of MS Word for Windows and Macintosh, WordPad for Windows, and recent versions of WordPerfect for Windows and Macintosh.

To use a form from the CD to create your documents you must: (1) open a file in your word processor or text editor; (2) edit the form by filling in the required information; (3) print it out; (4) rename and save your revised file.

The following are general instructions on how to do this. However, each word processor uses different commands to open, format, save, and print documents. Please read your word processor's manual for specific instructions on performing these tasks.

Do not call Nolo's technical support if you have questions on how to use your word processor.

Step 1: Opening a File

There are three ways to open the word processing files included on the CD-ROM after you have installed them onto your computer.

- Windows users can open a file by selecting its "shortcut" as follows: (1) click the Windows "Start" button; (2) open the "Programs" folder; (3) open the "Software Development Forms" subfolder; (4) open the "RTF" subfolder; and (5) click on the shortcut to the form you want to work with.
- Both Windows and Macintosh users can open a file directly by double clicking on it. Use My Computer or Windows Explorer (Windows 9x, 2000, Me, or XP) or the Finder (Macintosh) to go to the folder you installed or copied the CD-ROM's files to. Then, double click on the specific file you want to open.
- You can also open a file from within your word processor. To do this, you must first start your word processor. Then, go to the File menu and choose the Open command. This opens a dialogue box where you will tell the program (1) the type of file you want to open (*.RTF); and (2) the location and name of the file (you will need to navigate through the directory tree to get to the folder on your hard disk where the CD's files have been installed). If these directions are unclear you will need to look through the manual for your

word processing program—Nolo's technical support department will not be able to help you with the use of your word processing program.

Where Are the Files Installed?

Windows Users

- RTF files are installed by default to a folder named \Software Development Forms\RTF in the \Program Files folder of your computer.

Macintosh Users

- RTF files are located in the "RTF" folder within the "Software Development Forms" folder.

Step 2: Editing Your Document

Fill in the appropriate information according to the instructions and sample agreements in the book. Underlines are used to indicate where you need to enter your information, frequently followed by instructions in brackets. Be sure to delete the underlines and instructions from your edited document. If you do not know how to use your word processor to edit a document, you will need to look through the manual for your word processing program—Nolo's technical support department will *not* be able to help you with the use of your word processing program.

Editing Forms That Have Optional or Alternative Text

Some of the forms have check boxes before text. The check boxes indicate:

- **Optional text,** where you choose whether to include or exclude the given text.
- **Alternative text,** where you select one alternative to include and exclude the other alternatives.

We recommend that instead of marking the check boxes, you do the following:

Optional text

If you don't want to include optional text, just delete it from your document.

If you do want to include optional text, just leave it in your document.

In either case, delete the check box itself as well as the italicized instructions that the text is optional.

NOTE: if you choose not to include an optional numbered clause, be sure to renumber all the subsequent clauses after you delete it.

Alternative text

First delete all the alternatives that you do not want to include.

Then delete the remaining check boxes, as well as the italicized instructions that you need to select one of the alternatives provided.

Step 3: Printing Out the Document

Use your word processor's or text editor's "Print" command to print out your document. If you do not know how to use your word processor to print a document, you will need to look through the manual for your word processing program—Nolo's technical support department will *not* be able to help you with the use of your word processing program.

Step 4: Saving Your Document

After filling in the form, use the "Save As" command to save and rename the file. Because all the files are "read-only," you will not be able to use the "Save" command. This is for your protection. If you save the file without renaming it, the underlines that indicate where you need to enter your information will be lost, and you will not be able to create a new document with this file without recopying the original file from the CD-ROM.

If you do not know how to use your word processor to save a document, you will need to look through the manual for your word processing program—Nolo's technical support department will *not* be able to help you with the use of your word processing program.

C. Using United States Copyright Office Forms

Electronic copies of useful forms from the United States Copyright Office are included on the CD-ROM in Adobe Acrobat PDF format. You must have the Adobe Acrobat Reader installed on your computer (see below) to use these forms. All forms, their file names, and file formats are listed in Section D, below. These form files were created by the United States Copyright Office, not by Nolo.

These forms have fill-in text fields. To create your document using these files, you must: (1) open a file; (2) fill in the text fields using either your mouse or the tab key on your keyboard to navigate from field to field; and (3) print it out.

NOTE: While you can print out your completed form, you will NOT be able to save your completed form to disk.

Installing Acrobat Reader

To install the Adobe Acrobat Reader, insert the CD into your computer's CD-ROM drive and follow these instructions:

- Windows 9x, 2000, Me, and XP: Follow the instructions that appear on screen. (If nothing happens when you insert the Forms CD-ROM, then (1) double click the My Computer icon; (2) double click the icon for the CD-ROM drive into which the Forms CD-ROM was inserted; and (3) double click the file WELCOME.EXE.)
- Macintosh: (1) If the "Software Development CD" window is not open, open it by double clicking the "Software Development CD" icon; and (2) double click on the "Acrobat Reader Installer" icon.

If you do not know how to use Adobe Acrobat to view and print the files, you will need to consult the online documentation that comes with the Acrobat Reader program.

Do not call Nolo technical support if you have questions on how to use Acrobat Reader.

Step 1: Opening United States Copyright Office Files

PDF files, like the word processing files, can be opened one of three ways.

- Windows users can open a file by selecting its "shortcut" as follows: (1)

click the Windows "Start" button; (2) open the "Programs" folder; (3) open the "Software Development Forms" subfolder; (4) open the "PDF" folder; and (5) click on the shortcut to the form you want to work with.

- Both Windows and Macintosh users can open a file directly by double clicking on it. Use My Computer or Windows Explorer (Windows 9x, 2000, Me, or XP) or the Finder (Macintosh) to go to the folder you created and copied the CD-ROM's files to. Then, double click on the specific file you want to open.

- You can also open a PDF file from within Acrobat Reader. To do this, you must first start Reader. Then, go to the File menu and choose the Open command. This opens a dialogue box where you will tell the program the location and name of the file (you will need to navigate through the directory tree to get to the folder on your hard disk where the CD's files have been installed). If these directions are unclear you will need to look through Acrobat Reader's help—Nolo's technical support department will *not* be able to help you with the use of Acrobat Reader.

Step 2: Filling in United States Copyright Office Files

Use your mouse or the Tab key on your keyboard to navigate from field to field within these forms. Be sure to have all the information you will need to complete a form on hand, because you will not be able to save a copy of the filled-in form to disk. You can, however, print out a completed version.

Where Are the PDF Files Installed?

- Windows Users: PDF files are installed by default to a folder named \Software Development Forms\PDF in the \Program Files folder of your computer.
- Macintosh Users: PDF files are located in the "PDF" folder within the "Software Development Forms" folder.

Step 3: Printing United States Copyright Office Files

Choose Print from the Acrobat Reader File menu. This will open the Print dialogue box. In the "Print Range" section of the Print dialogue box, select the appropriate print range, then click OK.

D. List of Forms Included on the Forms CD-ROM

The following files are in rich text format (RTF):

FILE NAME	FORM NAME
Acknowledge.rtf	Acknowledgment of Obligations
Assignment.rtf	Copyright Assignment
Contractor1.rtf	Independent Contractor Agreement (Favorable to Hiring Firm)
Contractor2.rtf	Independent Contractor Agreement (Favorable to Independent Contractor)
Software.rtf	Custom Software Development Agreement
Website.rtf	Website Development Agreement
Nontechnical.rtf	Employment Agreement for Nontechnical Employees
Technical.rtf	Employment Agreement for Technical Employees
Shrink-Wrap.rtf	Shrink-Wrap End-User License Agreement
Click-Wrap.rtf	Click-Wrap End-User License Agreement
Negotiated.rtf	Negotiated License Agreement
Linking.rtf	Linking Agreement
NewEmployer.rtf	Letter to New Employer
Multimedia.rtf	Multimedia License Agreement
Release.rtf	Multimedia Publicity/Privacy Release
Nondisclosure.rtf	Basic Nondisclosure Agreement
Licensee.rtf	Nondisclosure Agreement for Licensee
BetaTester.rtf	Software Beta Tester Nondisclosure Agreement
Visitor.rtf	Visitor Nondisclosure Agreement
Interview.rtf	Interview Nondisclosure Agreement
Search.rtf	Search Request Form
WebLicense.rtf	Website License Agreement
Notice.rtf	Notice of Claimed Copyright Infringement
Counter.rtf	Counter-Notification In Response to Claim of Copyright Infringement

The following files are in Adobe Acrobat PDF format:

FILE NAME	FORM NAME
FORMCA.PDF	Form CA
FORMCON.PDF	Form CON
FORMDOC.PDF	Copyright Office Document Coversheet
FORMPAI.PDF	Form PA
FORMPAS.PDF	Short Form PA
FORMTXI.PDF	Form TX
FORMTXS.PDF	Short Form TX
FORMVAI.PDF	Form VA
FORMVAS.PDF	Short Form VA ■

Index